A BOWL FULL OF MEMORIES

A BOWL FULL OF MEMORIES

100 YEARS OF FOOTBALL AT THE YALE BOWL

Rich Marazzi

SPORTS PUBLISHING

Sports Publishing books may be purchased in bulk at special discounts for sales promotion, corporate gifts, fund-raising, or educational purposes. Special editions can also be created to specifications. For details, contact the Special Sales Department, Sports Publishing, 307 West 36th Street, 11th Floor, New York, NY 10018 or sportspubbooks@skyhorsepublishing.com.

Sports Publishing® is a registered trademark of Skyhorse Publishing, Inc.®, a Delaware corporation.

Visit our website at www.sportspubbooks.com.

10 9 8 7 6 5 4 3 2 1

Library of Congress Cataloging-in-Publication Data is available on file.

Cover design by Owen Corrigan
Cover photo credit: [top] Yale University Athletics Department, [bottom] Aerial Photography by Don Couture

Print ISBN: 978-1-61321-660-6
Ebook ISBN: 978-1-61321-683-5

Printed in China

The Kickoff

DEDICATION

To my dad, Reno Marazzi, for introducing me to the Yale Bowl and fostering my love for sports . . .

To the late Al Ostermann, who was in the Yale Bowl to witness 499 of the first 500 games ever played there. He is arguably Yale's greatest all-time fan. I interviewed Al in 1994 for *Sports Collectors Digest*. Several segments from that interview involving Yale football history appear in this book. Ostermann, who died on March 25, 2001, at age ninety-five, retired from the New England Telephone Co. and lived in Woodbridge, Connecticut, prior to his death. Throughout his life he kept the ticket from the first game ever played in the Yale Bowl on November 21, 1914.

And to all who ever played or witnessed any event in the Bowl . . .

CONTENTS

DIRECTORY OF CONTRIBUTORS

Many photographs in this book are from the archives of the Yale University Athletics Department. Photos from the archives of the Yale University Athletics Department will hereafter be credited as "Yale Athletics."

The following is a roster of non-players and coaches who were interviewed for this book.
Yale alums are listed with a notation of their graduation year throughout the book.

Erik Aaboe ('77) is Assistant County Manager for Santa Fe County. He resides in Santa Fe, New Mexico.

Mel Allen (posthumous) was the radio voice of the New York Yankees from 1939 to 1964 and is in the Baseball Hall of Fame. He also worked several football games in the Yale Bowl during a radio career that began in the 1930s. He died on June 16, 1996, at age eighty-three. The author interviewed him in 1979 at his home in Greenwich, Connecticut.

Michael Amato, from West Haven, Connecticut, is an off-track betting employee for the state of Connecticut.

Bob Barth, a resident of Shelton, Connecticut, serves as a Yale public address announcer in various sports including baseball, basketball, soccer and lacrosse.

Al Battipaglia was a Yale trainer from 1956-1992. The Hamden, Connecticut, resident passed away on January 7, 2014, at age eighty-six.

Tom Beckett, the Yale Athletics Director since 1994, resides in Guilford, Connecticut.

Norman Bender ('68), a resident of Woodbridge, Connecticut, is a freelance writer who was in the plumbing supplies business.

Karen Mckinnon Brown is the granddaughter of George Edward Weber, the longtime Yale football photographer. She was employed with the United States Department of Defense and lives in Colorado Springs, Colorado.

Vin Brozek was an administrator of heavy duty parts and executive vice president of Connecticut Wheel Rim. He resides in Branford, Connecticut.

Richard Butler, from Milford, Connecticut, was a senior office operations clerk at a brokerage firm and cashier for a major retailer.

Fred Cantor ('75) is an attorney and author from Westport, Connecticut.

Frank Carrano, who lives in West Haven, Connecticut, is a retired Master sergeant in the United States Army.

Joe Castiglione, a native of Hamden, Connecticut, has been the radio voice of Boston Red Sox baseball since 1983. He now resides in Marshfield, Massachusetts.

Stan Celmer, a former tool room foreman, lives in Hamden, Connecticut. Since the start of the '41 season, he has seen over 500 Yale football games.

Sam Chauncey ('57) was Vice president and Secretary of Yale University from 1971-1982. He also served as President of the Science Park Development Corporation and is a past President of Gaylord Hospital. A resident of New Haven, Connecticut, he has been involved in numerous nonprofit organizations.

Steve Cohen, who lives in Wallingford, Connecticut, is an AT&T customer service technician.

Stu Cohen is a chemical mixer who resides in Milford, Connecticut.

Bob Cumings, who lives in Winchester, Massachusetts, is the President of the Greater Boston Convention and Visitors Bureau.

John D'Antona, a regional manager for a coffee company, lives in Seymour, Connecticut.

Tony DeAngelo, a trust officer, makes his home in Pomfret, Connecticut.

Joe DeCrosta is a freelance writer/baseball reporter who resides in New Haven, Connecticut.

Jack Dolan, who resides in Wallingford, Connecticut, was an assistant Yale sports information director (1959-62; 1965-67). He lives in Wallingford, Connecticut.

Peter Easton, who lives in New Hyde Park, New York, was the Yale sports information director from 1973 to 1978 and the assistant SID from 1967 to 1973.

Merritt "Bud" Finch was an announcer and vice president and operations manager for 960 WELI radio. The Hamden, Connecticut, resident died on June 4, 2012, at age ninety-five. He was interviewed a few months prior to his death.

John Flanagan, a resident of Hamden, Connecticut, served as a probate court judge.

Gordon Ford, a retired technician from the Sikorsky aircraft company, lives in Ansonia, Connecticut.

Maria Gargano, a resident of Branford, Connecticut, is a driver for a senior community.

Chris Getman ('64) has been an assistant on the baseball and football coaching staffs. An investment advisor, Getman, who lives in Hamden, Connecticut, is the owner of Handsome Dan XVII.

Rocky Gillis, who lives in Westbrook, Connecticut, is the son of former Yale player Frank Gillis, a member of the 1944 Yale undefeated team.

Dick Graham, from West Haven, Connecticut, is a radio talk show host on WNHU 88.7 FM.

George Grande, a local and national sports broadcaster, was host for the very first broadcast of *Sports Center* on ESPN in 1979. He has been a play-by-play announcer for the New York Yankees, St. Louis Cardinals, and Cincinnati Reds. For thirty years the resident of Hamden, Connecticut, was host for the National Baseball Hall of Fame induction ceremonies at Cooperstown, New York.

Tom Hackett ('50) is an attorney who lives in Cheshire, Connecticut.

Don Harrison, who makes his home in Fairfield, Connecticut, is an author and formerly the *Waterbury Republican-American* Sports Editor.

Bill Kaminsky, who was a Yale trainer from 1969-2010, resides in Waterbury, Connecticut.

Robert Lewis is an attorney who lives in Branford, Connecticut and bleeds Yale blue. Thanks to his father, Sherman, a 1934 Yale graduate, he has the longest standing tailgate spot at the Bowl (Lot F Special) going back to 1958.

George Martelon, from Milford, Connecticut, is an attorney who serves as a spotter for Yale Bowl public address announcer Mark Ryba.

Catherine McKinnon is the granddaughter of former Yale football photographer George Edward Weber. A resident of Rocky Hill, Connecticut, she was a purchasing officer for the state of Connecticut.

Ernestine Weber McKinnon, the daughter of George Edward Weber, lives in Rocky Hill, Connecticut.

Steve McGill, the son of former great Yale running back Dennis McGill, is the Battalion Chief with the Jersey City, New Jersey, Fire Dept. where he resides.

Dan Mulvey Jr. is the son of former *New Haven Register* sports editor Dan Mulvey Sr. The Madison, Connecticut, resident is a retired English teacher and is also an author.

Don Nielsen is a retired telecommunications manager at SNET. The resident of Orange, Connecticut, is the Executive Director and past President of the New Haven Gridiron club.

Bob Norman was a newscaster and anchorman for over 20 years on WNHC-TV (Channel 8, now known as WTNH). For several years he teamed with Dick Galiette on 960 WELI radio covering Yale football. Norman, who served as mayor of East Haven, Connecticut, from 1985-1991, died on January 19, 2013, at age seventy-seven, about one year after he was interviewed for this book.

Ray Peach, an ardent Yale fan from North Haven, Connecticut, spent a career in banking.

John Pharr, the President of the Strand Development Company, lives in Myrtle Beach, South Carolina.

Tom Pepe from Ansonia, Connecticut, was Yale's Sports Turf Supervisor from 1985 to 2011.

Eileen Hellyar Peters is a retired Farrel's employee who resides in Forestdale, Massachusetts.

Al Proto, a resident of North Haven, Connecticut, was a school teacher and counselor.

John Resnik ('57), an attorney, lives in Woodbridge, Connecticut.

Dan Riccio is a welfare administrator for the town of North Haven, Connecticut, where he resides.

Dan Santoro is a vagabond rugby player from Fort Lauderdale, Florida.

Rich Schyner was the Superintendent of the Yale Fields from 1963 until 1988. He lives in Orange, Connecticut.

Bob Sheppard (posthumous) was the Yankee Stadium public address announcer for fifty-seven years (from 1951 to 2007) and did the PA for the New York football Giants from 1956 to 2006, including the Giants' years ('73 and '74) in the Yale Bowl. Sheppard died at age ninety-nine in 2010.

Walter "Bud" Smith is the President of the Orange Hills Country Club and a Connecticut Golf Hall of Fame inductee. The Orange, Connecticut, resident served in the 2nd infantry in World War II.

Carol Smullen, who lives in New Haven, Connecticut, is a teacher and director of the Orange, Connecticut, Chamber of Commerce.

Jon Stein, a former *New Haven Register* reporter, is currently involved with inside sales for Torrco in New Haven. He resides in Orange, Connecticut.

Frank Stolzenberg ('53), a press box spotter from 1948 to 1952, was the Director of Personnel for the Aetna Life and Casualty Company. He lives in Bloomfield, Connecticut.

John Sullivan is a retired ironworker who lives in Orange, Connecticut.

Jim Trapp is a former school teacher who resides in Milford, Connecticut.

Ron Vaccaro, ('04), the radio voice of Yale football since 2005, is also an editorial director for NBC Sports. He lives in Ansonia, Connecticut.

Francis T. "Fay" Vincent Jr., the son of Yale's 1930 football captain, Fay Vincent, served as Commissioner of Major League Baseball from 1989 to 1992. He lives in New Canaan, Connecticut.

William N. Wallace ('45 W, '49) was a *New York Times* sports writer and author. A resident of Westport, Connecticut, he died on August 11, 2012, at age eighty-eight in Norwalk, Connecticut, about one year after he contributed to this book.

James Walsh is the proprietor of the Stadium Museum Restaurant and Bar in Garrison, New York, where he resides.

SPECIAL RECOGNITION
JOEL SMILOW ('54)

Joel Smilow, the former chairman, CEO and president of Playtex Products Inc., never played football at any level but became an ardent supporter of Yale football as a student and sports director of WYBC, the Yale Broadcasting Co. In 1989 he made history as the first person to endow a Yale coaching position; his first seven-figure gift to the university endowed the head coach's chair in football. This led to a close relationship with head coach Carmen Cozza, first to hold the endowed position. A few years later, while Benno Schmidt was Yale's president, a much larger gift by Smilow allowed Yale to expand and renovate the Lapham Field House, which was renamed the Smilow Field Center.

His philanthropic leadership extended to other Yale sports. In 2003, the Southport, Connecticut, resident endowed the head coaching positions for men's and women's basketball and women's lacrosse. He also played a leadership role in the Yale Bowl restoration project.

Smilow's largest philanthropic donation came in 2009 with the lead and naming gift to create the Smilow Cancer Hospital, a part of Yale-New Haven Hospital. In 1992 he received the Yale Medal in recognition of his service to Yale.

TO THE READER

The first person entries ascribed to various individuals in this book are excerpted from interviews covering multiple subjects. Thus an individual may be quoted on different subjects at different points in the book.

Many comments were responses to questions not necessarily volunteered by the interviewee.

Occupations listed reflect their years of employment whether retired or not.

This book lists many players as having earned All-America honorable mention. Yale's media guide lists Yale players prior to 1956 who were first-team choices of All-America selectors recognized by the NCAA; for the years since 1956 Yale lists those who received any mention. For football's early days, the NCAA recognizes just two selectors: Caspar Whitney (*The Week's Sport*) and Walter Camp; by the 1940s that number had swelled to nine. In recent years the recognized selectors of Division I-A (Football Bowl Subdivision) All-Americans have been these five: The Associated Press, the American Football Coaches Association, Football Writers' Association of America, the *Sporting News* and the Walter Camp Football Foundation.

For years the AP and United Press (*later United Press International*) picked assorted All-East, All-New England and All-Ivy League teams. The lone recognized All-Ivy team today is selected by the league's coaches.

PREFACE

A Yale Fan Is Born

I have this recurring fantasy. I'm a Yale football player, standing on the field in the Yale Bowl after a Yale-Harvard game. The Bulldogs are victorious, and friends and family are greeting me, praising my heroics after beating haughty Harvard while the Yale and Harvard bands play "Down the Field" and "Ten Thousand Men of Harvard" under the fading November sun. My face is a football face—cut above the nose, bruised and battered. The helmet that I hold in my bloodstained hand has creased and reddened my forehead. The smeared eye black beneath my eyes is another reminder of what took place on this football afternoon.

Should a grandfather, who is on the back nine, be harboring such adolescent thoughts?

I say yes. I'm a certified, card-carrying, unabashed Yale football junkie. Not only have I attended virtually every home game in the last fifty years, but I attend practice on a fairly regular basis. Yale games serve as small anchors for my memory, reference points for marking where I was and whom I was with. The names of legends like Albie Booth, Larry Kelley, Clint Frank, Levi Jackson, Denny McGill, Brian Dowling, Calvin Hill, and John Pagliaro among others are eternally tattooed on my heart.

I never made it to the Bowl as a player but thanks to drum major David DeAngelis, a longtime friend, in 2007 I marched at halftime with the Yale Precision Marching Band, masquerading as a clarinet player. I simply followed the young Yalie on my right. My daughter-in-law Trisha trailed with a camera.

My journey into Yale football lore and the Yale Bowl began on Thanksgiving Day in 1948, when my dad and Uncle Leonard took a friend and me to the

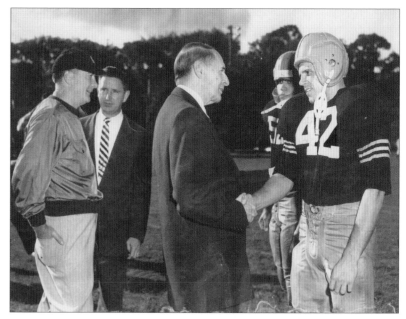

General Douglas MacArthur greets Army running back Bob Kyasky at a West Point practice. Coach Earl "Red" Blaik is to the far left.
(UNITED STATES MILITARY ACADEMY)

Bowl for the annual Hillhouse-West Haven High School football game. To borrow from *Atlantic Journal* writer Edward Weeks, "It was one of those brisk, bronze November mornings with the sun low and touching everything with gold."

I don't recall much about the game which Hillhouse won, 20-6. I do remember, however, the enormous crowd that numbered over 40,000 in the Yale Bowl that seemed bigger than life.

My second visit to the Bowl was November 5, 1955, when Yale hosted Army. I was focused on Army running back "Bullet Bob" Kyasky, who was the pride of my hometown, Ansonia, Connecticut, as Yale's Alex Thomas was in recent years. Kyasky's father and mine worked together at the Anaconda American Brass Company at a time when the local factories belched out smoke over the Naugatuck River throughout the day.

1955 Yale-Army game day program
(YALE ATHLETICS)

The pregame of marching cadets and martial music created a football environment second to none. The Army band proudly played...

On, Brave old Army team,
On to the fray,
Fight on to victory,
For that's the fearless Army way.

The Yale side answered with Bulldog, Bulldog. This was football heaven.

Although Army was a heavy favorite, on this day the Elis met the supreme challenge by upsetting the 19th ranked Cadets 14-12 after being humbled 48-7 the year before.

My dad died in September of 1979. The final game we attended in the Bowl together was November 4, 1978, when Yale dumped Cornell, 42-14. By this time I had been bitten by the storied history of Yale football and the consecrated Yale Bowl.

Writing this book has allowed me to become a small part of the Yale football story which I have attempted to tell in this book through the approximately 200 first-person interviews of the men who wore the blue, the coaches, the media and the fans.

Thanks to dad, my life has been A Bowl Full of Memories.

Author Rich Marazzi (No. 40) is flanked by family members L-R: Rachel (daughter-in-law) and son Brian, wife Lois, and son Rich with granddaughter Caitlin, and daughter-in-law Trisha with grandson, Richie.
(BILL O'BRIEN)

Walter Camp

PROLOGUE
SIR WALTER

*"What Washington was to his country,
[Walter] Camp was to American football:
the friend, the founder and father."*

—John Heisman

The 1876 Yale team. Walter Camp is standing in rear second from the left. The captain is Eugene Baker. It is believed that this is the first year that Yale wore the letter "Y" on their uniform. Numbers were not worn until 1916.
(YALE ATHLETICS)

IF THERE IS a high priest in Yale football history, it is Walter Camp. A native of New Britain, Connecticut, Camp captained the Yale team in 1878 and 1879 and served without salary as Yale's first head coach from 1888 to 1892. As coach, he compiled a 67-2 record, his teams playing a busy thirteen to sixteen games each year.

His position as sales manager of the New Haven Clock Company, where he later was treasurer and president, limited his time for coaching. The solution was that his wife, Alice, became in effect co-coach. She went to the field every afternoon, carrying Walter's instructions.

Walter Camp teaches passing to Billy Knox circa 1906.
(YALE ATHLETICS)

THE MASTER INNOVATOR

"Sir Walter" reshaped a game that was essentially English rugby into American football. He took the game from an ill-defined struggle to one with rules and organization of some sophistication. He pushed for teams of eleven men rather than rugby's fifteen. He replaced rugby's scrum with the scrimmage, from which set plays could be run, and he instituted scoring in points rather than the tally of goals as in soccer. He started the "downs" system. It evolved from three downs to make five yards to four downs to make ten yards by 1906. He used the earliest form of the T-formation, with the quarterback giving spoken signals.

The respect in which Camp was held reached all corners. A letter written in 1892 by Notre Dame coach James Kivlan to Camp reads, *"Walter Camp: Dear Sir, I want to ask a favor of you. Will you kindly furnish me with some points on the best way to develop a good Football Team...I know something of the Rugby game, but would like to find out the best manner to handle the men..."*

Changing Football's Rules

In 1905, President Theodore Roosevelt invited Camp and other college officials to the White House to discuss ways to make the game safer. T.R. loved football but he campaigned for reform because of the barbarous and brutal nature of the sport that resulted in many deaths and injuries.

As a result, the football rules committee chaired by Dr. Paul Dashiell agreed to major changes, making the forward pass legal in 1906. Dashiell supported Roosevelt and the reformers in legalizing the forward pass, which reduced the frequency of dangerous collisions between helmetless players. The committee's fourteen members included three Yale men—Camp, Amos Alonzo Stagg, and Dr. Harry Williams.

Despite Camp's innovative contributions to the game, he resisted the forward pass. His objections may have led to rules that today would be considered draconian. For example, a team could not score a touchdown on a forward pass. If a pass went out of bounds, the ball was turned over to the opposing team. And if the ball hit the ground without anyone touching it, the ball also went to the opposing team.

On November 1, 1913, Notre Dame beat Army 35-13 at West Point when Irish quarterback Gus Dorais passed for 243 yards in front of the New York press. Unlike today's pass-happy offenses, teams that amassed hundreds of passing yards were unheard of at the time. Although Notre Dame did not invent the forward pass, this game changed the way the game would be played.

Camp's Legacy

For decades Camp selected an All-America team, which was intended to recognize outstanding play and accomplishment. Whether the idea came from Camp or Caspar Whitney, manager of a magazine called *The Week's Sport,* is open to argument, but Camp either chose or collaborated on an All-America team every year from 1889 through 1924.

During World War I the hunch-shouldered Camp, who wore a distinctive blond mustache, was Chairman of the Athletic Department of the Navy Commission on War Training Camp Activities. He developed a "Daily Dozen" fitness program for servicemen that was adopted by many Americans.

On March 14, 1925, Walter Camp died in his sleep between sessions of the intercollegiate football rules committee meeting in New York City. Camp served on or advised every national rules committee from the time he was a student-player in 1878 until his death. Accounts in the *New York Times* indicate Camp, who was three weeks shy of his sixty-sixth birthday, was not visibly ill when he turned in for

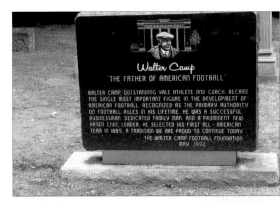

Walter Camp gravestone
(Rich Marazzi)

the night at the Hotel Belmont. The next morning Princeton coach Bill Roper, the hotel manager, and a carpenter went to his room and found Camp dead after he failed to show for the meeting. Legendary Notre Dame coach Knute Rockne said of Camp's death, "His loss to the sporting world is irreparable. He was not only one of the leading figures of football, but of all college sports and physical education as well. He has done more for college football ... than any other man may ever do."

Camp is buried at the Grove Street Cemetery in New Haven alongside his wife and son, Walter Camp Jr., who lettered in football at Yale in 1911 and 1912.

In 1988 Walter Camp Football Foundation past President Bill O'Brien initiated a drive to get Camp placed on a U.S. postal stamp. Thanks to the efforts of O'Brien, past Walter Camp President Kenneth Dagliere, former U.S. Senator Joseph Lieberman, and then U.S. Postal Board Governor John Walsh, Camp was honored on a stamp that also included football icons Bronko Nagurski, Ernie Nevers, and Red Grange. The first day of issue was August 8, 2003.

The Walter Camp Memorial Gateway

Dedicated on November 3, 1928, before the Yale-Dartmouth game, the Walter Camp Memorial Gateway on Derby Avenue is the eye-catching entrance to the Walter Camp Field, of which Yale

Bowl is one unit. Designed by John W. Cross ('00), the Gateway is a series of lofty stone pillars, flanked on each side by low walls of stone and brick extending 400 feet. Tablets set into the walls on each side of the gateway bear the names of the 224 colleges and the total number of prep and high schools all over the nation that joined with Yale in honoring the memory of Camp by helping to finance the structure that cost $300,000. But even the best laid plans are subject to error. The name Rensselaer is misspelled "Rensselear."

REMEMBERING MR. CAMP
Al Ostermann

"A few years after the Bowl opened I received my first football, and would you believe, it was from Walter Camp, 'the father of modern football,' and Tad Jones, a legend, who like Camp, both played and coached at Yale."

"My mother had a cousin who was a German professor at Yale. He was a roommate of Tad's and he knew that I was interested in football but didn't have my own football. My mother had another cousin who worked at the Yale Library. I was told to go there and someone would give me a football. When I got there, Walter Camp and Tad handed me the football. Camp said, 'I hope someday you'll come to Yale.'

"Unfortunately, I don't have the football. When I was a kid and you had a ball, you were a pretty popular guy. We played pickup games with that ball and it didn't last long."

Bill O'Brien

"George 'Papa Bear' Halas, the legendary Chicago Bears coach and owner, was the recipient of the Walter Camp Distinguished American Award for 1980. He wanted to visit the Bowl. So we drove down route 34 and through the entrance of the Walter Camp Memorial Archway. I took his picture standing in front of the columns. We became close friends over the years and I cherish the 14 letters he has sent me."

George Grande

"I've had the prestigious honor to emcee the annual Walter Camp banquet at the Yale Commons on three different occasions. And from 1972-78 my brother, Carlo, and I did a broadcast from the event on WNHC radio.

George "Papa Bear" Halas stands in front of the Walter Camp Memorial Gate in 1981.
(BILL O'BRIEN)

"The night before the dinner when we honored George 'Papa Bear' Halas and Gale Sayers, there was a reception and cocktail party at Mory's [a private club adjacent to the Yale campus, founded in 1849]. Sitting in the back of the room were Mr. Halas and George McCaskey, the founder and owner of the Chicago Bears. I got to know Mr. Halas from covering the NFL on ESPN and CBS-TV.

"When I greeted Mr. Halas he beamed, 'Oh Grandy, how are you?' And referring to himself, he went on, 'Who ever would have thought that some broken-down football player is here at Yale and is going to be a part of the Walter Camp Football Foundation? Do you realize who Walter Camp was?'

"'Papa Bear' knew everything about Camp. He then pointed his finger at me and asked, 'Do you know what the greatest football program in America was? It wasn't the Chicago Bears; it wasn't the New York Giants; it was Yale!'

"That night Mr. Halas bought each of us a Mory's cup and saucer as a memento of the night. I'll always cherish that gift."

PART I

The Yale Bowl

100 Years of Memories

The Yale Bowl, 1914.
(YALE ATHLETICS)

Chapter 1

THE BIRTH OF THE BOWL

*"When you walk out of the tunnel
onto the field you feel like a gladiator
entering the Colosseum."*

—Carmen Cozza

THE HISTORIC YALE Bowl with its Class of 1954 Field is where titans have wrestled for glory for a century and is a magnet of civic pride. It is the proud child of one of college football's most storied programs and one of the oldest Division I stadiums in the country. One week after Princeton's Palmer Memorial Stadium opened, the Bowl was unveiled for the Yale-Harvard game on November 21, 1914. At the time, it was the largest stadium in the world and the first stadium with seating that completely encircled the field.

The famous man-made crater that covers 12.5 acres of land lies under the lean shadow of West Rock. It is a venue shaped by history. In 1987 it was declared a National Historic Landmark and was chosen by the *Sporting News* as one of the 40 best college football stadiums in its 2005 book, *Saturday Shrines*. Unlike Harvard Stadium that is modeled on the ancient dignified stadiums of Greece and Rome with its ivy-clad arches and classic Doric colonnade, Yale Bowl is more expansive and pragmatic.

Other stadiums have copied the Bowl's design without capturing its charm. Born the same year as Wrigley Field in Chicago and two years after Fenway Park opened its gates in Boston, the Yale Bowl became a model for other stadiums such as the Rose Bowl and Michigan Stadium, the "Big House."

THE TRAIL TO THE BOWL: YALE FIELD I AND YALE FIELD II

Yale initially played its football games at Hamilton Park in New Haven from 1872 to 1883. Originally called Brewster Park, it was located at the intersection of Whalley Avenue and West Park Avenue. Built in the 1850s, the park served as home to every Yale athletic event. The *New Haven Register* reported that Yale fielded its first baseball team there in 1865 and seating was limited with just one grandstand that held 198.

In 1881, a tract of land was secured on the south side of Derby Avenue two miles west of the Yale campus with the assistance of two members of the class of 1881, Adrian S. Van Der Graff, and Charles S. White. This would become Yale Field where baseball and football games were played starting in 1884. Any playing venue (baseball or football) on the site was referred to as "Yale Field."

There has never been a formal distinction such as Yale Field I and Yale Field II as separate Yale football venues. But perhaps there should be since Yale played football games on two different physical locations at Yale Field.

Based on images provided by Sam Rubin, the assistant director of sports publicity at Yale, in 1884 Yale played on a field that ran perpendicular from center field of the current baseball field westward toward what is now the Clint Frank Field in the DeWitt Cuyler Complex where the J.V. team plays their games and the varsity team currently practices. There were no seats and spectators gathered around the sidelines. I have designated this "Yale Field I," a venue previously ignored by historians.

Yale Field II

Yale Field II ran north and south in what is now the DeWitt Cuyler complex. It is difficult to determine exactly what year Yale Field II was established. Photos as early as 1892 show a grandstand. In 1897, an apparent expansion of wooden grandstands were installed at a cost of $16,000 to accommodate 15,000. In 1903 the seating capacity increased to 29,000, then to 32,000 in 1906. It topped out at 35,000 (some sources say 33,090) in 1908 making it the largest wooden stands field ever constructed. Yale Field II served as Yale's home field until Yale

The 1910 Yale-Harvard game ended in a scoreless tie before an overflow crowd at Yale Field II.
(Library of Congress)

Bowl's inauguration in 1914. Because of the lack of facilities, the teams remained on the field at halftime reviewing instructions from the coaches.

Before 1900, it was clear that the football program was a profit-generating machine and that a larger stadium was needed. "By the 1890s, Yale's football receipts accounted for one-eighth of the institution's total income, an amount greater than its expenditures on law and medicine," wrote George Will in the January 5, 2013, edition of the *New Haven Register.*

But Yale Field II could not meet the demand of the large crowds. It was reported that in the seven years prior to the completion of the Bowl, the Yale Athletic Office lost $100,000 in ticket sales because of insufficient seating. Also, the annual expense for repairs amounted to between $10,000 and $12,000.

THE COMMITTEE OF TWENTY-ONE

Recognizing that Yale Field was undersized to meet the demands of ticket requests, the Yale Corporation appointed a committee of seven graduates to study the issue and make recommendations. S.J. Elder (1871) chaired the committee that reported the necessity of a new structure. In 1910 the Yale Corporation appointed and incorporated the Committee of Twenty-One to study ways of improving the athletic facilities. Thomas DeWitt Cuyler (1874), chairman, and David Daggett (1879), secretary,

headed the Structures Committee within the Committee of Twenty-One.

The Committee purchased eighty-five acres of land across the street from Yale Field. The land was reserved for different sports including tennis and squash. The northeast corner was chosen as the site for the Bowl. Yale alumnus Arthur Thompson donated a large parcel of land and sold another section to the Committee below market price. Another unnamed graduate advanced a large sum of money at a low rate of interest. The plot given by Thompson was named Anthony Thompson Field located near the current site of the Armory where the polo horses were housed near Lot D. Another section was named Gordon Brown Field after Yale's four-time All-America guard.

PLANS FOR A
MULTI-SPORTS COMPLEX

Plans called for the new stadium to be part of a complex serving several sports so that the space would not sit idle for ten months of the year. A sketch in the June 9, 1912, *New York Times* shows existing and proposed sites for track, baseball, hockey, tennis, and squash as well as a clubhouse. After lengthy debate and the demolition of the football stadium named Yale Field, track competition was relocated to the site on which it stood, now the DeWitt Cuyler Athletic Complex. The hockey rink that opened in January 1912 on Derby Avenue near the West River served Yale only briefly. Soil problems and the opening of the first New Haven Arena, located downtown at State and Wall streets, led Yale to move its home games to the Arena in January 1914.

Multi-Sports Complex

Members of the Yale Field Corporation engaged Leoni Robinson, a prominent New Haven architect, to prepare a preliminary design for a closed-end stadium on the site of the current baseball field that would exceed Harvard's seating capacity of 38,000. The Yale Field Corporation presented Robinson's drawings and proposals to the Alumni Advisory Board that appointed a committee to study the stadium problem in 1911.

According to William A. Wiedershein ('40), in an article written for the 1989 Yale-Harvard game day program, "Robinson drew up five different stadium plans, seating between 37,608 and 50,628. The proposals were for an above ground structure." Under Robinson's plans access and exiting would have been difficult which is most likely why they were never used. Robinson's designs and drawings were found in the late 1980s in the carriage house of his summer home in Maine.

The problem was solved when a design of a new stadium was submitted to the Committee of Twenty-One by architect Charles A. Ferry (Sheffield 1871). Sheffield was the scientific school at the Yale College. Ferry's design partially echoed the campus's neogothic design. It also met the challenge of creating a stadium that would hold at least 60,000, have ample entrances, be strong and durable with low cost for construction and maintenance, be safe for spectators, be fireproof and structurally sound, and have adequate access and exiting. The issue of fireproofing was especially important to the

Charles Ferry, designer of the Yale Bowl
(YALE ATHLETICS)

Committee because during this time fires in various large stadia in Europe and the United States had resulted in many casualties. The South End Grounds in Boston, Sportsman's Park in St. Louis, and Philadelphia's Base Ball park are some examples. It is believed that many fires resulted from cigars that were not properly extinguished.

To meet all of these criteria, the Committee settled on an oval stadium constructed of earth faced with concrete, a concept somewhat similar to reservoir construction, from which the idea derived. The oval shape of the Bowl allows every spectator to have an unobstructed view of the four corners of the playing field. The architectural features of the Bowl were worked out by Donn Barber (1893, Sheffield). The estimated cost of the construction of the football stadium was $300,000. In addition, the purchase of land was estimated at $150,000); improvements of the new grounds $100,000, a new clubhouse $100,000, and stands for the baseball field $50,000, for a total estimated cost of $700,000. The final cost of the Bowl was reported to be $750,000. This included the improvements made to the fields around it. If it had been built entirely above ground level, it is estimated that costs would have doubled to about $1.5 million. According to *DollarTimes.com* $750,000 in 1914 would have an approximate calculated value today of $9.2 million considering an annual 2.71 inflation rate.

FINANCING THE BOWL

In 1900 Walter Camp became treasurer of the Yale Field Corporation and quietly accumulated an enormous sum of money which formed the nucleus of the fund used to build the Bowl.

According to Tim Cohane, author of *The Yale Football Story,* Camp had saved $135,000. It had been agreed that when Camp retired from all formal connection with Yale athletics in 1910, the money would be turned over to the construction of a new football stadium. But more funds were needed.

The question of financing such a project became an issue of concern for the Committee of Twenty-One. Its members concluded that Yale should not fund a football stadium. Instead, the Committee constituted itself a holding guaranty company that was authorized to raise funds by subscription. Yale alums, undergraduates, and friends of the University were offered preferred rights to tickets. The "Ticket Privilege Contract" would give subscribers the right to apply for tickets to all games in the Coliseum (Bowl). A subscription of $1,000 or more entitled a subscriber to ten tickets per game on a multiyear basis. The plan scaled down to $100 certificates. "The majority of subscribers' rights expired in 1930," according to an article in the October 22, 1927, Yale-Army game day program. This was good news for disgruntled alums who had been unable to obtain the premium seats that had been set aside for subscribers.

NAMING THE NEW STADIUM

There was a major dispute among Committee members over what to call the new structure. Should it be named "Yale Bowl," "Yale Stadium," "Yale Coliseum," "Yale Arena," or "Yale Amphitheater"?

David Daggett, the secretary of the Committee of Twenty-One, said in an interview with the *Yale Daily News:* "The name 'Bowl' was first suggested by Mr. Noah H. Swayne Jr. (class of 1893), one of our Committee, and my recollection is that a vote was passed endorsing its term. The word 'Bowl' has the added advantage of being short and suggestive of

the general appearance of the structure looking at it from the top down."

Speaking at the 1912 commencement exercise, Yale University's President, Arthur Twining Hadley, endorsed the name when he said, "I am glad that Yale, in spite of its classical traditions, prefers the good old word 'Bowl,' with its savor of manly English sport, to the 'coliseum' of the Romans or the 'stadium' of the Greeks." At the time, the title "Bowl" for an outdoor athletic facility had never been used before.

Hadley led the groundbreaking on Monday, June 23, 1913, at 5 p.m.

THE EARLY STAGES OF CONSTRUCTION

The building permit for the Bowl was issued on July 19, 1913, by the city of New Haven through Building Inspector J.E. Austin. The Committee of Twenty-One was listed as owner of the land. The purpose of the building was listed as "Foot ball amphitheatre." The cost of the construction listed for this phase was $175,000. Construction was scheduled to begin on August 1, 1913.

Construction lasted sixteen months with a crew of about 145 men hired by the Sperry Engineering Company of New Haven. Yale grad Everard Thompson directed the construction details and also coordinated the allotment of 70,000 tickets for the first game.

The Bowl attained national fame during its construction. Its engineering feat has been compared to the digging of the Panama Canal.

Before the excavation or digging process began, wood gated portals were constructed around the perimeter of the future Bowl. Then a process called "cut and fill" was used. Simply stated, the plan was to dig a hole, then use the 320,000 cubic yards of soil to build the surrounding walls or berm. The Coliseum

Portal development
(YALE ATHLETICS)

of Pompeii in Italy was the only other known structure in the world with the same architecture.

From ground level an excavation was made about 27 ½- feet to the floor (playing field) which was called the "cut" process. The material or earth that was dug up was used for building the surrounding berm or embankment to a height of 26 feet. This was the "fill." Therefore, the top to the bottom of the Bowl measures 53 ½- feet.

The design allowed for two tunnels that serve as the entrance to the playing field for the players and coaches. The sides and roof of each tunnel were reinforced with steel.

William Sperry, the contractor for the project, built a circular track just outside the outer wall and placed two high towers, from the tops of which large cables ran to heavy posts set on the farther side of the "Bowl." A large drag bucket was operated from each tower, running out on the main cable and being dragged back by another cable. Two small rotary steam shovels were used to dig what the towers could not reach.

Horses were used during the construction for grazing the field and pulling the cable on the earth bucket. They also carried away receptacles brimming with soil before the advent of the bulldozer.

Although there is no concrete evidence, it's possible that some horses are buried under the Bowl's turf.

"If a horse died during the Bowl's excavation, most likely it was buried under the playing field of the Bowl," said former Yale's Sports Turf Supervisor Tom Pepe. Although it has been widely speculated that the steam shovels used in the excavation are buried under the Bowl turf, there is no evidence of that. Some believe that sections of the shovels were dismantled but parts were buried.

According to documents in the Ferry files at the Yale University Library, during the Bowl's construction "a sandstorm whisked and whirled tons of loose

Cable tower used for excavation
(YALE ATHLETICS)

Excavation towers outside Bowl complete the "cut" process.
(YALE ATHLETICS)

earth and grit through the city and out over the harbor...in the most Saharan style." Although no date was given, it was most likely May 27, 1914. The *Hartford Courant* reported that at the end of the first half inning of the Yale-Holy Cross baseball game, "a blinding sand-storm made the teams leave the field." The game was eventually rained out after three delays.

LATER MODIFICATIONS

In 1920 the temporary bleachers on the upper portion of the Yale Bowl were replaced by permanent facing of concrete, built in steps, and new bleachers with malleable iron standards, all similar to the lower portion of the Bowl. The press box was also erected at this time.

"The original concrete construction was only for the lower half of the Bowl," explained Pepe. "The upper half of the Bowl was constructed with temporary wooden bleachers built on soil into the dirt embankment. At the time, there were no mechanical means to compact the soil for the embankment. The engineers knew that if they waited several years, the soil for the embankment would settle and harden enough to support the concrete."

The cost of this phase was $175,000 and was again funded by ticket privileges (15 years) for Yale men. Subscriptions were eventually opened to the public.

Once the 30 feet of walls were formed around the Bowl to support the top rows of seats, the wooden-backed seats were installed. In 1931 ornamental 7-foot × 7-foot iron gates replaced the wooden gates at the portals.

The original bleachers, constructed of Oregon Douglas fir, were painted gray but repainted to true blue in 1959. (Some of the old bleachers from the Bowl were installed at the Shake Shack, a popular Yalie burger spot on Chapel Street in New Haven.)

Berm or "fill" from excavated soil creates the outer wall of the Bowl.
(YALE ATHLETICS)

Size and Seating Capacity

The Bowl is 930 feet long and 750 feet wide. "The Woolworth Building could be put to bed within its walls," reported the *New York Times* in 1921, referring to the tallest building in the world at the time.

There are sixty concrete steps from the surface of the Bowl to the top in each of the spaces between portals. The inner slope that serves as a foundation for the sixty steps was given a dished shape so that a person in the top seat has the same ability to see over the heads of people in front as someone in the second row.

The original design provided for 60,617 permanent seats, with each of the 30 portals handling about 2,000 spectators. There was space for 600 in the press area and 50 in the photographers stands, of these 249 were provided with seats. A 1912 rule change that shortened the playing field from 110 yards to 100 saved space and allowed for more seating. Bleacher seats built on the promenade around the top of the Bowl expanded capacity to nearly 71,000, and on certain occasions bleachers were installed inside the Bowl's inner wall, practically at field level, to handle crowds exceeding 75,000. Of the ten largest crowds in Bowl history, most were for games against Army.

In 1921 Ferry had a plan to increase the seating capacity of the Bowl from 64,015 to 117,000 by adding an upper deck but it never gained traction. Clarence W. Mendell, chairman of the Yale Athletic Advisory Committee, called the proposal "a pipe dream."

Before 1994 the seating capacity was 70,869. Because of subsequent alterations and a major restoration in the 2000s, it is now 61,446.

An Idiosyncratic Stadium
Optical Illusion

According to the Ferry report only 20,000 seats are enclosed between the goal lines extended, and that more than 40,000 are in the end zones. This optical illusion translates into two-thirds of the spectators sitting in the end zones when the Bowl is filled to capacity. The late David Halberstam, a prominent author and Harvard man, once described the Yale Bowl as "the most democratic of arenas where there were no bad seats, and for that matter no good seats."

A Yale man might counter, "Harvard Stadium is like sitting on a block of ice."

Hamden, Connecticut, native and veteran broadcaster George Grande disagrees with Halberstam. "In my opinion the Yale Bowl remains the best place to watch a football game in America," said Grande. "I played freshman football at USC and recall running onto the field at the Los Angeles Coliseum and how immense it was. I've been to Notre Dame, Ohio State, Michigan, and others. There is no place that is as perfectly constructed and puts you as close to the action as the Bowl does."

An Auditory and Astronomical Wonder

According to a report written by Ferry to the "American Society of Civil Engineers" on November 15, 1916, "Under favorable conditions when there are only a few people in the stadium, a whisper spoken at the center of the field can be distinctly heard at the tunnel portals where the players enter and exit. A conversation in an ordinary tone of voice can be carried on between persons stationed on opposite sides of the Bowl which is also referred to as an amphitheater."

The report added, "The Yale Bowl is also an astronomical wonder. The designers positioned the Bowl so that the minor axis points to the sun at 3 p.m. on Nov. 15th. Thus no football player in the Bowl would ever have to look into the sun when Yale plays its big games against Princeton and Harvard."

Approximately two-thirds of the 60,617 seats in the Bowl are in the end zones.
(YALE ATHLETICS)

The Mystery of the Rest Rooms

The 1916 Ferry report stated, "The plans for the permanent toilets and the permanent fence have not been finally settled." Ferry also wrote that the cost of permanent toilets was not included in the original estimate of the Bowl. Is that to be interpreted as an oversight when construction of the Bowl began, or was the issue of the rest rooms and a permanent fence, items for discussion? Chances are this was an oversight since it would hardly seem logical that plans for a stadium as large as the Yale Bowl would not include rest rooms in its original architectural plans. Temporary toilets, located outside the stadium, were used from 1914 through the 1930 seasons. The current eight exterior rest rooms that surround the Bowl were added in 1931 at a cost of $80,000 by the Dwight Construction Co.

LAPHAM FIELD HOUSE

Fans often have wondered why there are no dressing rooms in the Yale Bowl. According to Pepe, "There were two gate-houses that were scheduled to be built for showers, dressing rooms etc. for the teams at the entrances of both tunnels where the teams enter the field but construction never took place because of a shortage of funds."

In 1923 the Lapham Field House was built on a tract of land off Derby Avenue. Henry G. Lapham ('97), a wealthy Boston investment banker and president of the Boston Garden-Arena Corporation, donated $350,000 for the construction of a clubhouse to be used by athletes in all forms of outdoor sports.

"Lapham stipulated that he would make a pledge for such a structure but it would have to be free-standing and separate from the Bowl with his name on it," explained Pepe.

Thanks to a $5.37 million gift from Joel E. Smilow ('54) and another $1.7 million gift from other alumni, the Lapham Field House was renovated and expanded and is now called the Smilow Field Center.

CHAPTER 2

THE GRAND OPENING

"As a spectacle it was of an indescribable sort; people saw it from the outside as a low but huge green fort, only to come out at the thirty portal ends into a vast and sunlit arena"

—*Yale Alumni Weekly*
(November 27, 1914)

The first scrimmage in the Yale Bowl, 1914
(LIBRARY OF CONGRESS LC-US262-12893)

YALE HAD HOPED to open the Bowl against Notre Dame on October 17, 1914, but the new stadium was not ready until November 21. The two teams played at Yale Field II with the Bulldogs blanking the Irish 28-0.

On November 10, a large crowd of city and college enthusiasts gathered downtown at 1:45 p.m. and proceeded to march to the Bowl. They went on to the field where they sang their battle songs and practiced cheering. Of course, the singing and cheering reflected genuine enthusiasm, but it was also intended to measure how the noise would affect the opposing quarterback when giving signals.

The following day, led by coach Frank Hinkey, Yale scrimmaged in the new facility. Although it was reported that several thousand fans turned up, the above photo taken on that day indicates otherwise.

PREPARING FOR THE GRAND OPENING
Shopping

In anticipation of the opening game against Harvard, there were multiple retailers in the *New Haven Evening Register* advertising heavy outer wear and other items to prepare for the late November chill. Muhlfelder's on Chapel St. pushed fur coats, Hudson seal, pony, raccoon and leopard for as low as $25 and as high as $350. The Edward Malley Co. department store advertised heavy Shakir Knit Worsted Sweaters with a large shawl collar from $5 to $7. Other items included straw seats (5 cents), flasks (65 cents to $4), Yale flags, pennants, arm bands, warm gloves, raincoats, and umbrellas. Warm wool Steamer Rug blankets sold from $4.50 to $12. The Davis Drug Co. sold field and opera glasses "so that no matter where your seat is you can see every play." Women in search of evening gowns for the big weekend could find one at the Shartenberg and Robinson Co. for $19.85.

Scalpers and Betting

The Bowl was reported completed on November 17. Even though there were 70,055 available seats—excluding the media area or "stand" for the nearly 300 newspapermen and telegraphers who would cover the game—there was intense demand for the two-dollar tickets. Scalpers, or "speculators," were selling them for five to ten dollars each. One such speculator, Carlos Greeley of Brooklyn, New York, was arrested when he offered a detective two tickets for twenty-five dollars. He was fined ten dollars and court costs. The *New York Times* reported that a Chicago businessman paid five hundred dollars for five tickets.

The Yale ticket office, aware of the scalping, established a policy forbidding graduates to sell to speculators. Everard Thompson of the Yale ticket office was deluged with requests. Harvard applied for 25,000, Yale grads asked for 27,322, undergrads requested 11,042, and the "Committee of Twenty-One" wanted 3,268. By November 20, the day before the game, applications for tickets passed the 80,000 mark. The orderly line at the ticket office in Durfee Hall turned into a surging mob. Thompson, who also had overseen the Bowl construction details, collapsed—apparently from stress and exhaustion.

Betting was active. A $7 wager on underdog Yale might have won $10. The Harvards wanted even money. A group of Yale students collectively wagered $1,500 on the Bulldogs, and a group of Harvard Cantabrigians confidently sent $3,000 to New Haven to be laid out at odds of 5 to 3.

Security and Safety

The New Haven police department was in uncharted waters in dealing with a crowd of more than 70,000. City officials made provisions for an emergency hospital near the Bowl. Soliciting nurses, doctors, ambulances and cots was part of the planning.

The city's force of 304 police officers (including supernumeraries) was spread thin. Police Chief Philip T. Smith warned citizens to lock their doors and windows. Out-of-town detectives were brought in to help the local gendarmes.

The Teams Work Out

The Harvard team stayed at the Mohican Hotel in New London, Connecticut, and journeyed the roughly fifty miles to New Haven in two waves. The vanguard, which arrived on Thursday, November 19, consisted of coaches and nineteen players, limited to backs and centers. The remaining linemen arrived at 1 p.m. the next day.

The backs and centers were taken to the Bowl on Thursday afternoon to get oriented. The turf was soggy, the result of an earlier snowstorm that had turned to rain. The Yale team worked out in the Bowl after Harvard's practice. On Friday a steamroller was used to force the water out of the turf, which had been laid six weeks earlier. However, the excellent drainage system had carried off most of the water. A thick covering of hay was spread nightly during the week to protect the turf and keep it as hard as possible.

November 20, 1914

Since there were no locker rooms in the new Bowl and the field house hadn't yet been built, the Yale team dressed in the gym to prepare for practice. At that time the gym was located at the present site of the Trumbull College dining hall on the north side of Elm Street between York and High Streets. The team held a light practice at the old Yale Field II and according to the *New York Times* celebrated their departure by "cheering the historic structure lustily."

The Elis only used the hay-covered Bowl field to practice punting and drop kicking. After their light workout, they went to the Quinnipiack Club on Church Street for dinner. Later that evening the team held a signal drill in the baseball cage.

A full contingent of Harvard players came to New Haven and had lunch at the Hotel Taft. They then took special trolleys to the Bowl and dressed in the Yale trackhouse before working out on Friday afternoon at the baseball field, located at the site of the current field. Following the workout, the Harvard team returned to New London.

Pregame Atmosphere

Despite miserable weather, the Elm City and the Yale campus were bustling with excitement on the eve of the game. An estimated 20,000 clamored for rooms. A University Bureau of Information was placed in Osborn Hall for their convenience. The University dining hall, the Dwight Hall grill and the University Club were among those holding open houses. Guests filled the local hotels and boarding houses to the brim. The Hotel Taft, which held its grand opening only two years earlier, reportedly had 676 guests and served 6,900 dinners. Because the city was unable to adequately house the overload of spectators, many had to find lodging in surrounding cities and towns.

Yale alumni returned and partied at Mory's, Tut's, Heub's, and other student watering holes. There was a joint concert of the Yale and Harvard musical clubs at Woolsey Hall and an all-night dance at the Hotel Taft. Popular songs of the day included *Alexander's Rag Time Band* and *It's a Long Way to Tipperary*. Advance ticket sales for the local theaters were heavy. The historic Shubert Theater was quiet with its opening three weeks away.

Old Yale gridiron notables like Walter Camp, Ray Biglow, Ray Tompkins, Malcome McBride, Jack Owsley, Jack Field, and others relaxed in the coaches counsel in room 117 of the Hotel Taft.

Game Day: November 21, 1914

It was sunny and not very cold. A light northwest breeze came puffing down from the Connecticut Hills. World War I in Europe (then referred to as the Great War) seemed like a million miles from New Haven with so much interest centered on the opening of the spectacular amphitheater. The Bowl was mega news and was heralded as the greatest athletic structure in the world. The *New Haven Evening Register* proudly proclaimed, "Made in New Haven. The Greatest Amphitheater in the World. The New Mammoth Yale Bowl."

Mass transportation played a major role in getting fans to and from the game. According to Yale historian Thomas Bergin, "The New Haven Railroad ran twenty-five specials from New York and fifteen from Boston; about 35,000 arrived by train."

Once in New Haven, thousands boarded the 150 trolleys that buzzed through the city. It was recommended by some that walking to the Bowl was the best bet.

Chapel Street was like Times Square on New Year's Eve with hucksters and fakers dispensing Yale-Harvard memorabilia. The *New York Times* reported, "In every store window in the city was a big bulldog with its collar of blue silk ribbons."

Some well-heeled old Blues most likely drove up in their glitzy Stutz Bearcats and parked in one of the 6,000 spaces available. Elm Street was so snarled with auto traffic that crossing the street at noon was impossible. Special automobile routes were established from the outlying towns.

A special train carrying the Harvard team left New London at 9:45 a.m. and was scheduled to arrive in New Haven at 11 a.m. The team remained in the parlor cars and went directly to the Bowl. This leaves one to speculate that they dressed in their New London hotel.

The First Fan in the Bowl

Most likely the first fan to make his way into the Bowl was Al Ostermann, an eight-year-old from the neighborhood. "The night before the first game, I dug a hole under a fence and put leaves in the hole," said Ostermann. "I made my own tunnel. The next day I crawled into the hole to get through the fence. I then entered the Bowl through a portal about 7:30 in the morning.

"I made a position for myself inside at the top of the Bowl, under the seats. A lot of kids who snuck in were seated just above the portals at midfield where the players come out, and they were thrown out.

"At 11 a.m. the crowd started to file in for the grand opening. An older couple found me curled up like a squirrel, chilled to the bone, and offered me a cup of coffee. It was the first cup of coffee I ever had.

"Of the first 500 games played in the Yale Bowl, I saw 499 of them. The only game I missed was because I attended an Army game. A few days after the 1977 Yale-Harvard game, I suffered a heart attack. When my wife, Eleanor, visited me in the intensive-care unit of the hospital, I whispered to her, 'At least I made it through the end of the season.'"

The Arrival of the Fans

Once the fans arrived at the Bowl they were greeted by throngs of vendors hawking pennants, badges, and buttons, along with hot dogs, sandwiches and fruit. Some fans entered the Bowl immediately upon arrival while others watched the Yale-Harvard soccer game that was being played across the street at Yale Field II. If they were lucky they could have caught an intercollegiate cross country race involving eleven colleges that started and ended in the Bowl, perhaps the first official sports event held (partially) in the Bowl.

Yale issued a special eighteen-page program to commemorate the grand opening. This program featured full-page color illustrations of the Yale Bowl before, during, and after its construction. For fans who did not attend Yale or Harvard games regularly, identifying the players was difficult since the players' jerseys were not yet numbered.

During the game an airship flight advertised over the Bowl added a spectacular touch.

Al Ostermann saw 499 of the first 500 games played in the Yale Bowl and was most likely the first spectator to step into the Bowl.
(NEW HAVEN REGISTER)

A total of 1,400 attendants were tasked with ushering approximately 70,000 fans, the largest crowd ever to attend a sporting event in the United States. "The Roman Colosseum with its grim drama of human torture, the great stone arena of Pompeii, the massive amphitheatre at ancient Carthage were never so densely populated with humans as the Yale Bowl was," wrote the *New York Times*.

At the time there were no fences surrounding the Bowl so ticket holders were not required to show their tickets until they reached the entrance to one of the portals.

The total take for the Bowl's opening day was more than $139,000, which was split between the two schools.

Yale Bowl opening commemorative program illustrated by the Tuttle Printing Co. described the construction of the Bowl.
(YALE ATHLETICS)

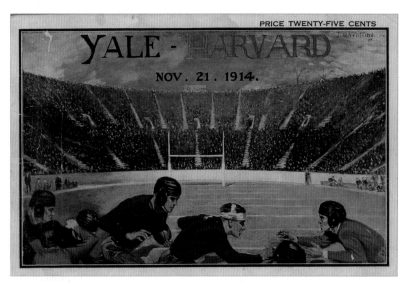

The Yale-Harvard opening-game day program
(YALE ATHLETICS)

Harvard Spoils the Party

Harvard came into the contest undefeated (6-0-2) and on a twenty-eight-game unbeaten streak that started in 1911. They would extend their run to thirty-three games, a streak that would end in the middle of the 1915 season. Yale captain Nelson Talbott predicted victory and trainer Johnny Mack declared the 7-1 Elis "fit for the game." But Harvard dominated the Bulldogs, winning 36-0. One journalist-wag wrote, "Yale had the Bowl but Harvard had the punch." Talbott took the loss hard. "He was so despondent because Yale lost that he walked the streets of New Haven all night," said

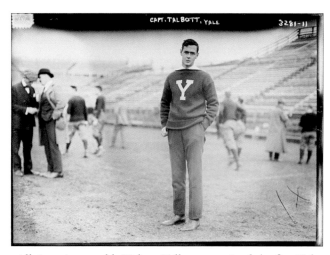

All-American tackle Nelson Talbott captained the first Yale team to play in the Yale Bowl.
(LIBRARY OF CONGRESS CCDIG-GGBAIN-17712)

Nelson Talbott Jr. who wore the Yale blue in the early '40s.

Harvard All-American end Tack Hardwick, whom Grantland Rice called "dynamite on the football field," scored the first touchdown and points in Bowl history on a five-yard pass from All-American Eddie "Packy" Mahan, who kicked the first field goal at the Bowl in the second quarter. Mahan also caught a touchdown pass and personally accounted for 15 points that day.

History was made in another way as well, when Harvard's All-American end Thomas Jefferson Coolidge returned a fumble 98 yards. Coolidge's play still stands as the longest fumble return at the Yale Bowl.

The first Bowl game was not without controversy, albeit minor. All-American back Charley Brickley had missed most of the season because of an appendectomy. The Harvard players wanted Brickley to play against Yale in the new Bowl but the doctors nixed the idea. Despite that, Brickley entered the game late in the fourth quarter under bogus circumstances. He was allowed to stand behind the action and watch while the other ten Harvards drove down the field for the final touchdown. Brickley then kicked the extra point.

At the end of the game (4:17 p.m.), Yale students and grads acknowledged defeat by singing *Bright College Years*, Yale's unofficial alma mater. The Harvards celebrated victory by doing the first snake dance in the new Bowl and launching a startling fireworks display at the tops of the goal posts. The stunt was conceived by Harvard alum George S. Prouty, who was unable to attend the contest.

That night the streets were quiet in the Elm City with the exception of seven Harvard students who extended their celebration and were each fined $5.29 for disturbing the peace. The revelry

Tack Hardwick scored the first touchdown in the Yale Bowl.

and pregame excitement of the night before was just a memory. The Yale coaching staff sequestered themselves in a room at Mory's.

In the wake of the Bowl's grand opening the big winners were New Haven mayor Frank Rice, police chief Philip Smith, and the various city departments that were responsible for planning the big event. Despite the massive crowd, there was nary an incident. The transportation system flowed smoothly, with streetcars moving thousands of fans without a glitch. Security problems were virtually nonexistent.

Harvard scoring in 1914 game. Notice the players are not numbered.
(YALE ATHLETICS)

THE SECOND GAME—NEARLY ONE YEAR LATER

The second game ever played in the Bowl was on September 25, 1915, when Yale defeated Maine 37-0. The first Yale touchdown in the Bowl was recorded by an otherwise anonymous player, Beverly V. Thompson. A popular feature of the contest was the public address announcer who was positioned on the field with a megaphone and announced the names of the players who scored touchdowns.

Despite the attraction of the new Bowl, the game was played before a sparse crowd of about 7,000. Strange but true, this was reported as the largest number to ever attend a Yale opening game. The reason for the light turnouts? Apparently the Yale

fandom had the perception that in opening games the Bulldog faced only inferior competition. And statistics seemed to bear this out. From 1876-1932, Yale played fifty-six openers yielding an amazing total of only three points when they defeated Wesleyan, 10-3, in 1912. Also, baseball on the state and major league level was still very popular at this time of the year.

The unusually warm weather was possibly a factor. The game started at 4:00 p.m. instead of the normal 3:00 p.m. start because of the heat.

By now the Yale Bowl had built a reputation as the most spectacular sports stadium in the world. It would not only provide a home for Yale football teams for over a century, but would be the site for multiple sports and non-sports events for decades.

(Yale Athletics)

CHAPTER 3

THE YELLOW LADIES OF THE TRACK

"The lighthearted crowds made a rush for the open trolleys, and clung like swarms of bees on the sagging sideboards."

—George Wilson Pierson,
emeritus historian of Yale University

THERE WAS A time when the rush of passengers boarding the open trolley cars to the Yale Bowl from downtown New Haven and the city's outskirts was as much a part of Yale football as touchdowns, field goals, and marching bands.

The electric trolley system around New Haven proliferated in the first two decades of the twentieth century. By 1920 more than 400 cars were rumbling along New Haven streets. The trolley was the most efficient and practical way to transport an ever-growing population that numbered more than 162,000 by 1930.

The trolley system was Yale Bowl's conduit deluxe for most of the pre-WWII era. According to John D. Somers, author of *Yale Bowl and the Open Trolleys*, the trolleys carried 33,000 passengers to the Bowl when it opened on November 21, 1914, for Yale's game with Harvard.

Of the 1936 Yale-Harvard game, he writes, "Between 1-2 p.m. 92 trolleys passed the corner of Chapel and College. They clanged, clattered and swayed their way to the Bowl, handling almost 15,000 passengers in 2 ½ hours."

The Connecticut Company, a subsidiary of the New Haven Railroad, used its open-sided trolleys on Yale game days, regardless of weather, because the open "breezers" could carry more passengers than the enclosed cars. The average car, forty-five feet long and about eight feet wide, could seat seventy-five while thirty-five to forty more passengers stood on the running boards. "The trolleys moved about 15-20 mph with a 45-second headway between them," wrote Somers.

Under the direction of the Connecticut Company, the trolleys were painted yellow with white trim and red stripes.

In downtown New Haven, the route to the Bowl began at Church and Chapel Streets, going out Chapel to Derby Avenue. The fare was 10 cents, or three tokens for a quarter. After games, the trolleys were lined up on Derby Avenue ready to go downtown to Chapel or to the railroad station. A passenger who disembarked at Church and Chapel after a Yale win might have visited the Hofbrau Haus, an old-fashioned landmark in Yale life.

The final trolley rush for a Yale game was on November 22, 1947, for the Yale-Harvard game. The last excursion to the Bowl was five days later on Thanksgiving Day for the annual high school game between Hillhouse and West Haven. All trolley service ceased in Connecticut the following September.

During the throes of the Great Depression in the 1930s, trolleys became a financial burden for the Connecticut Company which, along with the increasing popularity of cars and busses, led to their demise.

After the trolleys had transported countless Yale fans to and from the Bowl, the era of the "Yellow Ladies of the Track" had ended.

Artist Jim Fogelman captures the gay mood of the fans on the open trolley on the front cover of the November 1, 1947, Yale-Dartmouth game day program.
(YALE ATHLETICS)

Passengers are dropped off in front of the Walter Camp Memorial Gateway on Rt. 34-Derby Avenue.
(YALE ATHLETICS)

Open Trolley on display at The Shore Line Trolley Museum in East Haven, Connecticut. Notice the old Yale Field sign.
(BILL O'BRIEN/THE SHORE LINE TROLLEY MUSEUM IN EAST HAVEN, CONNECTICUT)

JOHN RESNIK ('57)

"The early 1930s were the heyday of the trolley. Trolley lines were spread all over New Haven. The Yale campus had tracks going through it, around it, and alongside it.

A pair of trolley tracks ran down the middle of the street. Cars passed on the right while people were getting on and off the trolley. With the exception of Yale game day, most of the trolley cars were closed and had doors on the right-hand side in the front and back. It took two people to operate them. While the motorman drove, the conductor would collect the fare.

But the 1930s was also the decade of the Great Depression. A trolley ride may have cost a nickel or a dime, but not everyone had the money. It was not unusual to see people hanging onto the side of the slow-moving trolley or for boys to come alongside with their bikes and hang on for a free ride. Al Capp, the cartoonist who created *Li'l Abner*, lost a leg at age nine in 1919 when he lost his hold and fell from the back of a New Haven trolley.

Yale College was all male in the '30s but you would never know it on big social weekends. The women arrived from the Seven Sisters on Friday afternoon and stayed until Sunday. They would charter a limo that sat seven.

The money seemed to be flowing as much as the booze. Jeans and T-shirts were not worn to the game—it was ties and jackets for the Yale students, and skirts and corsages for the coeds. No one had told them that the '20s had ended, so there were still some raccoon coats around. Hawkers were outside the Bowl selling banners,

pins, Yale feathers and flowers. The Depression was forgotten.

Everyone had to get to the Yale Bowl, of course, and there was the trolley. The tracks ran straight from downtown to the area of Coxe Cage on Derby Avenue.

Along both sides of the open trolley were double running boards and vertical poles used for holding on. Watching the cars going to the Bowl was like viewing an old silent movie. To avoid paying, when the conductor came to collect the fare, passengers would jump off the running board, run alongside the trolley, and then jump back on."

"Scramble"

"During the late 1930s, I lived on the Chapel Street route. My father and uncles had gone to Yale and would go to the games, but I was too young. I really didn't mind, because I used to wait for the trolley return trip. By then the flasks were empty and everyone was in a happy mood—especially if Yale won. We would yell, 'Scramble,' and money would be thrown to us. We then scurried to pick it up. The bigger the game, the more money there was. I remember the 1938 Harvard game in particular, when I picked up $3.52 in less than an hour. That was more than our maid earned for an entire week!

The trolleys are gone. So are the raccoon coats, neckties and jackets, banners, corsages, and a packed Yale Bowl. They have been replaced by parking lots jammed with tailgaters, many of which don't even go into the Bowl and watch the game."

A packed trolley heads to the Yale Bowl.
(The Shore Line Trolley Museum in East Haven, Connecticut)

AL OSTERMANN

"My father owned a florist in New Haven on the corner of Church and Chapel. He would sell 50,000 violets for every home game to the waiting passengers."

VIN BROZEK

"When I was in high school I worked behind the counter at the El Dorado Pharmacy as a soda jerk. The pharmacy was on Chapel Street, next to the Hotel Duncan. When Yale would play on a Saturday, the pharmacy was jammed with customers. They would get off the trolley, come into the store to get booze and sandwiches, then hop back on the trolley to the Bowl."

FRANK STOLZENBERG

"I walked up to Chapel Street and caught the last ride on Thanksgiving Day in 1947 for the Hillhouse-West Haven game. Jumping on the side of the open trolleys was easy."

TOM PEPE

"In the winter of 2010 there was a pothole in the driveway in front of the Smilow Center. When the ice and snow melted, we saw the remnants of a trolley track that apparently went into the Cullman Loop in front of the Coxe Cage."

World Cup soccer in the Yale Bowl.
(Bill O'Brien)

CHAPTER 4
A FRIENDLY HOST

"The game was just about to begin, and Babe Ruth lifted a gallon jug from under the bench. He poured something into a paper cup for himself and poured one for me. They looked like whiskey sours. He handed me a cup. 'To Eli Yale,' he said. Babe grinned at me. We raised our cups and drank."

—William White

ENTERING THE 2014 season, Yale has played 600 football games in the Yale Bowl. The Bulldogs have won 377 against 201 losses and 22 ties. Although the Bowl is historically linked to Yale football, it has been host to both sport and non-sport events. And some of the world's most popular figures have entered its dark portals.

ARMY-NAVY AND THE WORLD SERIES?

Because the Bowl could hold 25,000 more than any other football stadium at the time, there were plans to have the Army-Navy game played there on November 28, 1914, one week after the Yale-Harvard game. But Navy had a rule against its contingent spending the night away from Annapolis and the idea never came to fruition.

As incredible as it may sound, the Bowl was considered as a site for the 1915 World Series. About a month before the Bowl opened, Harry Hempstead, president, and John B. Foster, secretary of the New York Giants National League Club, came to New Haven as guests of Everard Thompson to explore the possibility of playing the '15 Series in the Bowl. Since the giant saucer could hold approximately 72,000, the profitability of the scheme was intriguing.

Hempstead and Foster took measurements and concluded the Bowl was adequate for baseball. On November 2, 1914, the *Hartford Courant* reported, "It was determined that there was more room in the Bowl for a baseball game than was provided in the crowded Fenway grounds at Boston on Columbus Day (1914) for the Athletics and Braves...." That game drew 35,520.

For reasons unknown, the idea never got off the ground.

THE BABE AT THE BOWL

On June 5, 1948, a dying Babe Ruth presented a manuscript of his autobiography to the Yale library in a ceremony that took place at Yale Field prior to a Yale baseball game. George H. W. Bush, captain of the Elis, accepted on behalf of the university. The popular photo is normally how fans connect the Babe to Yale.

Ruth, however, was no stranger to Yale. He had played exhibition games in the Elm city numerous times. And it appears that the Bambino enjoyed watching Yale football in the Bowl. Ruth and his wife were present at the 1932 Yale-Harvard game, which was played in a torrential rain. The *New York Times* reported the details of Yale's 19-0 victory.

"Babe Ruth sat in the downpour with Mrs. Ruth until his massive physique could not stand it any longer. He left in the fourth quarter totally unnoticed. He was just another bedraggled figure heading for the exits."

In 1985 *New York Times* writer Ira Berkow added to the story through an interview with William White, a professor emeritus of English at Miami University in Oxford, Ohio.

White talked about entering the Bowl on that rain-swept day as a seventeen-year-old Yale freshman. He sat alone on the 30-yard line, then moved to the 50 where fans were huddled together. "I had been sitting there only a moment or so when I felt someone tapping me on the shoulder," White recalled. "The man behind me said, 'Come sit with us.' The man was with a woman. The couple held a large strip of linoleum to protect them from the rain. I recognized him immediately. I said, 'I know you, you're Babe Ruth!'

Babe Ruth, presenting his autobiography to Yale baseball captain George H.W. Bush in 1948, enjoyed visiting the Yale Bowl.
(YALE ATHLETICS)

"He had a wonderful smile and he introduced me to his wife (Claire). I was aghast. She said, 'Come under, you don't want to get wet.'

"At about this time, the Yale and Harvard teams came sloshing onto the field and the modest crowd cheered. The Yale band struck up *Boola Boola*."

THE FRENCH CONNECTION

Marshal Foch, the Commander of the Allied forces during the closing months of World War I, attended the 1921 Yale-Princeton game. The following year French premier Georges Clemencau was in the Bowl for the Harvard contest. Like Foch, he diplomatically moved from the Harvard side to the Yale side at halftime while both bands played the *Marseillaise*. Actress Gloria Swanson attended the 1925 Yale-Princeton game with her titled husband Henri, Marquis de la Falaise de la Coudraye.

PRESIDENTS IN THE BOWL

Former President William Howard Taft (1909-1913), a Yale alumnus, rowed on the Yale crew and was an accomplished wrestler. He returned to the university after leaving the White House in 1913 to teach law. Taft was a member of the Yale Law faculty until 1921, when he was appointed Chief Justice of the Supreme Court. Because his son, Charley, lettered at Yale as a center in 1916 and 1918, it's safe to assume that during this time Taft attended games in the Bowl.

The 1995 Special Olympics was a memorable spectacle.
(BILL O'BRIEN)

Herbert Hoover, the 31st President of the United States (1929-33) attended Yale's 15-7 win over Army on October 16, 1937, and reportedly attended the 1940 Yale-Harvard game.

Former Michigan star Gerald Ford, who became president when Richard Nixon resigned, served Ducky Pond as an assistant coach from 1935 to 1940 while attending Yale Law School.

Harvard grad and future president John F. Kennedy was a spectator at the 1955 Yale-Harvard game to cheer on his brother, Ted, and the Crimson.

You can bet that Yale alums George H.W. Bush and George W. Bush, sang *Bulldog* a number of times before taking residence in the White House.

Bo Jackson and former Yale running back Rich Diana meet in New Haven during the 1995 Special Olympics World Games.
(BILL O'BRIEN)

Future President Ronald Reagan showed up for the October 2, 1976, Lehigh game during parents weekend—his son, Ron, was a Yale student—and dined at Mory's following the game.

The 1995 Special Olympics World Games involving 140 countries were hosted by New Haven from July 1-9 with the opening and closing ceremonies taking place in the Bowl. President Bill Clinton and First Lady Hillary Clinton, both Yale Law School grads, attended the opening ceremonies with about 60,000 on hand. It is believed to be the only time a sitting president visited the Yale Bowl.

WORLD WAR I AND CAMP YALE

Because of the Great War, Yale did not field a team in 1918, but there was football in the Bowl when the Newport (R.I.) Naval Training Station played trainees from Pelham Bay (N.Y.) for the Eastern football championship of the U.S. Navy. Walter Camp helped bring the game to the city in his role as head of fitness programs for the Navy and the Army Air Service.

The war transformed the area surrounding the Bowl into a military base known as "Camp Yale." In April 1917, America mobilized its National Guard forces. The 1st Connecticut, from the Hartford area, and the 2nd Connecticut, from the New Haven area, were sent to Camp Yale for training. The

1st and 2nd combined to form the 102nd Infantry and were made part of the 26th (Yankee) Division of Massachusetts. (The "102nd" designation represented the numbers 1 and 2 with "nothing" in between.)

Military tents spread out over the current site of the Coxe Cage, the tennis courts, the soccer and lacrosse stadium, parking lots B, C, D, E and F. The officers were quartered in tents across the street at what is now DeWitt Cuyler Field, adjacent to the Yale baseball field. A 102nd Street sign still stands on the corner of Central and Derby Avenues. The armory by Lot D where the polo horses were housed, was built during World War I to shelter the cavalry horses.

Before the soldiers were shipped overseas they were treated to a vaudeville show staged by citizens of New Haven that drew 50,000 in the Bowl. It was an evening event with portable lights with the stage set in the middle of the field. Acts arrived from all points of the globe including Australia, Japan and the United States. The two-hour program finished with the "Great White Circus."

STUBBY: THE MILITARY DOG

There was no Handsome Dan, the Yale bulldog mascot, during this time, but a mongrel named Stubby wandered into the encampment and befriended the

View of the grounds outside the Bowl occupied by Camp Yale. This 1917 photo was most likely taken on the berm or atop the Bowl above Portal 16 facing what is now the tennis courts and the Smilow Field Center.
(WEST HAVEN VETERANS MUSEUM AND LEARNING CENTER)

Stubby was a WWI hero.
(West Haven Veterans Museum and Learning Center)

soldiers. When the unit was deployed to France in October 1917, Stubby was smuggled aboard the troop ship *SS Minnesota* by Pvt. J. Robert Conroy and became the official mascot of the 102nd. Stubby was with the troops in seventeen battles, making morale-lifting visits up and down the line. With his sensitive nose, he gave early warnings of poisonous gas attacks, and he saved lives by leading medics to wounded soldiers. Stubby himself was wounded by shrapnel from a German grenade.

After the war Conroy brought him back to America and he became a celebrity, receiving awards from both French and American armed forces and twice visiting the White House. When Conroy enrolled as a law student at Georgetown, Stubby became the Hoyas' mascot, nudging a football around the field. He died in Conroy's arms in 1926.

Local Club Football

The local community has made frequent use of the Bowl. On November 28, 1920, two New Haven neighborhood teams, the Washington Glee Club and the Williams Athletic Club, played to a scoreless tie before a crowd of 10,000. Several days later the Glees played the professional Canton Bulldogs, led by Olympic legend Jim Thorpe in a heavy rain at Weiss Park, a baseball field in nearby Hamden built by George Weiss who grew up on Whalley Avenue in New Haven. The future New York Yankees and New York Mets general manager attended Yale but never graduated.

Both Yale and Harvard started 150-pound teams (also then known as lightweight football) in 1930,

when they played at Harvard with Harvard winning 7-0. On November 14, 1931, Yale won 14-0 in the Bowl on two touchdowns and a safety in front of 1,200 fans.

High School Football

The Bowl also has been used for interscholastic football. The first high school game played there took place on November 21, 1931, when Hillhouse defeated Commercial (now Wilbur Cross) 46-0 before a crowd that numbered over 16,000. Proceeds from the game went to the Community Chest, a forerunner of the United Way. This was the only high school game played in the Bowl until 1939 when Hillhouse met West Haven. From 1939 through 1957 the two schools played their traditional Thanksgiving Day game there. Hillhouse dominated the series going 14-2-3. The 1948 game drew a state record 40,504 fans.

The Bowl was also the site of the Harvest Festival game between Hillhouse and crosstown rival Wilbur Cross from 1951-56. Yale did not charge a rental fee for these events. The schools paid for the personnel needed to staff the Bowl and then divided the remainder of gate receipts.

Hopkins School, then known as Hopkins Grammar, used the Bowl occasionally in the 1940s, as did Hamden High School when it played Hillhouse. The Nutmeg Bowl, a Connecticut scholastic all-star game, was staged there in 1975. The last high school game played at the Bowl was on December 1, 1984, when Hand defeated Wilton 14-7 in a C.I.A.C. (Connecticut Interscholastic Athletic Conference) playoff game.

It should be noted that Yale allowed use of its facilities for high school football long before there was a Yale Bowl. On November 3, 1894, the semifinal football game for the championship in the

The scoreboard was originally on the visitors or east side of the Bowl.
(YALE ATHLETICS)

Bobby Hertz, the "Human Semaphore"
(YALE ATHLETICS)

Connecticut Interscholastic Football League was played at Yale Field I with Bridgeport High School defeating New Haven High School, 10-4.

BOBBY HERTZ AND SCOREBOARD HISTORY

Yale Bowl's original scoreboard was located across from the press box above Portal 2 on the east side or visitors' side of the Bowl. Eventually the board was placed behind the north end zone for the start of the 1937 season where it has since remained. The Western Union clock was prominently displayed on that scoreboard.

The first electrified scoreboard appeared in the Bowl in 1958 and was financed by the Bobby Hertz Memorial Fund, a project spearheaded by the New Haven Gridiron Club in memory of Hertz, who died the year before. Hertz spent fifty-one years walking the sidelines at Yale Field and the Bowl, giving semaphore signals with his arms to the scoreboard operator, who would post the ball's position, down and yards to go by hand. He earned the nickname "Human Semaphore." Hertz was distinguished by his white flannel sweater with black stripes on the sleeves, white flannel slacks and white shoes.

The current scoreboard was installed in 2008.

FOOTBALL LUMINARIES IN THE BOWL

Six Heisman Trophy winners played in the Bowl Including Larry Kelley and Clint Frank (Yale), Tom Harmon (Michigan), Glenn Davis (Army), Dick Kazmaier (Princeton) and Doug Flutie (Boston College). Except for Kelley and Frank, all played in the Bowl as underclassmen, before their Heisman years.

Distinctive actors who have left cleatmarks in the Bowl include Ed Marinaro (Cornell); Harvard's Tommy Lee Jones; Brian Clarke and Kip Pardue (Yale); Brian Dennehy (Columbia); and Dean Cain (Princeton). And the Bowl has had its share of TV personalities including Stone Phillips and Jack Ford (Yale) and Dan Jiggetts and James Brown (Harvard).

PRO FOOTBALL, SOCCER, AND MORE

The New York Giants played thirteen exhibition games in the Bowl, beginning in 1960. Also, the team played most of its regular season games there in 1973 and 1974. (For more on the Giants at the Bowl, see Chapter 5.)

The Yale Bowl also has been the site of international soccer, lacrosse, tennis, concerts and even an open-air flea market sponsored by the *New Haven Register* Fresh Air Fund in '1976.

Brazil defeated Italy 4-1 before 36,096 fans including Secretary of State Henry Kissinger to

World Cup soccer action
(BILL O'BRIEN)

In 1997 the University of New Haven football team enjoyed NCAA playoff wins in the Bowl.
(UNIVERSITY OF NEW HAVEN DEPARTMENT OF ATHLETICS)

capture the American Bicentennial Soccer Cup on May 31, 1976. The worldwide TV audience was expected to be 130 million, most likely the most widely watched event ever from the Bowl.

The Bowl served as home field for the Connecticut Bicentennials of the North American Soccer League in 1977. The franchise opened the season against the New York Cosmos and Pele, the Brazilian superstar. The game drew 17,302, more than four times the average for 13 home matches. When the game ended, a mob ran onto the field and chased Pele into the visitors' tunnel on the east side of the Bowl. Pele praised the Bowl and said, "I loved being on the field because it has beautiful grass." But in general the soccer people did not favor playing on a crowned field.

On June 6, 1993, the U.S. played Brazil in a World Cup Soccer game in front of 44,579 fans.

In 1997 the University of New Haven football team, en route to the NCAA Division II finals, defeated Slippery Rock and Cal Davis in the second and third rounds of the playoffs played in the Bowl.

On August 24, 2009, the Bowl was turned into the largest tennis court in the world. In conjunction with the Pilot Pen Tennis Tournament at Yale's Cullman-Heyman Tennis Center, Caroline Wozniacki faced Flavia Pennetta. The sponsors exhibition, a publicity stunt with no fans on hand, was billed as a "Football Tennis" match.

CONCERTS

Not long after the Yale-Harvard game in 1914, world famous opera tenor John McCormack was invited to sing to an empty Bowl to test its acoustics and sound. Everand Thompson sat at a distance and determined that a grand opera would be a success there.

The first concert was held on May 15, 1915, when the Yale Dramatic Association performed *Euripides' Iphigeneia in Tauris* before 14,000. In 1916 *Die Walkure* was performed there.

On July 6, 1945, a series of five summer concerts promoted by the New Haven Junior Chamber of Commerce began under the direction of Harry Berman before a crowd of 10,000. The concerts, patterned after the famous Boston Pops, were supported by the 80-piece New Haven Symphony orchestra.

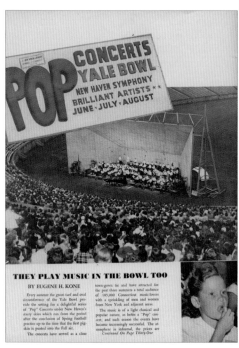

THEY PLAY MUSIC IN THE BOWL TOO

BY EUGENE H. KONE

Every summer the green turf and oval circumference of the Yale Bowl provide the setting for a delightful series of "Pop" Concerts under New Haven's starry skies which run from the period after the conclusion of Spring football practice up to the time that the first pigskin is punted into the Fall air.

The concerts have served as a close town-gown tie and have attracted for the past three summers a total audience of 185,000 Connecticut music-lovers with a sprinkling of men and women from New York and adjacent areas.

The music is of a light classical and popular nature, as befits a "Pop" concert, and each season the events have become increasingly successful. The atmosphere is informal, the prices are reasonable.
Continued On Page Thirty-One

The Pop concerts and rock concerts provided fine entertainment on warm summer evenings.
(YALE ATHLETICS)

New Haven mayor Dick Lee emceed many concerts during his tenure. Actress Martha Wright was one of the guest stars. Glenn Miller, head of the Army Air Forces band, Benny Goodman and other famous band leaders played in the Bowl with the New Haven Pops. Leroy Anderson, the preeminent composer, was a guest conductor at a summer Pops in the Bowl.

Over the years such stars as Johnny Mathis, Simon and Garfunkel, Sonny and Cher, Ray Charles, Jack Jones, James Taylor, Linda Ronstadt, Anne Murray and Eric Clapton appeared in concert as well as noted groups like Peter, Paul and Mary, the Beach Boys, Chicago, Seals and Crofts, Led Zeppelin, Three Dog Night, The James Gang, The Lovin' Spoonful, Grand Funk, Yes, The Grateful Dead, and The Who. For most concerts the stage was at the south end of the field, opposite the scoreboard. Spectators used the approximately 20,000 seats behind the end zone.

The term "pop concert" changed to "rock concert" with time. Concerts ended after an event titled "Summer Jam 1980" on June 14 of that year. The Eagles, Heart and The Little River Band performed and 67,000 spectators attended, paying $15.50 each for a gross of more than $1 million. Yale received $100,000 for the rental; $20,000 went to charities.

"People were on the grass, in the bleachers and stuck in the portals," said Rich Schyner the Superintendent of Yale Athletic Fields from 1963 to 1988. "Unlike the concerts in the 1950s and '60s, the stage was set up in the end zone area on the scoreboard end of the field. There were large video screens on the stage to assist the viewing."

Police made only twelve arrests, but the rowdy crowd left residents in the neighborhood fuming. When a Paul McCartney concert was scheduled for June 1990, local opposition was so vehement that the event was called off and rescheduled for Chicago.

CELEBRATIONS AND SPECIAL EVENTS

The Bowl has been Yale's home field since its opening, with one exception. In the fall of 1916 Yale staged an elaborate pageant to celebrate the 200th anniversary of its move from Saybrook, Connecticut to New Haven in 1716. The rehearsal, involving a cast of 8,000, forced the October 14 game with Lehigh to be held across the street at Yale Field II and because the pageant itself was on a Saturday, October 21, Yale met Virginia Tech in the Bowl that Friday. It was the only Friday game ever played in the Bowl by the Yale varsity.

In 1938 a part of the tercentenary celebration of New Haven's founding was conducted in the Bowl. From June 7-10, a spectacular pageant re-enacted New Haven's history.

On October 5, 2001, the Bowl was used for the closing ceremony of Yale's own tercentenary. To allow time for cleanup afterward, the scheduled game with Dartmouth was shifted to October 7, a Sunday, the only time Yale football has had a Sunday varsity game.

The Yale Bowl's Only Wedding

A wedding was staged in the Bowl when two former Yale band members tied the knot on October 10, 1992, at halftime of the Yale-Fordham game.

"My daughter Rori married Jim Lockman at halftime of the Yale-Fordham game," said Carol Smullen. "Both were former members of the Yale Precision Marching Band and fell in love. Jim (1989) was the drum major and Rori (1992) did the props. I walked her down the 50-yard line and Judge Riley performed the ceremony. Members of the Yale band were in the wedding party and the bridesmaids had flowers draped on their instruments. Following the ceremony we marched off with the band and that evening held a reception in Guilford. The only wedding in Yale Bowl history got national media coverage, and I received phone calls from people I hadn't seen in years.

James Lockman, '89 Saybrook, and Rori Myers, Branford '92, greet the assembled crowd following their wedding on the 50-yard line in the Yale Bowl on Oct. 10, 1992.
(Michael Marsland/Yale University)

"Tom Duffy, the director of bands at Yale University and professor (adjunct) in the Yale School of Music, authorized the ceremony. The Yale administration wasn't aware this was going to take place in the Bowl, and I don't think they would ever allow this to happen again.

"Jim and Lori are happily married with three children and live in Maine. The license plate on their car reads: 'YPMB.'"

In celebration of their 20th wedding anniversary, the couple renewed their vows in the Bowl at halftime of the Yale-Lafayette game on October 13, 2012. Joining the celebration were their children, Arthur, Theodore, and Ezekiel.

Clouds Over the Bowl

Although the Bowl has been the site of mountains of thrills and memorable events, it has had its share of tragedies. On June 1, 1919, three military planes flew over the area of the Yale Bowl when two collided 1,000 feet in the air. Two aviators, Lieutenant Melvin B. Kelcher and Corporal Joseph Katzman were instantly killed when their plane crashed in a sandy terrace in front of the property of C. E. Libbey on Westwood Avenue near Yale Avenue. The plane narrowly escaped falling on several houses and among a dozen people.

The plane that struck them was piloted by Lieutenant Howard D. Norris. The Norris plane had trouble in alighting. It was, however, able to make a safe descent after the crash but in landing ran into the backstop at Pratt Field smashing the propeller and both wings.

On October 24, 1931, 75,000 packed the Bowl for the Army game. Army scored on the first play in the fourth quarter to take a 6-0 lead but missed the extra point. Army then kicked off and Bud Parker ran it back 88 yards, tying the game 6-6. But Yale missed the conversion and the score remained tied. The rule for many years in college football was that the team scored on had the option of kicking off or receiving the kick. Army elected to kick off after Yale scored apparently thinking they would subsequently grab good field position.

West Point cadet Richard Sheridan lost his life resulting from injuries in the 1931 Yale-Army game. (YALE ATHLETICS)

Yale's Bob Lassiter returned the kickoff and was hit by Richard Sheridan, a slender 149-pound end who was trying to bust Yale's "flying wedge" (The flying wedge was a V-shaped formation which had its origins as a military tactic.) Lassiter's knee struck Sheridan in the back of the neck fracturing his fourth and fifth cervical vertebrae. He fell unconscious and was rushed to New Haven Hospital where he underwent emergency surgery. The cadet died two days later, the first and only on-field fatality in Yale Bowl history.

The flying wedge had by then been banned, but was still permitted on kickoffs.

Major Ralph Sasse, Army's head coach, went to Sheridan's bedside after the game and remained with him for two days before he died on Monday, October 26.

Sheridan's body lay in state at West Point and was buried with full military honors on October 29. Yale coach Mal Stevens and team captain Albie Booth attended the funeral.

At the close of the 1931 season, the American Football Coaches Association appointed Yale coach Mal Stevens to head a committee to investigate injuries and fatalities in college football. A staggering total of 43-50 football-related deaths was recorded in 1931, seven of which occurred on the collegiate level. Stevens had a medical degree from Yale and taught orthopedic surgery when he wasn't coaching. His findings led to several changes to make the game safer. Defensive players were forbidden to strike opponents on the head, neck or face. And the use of the flying wedge was barred under threat of penalty, including during kickoffs.

The unusual sight of four teams appearing in the Bowl on the same day occurred on December 5, 1931, when Yale, Brown, Dartmouth, and Holy Cross competed in an exhibition to raise money for charity amid the Great Depression. According to former Dartmouth Sports Information Director Jack DeGange, *The Dartmouth* called the spectacle, "a gridiron rodeo... the most amazing football circus ever concocted."

Spectators paid $2 for the event that was described as "The Gloomy Bowl." A total of 9,232 programs were sold at 25 cents each. Several such charity events were held across the country.

Each game in the Bowl consisted of two twelve-minute periods. Dartmouth opened against Brown followed by Yale and Holy Cross. Yale beat Holy Cross 6-0 and had a scoreless game with Brown. A panel of judges from Trinity, Tufts, and Bowdoin awarded Yale the championship on the basis of a complicated scoring system. Points were awarded or subtracted for yards gained, fumbles, interceptions, and so on.

The event drew somewhere between 22,000 and 28,000 spectators, raising almost $50,000.

The four team exhibition ended on a sad note when James C. Kelly, 35, a chain store grocer, died at New Haven Hospital three days later as a result of falling to the pavement as he was leaving the Bowl following the game. His skull was fractured and he lapsed into unconsciousness several hours after the fall. An emergency operation could not save his life.

Despite these and other sad events, the Yale Bowl has, for the most part, been the site of enormous enjoyment. It is a unique venue where sports and non-sports legends have performed for a century. These performers have given the Bowl its face, but it is the fans who have given the stadium its personality.

CHAPTER 5

THE GIANTS IN THE BOWL

*"Considering the amount of beer in
there, I think the fans did pretty good."*

—A New Haven police spokesman after the
New York Giants' first regular season game in
the Bowl on October 7, 1973

THE NEW YORK Giants played most of the 1973 season and all of the 1974 campaign in the Yale Bowl. The Gotham Gang was quite familiar with the surroundings. They had played thirteen exhibition games in the old saucer beginning in 1960. The first three were played to provide construction funds for the Albie Booth Memorial Boys Club in New Haven. Later, Yale partnered with the United Way, and the annual exhibition was known as the Yale-United Way Game.

The first Albie Booth game, on September 11, 1960, saw the Giants and Detroit Lions battle to a 16-16 tie in a steady drizzle. Connecticut natives Andy Robustelli of Stamford and Nick Pietrosante of Ansonia were key attractions. Both had dreamed

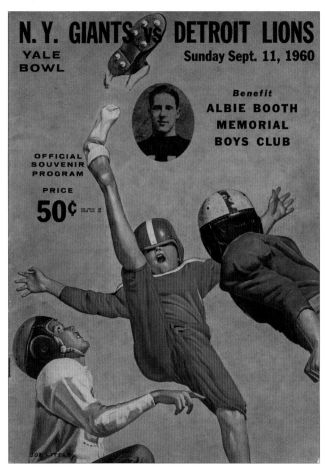

1960 program of the first Albie Booth Memorial NFL exhibition game
(BILL O'BRIEN)

of playing in the Bowl. The Lions' Pietrosante scored the tying touchdown late in the game on a one-yard plunge, but Jim Martin missed the extra point.

The following year, on September 10th, Johnny Unitas and the Baltimore Colts crushed the Giants 49-20 in sweltering 89-degree heat. The vendors weren't quite prepared for the parched 50,737 fans. Arguably the greatest quarterback to ever play in the venerated Bowl, Unitas passed for 246 yards and four touchdowns in the first quarter. He added another score in the first half. For the day he threw for 327 yards.

"My most memorable experience at the Bowl was when the Giants and the Colts played the Albie Booth Memorial exhibition game," said longtime fan Al Proto. "At the time I lived on Huntington Avenue in the Annex part of New Haven. I didn't have a ticket, but I met a detective at the turnstile and he took care of me. He told the guy taking the tickets that I was with him, like I was in custody.

"We entered the portal under the scoreboard as the game was in progress, and I sat on the steps since I didn't have a ticket. If someone asked to see my ticket, this detective would cover me and say, 'He's with me.'

"It was a brutally hot day. I think Giants' lineman Rosey Grier lost 15 pounds. The vendors ran out of soda, and they were selling ice for 25 cents a cup. I looked around for some relief. The only place I could see any shade was the scoreboard. So I went up and snuck behind the scoreboard and watched the game through the open slats. I didn't get a panoramic view but I was glad to see what I saw.

"I had one of the coolest seats in the Bowl—not bad for a kid in custody without a ticket."

Fullback Chuck Mercein, who starred for Yale in the early 1960s, returned to the Bowl in '66 as a member of the Giants when they played an exhibition game against the Pittsburgh Steelers.

"I kicked a 45-yard field goal thanks to Joe Morrison, the holder," recalled Mercein. "The snap was high and Joe had to grab it and place the ball down properly with the laces of the ball away as always. Because it was a bad snap, it took Joe longer for that to happen, which screwed-up the timing on the kick. Morrison did a great job of getting the ball down under the circumstances."

Playing in the NFL out of an Ivy League school posed a challenge for the former Yalie. "I took my share of kidding by my teammates," stated Mercein. "They used to call me 'Boola, Boola,' but not often. What did bother me is when Giants' coach Allie Sherman would make a wise comment like, 'Don't think you're playing against Harvard this week,' which was his way of demeaning Ivy League football. Didn't he realize that I was recruited by schools all over the country? I didn't see eye to eye with Sherman. Here was a little guy from Brooklyn with a Southern accent. He was a phony."

SUBURBAN SUPER BOWL I

On August 17, 1969, the New York Jets beat the Giants 37-14 in an exhibition billed as Suburban Super Bowl I. The game drew 70,874, the largest crowd to witness an NFL game in the Bowl. "The Super Bowl was one thing, but playing in the Yale Bowl before 70,000 people for an exhibition...that was another kind of Super Bowl," said Jets wide receiver Don Maynard to the *New Haven Register.* "That game meant something."

Tickets sold out in twenty-four hours. The Jets came to New Haven off their Super Bowl win against the Colts with charismatic quarterback "Broadway Joe" Namath as the main attraction The team's share from the sellout was $87,545 with players receiving $250 for the game. Jets business manager John Free

"Broadway Joe" Namath in the Yale Bowl
(SABBY FRINZI)

reportedly lost the check in the team's locker room. "Overall the two teams played seven exhibitions in the Bowl from 1969 through 1975, the Giants going 4-2-1," according to Giants' football historian Don Kosakowski.

WELCOME GIANTS

The Giants were interested in using the Bowl in 1973 and 1974 for regular season games because of renovations at Yankee Stadium and the still-unfinished construction of Giants Stadium in New Jersey's Meadowlands. (In March 1973, Princeton University had turned down the team's request to play home games at Palmer Stadium.)

"Giants' owner Wellington Mara and general manager Ray Walsh made a visit to New Haven to research the possibility and assess the conditions and facilities of the Bowl which was almost sixty-years-old and in a state of disrepair," stated broadcaster George Grande. "I was privy to a luncheon meeting with them and the Yale powers to be at 'Patricia's' restaurant on Broadway. Mara, who had a great sense of Yale Bowl history said, 'My father took me here and I remember what a special place it was. We're looking for a place to play. Can you people help us?' He added, 'One thing I hope we can do is help restore the glory and grandeur of the best place to play football in America.'"

Yale administrator Sam Chauncey was directly involved in the negotiations with Mara that proved to be a cash cow for Yale. "They paid us one million dollars for using the Bowl for almost two years," he revealed. "In addition, the Giants renovated the halftime rooms in the Bowl and improved the facilities in the Lapham Field House. Overall the deal was worth about two and a half million dollars to Yale. That was big money then. The cities of New Haven, West Haven, and Yale all got a cut from gate and concession receipts. Jack Blake, our ticket manager at Yale, wanted to know if Yale would be involved in selling tickets for the NFL games. When I asked Mara about this he responded, 'We've never sold tickets because of the season ticket holder sale.'"

From the outset, the Giants presence in the Bowl was not a positive experience for everyone. Aside from disgruntled residents in the neighborhood near the Bowl, Rich Schyner, who succeeded Bill Humes as the Superintendent of the Yale Athletic Fields, was not a happy camper.

"My biggest challenge over the years was when the New York Giants played in the Bowl," lamented Schyner. "If there was a Yale game on a Saturday and a Giants game the next day, I would be working from 6 on Saturday morning to about 9 on Sunday night. That's almost forty hours. And all I got for that extra work was $50. I felt like telling them that you can put that $50 where the sun don't shine. They were long days, and I would only get about three hours of sleep in the halftime room that the Yale team used."

The differences in rules between college and pro football necessitated some fast changes to the field. "We had to dismantle the goal posts that were used for the Yale games, which were ten yards behind the goal line, and install the pro goal posts, which were narrower, on the goal line," said Schyner.

"The Friday before a Giants game, one of their trainers would drive to New Haven with the pro goal posts; he'd take them back after the game. In addition, the pro hash marks were closer together and we had to adjust those as well. My crew of about 21 would also work on the divots from the Yale game to make the playing field as smooth as possible. We used to also bring in fifty to sixty temporary workers for the trash.

"I used to charge the Giants $5,000 a game, and they made a stink. Keep in mind that I paid my guys time and a half. All the Giants cared about when they were here was making money. They weren't concerned about the game or the people. Before the game ended, they would split the money with the visiting team and Yale would get a cut. I've hated the Giants ever since.

"Fans from New York would arrive at 8 a.m. Sunday and ask what time the bars opened. I'd say, 'You're in Connecticut.'" (At the time, Connecticut's Blue Laws prohibited the sale of alcohol in taverns on Sundays.)

Rich Schyner, former Superintendent of Yale Athletic Fields (Tom Pepe)

Traffic was another issue. Bob Sheppard, the mellifluous public-address announcer at Yankee Stadium and Giants Stadium for many years, handled the PA when the Giants played in the Bowl. "I did not enjoy going up to New Haven from my home in Long Island because of the traffic," said Sheppard candidly prior to his death in 2010. "It was terrible."

The Hapless Giants

In 1973 the Giants played their first two games at Yankee Stadium before moving to the Bowl for their final five. Tickets were priced at $8.

Writing in the *New York Times*, on May 20, 1973, Arthur Daley had described the impending move this way: "The New York Giants will turn loose their football forces on the sacred sod of the Yale Bowl for most of their home games for the next two seasons because they are relying on the unflinching devotion of longtime, hardcore followers who will stay with them through thick and thin, hell and high water." When the Giants took the field almost five months later, it wasn't long before the fans' devotion was sorely tested.

The first regular season NFL game played in the Bowl was on October 7, 1973, when the Green Bay Packers beat the Giants, 16-14 in front of a hostile crowd of 70,050. "The fans were vicious, and lit into players and coaches throughout the game," wrote Chip Malafronte in the *Register's* "200" series in 2013. "When it was over, a beer bottle hurled in disgust splattered against the side of the team bus as it pulled away from the stadium." Despite the angry crowd only six arrests were made, including two for intoxication. It marked the first time that beer was sold in the Yale Bowl.

These were not the Giants of Y.A. Tittle, Phil Simms, and Eli Manning but rather the Giants of Craig Morton, Norm Snead, and Pete Athas. During their almost two full-season stay, the hapless "Mara-men" went 1-11, their only win coming against the St. Louis Cardinals in '73. Despite their futility, four of the five home games that year drew over 70,000. Including exhibition games, the Giants were 8-15-2 in the Bowl going back to 1960.

NFL History Made in the Yale Bowl

The 1974 season was the first year the NFL used the overtime rule for regular season games. On November 10 the Jets beat the Giants in overtime marking the first time a regular season NFL game was won in overtime. The Jets' win was punctuated by a three-yard bootleg by Namath, the limping Jets QB, that tied the score. His five yard pass to halfback Emerson Boozer won the game in overtime, 26-20.

Because there were no sellouts in '74, all seven home games were blacked out locally on TV. The Giants played the Philadelphia Eagles in their

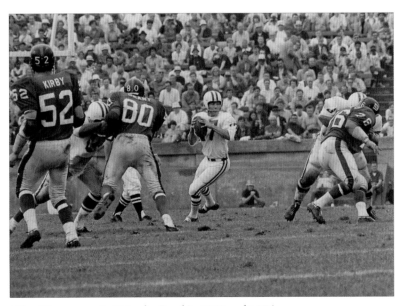

The Giants were 1-11 in the Bowl in 1973 and 1974.
(Yale Athletics)

Giants quarterback Craig Morton looks down field at the Yale Bowl during a muddy game against the Philadelphia Eagles on December 8, 1974. This was the Giants' last game in the Bowl.
(AP)

final game in the Bowl on December 8, 1974, in front of a sparse 21,170. Ten days later the team announced that it would be playing its home games in '75 in Shea Stadium. *Register* sports editor Bill Guthrie quipped, "The fastest the New York Giants moved all year was out of town."

WELCOME HOME CALVIN

The Giants playing in the Bowl allowed Calvin Hill (Yale/Cowboys), Ed Marinaro (Cornell/ Vikings) and Pete Gogolak (Cornell/Giants) to boast that they were the only players to play in regular season games in the Bowl as collegians and pros.

"I returned to the Yale Bowl as a member of the Dallas Cowboys on November 11, 1973 and October 27, 1974, to play against the Giants," recalled

Calvin Hill
(YALE ATHLETICS)

Ed Marinaro
(CORNELL UNIVERSITY ATHLETICS)

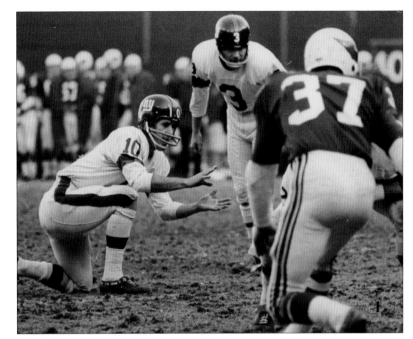

Pete Gogolak
(CORNELL UNIVERSITY ATHLETICS)

Hill. "When we arrived in '73, we stayed at a hotel in West Haven. On the way from the airport I sat in the front seat of the bus and told the driver how to get to the hotel. Without telling my teammates, I had the bus driver tour the Yale campus. The players were really getting pissed off at me. They were tired from all the travel and wanted to get to their rooms. Mark Washington and Robert Newhouse, two Cowboy teammates, accompanied me to dinner at Mory's and we walked around the campus.

"On the day of the game we dressed at the Lapham Field House and walked to the Bowl, just like I did when I played at Yale. For many of the Cowboys that

was a negative, but they were shocked how big the Bowl was. I was greeted by many well-wishers, who remembered me. Our bench was on the visitors' side in the Bowl. It seemed strange at first but I soon got adjusted. After the game, I walked back to the field house and signed autographs.

"It was a great day!"

Broadcaster/attorney Joel Alderman ('51) interviewed Hill when he returned to the Bowl as a member of the Dallas Cowboys.

"In the '73 game he had 19 carries for 95 yards and the following year had 23 carries for 73 yards," recalled Alderman. Calvin said, 'Never in my wildest imagination when I graduated from Yale did I think someday I would play another game in the Yale Bowl.'"

The Giants never played in the Bowl again. The team did not miss playing in a venue without a clubhouse and the fans, as evidence by their paltry attendance, did not miss the Giants.

The newly-restored Yale Bowl.
(WOODRUFF/BROWN ARCHITECTURAL PHOTOGRAPHY)

CHAPTER 6

SAVING THE BOWL—A MAN, A CLASS

"The Bowl is beginning to look perilously like the ruins of the Roman amphitheaters that inspired its design"

—Marc Wortman, *Yale Alumni Magazine* (November 1992)

"What you will see going into the Bowl this Saturday is the work on the outside... The inside is complete. It's magnificent."

—Yale Athletic Director Tom Beckett *(Hartford Courant,* September 13, 2006)

BY THE LATE '70s, what was once the most august football facility in the nation had grown old and antiquated. Decades of weathering and corrosion caused excessive amounts of moisture in the concrete forcing the surface to peel or flake, a condition known as spalling. Unplanted trees had grown between the interior and exterior walls of the Bowl. "The trees had root systems the size of some tree trunks, many of which played a key role in the destruction of the exterior walls," wrote Sean Barker in the *New Haven Register.*

In addition, new drainage lines were needed and utilities called for repair. The thirty portals including the entrances and wing walls at the exits were in need of refurbishing. Along with the decaying walls, the seats became decrepit.

Some called for the tired looking structure to be bulldozed. In 1989 members of the Yale Precision Marching Band gave it a cursory facelift by repainting the seventeen miles of seats that were in utter decay.

"The concrete within the bowl and on the outside of the bowl was severely deteriorated and falling apart," said Carmine Capasso, the projects manager for the restoration. "There was no waterproofing back in the day when the Bowl was built, so the harsh freeze thaw cycles caused the concrete to split and deteriorate. As part of the restoration project, the deteriorated concrete was sounded out and removed and new concrete was formed and poured."

G.L. Capasso Inc. was awarded the contract to waterproof the new concrete with Kemper waterproof and also replace all of the joint sealant and expansion joints within the stadium. Capasso added, "With a fast track schedule, the crews worked tirelessly installing new Kemper Waterproof Coatings as well as new joint sealants and expansion joints. We were pleased to be a part of this project and look forward to performing more work for Yale University in the future."

Official restoration of the Bowl, spearheaded by athletic director Tom Beckett and former coach Carmen Cozza, began in the spring of 2005. Under Beckett's direction and the many generous donors, there have been numerous renovations of athletic facilities at Yale—most notably, the Yale Bowl.

Tom Beckett

YALE DIRECTOR OF ATHLETICS (1994-PRESENT)

Tom Beckett, Yale's 17th athletic director, is a 1968 graduate of the University of Pittsburgh where he captained the Panthers' baseball team in 1968. He earned a master's degree from his alma mater and played in the San Francisco Giants' organization for five seasons. The Guilford, Connecticut, resident coached at the University of Pittsburgh and Butler Community College (Pa.), and was an athletic administrator at San Jose State University before moving to Stanford, where he served from 1983-94 as associate director of athletics.

"I think one of the really powerful things for me was during my very first visit to interview for the

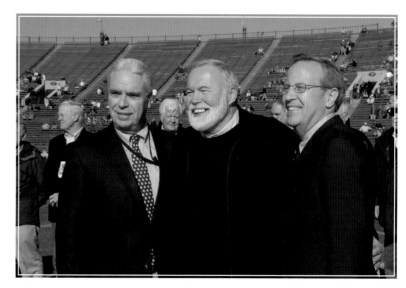

L-R: Tom Beckett, Mike Pyle (1960 captain) and former Yale president Richard Levin stand in the Bowl at the 50th year reunion of the 1960 team on November 13, 2010.
(BILL O'BRIEN)

Top: a crumbling portal; Bottom: a restored portal
(YALE ATHLETICS)

Director of Athletics job in Feb. of '94. The chair of the committee, Stan Wheeler, took me to the Yale Bowl which was snow-covered. I thought it was one of the most spectacular facilities I had ever seen. I had been to the Rose Bowl while at Stanford, but I had never seen the Yale Bowl before. I was told that both the Rose Bowl and 'The Big House' at Michigan were copies of the Yale Bowl.

"After accepting the Director of Athletics position at Yale I got to see the Yale Bowl up close and the snow was gone. It was hard to believe that this venerable facility (Yale Bowl) was turning into the Roman Colosseum. One game day I was walking around the outer promenade of the Bowl after we had played the University of Pennsylvania. I saw a Penn player point to one of the decaying cracks and overheard him say, 'Do you think Yale is going to recruit somebody to play in a facility that looks like this?' That certainly got my attention.

"The deterioration of the Bowl was not a health or safety issue. It was just that the crumbling of the concrete and the exterior wall of the Bowl were becoming unsightly. You could see the spalling of the concrete. It was clear that something had to be done to preserve this national treasure.

"There was talk of razing the Bowl and no one wanted that to happen. But we had to figure out a way to restore the Bowl or it would turn into a facility that would be condemned as was Princeton's Palmer Stadium. I was at the last game at Palmer Stadium in '96. They had huge nets underneath the stands collecting falling concrete. There were giant pieces of concrete in the net and people were walking into the stadium wondering if Palmer Stadium would remain standing for the duration of the game. They tore it down after that season and rebuilt it. It took a year and a half to build the new stadium that is now called Princeton University Stadium. In '97 Princeton played all their games on the road.

"Nobody at Yale was in favor of doing what Princeton was required to do. I met with Coach Cozza, who was still the head coach at the time, and we talked about a fundraising project to restore the Bowl. Our idea was to get generation after generation of Yale football men to support the project. Carm did a fantastic job of reaching out to all of the men who played for him about this idea and got their support.

The Class of '54

"Wow! 32 million dollars later the Yale Bowl was preserved as one of college football's great venues primarily because of the efforts and generosity of Yale's Class of 1954 led by its class secretary Joel Smilow and Charlie Johnson, the largest contributor

to the Bowl project. Prior to my arrival at Yale Joel had endowed the Yale Football Coach position and made the naming gift to expand and renovate the Lapham Field House containing the football locker rooms. Because of his interest in and passion for Yale Football, he made continued contributions. He helped jump start the Bowl project via the idea of creating 30 naming opportunities for significant contributors or groups of contributors who wished to be identified with each of Yale's portals. Yale '54 classmates including Ed Toohey, Charlie Johnson, Joe Fortunato, Harris Ashton, and Irv Jensen (with his three brothers from other Yale classes) "bought" five more portals—giving Yale '54 almost twenty-five percent of the portals which were all sold. Chris Forester was also a key figure.

"Still short, Johnson, who had previously created Yale's first outdoor all-weather multi-use field and stadium, stepped back in with the most important transformational gift—matched by Yale '54's 50th reunion matching gift fund—thereby creating the 'Yale Class of 1954' Field at the Yale Bowl.

"The playing surface of the Bowl is now called The Class of 1954 Field in honor of their most generous gift. These alums love the Bowl and they wanted to see it restored. Several of them made major gifts to this restoration effort. Their names are on a perman-ent plaque outside of Portal 15 at The Bowl. The Yale Community shall be forever grateful to this most generous Yale Class of 1954.

"Two additions to the Bowl were dedicated during the 2009 season, the Kenney Center and Jensen Plaza, the result of very generous donations from the Kenney and Jensen families. The Kenney family (Brian R.,'61, Jerry P., '63, Robert D., '67 and Richard L., '71) is the only family to have four brothers play for Yale. Robert's son, Jeffrey S., '93, also played for the Bulldogs. It is a three-story building attached to the Bowl that houses team rooms and a reception area that opens up the inside of the venue. Before the Kenney Center was built the Yale team used a small halftime room.

"The first floor Team Room, the 'Undefeated and Untied 1960 Championship Team Room,' is named in honor of that great Yale team. The second floor Team Room is named in honor of Sandy Cutler, a member of the Class of 1973 and a three year starter

L-R: Erik, Colin, Irving and Mark Jensen. Colin ('57) and Erik ('63) lettered in football.
(YALE ATHLETICS)

The Kenney brothers gather at the 2013 Blue Leadership Ball where Jerome Kenney was honored as a George H.W. Bush '48 Lifetime Leadership Award recipient. L-R: Brian, Jerome, Robert, and Richard.
(JAMES R. ANDERSON / PHOTOG.COM)

for Coach Cozza. The top floor is called 'The Kenney Family Champions Room,' a truly spectacular addition to the Bowl Complex.

A Wider Concourse

"When the Bowl went through its restoration process one important change that was made was the width of the concourse that circles the Bowl upon entering. The architect did a two-year interior stadium traffic study by attending the Princeton and Harvard games. He wanted to assess the flow of the spectators. He wanted to see what it would be like

The Kenney Center
(BILL O'BRIEN)

when there were 20,000 in the Bowl for the Princeton game vs. 60,000 for the Harvard game. For the Princeton game, 90 percent of the 20,000 would be sitting on the sidelines with about 500-1,000 spectators in the end zones. The traffic from the 50-yard line to the goal line was just as congested as when there are 60,000 people in the Bowl. There was a noticeable traffic jam so the architect decided the way to remedy this was to double the width of the concourse that separates the lower section of stands from the upper section.

"This did not sit well with a few preservationists because they felt it would change the original design of the Bowl. President (Richard) Levin asked how a wider concourse would affect the Yale Bowl architecturally. He was told that a wider concourse would maintain the feel of the concentric ovals of the Bowl and a wider concourse would make a mass exodus in case of an emergency much safer. They agreed and today the Yale Bowl remains one of the most beautiful college football facilities in the country. And I personally think the wider concourse beautifies the Bowl.

"If there's one thing I would hang my hat on during my tenure as Director of Yale Athletics, it would be the successful restoration of the Yale Bowl."

An unidentified Yale fan celebrates a Yale victory in the Bowl.
(YALE ATHLETICS)

CHAPTER 7

THE FANS REMEMBER THE BOWL

*"The first time I visited the Bowl was in 1937
when I was seven years old.... I remember being a
little scared walking through the tunnel, but the
sight that greeted my eyes stunned me by the vast
size of such a place and the thousands of people."*

—Frank Stolzenberg ('53)

THE YALE BOWL was named a National Historic Landmark in 1987. In the years prior to this designation and ever since, an untold number of people have passed through its portals. And each of those fans has a distinct memory of what the experience was like—although not everyone recalls details of the game they were there to watch. Some visited the Bowl for the first time as children and were awed by the stadium's vastness and the size of the crowd. (Many adults had a similar reaction.) Others attended events in the Bowl that had nothing to do with football, and still others have some sort of family connection to its construction.

This chapter is a potpourri of memories of the Yale Bowl collected from fans, writers, broadcasters, and a Yale player whose father played in the first game ever in the Bowl.

JOHN D'ANTONA

"My cousin, Mike Patricelli, whom we all called 'Uncle Mickey,' was in the Yale Bowl the day it opened in 1914. He was five years old and lived in the area of the Bowl when it was being constructed. He would tell me that the first thing they did when the Bowl was constructed was build the portals, or tunnels. He thought they were funny-looking houses. He and his brother used to slide down the big piles of sand they dug up until the boss of the work crew would chase them away.

"Many fans clamored to get in the Bowl the day it opened including Uncle Mickey. But they wouldn't let him and his friends in because they didn't have a ticket. However, around halftime, a guard let them in.

"I grew up on Legion Avenue in New Haven. We used to ride our bikes to the Bowl and hide them in bushes before sneaking in. Over the years I wonder how many kids snuck into the Bowl. In the late '50s Uncle Mickey got me a job as a rope guard there. Of course, that was a great way to watch the game for free.

"All I can say to Uncle Mickey is, 'Thanks for the memories—and rest in peace.'"

BUD FINCH

"My roots to Yale football and the Bowl go back to my dad, Arthur, who grew up in New Haven and was there when they were building it. They started with a steam shovel that was buried in the middle of the field because they had no way of getting it out unless they disassembled it. That's a popular story. I'm not sure if it's apocryphal but my father always said it was true."

GORDON FORD

"My great-grandfather, a black man from Virginia, was part of a crew en route to Canada looking for work when they got word that help was needed to construct the new Bowl. So my great-grandfather went to New Haven and helped build the Bowl. He helped load the mules that carried sacks of earth from the ground to the exterior of the Bowl. He then found employment in Ansonia, Connecticut, where he settled.

"I've often wondered where I'd be had it not been for the Yale Bowl."

RICHARD BUTLER

"The eternal question is, did the architect who helped design the Bowl forget to install rest rooms inside the Bowl?

"In the 1960s I was working for a brokerage firm In New York City. In the summer of '69, I had tickets for the Jets-Giants exhibition game in the Yale Bowl. I told John Hanley, one of my colleagues, that I was going to the Bowl and he said, 'You mean you're going to 'Hanley's Folly.' He explained, 'My uncle was the architect, and he forgot to put in the bathrooms.'

"The Jets beat the Giants 37-14. I began going to sporting events in 1952, and this game, played under azure blue skies in the majestic Yale Bowl, was the greatest thrill of my life—even if I had to exit through a portal to go to one of the rest rooms that surround the Bowl."

Although research hints strongly that the lack of rest rooms at the Bowl when it was constructed was an architectural oversight, no evidence has been found documenting Mr. Hanley and the term "Hanley's Folly." The Bowl was designed by Charles A. Ferry.

EILEEN HELLYAR PETERS

"My family had friends from England named Gallagher who lived on a side street just off Derby Avenue, close to the Bowl. On game day they would let people park in their yard for a small fee. The Gallaghers had kids my age, and during a visit in 1927 when I was nine years old, they took me to the Yale Bowl, which was open to the public. It was there that I learned how to ride a bike in the aisles or concourse that circles the interior of the Bowl."

WILLIAM N. WALLACE ('45 W, '49)

"Everyone remembers their first visit to the Yale Bowl—the walk through the pinched, dark tunnel and then: Boom. Suddenly the big Bowl is there, spread all the way around in a world of its own.

"My experience was no different from that of anyone else, except it had a postscript that took place about thirty years later.

"The date—I had to look it up—was Nov. 7, 1931, a beautiful balmy day. I was seven years old and was taken to the Bowl in company with my Rye, New York, playmate, John W. Hanes Jr., his mother, Agnes, and my mother, best of friends. A chauffeur drove the Hanes' Isotta Franschini sedan and did the tailgating picnic tasks from a Fortnum & Mason wicker basket—many years before the term tailgating evolved.

"Bob Lassiter, John Hanes' cousin, was a sophomore halfback for Yale that day and two years later its captain. I was told his number and to look out for him. Maybe I did.

"The final score was 52-0, the opponent a lamb that Yale had scheduled prior to the two final games that mattered, Princeton and Harvard. The victim was tiny St. John's of Annapolis, an academic institution across the street from the Naval Academy and renowned for its great books curriculum, but not then nor ever afterward for its athletic prowess. I recall nothing of the game itself, even though the great Albie Booth was Yale's captain and Joe Crowley scored a modern-record five touchdowns.

"Kindly Agnes Hanes told me I'd remember the final score because it was equal to the number of cards in a deck. She was correct on both counts.

"The years rolled by. I was a sportswriter for the *World Telegram & Sun* in New York, covering college football, when I came across an administrative aide to Asa Bushnell, the commissioner of the Eastern College Athletic Conference, with headquarters in the Hotel Biltmore near Grand Central Terminal. The administrator's name was Danny Hill, a pleasant chap with whom I struck up an easy conversation. Where did he go to college?

'A place you never heard of, St. John's of Annapolis,' he said.

'Oh, yes, I have,' I said.

"Could he possibly....?

'Did you play football?'

'Yeah, I did. They haven't had a team in years. But they did then.'

'Do you know that your St. John's once upon a time played Yale in the Yale Bowl?' Hill kind of jerked upward. 'I certainly do know. I was there. I played in that game. Never forget it.'

"He went on to tell me that St. John's had accepted the game because of the nice guarantee Yale would pay. 'We went north with 18 players,' he said. 'Near the end there were only about 11 of us who could still line up.'

'You wore red jerseys?' I asked. He nodded.

"That I did remember."

WALTER "BUD" SMITH

"On October 14, 1933, at age nine, I went to the Yale Bowl with my father and saw Yale beat Washington & Lee, 14-0. It was my first visit to the Bowl and we entered through Portal 24. I didn't want to go. Here it is over eighty years later and I'm still sitting by Portal 24."

SABBY FRINZI

"I was born in Sicily and came over here as a young boy. I remember seeing Larry Kelley and Clint Frank play in the Yale Bowl when I was fourteen or fifteen years old. Who would ever think that I would one day be the official Yale football photographer.

MEL ALLEN

"I earned a law degree from the University of Alabama in 1936 and taught a speech course there in the fall semester. During the Christmas vacation that year, I drove five of my former classmates to New York, New Jersey, and Connecticut. I borrowed my daddy's Ford and drove 36 hours nonstop with my friends. It was standard procedure for students to pay $20 round trip.

"One of the guys with me was Irving Berlin Kahn, the nephew of Irving Berlin, the great song writer. I dropped him off in Newark, New Jersey. I then dropped three guys off in midtown Manhattan before I took Burt Levey to New Haven. I always wanted to see the Yale Bowl, so while I was in New Haven, I visited the Bowl, which was snow-covered. I remember walking out to the middle of the gridiron on the 50-yard line surrounded by 70,000 empty seats on a cold New England day.

"On that trip I went to CBS radio in New York and asked for an audition. I did it on a lark. I was hired as a staff announcer and became an understudy to Ted Husing and Bob Trout.

My parents weren't happy about it, since I studied to become a lawyer."

JOHN DOWNEY (GUARD) '50

"It was great playing in the Yale Bowl. Growing up in Wallingford, Connecticut, my father took me to the Bowl in the '30s. I told my father that one day I would play for Yale. I did and it was a thrill."

FRANK STOLZENBERG ('53)

"The first time I visited the Bowl was in 1937 when I was seven years old. My father took my brother, Allan, and me to see my first college football game. I remember being a little scared walking through the tunnel, but the sight that greeted my eyes stunned me by the vast size of such a place and the thousands of people.

"My brother sat on an Indian design brown and white blanket. He currently lives in Hamden and attends every Yale home game. And would you believe he sits on the same blanket that is over eighty years old!"

DON NIELSEN

"The first time I ever walked in the Yale Bowl was November 5, 1938, for the Yale-Brown game. I was nine years old and went with my father and grandfather. We walked through Portal 19 and I was amazed at how low the grass (field) was to the street level. My father said, 'The Yale Bowl is just as far in the ground as it is above the ground.' I have seen 470 Yale games; that includes many on the road."

VIN BROZEK

"I grew up in New Haven and saw Kelley and Clint Frank play. I remember dancing on the field of the Bowl when New Haven celebrated its 300th anniversary in 1938."

STAN CELMER

"The first game I ever saw in the Bowl was when Yale upset a strong Virginia team in '41. It was a time when Yale football had reached rock bottom. I have seen almost every game in the Bowl in the last 70 years."

JON STEIN

"My memories of Yale football go back to the 1948 Dartmouth game. It was a family civil war: my dad Jerry was in the Yale class of 1940, and his brothers Morris, Joe and Harold were Dartmouth alums. Dartmouth kicked Yale's behinds that day, 41-14."

DON HARRISON

"I was twelve years old when I visited the storied Yale Bowl for the first time. A seventh-grader in the East Haven school system, I signed up as a volunteer usher for The Game. The date was November 24, 1951. I was astounded when I entered the Bowl; I had never seen so many people gathered in one place.

Yale fan deluxe Stan Celmer

"About mid-way through the second quarter, I was able to secure a seat in the outer reaches and watched Yale and Harvard battle to a 21-21 tie. I didn't realize it at the time, but this would be Herman Hickman's final game as the Bulldogs' head coach. And certainly I had no premonition that I, by 1968, would begin chronicling many of the historic moments in Yale football history."

JOE CASTIGLIONE

"I grew up in Hamden, Connecticut, in the shadows of the Yale Bowl. My father, who was from New Haven and a Yale alum ('36), followed Yale football all of his life. He was a fan of Albie Booth and knew him well. My father, a dermatologist, was on the Yale faculty and we went to all the games. My first Yale game was on October 25, 1952, when Yale crushed Lafayette, 47-0.

"In '62 and '63 I served as a rope usher. When I was informed that I would be stationed in the Yale student section, I was excited thinking I would make some good tips. But I never got one."

JOHN SULLIVAN

"I grew up in New Haven and remember going to the Yale Bowl for the first time in 1942 to see Yale play. While at Hillhouse High School I played in the Bowl for the traditional Thanksgiving Day game against West Haven from 1948-50.

"It was a thrill to play in the Yale Bowl. We used to dress at the high school and get bused to the Bowl. We would enter through the tunnel on the Yale side which is the side of the field where our bench was.

"I played for Sam Bender and was a halfback in the T-formation. I scored two touchdowns in the

'49 game and three touchdowns the following year. We had some great players at Hillhouse like Joe Johnson, who went on to play with the Green Bay Packers, Pat Musto, and Ray DeFrancesco. West Haven had their share of talent with guys like Billy Irons, 'Harpo' McNulty and Freddie Robinson. It was seldom that they beat us. Hillhouse was a much larger school and West Haven coach Whitey Piurek used to say that Hillhouse had more band members than he had players try out for the team.

"It was a thrill watching my son, Mike, play in the Bowl. I was sitting in the end zone on the scoreboard side with my wife, daughters, and their friends when he ran 66 yards for a touchdown in the '77 Yale-Harvard game. He ran right at us and he had to beat one Harvard player. I knew he was going to run him over if he wasn't blocked.

"There aren't many fathers and sons who can share the experience of playing football in the Yale Bowl as Mike and I did."

FRANK CARRANO

"My father was a custodian at Hillhouse High School in the '40s. When Hillhouse and West Haven played in the Bowl, the custodians and their kids would ride the team bus. When Hillhouse lost (1940 and 1942), the players would wreck the bus."

MICHAEL AMATO

"My greatest memories of the Bowl were back in the '50s, when on Thanksgiving morning my father would take the kids to the annual West Haven-Hillhouse game. Hillhouse won two of the games I saw 25-7 and 45-13, but the best game was when the teams battled to a 13-13 tie in '57 after a last-second field goal attempt by Hillhouse was blocked by a West Haven lineman. The thrill I felt going to the Thanksgiving games in the Bowl made Thanksgiving the holiday I loved most."

GEORGE GRANDE

"Although I had been there earlier, the first game I remember seeing in the Bowl was the 1957 Yale-Harvard contest when the Bulldogs dispatched Harvard 54-0. I went with my father, Carlo, and brother, Carlo. At halftime the Elis led 34-0, and the sight of Yale fans dressed in their traditional raccoon fur coats, waving their white handkerchiefs in celebration of their imminent victory, is something that I'll never forget. It was such a lopsided game, and in the second half I asked my father when we were going to leave. He said with authority, 'When the game ends!' That's a lesson I've learned throughout my life—leave when the game ends. Didn't someone say, 'It's not over till it's over'?

ROBERT LEWIS

"I was a sideline ball boy for six seasons. My job was to throw in a new ball when necessary. I worked the sidelines with freshman coach Gib Holgate's son, John. I normally worked the Yale side but I was on the Dartmouth sideline for the 1966 game.

"Early in the game Yale punted on their own 15- or 20-yard line, facing the scoreboard. The ball reached midfield and grazed a Dartmouth player's helmet on the way down. I was standing about 8 feet away and I was screaming for Del Marting to jump on the ball. Marting dives on the ball and the referee says, 'First down, Yale.' Dartmouth coach Bob Blackman turns to one of

the referees and barks, 'Get that son-of-a-bitch kid off my sideline.' The bad news about the story is that Dartmouth won that game 28-13."

DICK GRAHAM

"I was tailgating before the '67 Harvard game. As the Harvard band was about to enter the Bowl, I decided to sneak in with the band. I then exited to the stands on the Harvard side where I met Skip Falcone, a friend who had gone to Harvard. In reference to me, one of Skip's friends asked, 'Did you see that damn fool marching with the band?' I said, 'No. I couldn't see from where I was sitting.'"

STEVE COHEN

"I started going to the Bowl in the '60s when my parents, Fran and Shep, started taking my brother Stu and me to the games. My mother used to roller skate around the inside of the Bowl when she was a kid. My father grew up on George Street and had two brothers who attended Yale. My mother attended the games faithfully as long as her health allowed.

"I became a rope guard when I was in Cub Scouts and then an usher when I was in my teens. I now have a lifetime pass for the football games, which was given to all of the volunteer ushers who remained when the school did away with those positions."

STU COHEN

"I was an usher for twenty-six years (1974 to 1999) at Portals 1 and 2. I used to tell people that a big steam shovel used to excavate the ground was trapped inside after the Bowl was built. Being too big to get out, it was buried under the field. You would be amazed at how many people believed that story. I still attend games with my dad who is ninety-one, and brother Steve. I have seen nearly 300 Yale home games and have only missed two since 1964. I also saw all of the Giants' games when they played in the Bowl."

BILL O'BRIEN

"My first day in the Bowl was the 1948 Vanderbilt game. But one of my best memories centers around a winter day in 1982 when the Bowl was empty.

"Harold 'Red' Grange, 'The Galloping Ghost,' out of the University of Illinois, received the Walter Camp Distinguished American Award for 1981. Grange had broadcast games from the Bowl and he wanted to revisit the historic venue. So Don Scharf arranged for Grange, Marcus Allen, the great USC All-American running back, and I to drive through the visitors' tunnel that leads

L-R: Harold "Red" Grange, "The Galloping Ghost," Bill O'Brien, and USC All-American Marcus Allen visit the Bowl during 1981 Walter Camp weekend.
(SABBY FRINZI)

to the field. I had an old leather football helmet from football's early days and gave it to 'Red.' He held the helmet in his hand and standing on the turf of the Yale Bowl he said, 'I look around this place and I feel like suiting up to play.' That was pretty good for a 79-year-old man. Marcus wore my trench coat to escape the cold weather."

TOM HACKETT ('50)

"I was at the Bowl in '83 for 100th Yale-Harvard game. I took my 18-year-old daughter and it was so crowded, we had to sit on the concrete steps. My daughter asked if the Bowl was always this crowded? I said, 'No, only every 100 years.'"

FRED CANTOR('75)

"I have an original program from a Supremes/Four Tops concert from July 1967 (my first concert ever). Only three of the Four Tops actually appeared. I believe it was Levi Stubbs who explained to the audience that the missing member wasn't feeling well because 'Yesterday we were at a lawn party and he had too much of the lawn.'"

CAROL SMULLEN

"Many years ago I began the practice of giving the band members candy before they entered the Yale Bowl. When they see me outside Portal 25, they stop and play a song. The tradition exists today."

JIM LITTLE (HALFBACK) '59 FRESHMAN

"As an undergraduate at Yale in the early '60s, I and my classmates went to all of Yale's home games at the Bowl. At that time, the men's rooms at the Bowl had building-length urinals that consisted of a gutter that the men stood next to, a wall that the men peed against and a pipe about six-feet high on the wall that constantly dripped water to rinse the wall and flush the gutter that drained away into a sewer.

"I went to the men's room at halftime and stood at the gutter next to two handsomely dressed alumni who were probably in their 60's. One of them said to the other, 'When I was a student, my stream could hit that pipe up there. Now, I can barely make it into the gutter.' At the time I thought that was very funny. In 2011, I understood what he was saying.'"

TOM PEPE

"They're Peeing on the Walls"

"Yale football is passed down from father to son. My father, who was an usher in the '50s, would take me with him on occasion, and I would sit in the area of Portal 12. During my working years at the Bowl, I would sometimes sit in an empty Bowl in the same seat I sat in as a kid and reflect on those wonderful days. When I took my son to his first game, he was eight or nine years old. At halftime we walked into the bathroom and he started laughing like crazy. He said, 'Dad, they're peeing on the walls.' Stainless steel troughs were installed several years ago, so fans no longer pee on the walls."

LOISANN MARAZZI

A Family Tailgate and a Bank Robbery

"On a chilly Saturday in the late '80s our family set out for the Yale Bowl. Once there, we began tailgating in Lot D by grilling on a hibachi and enjoying our hamburgers, salads, etc. My husband Rich and our sons, Rich and Brian, threw a football around while I savored my specially brewed hot coffee from the large thermos I made because the concession stand coffee would never put Dunkin Donuts out of business! When it was time to head into the Bowl, my husband emptied the red hot coals from the hibachi onto the dry grass which immediately ignited. As the fire spread, he attempted to put it out with his gloves which began to blister. He grabbed my thermos of specially brewed coffee and emptied it to extinguish the flames as I looked on in utter dismay. Adding insult to injury...Yale lost that day. And to make matters worse, the disastrous weekend continued.

"While at school the following Monday, the principal called me to the office as my husband was on the phone with an urgent request. Rich told me to go to the faculty parking lot and check to see if my car's license plates were missing. They were! When I informed him of this, he explained that our local Ansonia police had contacted him. My license plates, apparently pilfered in the Bowl parking lot, were placed on a stolen car which was used in a bank robbery in Norwalk. I wonder if the thieves passed a note which read, 'Boola Boola, give us the moola'!!!"

FOR MOST, ENTERING the Yale Bowl for the first time is a visceral experience that one never forgets. The historic structure has meant so much to so many for 100 years. Later in the book, the men who played in the Bowl tell us what the Bowl has meant to them.

In the next chapter we'll explore the early history of Yale's fabled football program when the Elis ruled the world of college football.

PART II

Yale Football

The First Half (1872-1940)

OFFICIAL PROGRAM 1902

HARVARD • YALE

(Yale Athletics)

CHAPTER 8
A GOLDEN ERA (1872-1926)

*"I'd rather beat any team in the country
than Yale. For to me and most of us,
Yale means American football."*

—Harry Mehre, former Notre Dame player
and University of Georgia coach (1928-1937)

ENTERING THE 2014 season, Yale University has played 1,291 football games, amassing an impressive record of 876-360-55. The first college program to win 800 games, Yale has won or shared fourteen Ivy League titles since "the Ancient Eight" began formal play in 1956, more than any other member except Dartmouth and Penn.

No institution has a richer football history than Yale. For many years it was college football's bellwether program. More than 100 All-Americans, including two Heisman Trophy winners, have worn the Yale Blue. Twenty-six Yale players and four coaches are enshrined in the College Football Hall of Fame, and Yale has sent twenty-four players to the NFL.

Excluding 1918, when the football program was suspended because of World War I, Yale has played competitively every year since 1872. But the early brand of football at Yale was not the game we know today.

THE DAWN OF YALE FOOTBALL

On October 31, 1872, David S. Schaff, Elliot S. Miller, Samuel Elder, and other members of the class of 1873 called a meeting of the student body. From that meeting emerged the Yale Football Association, the first formal entity to govern the sport at Yale. Schaff was elected president and team captain.

Three years after the first intercollegiate football contest between Princeton and Rutgers, Yale played its inaugural game. Historians consider the November 16, 1872, Yale-Columbia game at Hamilton Park in New Haven Yale's first football game. In fact, the game resembled a soccer match with twenty players on a side, a 400- x 250-foot field, and a final score measured in goals (Yale won, 3-0). Tommy Sherman

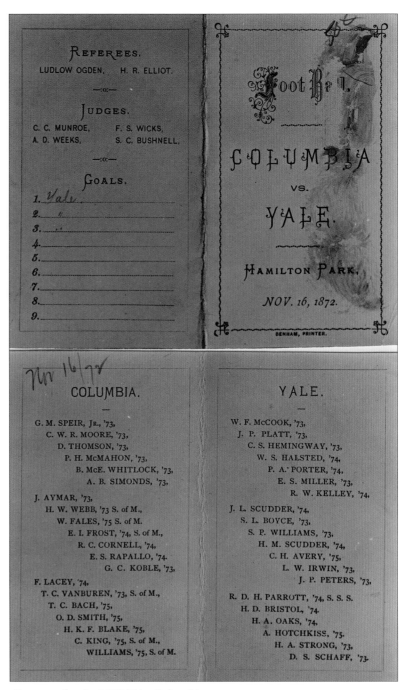

Program for the 1872 Yale-Columbia game
(YALE ATHLETICS)

booted the first Yale goal and Lew Irwin kicked the other two.

About 500 fans attended and paid a 25-cent admission fee. According to the *New Haven Register,* "The contest excited considerable applause," and "Yale discipline prevailed over Columbia muscle." After the game the teams enjoyed dinner together at Lockwood's Restaurant."

The 1873 team. Captain William Halstead (front row center). Notice the soccer shaped ball.
(Yale Athletics)

Before the turn of the 20th century, teams would give out sheets of paper instead of full programs. "This goes back to 1872 when Yale played its first football game," said Al Ostermann. "The initial program was a four-page folder listing only names and classes of the members of the Yale and Columbia University squads, together with the officials of the contest."

In 1880 football became an eleven-man game and the scoring system was modified "Point values changed frequently between 1883 and 1912," said Yale football historian Bob Barton. "In 1886 a touchdown was worth two points, a conversion two, and a field goal five."

In the embryonic days of Yale football, Wesleyan was an annual patsy. In 1884 the Elis, playing a nine-game schedule, shut out Wesleyan three times, by scores of 31-0, 63-0 and 46-0. The 46-0 game, played on November 5, saw Wyllys Terry set a record by running 110 yards from scrimmage for a touchdown on a field that measured 110 yards. Over the next few years Yale scored more

than 100 points in a game four times, and three times Wesleyan was the victim. On October 30, 1886, Yale mercilessly humbled "the Methodists" (now nicknamed the Cardinals) 136-0 as Henry Ward "Harry" Beecher, a grandson of the famous preacher and abolitionist of the same name, scored 11 touchdowns. In his three-year career Beecher scored a record 66 TDs. In that game, George Watkinson made 22 of 23 kicking conversions, good for 44 points, a national record that still stands. (Watkinson died of typhoid fever shortly after playing in a pouring rain in the final game that year against Princeton.)

A Golden Era

From 1872 to 1927, Yale football sat atop Mount Olympus, gaining recognition as national champion or co-champion twenty-seven times in this fifty-five year period. The championship count is based on selection systems listed by the Official NCAA Football Records Book.

The golden age of Yale football ran from 1872 through 1909, when the Bulldogs accumulated 324 wins against only 17 losses and 8 ties. Yale boasted a cavalcade of stars that formed the bedrock of Yale football history. From 1889 through 1927 the Bulldogs produced seventy-five All-Americans.

Ray Tompkins, a guard, captained Yale's national champions of 1882 and 1883. After the deaths of Tompkins and his wife, Sarah, it was announced in 1931 that she had left $3 million to Yale. A portion of the bequest was used to build the Ray Tompkins House on Tower Parkway in New Haven, which houses the offices of the Yale Athletic Department.

Pa Corbin was captain of the 1888 team, which finished 13-0 and outscored its opponents 698-0.

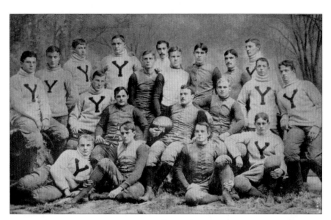

The 1891 team with captain "Bum" McClung in front center with ball.
(YALE ATHLETICS)

Four time All-American Frank Hinkey served as Yale's head coach in 1914 and 1915.
(YALE ATHLETICS)

In one stretch that team played four games in eight days.

One of the great early running backs was Thomas L. "Bum" McClung, who scored 438 points in four seasons (1888-91) and captained the 13-0 undefeated and unscored-on 1891 squad coached by Walter Camp. In 1909 McClung was appointed the 22nd treasurer of the United States by President William Howard Taft.

Frank Hinkey was a skinny 5-foot-9, twenty-year-old freshman end on the 1891 team and captained the 1893 and 1894 teams. Yale suffered defeat only once during his playing career. Pop Warner called him "the greatest player of all time." Camp referred to him as "a disembodied spirit."

Hinkey is one of four players to be named an All-American four times. He played with a reckless abandon, hurling his body at opponents without regard for the consequences. He was known to keep late hours, smoke cigars (despite having a lung condition), and drink the worst brands of whiskey. Hinkey was Yale's head football coach in 1914 and 1915 when Harvard outscored the Elis 77-0.

William "Pudge" Heffelfinger was a three-time All-American (1889-91). Standing 6 feet 3 and weighing about 210, he revolutionized offensive guard play by pulling out to lead interference. He also was used as a ball carrier and is credited with 27 touchdowns. In 1892 the Allegheny Athletic Association paid him $500 to play a game in Pittsburgh, making him the first pro football player. He coached at Lehigh, California, and Minnesota. Legend has it that in 1916, at the age of forty-eight, he scrimmaged against the Yale varsity and gave Mac Baldrige, playing tackle opposite him, two broken ribs. Grantland Rice wrote, "There never will be another Heffelfinger. His kind will never pass this way again."

"I met William Walter 'Pudge' Heffelfinger at a dinner," said Dr. Len Fasano, a lineman who played in the late forties. "He was an animal who was built like a gorilla. At 6-3, 210 pounds, he wasn't too pudgy. He was a great guard and has been credited as the first lineman in football history to pull out and block on end sweeps.

"Pudge" Heffelfinger
(THE TOPPS CO., INC.)

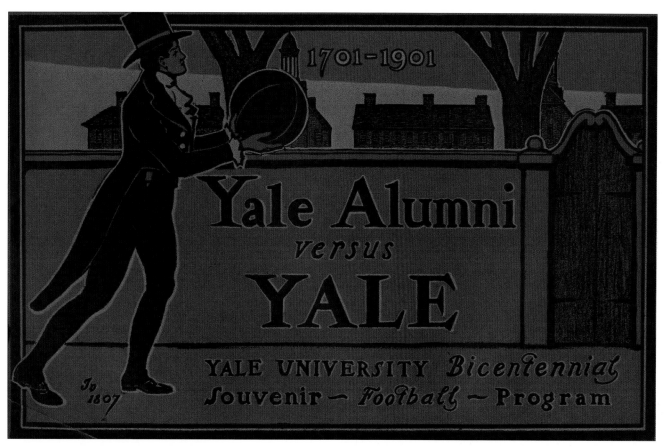

Yale v. Alumni souvenir Football program.
(YALE ATHLETICS)

"When he was fifty-three years old he played fifty-six minutes in an all-star game in Columbus, Ohio, with a group of outstanding college players."

The Team of the Century

At a time when William McKinley occupied the White House and the first year Yale used cheerleaders, Yale's 1900 juggernaut eleven led by four-time All-American captain (Francis) Gordon Brown, a Phi Beta Kappa student, Yale claimed the national championship by virtue of a 12-0 record that included ten shutouts. The Elis gave up two touchdowns (then worth five points) the entire season in wins over Columbia (12-5) and Princeton (29-5).

Harvard, which brought a 32-game unbeaten streak into New Haven, was burned 28-0 by the Blue. Yale played the entire game using twelve players. All Yale starters with the exception of All-American center Beau Olcott played the full game. In reference to Yale's dominance in this era, the *New York Times*

wrote, "She is past mistress of the art (of football), and whoever wins from her wins by playing of the highest order."

In addition to Brown and Olcott, five other Yale players made Walter Camp's All-American team. They were tackles George Stillman and Ralph Bloomer, and backs Bill Fincke, George Chadwick, and Perry Hale.

FIGHT SONGS

There are a number of fight songs associated with Yale athletics. The one most closely connected with the program is *Boola, Boola*, which was first sung during Yale's 28-0 victory over Harvard on November 24, 1900. It appears that three Yale students, Allan M. Hirsh, F.M. Van Wincklen, and A.H. Marckwald, wrote the words of *Boola, Boola* to fit the tune of *La Hoola Boola*—a song African American entertainers Bob Cole and Billy Johnson performed in New Haven in the 1890s. According to Philip Hirsh ('60), Allan Hirsh's grandson, "John Philip Sousa played *Boola* at a concert in New Haven in April 1901. And it sold more sheet music in the first half of that year than any other song in the country."

Another Yale song, *Down the Field,* made its debut in 1904 at Princeton's University Field, where the Bulldogs downed the Tigers 12-0. The song was composed by Stanleigh Friedman ('05) and written by C.W. O'Connor. It has long been a tradition for the Yale Precision Marching Band to play *Down the Field* as its exit song at the conclusion of the halftime show and when leaving the Bowl after the game.

Yale's most popular song, *Bulldog,* was written by Cole Porter ('13) during his junior year and is played by the Yale band when the team enters the playing field and after every Yale score.

Porter composed over 300 pieces while an undergraduate, including the music and lyrics to what have become two on a short list of the most traditional and best-known college fight songs, *Bingo Eli Yale* (1910) and *Bulldog* (1911). The Yale band traditionally strikes up *Bulldog* when the Elis run out of the tunnel and after every score. But perhaps its largest audience was not on a football field.

"In 1989 a little bit of Yale football was taken to the presidential swearing-in of George H. W. Bush, who, remembering his years under the Elms, had invited the Yale band to take part in the inaugural parade," said Joel Alderman ('51). "Upon reaching the reviewing stand the musicians broke into Cole Porter's *Bulldog.* The new President and First Lady showed immediate recognition with their signs of delight, and Barbara, as viewed on world-wide television, clapped her hands in time to the familiar strains. It was no doubt the largest audience a rendition of *Bulldog* has ever had or will have."

Bulldog, Bulldog, bow,wow,wow, Eli Yale,
Bulldog, Bulldog, bow wow, wow,
Our team can never fail,
When the Sons of Eli break thru the line
That is the sign we hail,
Bulldog, Bulldog, bow, wow, wow, Eli Yale.

DASHING TOM SHEVLIN

From 1905 through 1907 the Bulldogs went 28-0-2, claiming the national championship all three years.

Tom Shevlin
(NEW HAVEN REGISTER)

Tom Shevlin, a three-time All-America end who is in the College Football Hall of Fame, captained the '05 team, which went undefeated and outscored its opponents 227-4. The Alpha Male, Shevlin was one of the most charismatic players in Yale football annals. He had matinee-idol looks, was the son of a millionaire, and excelled at numerous sports. Shevlin once sparred with heavyweight boxing champ "Gentleman Jim" Corbett in the Yale gym and held his own. His romance and eventual marriage to Elizabeth Sherley, daughter of one of the wealthiest families in Louisville, Kentucky, drew national press.

After graduating, Shevlin joined his dad's lumber business and served as an assistant coach at the University of Minnesota under Dr. Henry L. Williams, who designed the "Minnesota shift," forerunner of all quick shifts in American football. Shevlin introduced the shift to Yale when he returned to New Haven as a coaching advisor late in the 1910 season. The Elis used the shift to beat Princeton and played a scoreless tie with Harvard. Shevlin died prematurely at the age of 32, after contracting pneumonia.

THE 1909 TEAM HITS THE TRIFECTA

The celebrated 1909 Yale team is one of a handful of major-college teams since 1900 that have enjoyed seasons in which it was undefeated, untied, and unscored-on. In the first year that field goals counted as three points instead of four, the Bulldogs went 10-0 under 24-year-old coach Howard Jones and outscored their opponents 209-0. One of the team's most potent offensive weapons was three-time All-America fullback Ted Coy, a fierce runner who led all scorers despite missing four games after an appendectomy. That season Yale beat Syracuse, coached by Jones's brother Tad, 15-0, marking the

first time brothers coached against each other on the major-college level. The Jones boys had played together at Yale during the Shevlin era.

Coy was a boyhood hero of F. Scott Fitzgerald and the basis for the character Ted Fay in Fitzgerald's 1928 story, *The Freshest Boy*. Several months after Coy's death in 1935, *Time* magazine reported that Coy's widow (his third wife) had to pawn his most prized possessions, including a gold Yale football pin.

With expectations high after the undefeated '09 season—after which Howard Jones departed for Ohio State—Coy was chosen as head coach for 1910. He failed to last through the season. After a 21-0 loss to Brown—Yale's second of the season, against five wins and one tie— Henry Holt took over for the final two games, against Princeton and Harvard. The team finished the season 6-2-2. That year games changed from two thirty-five-minute halves to four fifteen-minute quarters.

The 1912 season was noteworthy for several reasons. The value of a touchdown was stabilized at 6 points and the field was reduced from 110 to 100 yards. Downs increased from three to four to gain

1909 Captain Ted Coy's 1955 Topps All-American football card
(Topps, Inc.)

10 yards. The November 2nd Yale-Colgate game was canceled after Theodore York, a sophomore right guard on the Yale team, died in the college infirmary. After breaking two ribs in the Army game at West Point on October 19, York developed blood poisoning and pneumonia set in, The *New York Times* reported. York's parents were at his bedside when he died.

Yale's failure to beat Harvard from 1910 through 1912 drove the program in the direction Harvard had gone—toward having a permanent, paid coach. Howard Jones, who had moved on to Ohio State in 1910 and spent a couple of years in private business, returned to Yale in 1913 and was paid $2,500, making him the first salaried Yale coach.

Jones stayed just one year before taking his coaching talents to the University of Iowa, Duke University, and the University of Southern California. At USC, Howard's teams went 121-36-13 and won five Rose Bowls. His overall coaching record stands at 194-64-21 and includes five national championships, one at Yale in 1909 and four at USC.

YALE 28 NOTRE DAME 0

Hinkey succeeded Jones in 1914. His two-year run peaked early when Yale upended Notre Dame 28-0 at Yale Field on October 17, 1914, ending the 27-game unbeaten streak of the Irish. According to Yale football historian Tom Bergin, "Hinkey was the first coach to use movies [game films] as an educational adjunct."

The legendary Knute Rockne, a Notre Dame assistant coach at the time, wrote in his autobiography: "They [Yale] lateral-passed Notre Dame out of the park and knocked our ears down to the tune of twenty-eight to nothing—the most valuable lesson Notre Dame ever had in football. It taught

us never to be cocksure. Modern football at Notre Dame can be dated from that game, as we made vital use of every lesson we learned."

Thomas Albert Dwight (Tad) Jones, a former Yale All-American quarterback (1907) succeeded Hinkey as head football coach in 1916. After an absence during World War I, he returned in 1920.

Tad led the Elis to an 8-1 record in '16, their best record of the decade. Their only loss came at the hands of All-American Fritz Pollard's Brown team.

The first African American to play in the Yale Bowl, Fritz Pollard was not well received. Reportedly fans serenaded him with *Bye Bye Black Bird*. (BROWN UNIVERSITY ATHLETICS)

Pollard, a 5-foot-8, 165-pound halfback was the first African American to play in the Yale Bowl when he led the Bruins to a 3-0 victory in 1915 with long runs and exciting punt returns.

Pollard was received with racial animosity from the Yale side. In an article written by '65 Brown graduate John M. Carroll for the Oct. 1992 *Brown Alumni Monthly,* Carroll wrote, "Before the 1915 Yale-Brown game in the Bowl, Pollard was instructed to enter the field by a separate gate in order to avoid an ugly incident or possible injury at the hands of some unruly Yale fans."

William A. Ashby, an African American Yale student who attended the game, sat on the Brown side. Ashby was quoted in the article, "Each time Pollard returned a punt, the Yale stands arose and screamed, 'Catch that nigger. Kill that nigger... Ashby hollered, 'Run, nigger, run. Go Fritz go.'

"After the game Yale's Jim Sheldon, who was from Atlanta, burst into the Brown locker room and demanded to see the Bruin halfback. As Pollard emerged from the dressing cage, according to William Ashby, the large Yale lineman approached Fritz, thrust out his hand and said, 'You're a nigger, but you're the best goddamn football player I ever saw.'"

YALE FOOTBALL BY THE NUMBERS

Jersey numbers did not appear at Yale until the 1916 season. According to the NCAA record book, the numbering of football players began at Washington and Jefferson in 1908.

The issue of numbering uniform jerseys was a heated one. Sports writers clamored for numbers to make it easier to report the games. But opponents claimed that numbering players would accent the individual rather than the team and for many years team captains vetoed the idea.

The *New York Times* reported in 1921 that Yale wore numbered jerseys for the Princeton and Harvard games in 1916 and 1920 but it wasn't until 1921 that they were tagged for a full season. By '21, the Big Three all agreed to outfit their players with numbered jerseys.

Cupe Black, the 1916 Yale captain, was issued No. 1. In the March 23, 1916, edition of the *Yale Daily News,* Black spoke out against jersey numbers but reportedly changed his mind during the '16 season. Black's reasoning for changing his mind is unknown. Most likely he went with the flow of the "Big Three" thinking of the time. That year Yale players were numbered during "The Game" against Harvard. (The Crimson players were not.) In 1920 Yale captain Tim Callahan wore number one and the rest of the team was numbered alphabetically, according to last name. This apparently was the only year that this was done.

Unlike many other college programs, Yale does not retire numbers. In the '30s and '40s, the number 45 was set aside in tribute to Norman Hall ('27, '28), who died of shock and exposure during Christmas recess in 1928, his junior year. After rescuing a Yale classmate's sister from a frozen pond, he went back for the classmate and disappeared. By the time the firemen fished him out, he couldn't be revived.

For a time, the numbers 17 and 69 were not issued out of respect for former quarterback Ed McCarthy (a '62, '63 and '64 letterman) who was killed in a car crash following his senior season and Brent Kirk ('73, '74) who drowned. According to the September 16, 1975 edition of the *Football Y News,* Kirk and his brother, Philip, were in an aluminum canoe at Yellowstone National Park on Aug. 6, 1975, when lightning struck the boat. Both were thrown overboard into the cold deep water. Philip was stunned by the bolt and was eventually pulled to safety by park rangers, but Brett vanished without a trace and his body was not found.

WORLD WAR I

The United States formally entered World War I, known then as "The Great War," in April 1917. Young men's enlistments drained the nation's colleges of student-athletes. Twenty-one of the twenty-two players who lettered at Yale in 1916 were in the military the following year.

On October 20, 1917, Yale held its first wartime athletic event, with a freshman team made up of ROTC students defeating Phillips Exeter Academy 20-0 in front of 2,000 in the Bowl. The "Bull-pups" played a five-game schedule, finishing 4-1. An informal varsity team, mostly ROTC students, played three games in 1917, beating Loomis Institute, the New Haven Naval Base, and Trinity. Varsity coach Tad Jones, who coached the Yale freshmen against Exeter, was soon ordered by the government to service at the Ames Shipbuilding plant in Seattle. In his absence, Dr. Arthur E. Brides and trainer Johnny Mack ran the program.

Numerous Yale lettermen served in the war, among them George Moseley, an All-America end in 1916. He was with the Lafayette Flying Corps, a group of American volunteers who flew for the French. George's son, Spencer, was an All-America center and linebacker who captained the '42 Elis. The Moseley's are the only father-son tandem All-Americans from Yale.

Chester "Chet" LaRoche, the 1916 Yale quarterback, served as a lieutenant in the Navy. He went on to become a founder and chairman of the National Football Foundation and Hall of Fame. John Reed Kilpatrick, an end who earned All-American honors

in 1909 and 1910, served in both world wars. Kilpatrick is enshrined in the College Football Hall of Fame as well as the Hockey Hall of Fame for his role as president of Madison Square Garden and overseeing the operations of the New York Rangers from 1934-1960.

John Reed Kilpatrick
(YALE ATHLETICS)

The harsh realities of war also touched the Yale football program. Yale's 1915 football captain, Alex Wilson, became an infantry captain and was killed in combat near Breiulles, France, in 1918. According to Tim Cohane in *The Yale Football Story*, three other former Yale players lost their lives in WWI—Joseph Stillman, starting right end in the 1914 Harvard game; James E. Miller, a 1903 starter at guard; and Andrew C. Ortmayer, an end on the 1904 squad. As in World War II, many Yale students served but did not return. Their names are listed in the memorial panels in Yale's Woolsey Hall rotunda.

Yale played the University of North Carolina in the Bowl every year from 1919 to 1924. These weren't the Tar Heels of Charlie "Choo Choo" Justice, who starred at UNC in the late forties, or Lawrence Taylor, who did likewise in the late seventies. The Elis won all six games, outscoring the overmatched Southerners 187-7. The only North Carolina touchdown was pulled off in the 1919 game by "Chuck" Pharr, described as "midget Pharr" by the *New York Times*. Only 5-feet-6 and weighing in at 150 pounds, Pharr may have been the smallest opponent to score a touchdown in the history of the Yale Bowl. "My dad scored on a trick play," said John Pharr, son of

1915 Yale captain Alex Wilson lost his life in WWI.
(LIBRARY OF CONGRESS LC-DIG-GGBAIN-10969)

Yale alum Rudy Vallee, seated on the far right of the bench in this 1920s photo, became a popular pop singer and band leader.
(YALE ATHLETICS)

Chuck Pharr might be the smallest opponent to have scored a TD in the Yale Bowl.
(JOHN PHARR)

the former Tarheel. "Yale was not expecting a punt. When the ball was punted it deflected off a Yale player. My father recovered the ball and ran into the end zone for a touchdown."

Fred "Chuck" Pharr was hailed as a local hero for many years in his home town of Charlotte, North Carolina, where he lived until age ninety-six.

FOOTBALL IN THE 1920S

The Roaring Twenties was a time when the well-dressed Yale man shopped at Brooks Brothers in New York City and wore a Mallory hat and Gunther Raccoon coat. The Hotel Elton in Waterbury, Connecticut, hosted dinner dances following Yale games. Attendance soared in this era when the average attendance at Yale games was 37,405. From the 1920s through the1960s, crowds averaged more than 31,000 per game.

The Elis went 58-20-5 in this glorious era highlighted by an undefeated and untied season in 1923. Of the 83 games played in the decade, 72 were in the Bowl for economic reasons. It was in the best interest for Yale and their opponents to play in the Bowl because of its extensive seating capacity and large crowds. The Bulldogs enjoyed their winningest decade in their own den going 54-13-5.

"In the 20s I used to sit on the bench and watch the Yale players practice," said Al Ostermann. "Rudy Vallee, who went on to a radio and film singing career, would arrive in a raccoon coat, throw me the coat and say, 'Hey, kid, hold this for me.'"

Vallee, who was arguably the first crooner and first mass media pop star, made his presence felt in the Bowl. "My uncle played with the Yale band," said Joel Alderman. "He once told me that Rudy Vallee, who played the saxophone, would play a solo with the Yale band at the Bowl. Vallee formed a band called the 'Connecticut Yankees.'"

HOWARD VS. TAD

With his brother, Howard, now coaching at the University of Iowa, Tad Jones returned to Yale

Collector Dan Riccio traded a 1956 autographed Topps Mickey Mantle baseball card plus other items for the Oct. 22, 1921, Yale-Army game day program.
(Don Kosakowski)

in 1920, succeeding Albert H. Sharpe, a former All-America half-back (1899) whom some considered the greatest Yale athlete of his time. Sharpe, who was also a medical doctor, coached the 1919 Bulldogs to a 5-3 mark that Jones matched on his return. Yale's 24-0 victory over a much bigger West Virginia team in the Bowl was a satisfying win for Jones. One his stalwarts was QB/HB Fido Kempton who also ran out of the halfback spot in the single wing.

"My memories go back to the days of the flying wedge and a time when players were not mandated to wear helmets," recalled Ostermann. "One particularly brave Yale player was a warrior named Fido Kempton (1919-20). He fielded punts and ran them back like a madman without his helmet on. You could see his hair flying in the wind."

Although some players wore leather helmets before 1900, it became a more common practice by World War I. The NCAA did not mandate the wearing of helmets until 1939.

Tad's 1921 squad won the first eight games of the season, including a 14-7 win over Army in the Bowl, before the bubble burst on the road at Harvard. It would not be the last time the Crimson would spoil a perfect season for the Elis.

The Jones brothers renewed their coaching rivalry in 1922 when Howard's undefeated Iowa Hawkeyes edged Yale 6-0 in the Bowl. Howard beat Tad a third time in a demonstration game in Los Angeles during the 1932 Olympics. Howard's

L-R: Brothers Howard and Tad Jones had successful coaching tenures at Yale.
(Yale Athletics)

West All-Stars triumphed 7-6 over his brother's East squad, composed of players from Yale, Harvard and Princeton.

The Great 1923 Team

Some regard the undefeated, untied team of 1923 as the greatest Yale squad ever.

The '23 Elis outscored their eight opponents 230-38, shutting out North Carolina, Georgia, Brown, Princeton, and Harvard. (This was welcome relief to old Blues, who had seen the Elis go 24-10-1 the previous four years but only 1-7 against Princeton and Harvard.) Captain "Memphis Bill" Mallory, a plunging runner and punishing blocker, led a contingent of stars that included Century Milstead (tackle), Mal Stevens, Ducky Pond and Newell Neidlinger (halfbacks), Win Lovejoy (center), Tex Diller (guard) and Lyle Richeson (quarterback).

"Memphis Bill" Mallory, captain of the great 1923 team, lost his life on a transport plane in WWII.
(YALE ATHLETICS)

Stevens and Pond would later become Yale head coaches.

Milstead got his unusual first name by being born on January 1, 1900. He was also one of four transfers on that team, together with Stevens, Richeson, and Widdy Neale. Milstead, Stevens, and Richeson played only one year at Yale. Tim Cohane wrote, "Through the years the whisper of a legend has taken growth that Yale ... scoured the country for every tramp athlete on the loose to build the '23 team."

On November 3 the Bulldogs beat Army 31-10 in front of an estimated 80,000 fans in the Bowl. Ted Blair, a tackle, recovered a fumble forced by Mallory for Yale's first touchdown. It was never really a contest after that. (Blair later served as a member of

the Yale Corporation—the university's board of trustees—and was the founder and president of the Yale Football Y Association.)

A WIDE RANGE OF VISITORS

During the '20s Yale University and the Bowl attracted a wide range of visitors and tours of the campus were popular.

"My dad, Carlo, was a 1926 Yale graduate," said broadcaster George Grande. "He received a scholarship to Yale, and one of the conditions of his scholarship was to conduct campus tours of the university. He had the fortune of giving tours to Gen. John J. Pershing, who commanded the Allied Expeditionary Forces in World War I, and Gene Tunney, the great world heavyweight boxing champ in the late '20s.

Century Milstead
(YALE ATHLETICS)

"My father's roots were not typically Ivy League growing up in Lawrence, Massachusetts, a mill town where people worked long days and were of modest means. He went out for football in 1922, but there wasn't much opportunity for a guy who weighed 130-140 pounds. He was not in the class of a 'Ducky' Pond, Bill Mallory, or Win Lovejoy. He made his mark on the crew team and boxed in the lightweight class."

Yale University has a reputation as one of the great universities in the world but we should not assume that all identified Yale as a university of higher learning during this era. Stamford, Connecticut, native Tony DeAngelo learned this firsthand. "Stamford in the 1920s and 1930s was a factory town," explained

DeAngelo. "One of the most noted factories was the old Yale & Towne lock company in the South End, where many immigrants of all nationalities worked. A number of them, including my elderly old friend, Gus Karukas, began to follow the Yale football team passionately.

"They posted clippings on the bulletin board. They listened to radio reports. They drove to home games at Yale Bowl every Saturday in the '20s, before any highways were built.

"They were absolutely in love with this team. But all of them had one thing in common. They thought that this was the Yale & Towne shop team and Dartmouth, Princeton, and Brown were just other factories that Yale was playing.

"One day someone spoiled their fun and told them that this is a college team. Dejected, they all returned home and stopped rooting.

"Except for Gus.

"To his dying day in the 1980s, he followed every Yale game, as he always had. The other guys asked him how he could do this, to which Gus would respond: 'I am a Connecticut man! I will ALWAYS follow Yale! For Yale IS Connecticut!'"

Yale football would never enjoy the dominance it did in its first five decades. But it would continue to be a national power that prided itself on its success in producing great players and many outstanding teams for almost the next ninety years.

CHAPTER 9

AN ERA OF LEGENDS—1927-1940

"Larry Kelley, TC '37, won the second Heisman ever, and teammate Clint Frank, '38, won the third. A few years before them, however, there was a 140-pound star named Albert 'Albie' Booth, '32."

—Peter Smith, *The Yale Herald*, 1997

WHILE THE CLAWS of the Great Depression gripped the nation, Franklin Delano Roosevelt, who had succeeded Herbert Hoover, began his first of four elected terms in the White House. In 1932, Amelia Earhart became the first woman to fly across the Atlantic, setting off five years to the day after Charles Lindbergh. Jesse Owens won four gold medals in track and field in the 1936 Olympics in Berlin, angering Adolf Hitler and effectively rebutting his message of Aryan superiority. During this time, Yale produced a trio of legends including two Heisman winners that would forever stand atop Yale football's Mount Rushmore.

A name that is lost in the dusty archives of Yale football lore from that era is Bruce Caldwell.

CALDWELL-GATE

Of the more than 3,000 athletes who have earned football letters at Yale, only one went on to play in both the NFL and major-league baseball after college. That player's name is Bruce Caldwell. Caldwell's college career was not without notoriety. His abrupt dismissal from the '27 team was perhaps the most celebrated and sensational college sports story of the time. In 1927 Caldwell, then a senior, was considered one of college football's elite athletes. *New York Times* writer James Harrison lionized him as "one of the greatest halfbacks who has ever worn a white 'Y,' and added, "When you run the list of great halfbacks from Jim Thorpe to Red Grange, don't forget to reserve a niche for Bruce Caldwell."

A tailback from Ashton, Rhode Island, Caldwell enrolled at Yale in 1924 and played that season with the freshman team. He became a starter in his junior season, which ended abruptly when he broke his ankle in the Bulldogs' second game against Georgia, a 19-0 victory.

In the fourth game of the 1927 season, on October 22nd, Yale faced a powerful Army squad. Seventy-seven thousand fans packed the Bowl and watched Caldwell pass, run, and kick the Elis to a 10-6 victory. His 96 yards rushing and 46-yard field goal were pivotal. He completed two passes in six tries, one producing Yale's touchdown on a 34-yard tackle-eligible play to Sid Quarrier.

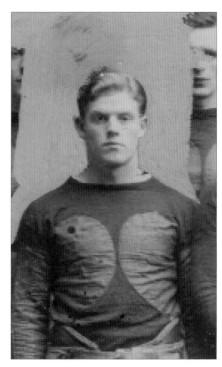

Bruce Caldwell is the only Yale football player to play in the NFL and the major leagues.
(YALE ATHLETICS)

On November 8, three days after Yale had crushed Maryland 30-6, the *Providence Bulletin* disclosed that Caldwell had played as a freshman at Brown in 1923 before transferring to Yale. The writer cited a Yale-Harvard-Princeton agreement not to use any player who had competed for another college football team. The idea of the agreement was to prevent "tramp athletes" from hopping from school to school, a widespread problem after World War I.

Tad Jones telephoned Brown and was told that Caldwell competed in three freshman games in '23. Some sources say he played in two.

The Yale University Athletic Association was then under the control of the alumni and was headed by Professor George H. Nettleton. A committee that included students, among them football captain William A. Webster, voted unanimously to declare Caldwell ineligible and he was dropped from the squad.

Outraged Yale students staged demonstrations and rallies, protesting what they perceived as a cold and unjust treatment of a student athlete. Harvard and Princeton encouraged Yale to waive the agreement and let Caldwell play the final two games of his college football career. But Nettleton and his group did not bend.

A follow-up revealed that Caldwell had signed a printed questionnaire when he came to Yale that stated he had never played football at Brown. It's quite possible that Caldwell thought that playing obscure time in a couple of freshman games did not violate any agreement made by the "Big Three." His intent is unknown, and the Yale Athletic Association never followed up on it. For this, Yale drew criticism from angered alumni. Unlike Yale's policy in the post WWI years, there was no one-year residency requirement in 1928 which would have required that Caldwell sit out for one year.

Without Caldwell, the Bulldogs went on to beat Princeton and Harvard. Yale compensated Caldwell by awarding him a varsity letter. He later wrote, in the *Saturday Evening Post,* that the Yale Athletic Association broke its own rule in awarding the letter. He also revealed that a New York paper offered him $1,000 for his story. Who, if anyone, tipped off the *Providence Bulletin* writer remains a mystery. None of Yale's opponents claimed responsibility.

Though barred from football, Caldwell, an outstanding second baseman, continued to play baseball for Yale under coach Smokey Joe Wood, hitting .413 in 1928.

After graduating magna cum laude, Caldwell had a 25-game major-league career with the Cleveland Indians (1928) and Brooklyn Dodgers (1932), seeing limited action as a right fielder, first baseman, and pinch hitter. He also played one season (1928) as running back with the New York football Giants, scoring the only touchdown in the Giants' 6-0 win over the Green Bay Packers on October 7th.

While dabbling in pro sports he attended Yale Law School. He later served as a lieutenant commander in the Navy in World War II, practiced law in New Haven, and became a municipal court judge in West Haven, Connecticut. Caldwell died on February 15, 1959, in West Haven, just a drop-kick away from the scenes of his college sports achievements at Yale Bowl and Yale Field.

The eternal question remains. Was Caldwell delivered an injustice by the Yale administration? Was the decision by the Nettleton committee motivated by a desire to stop the movement of "tramp athletes" from school to school?

John Kieran brilliantly penned the following words in his Nov. 10, 1927, *New York Times* column: "The enemy rush line couldn't halt Bruce Caldwell, but he was stopped by a printed paragraph. The halfback who could dash through a broken field finally tripped over a scrap piece of paper."

TAD'S LAST HURRAH

Before the start of the '27 campaign, head coach Tad Jones made the shocking announcement that he would retire at the end of season. In a year the goal posts were moved from the goal line to the end zone line, Jones guided the Elis to a 7-1 record, losing only to Georgia, and they were among claimants to the national championship.

Jones finished his Yale career with a remarkable 60-15-4 record. Only Walter Camp (67-2) had a better winning percentage. Jones was succeeded by Mal Stevens, a Yale medical school student and member of the '23 team.

Jones remained in the area. "I worked part-time in Camp's market in Madison as a meat cutter for 30 years," said Dan Mulvey Jr. "Tad, who lived in Madison, would come in once a year and order an

Mal Stevens (left) succeeded Tad Jones (right) as Yale's head coach.
(YALE ATHLETICS)

8-10 inch sirloin steak. He would take it home and roast it."

LITTLE BOY BLUE

Yale opened the 1929 season on October 5th by walloping Vermont 89-0 in the Bowl. It remains the highest number of points and largest margin of victory by any team playing in the Yale Bowl.

Coach Stevens's star was Albie Booth, the 5-foot-6, 144-pound iconic tailback. What Booth lacked in size he made up for with boundless confidence, skill, and fortitude. It was written that "he was a snake on the field—cut left, right, spinned, turned and had a knack of landing on his tacklers." Some called him

Albie Booth 1955 Topps All-American card
(THE TOPPS CO. INC.)

"The Mighty Atom" but his most popular nickname was "Little Boy Blue."

"My late father, Dan Mulvey, was the sports editor of the *New Haven Register* for many years," said Dan Mulvey Jr. "He used to use some flashy headlines. For Albie Booth he would banner, 'Little Boy Blue.' Charles McQueeney, the editor of the paper, didn't like it and told him to cool it. But 'Little Boy Blue' stuck."

Booth established his legend against Army on October 26, 1929, three days before the stock market crashed and America hurtled toward the Great Depression.

With Army ahead 13-0 in the second quarter, it appeared the Cadets would be burning the bonfires of victory on the West Point plains that night. But Booth came off the bench and riddled the West Point defenses, scoring three touchdowns and drop-kicking three extra points in a 21-13 comeback win before an overflow crowd estimated at 80,000. Booth's heroics rank near the top in the pantheon of all-time Yale football performances. As *Time* magazine put it, Booth "stole the thunder" of Christian "Red" Cagle, Army's All-America halfback. In the large throng was Booth's mother, attending her first football game. He made her proud by rushing for 141 yards on 32 carries and scoring on a 72-yard punt return.

Booth was humble and modest, never forgetting to compliment his teammates. "I interviewed Albie in 1956," said Joel Alderman ('51). "[The broadcaster] Mel Allen used it on his ABC radio show that year. Albie said his greatest thrill was the '29 Army game when he scored all 21 points. He modestly credited his teammates for his success that game."

Fay Vincent Jr. (Yale Law School, '63), the former commissioner of major league baseball, is the son of Fay Vincent Sr., who played with Booth. He talked

Francis "Fay" Vincent captained the 1930 Yale football team.
(YALE ATHLETICS)

about his father's connection to the '29 Army game and coach Mal Stevens.

"My father was a 5-foot-11, 200-pound tackle who captained the 1930 football team and the 1931 baseball team," said Vincent proudly. "He was credited for throwing a wicked block on an Army player that allowed Booth to score one of his three touchdowns. In 1983 I sat with my father high in the end zone on the scoreboard side at the 100th anniversary of the Yale-Harvard game. I asked him where on the field did he make that great block. He pointed to the front of the visitors' bench on the east side of the Bowl.

"Although [Stevens's] record at Yale was pretty good (21-11-8), my father did not think highly of Stevens as a coach. He thought that he was too predictable and the offense lacked imagination. It was always 'Booth to the right.' Harvard beat Yale every year that my father played.

"By the way, my father was dating my mother while at Yale, and she had perhaps the best seat in the Bowl. Her ticket was in Portal 16, Aisle A, Row 1, which was the seat of the captain's date."

The 1930 Army game, played on a rainy field, ended in a 7-7 stalemate. The contest was marked by controversy, including allegations of dirty play. The Yale staff's review of the game film hinted that the Cadet touchdown was illegal. The Associated Press quoted Yale officials as saying Army ball carrier Tom Kilday was lifted over the goal line by teammate Ray Stecker after the Yale defense had stopped Kilday's initial charge. Pushing or lifting the runner off the ground called for a 15-yard penalty. The Yale Athletic Association, however, took the high road and never filed a protest. Some of the knights of the keyboard seated in press row said they had seen Strecker give Kilday a boost.

Because of the heavy rain, Booth did not start the game. Inserted on defense late in the second period, he intercepted an Army pass near the goal line and was met by a phalanx of Army tacklers after a short return. According to an AP report, after the ball had been ruled dead, "Army players ... leaped into the mass on the ground in which Booth was entangled." He was carried from the field on a stretcher.

No penalty was called, and the Yale fans booed loudly,

Was the chorus of Army tacklers payback for Booth's 1929 heroics or simply "brave old Army team" football? Dan Mulvey of the *New Haven Register* wrote that the ball had been thrown directly to Booth and that six Army players hit him. And in the pileup someone kicked him in the back of the head, stunning him. Conscious by the time he was carried off, Booth wanted to return to the game, but Stevens vetoed that, according to Mulvey.

1929 Yale-Army game day program
(YALE ATHLETICS)

Hank O'Donnell of the *Waterbury Republican* was not convinced it had been a premeditated assault. "For one thing, Army, trailing 7-0, had a receiver in the end zone, and Booth leaped to snare the pass," wrote O'Donnell. "He was hit at knee level by an Army player but shook him off. Two other Cadets, coming from his left and his right, then hit Booth at the same time." There was no fumble, but two other players dived into the pile as if there had been.

George Currie summed up the controversy this way in the *Brooklyn Eagle*, "Albie Booth's injury in the Yale-Army game . . . and the hot post-mortems over it overshadowed all other technical details of the play. Eli grads between the halves were fuming, and while nobody suggested lynching the Army team at least something pretty close to the thought was there. The day was too wet and soggy for direct action, but there was tall talk on both sides. "

Booth's injuries were described after the game as not serious. He returned to practice on Monday and played the full sixty minutes against Dartmouth the

Army cadets march on Yale Bowl before 1929 Yale-Army game.
(YALE ATHLETICS)

following Saturday. There was talk of breaking off the Yale-Army series but the rivalry survived.

In three seasons, playing tailback on teams that went 15-5-5, Booth rushed for 1,428 yards and ate up 1,138 yards of real estate on kick returns. He scored seventeen touchdowns and kicked twenty-four extra points. Despite his gaudy numbers, he never made an All-America first team. (He was voted into the National Football Foundation's College Football Hall of Fame in 1966.) The Topps Company, however, honored him in its 1955 All-America set with a bubble-gum card of his own, No. 86. In 1932 he was in a movie titled *The All-American,* with a cast that included fellow stars Red Cagle (Army), Frank Carideo (Notre Dame), and Ernie Nevers (Stanford).

Booth later served as an assistant coach at Yale under Howie Odell (1945-47) and was widely known as a football referee. Frank Stolzenberg ('53) has fond memories of Booth.

"I grew up on Yale Avenue," said Stolzenberg. "When I was in high school in the '40s I would go over to the practice area, near the horse stables that were used for the polo team. I would help bring out the equipment and shag balls for the punters and kickers. The football practice field had lights, but the lighting was poor. Albie was one of Howard Odell's assistant coaches.

"I was a pretty good drop-kicker and once challenged Albie to a drop-kicking contest. We started at the 5 and worked our way to the 25-yard line, which is where Albie put me away."

"Little Boy Blue" died unexpectedly of a heart attack on March 1, 1959, after attending a Broadway play. He was fifty-one years old. Just two weeks earlier, another Yale great, Bruce Caldwell, had also died prematurely at the age of fifty-three.

BULLDOGS VS. BULLDOGS

It is no coincidence that Yale and the University of Georgia share the nickname "Bulldogs." Abraham Baldwin, a native of Connecticut and graduate of Yale, was installed as the University of Georgia's first president in 1786. The teams first met on October 13, 1923, in the Bowl, with the Elis breezing to a 40-0 win. They played eleven times through 1934, with Georgia winning six games.

Yale played its first football game in the South on October 12, 1929, losing 15-0 to Georgia in the opening game at Sanford Stadium in Athens. The "Dawgs" were led by Vernon "Catfish" Smith and Spurgeon "Spud" Chandler, who went on to become a two-time 20-game winner for the New York Yankees in the 1940s.

Although they came away on the short end, the Yale contingent had received a warm welcome in the Peach State. According to the *New York Times*, "The Georgia governor declared game day a legal holiday in the state. The Yale band got off the train and paraded though the streets, with the sidewalks lined, and a burst of cheers greeted the blue-sweatered musicians as they broke into *Dixie*. (Rare footage of part of the game is available on the web: www.patrickgarbin.blogspot.com/2012/07/rare-northeastern-exposure.html.)

AN HISTORIC TIE

In 1931 Yale and Dartmouth played to a 33-33 tie when Dartmouth spooked the Bulldogs on Halloween by staging the greatest comeback ever by any Yale opponent, overcoming a 23-point deficit. At the time, it was the highest scoring tie game in college football history.

Dartmouth entered the game winless in fourteen meetings between the two teams. Initially, the game looked like Dartmouth would be getting more of the same. "It looked like a laugher for the Elis that day as they took a commanding 33-10 lead," said judge John Flanagan, who attended the game at age ten. "Albie Booth scored three touchdowns within an eight minute span in the second quarter. He had an electrifying 94-yard kickoff return, a 22-yard pass, and a 53-yard run. But the wheels came off the wagon in the second half.

"Dartmouth halfback 'Wild' Bill McCall ran back a kickoff and then scored on an interception. [McCall had scoring plays of 76, 92, and 60 yards.] That made the score 33-24. Dartmouth blocked a kick and scored making it 33-30. They then missed the extra point. As dusk was settling on the Bowl, All-American quarterback Bill "Air Mail" Morton kicked a 34-yard field goal and the game ended in a 33-33 tie. So the 1968 Harvard game was not the first time Yale lost a tie game, the '31 Dartmouth game was."

Yale opened the 1932 season with an unlikely scoreless tie against Bates, a small liberal arts college from Lewiston, Maine, before 20,000 in the Bowl. It marked the first time Yale did not win its opener. The Bulldogs had bludgeoned the Bobcats, outscoring them 175-0 in their previous five meetings and would cruise to a 48-0 win in 1951, against a Bates team coached by former Yale coach Ducky Pond.

A LEGEND RETURNS

The following week, on October 8th, former Yale All-American Amos Alonzo Stagg, the "Grand Old Man of the Midway," brought his University of Chicago Maroons to the Bowl, where they tied Yale 7-7. Stagg's team was reportedly the first to use

Amos Alonzo Stagg coached until age ninety-eight.
(YALE ATHLETICS)

the dormitory at the Ray Tompkins House for lodging.

The ageless coach, who lived to 102, had a long and successful head coaching career at Springfield (1890-91); Chicago (1892-1932); and College of the Pacific (1933-46); winning 314 games against 199 losses and 35 ties. From 1947-52 he served as co-coach with his son, Amos Jr., at Susquehanna in Pennsylvania and an advisory coach at Stockton Junior College from 1953-60. The ageless wonder retired at age ninety-eight.

Ferd Nadherny, who played in the Yale backfield in the late 1940s, talked about Stagg.

"One of my most interesting experiences at Yale was meeting Amos Alonzo Stagg, who was elderly at the time," he said. "Many called him 'football's Grand Old Man.' He was credited with many innovations in the game, such as the huddle, the direct pass from center, the onside kick, padded goal posts and the tackling dummy. One day he came to one of our practices and spoke to everyone."

FROM MAL TO REGGIE

After the 1932 season Stevens, having received his medical degree, gave up the head coaching position. He coached the Yale freshmen in '33 and later coached New York University (1938-41) and the Brooklyn Dodgers of the All-American Conference

(1946). He taught orthopedic surgery at both Yale and NYU and in 1947 served as team doctor for both the baseball and football New York Yankees. (The football team played in the All-American Conference.)

Reggie Root, a tackle on Yale's '24 and '25 teams, succeeded Stevens. His '33 team came out of the gate 3-0 before losing four of its last five, including the Harvard and Princeton games. The Princeton game was on December 2nd, the latest regular-season game Yale had played since 1900. According to Tim Cohane, Root "heard the lupine howl" of disgruntled alumni. He quietly returned to coaching the freshmen for the next nine years before going to Hillhouse High School in New Haven, where he coached the great Levi Jackson.

NO GOAL POSTS?

On November 2, 1935, Dartmouth beat Yale in the Bowl for the first time in nineteen tries in a game that was completed with the unlikely sight of a football field without goal posts. With seconds on the clock and the ball in the hands of the Indians, jubilant Dartmouth fans stormed both ends of the field, tore down the posts and removed the goal markers. When order was restored, the game ended on the next play. Fortunately, neither team had the opportunity to score by kicking.

In July 1936, new goal posts—six-inch-square steel girders sunk into fifty-eight inches of cement—were installed. Apparently, the tradition of tearing down goal posts started in the '20s. "The ones who would start the action, Yale authorities found, were professional pickpockets who had a heyday with all the shoving and pushing that went on in the free-for-all," wrote Ned Thomas in the *New Haven Register* on Oct. 25, 1964.

"DUCKY" POND

Raymond "Ducky" Pond, one of the heroes of Yale's famed '23 team, replaced Root and remained through 1940. He is the last Yale graduate to serve as head football coach. He earned an ignoble distinction as the first Yale coach to lose his first game, 12-6 to Columbia on October 6, 1934—but brighter days were ahead.

Pond mentored Larry Kelley and Clint Frank, back-to-back Heisman Trophy winners in 1936 and 1937. Pond's 30-25-2 mark against tough national teams was highlighted by his 1936 and 1937 teams, which both finished 12th in the Associated Press national rankings with records of 7-1 and 6-1-1 respectively.

THE KELLEY-FRANK ERA

Yale produced Heisman Trophy winners in back-to-back years in Larry Kelley and Clint Frank. Their deeds remain etched forever in Yale lore when the Bulldogs strived to maintain their image as a national power.

Larry Kelley had a quick, flowing wit and was confident to the point of cockiness. He came to Yale out of Williamsport High School in Pennsylvania and the Peddie School, a boarding school in Hightstown, New Jersey. While at Yale, the native of Conneaut, Ohio, was a member of Skull and Bones but never joined a fraternity. In his career the 6-foot-2 All-American end had 49 receptions for 889 yards and scored 15 touchdowns. Kelley, the 1936 Yale captain, was also a defensive giant.

In 1936, he won the Heisman Trophy in a landslide vote beating out such legendary gridiron greats as Sammy Baugh (Texas Christian) and Ace Parker

All-American end Larry Kelley
(YALE ATHLETICS)

(Duke). That year Kelley caught seventeen passes for 372 yards and scored six touchdowns in an era dominated by the running game.

In Yale's win over Navy in Baltimore on October 17, Kelley was involved in a play that had fans buzzing for a week. Navy was leading 7-6 when Yale's Tony Mott punted from Yale territory. Middie back Sneed Schmidt tried to catch it on or about the Navy 25-yard line when he fumbled the punt. Kelley, coming down in punt coverage, inadvertently kicked the ball to the Navy 3-yard line where he picked it up and stepped into the end zone for an apparent touchdown. But the ball was brought back to the 3-yard line because he could not advance a fumble. Two plays later Clint Frank scored to put Yale ahead 12-7 which proved to be the final score.

The kick was fodder for discussion. Were Kelley's actions intentional or not? Kelley always maintained that his kick was not intentional. Schmidt, in an interview decades with Bob Barton agreed. "From what I could observe," Schmidt said, "There was no way he could have avoided the damn ball."

Kelley's kick resulted in a supplemental note to the rule adding, "If a free ball is kicked accidentally, it is to be treated simply as if the ball had been touched."

Kelley never played professionally because he did not think that pro football had a good reputation in the late '30s. In 1937 he signed a contract to play for the Boston Shamrocks of the American Football League but reconsidered after a Sunday visit to watch the team play. He also nixed an $11,000 offer to play for the Detroit Lions.

A gifted athlete who also starred at baseball during his collegiate years, he was offered a $5,000 contract by St. Louis Cardinals vice president and business manager Branch Rickey. According to Dave Newhouse in his book titled, *After the Glory: Heisman,* Rickey promised Kelley, a first baseman, that he would never play lower than Triple-A. If he didn't make it to the big league club, he would get an

administrative position in the Cardinals' organization. Kelley declined.

Offers came in from other quarters as well. Hollywood dangled $1,500 a week in front of Kelley to make a movie of his life titled, *Kelley of Yale.* The handsome All-American would play himself. Again, the answer was no.

Kelley spent twelve years in the glove-manufacturing industry but most of his career following athletics involved education. He was a math teacher and alumni director at the Cheshire Academy in Cheshire, Connecticut, but most of his post college years were spent at the Peddie School where he served as a teacher, coach, and fund-raiser for the alumni association.

In 1969 he was elected to the National Football Foundation's College Football Hall of Fame.

On the weekend of the 1981 Yale-Harvard game Kelley and Clint Frank, the 1937 Heisman winner, presented replicas of their Heisman trophies for permanent display in the Yale gym. In a December 11, 2000, *Sports Illustrated* article written by Michael Bamberger, the always glib Kelley quipped, "I hope some potential Rhodes Scholars visiting Yale gain some inspiration. And I hope they can run, pass and kick."

At halftime of the game, the two Yale greats were ushered into the Yale team's meeting room. "We wondered who these old guys were," said Rich Diana, a star running back on the '81 team.

AUCTION

Kelley auctioned his original Heisman Trophy in December 1999 to benefit his large number of nieces and nephews. He and his wife, Ruth, never had children of their own and he admired the respect his family had given him. Although Jay Berwanger is

Larry Kelley's Topps football card
(THE TOPPS COMPANY)

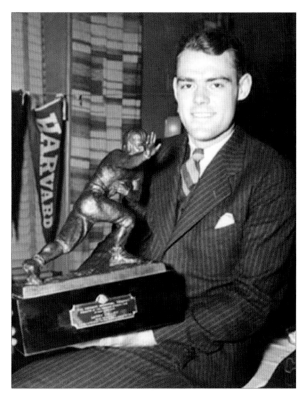

Larry Kelley holds the original Heisman
Trophy.
(YALE ATHLETICS)

considered the first Heisman winner in 1935, his
prize was the Downtown Athletic Club award. The
first Heisman as we know it in its present form was
given to Kelley the following year.

Kelley's 1936 Heisman trophy fetched the staggering sum of $328,110. The winning bid went to
the Walsh family, owners of a bar and restaurant
in Garrison, New York. Kelley visited the restaurant shortly after the
auction.

"In February
2000, two months
after my family won
the bid for Larry
Kelley's Heisman
Trophy, Larry came
up here with Ruth,
and 22 of his nieces
and nephews to
look at the trophy

James Walsh, the proprietor of the Stadium
Museum Restaurant and Bar, holds Larry
Kelley's Heisman Trophy in his restaurant.
(DON KOSAKOWSKI)

one last time," said James Walsh, proprietor of the
Stadium Museum Restaurant and Bar. "When he
came through the door he saw my signed Yale baseball photo of former President George H.W. Bush,
which caught his attention.

"When Larry noticed that the trophy was the
centerpiece of the whole building, he was driven to
tears. He was scared that someone would put it in
their living room and nobody would see it.

"We had lunch/dinner for five hours. Larry knew
how good he was but he was very unassuming. I've
met Michael Jordan and Joe Montana but I never
had the feeling I had meeting Larry Kelley."

At the age of eighty-five, Kelley died of a self-in-
flicted gunshot wound at his home in Hightstown,
New Jersey, six months later on June 27, 2000. Kelley had suffered a stroke a few months earlier and
had undergone heart bypass surgery. Although his
mobility was impaired his mind was still sharp. He
had no known fatal disease. His suicide was shocking to all. Although he reportedly did not have financial problems, some speculate he took his own
life so there would be something for the nieces and
nephews to inherit.

Kelley's wife found him dead in the basement
of their home after she returned from Mass, a daily
ritual for her. She found her husband sitting on
a chair with a small handgun on his lap, a gun she
never knew he had.

"As Larry's body was being taken from the house,
she (Ruth) asked the medics to remove his rings and
leave them with her. One was his class ring from
Yale. The other his wedding ring," wrote Bamberger.

The irrepressible Kelley holds a distinction as
the only player to score touchdowns in all six games
played against Princeton and Harvard from 1934 to
1936. John T. Brady wrote the following verse titled,
The Heisman, in tribute to Kelley.

CLINT FRANK

Two-time All-American halfback Clint Frank, who won the '37 Heisman Trophy, came to Yale out of Evanston Township High School in Evanston, Illinois. He was extremely nearsighted, but his football instincts were 20-20. The myopic back with a quiltwork of well-woven skills did everything but sell tickets from his spot in Pond's single-wing offense. He also returned kicks and called the plays. A power runner with ten second hundred-yard dash speed, he rushed for 1,244 yards and completed 59 passes for 937 yards and nine touchdowns in his Yale career (1935-37). After Yale's 27-7 win over Penn in 1937, the *New York Times'* Allison Danzig, alluding to Booth, referred to Frank as Yale's "Big Boy Blue." Defensively, he was an aggressive tackler and knocked down many passes from his safety position.

In 1937 he scored three touchdowns in Yale's 19-0 victory over Brown. The following week in Yale's 26-0 pounding of Princeton, he rushed for 190 yards, a Yale record that lasted for thirty-five years until broken by Dick Jauron. That year he won the Heisman, beating out University of Colorado running back (and future Supreme Court Justice) Byron "Whizzer" White.

Like Kelley, Frank turned down offers to play in the fledgling National Football League. In 1955 he was elected to the National Football Foundation's College Football Hall of Fame.

Ironically, Frank and Jay Berwanger, the first winner of the Heisman Trophy, played on the same rugby club on the North Side of Chicago prior to World War II. Another notable player on that team was Joseph Kennedy Jr. Frank and Berwanger developed a close friendship during their lives.

Frank became an advertising executive, but at sixty he retired from business and turned his attention to philanthropy. Yale remained dear to his heart. He donated $500,000 to renovate the DeWitt Cuyler Athletic Complex adjacent to Yale Field on Derby Avenue. The track's infield was named for Frank in 1985. He also was a champion of the arts and medical research and of special-needs children. When Frank passed away in 1992, Bob Barton wrote, "It has been said that the test of a great man is the way he treats the little people around him. By

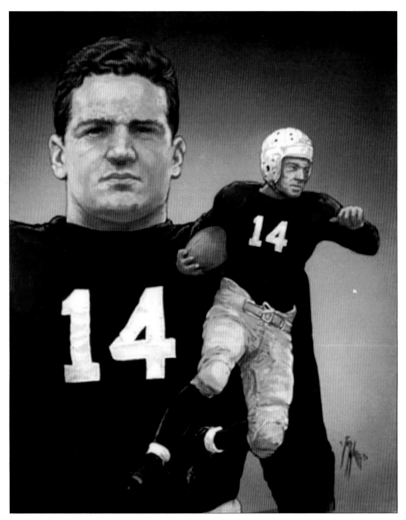

Clint Frank captained the 1937 team.
(YALE ATHLETICS).

that standard Clint Frank, a great athlete, great competitor, was a great man."

At this writing, Frank's Heisman trophy has never been sold. It is still held privately, presumably by the Frank family.

Paul Sortal, a running back and wide receiver in '70 and '71, recalled Clint Frank, the man.

"In the spring of my junior year (1972), I asked Carm Cozza if he had any ideas about a summer job. He put me in touch with Clinton E. Frank, the winner of the third Heisman Trophy and the first Maxwell Award (each intends to honor the best college football player in the country). Though I was working as a mailroom boy for $5/hour, Clint, the founder and owner of the fifth largest advertising agency in Chicago, treated me like a good friend from day one. At the end of the summer, he invited me to his home for Christmas, a tradition which continued for several years."

"That fall, Yale celebrated its 100th year of football and the night before the Princeton game, they held a huge black-tie dinner for 400 in the Commons. Clint was honored as Yale's greatest football player the second half of that century of competition and gave a long speech. The next day, on the very busy weekend he was honored with plenty of people to see in New Haven, Clint somehow located my room after the game, knocked on the door with his wife, Margaret, a.k.a. "Mike," and her daughter, Kathy, and presented me with a magnum of champagne, exclaiming, 'You played a great game!' I was floored by the magnanimous nature of that gesture. I was to learn over the years that he treated all manner of people that way."

Collector Dan Riccio had an unusual experience involving Frank. "I have the signatures of Larry Kelley and Clint Frank on a football card that was part of a Heisman Trophy football card set," said Riccio.

The Frank signed card was interesting in that I had sent a card and a photo. He signed both and wrote a nice note. Two days later (July 7, 1992) he passed away. His wife, Marge, sent me the materials."

Kelley and Frank donated replicas of their Heisman Trophies to Yale during the weekend of the 1981 Yale-Harvard game. Rich Diana, a running back for Yale at the time, chuckled, "At halftime of the game, two state policemen escorted them into our meeting room. We were all wondering who these old guys were."

TOP TEAMS INVADE THE BOWL

The Associate Press Top Ten poll originated in 1936. Yale (No. 5) and Dartmouth (9) played to a 9-9 draw on October 30, 1937. It marked the only time that top ten teams played in the Bowl. William Proxmire, later to be a senator from Wisconsin, was a member of Yale's '37 team, as was Eddie Collins Jr., son of the baseball Hall of Fame second baseman.

The University of Michigan edged Yale 15-13 on October 22, 1938. With Yale ahead 13-8 late in the game, a roughing-the-kicker penalty gave the Wolverines new life at their own 26-yard line. The magnificent Tom Harmon, who was to win the 1940 Heisman, sparked a 74-yard scoring drive with his runs and passes. Both teams wore blue jerseys. Yale's were a notch or two lighter than Michigan's. This was not Michigan's first trip to New Haven. The Wolverines lost to Yale at Hamilton Park in 1881 and 1883.

In 1939 the Elis played No. 3 Michigan at Ann Arbor and lost 27-7. Yale football had fallen on hard times.

Cornell came into the Yale Bowl on November 9, 1940, ranked No. 1 in the country and riding a thirteen-game winning streak under coach Carl Snavely. The Red Raiders led by All America tackle

Yale assistant coaches, 1938, L-R: Jimmy DeAngelis, Ivy Williamson and Gerald Ford, the future President of the United States. Ford was a center and linebacker on the University of Michigan teams from 1932 to 1934. (YALE ATHLETICS)

Nick Drahos and signal caller and blocking back Walt Matuszak, dispatched the Elis, 21-0. It was the only time a No. 1 AP poll ranked team played in the Bowl.

Nineteen-forty was Pond's final season as Yale's head coach. Pond's last three years proved to be a struggle, with the team going 6-17-1. Gone were the glory days of Booth, Kelley, and Frank. World War II, the most widespread war in world history, lay ahead—and its impact on Yale University and its football program would be profound.

CHAPTER 10

THE RIVALS—PRINCETON AND HARVARD (1873-1940)

"To many of the 'old Blues,' it's more important to beat Princeton and Harvard than it is winning the Ivy League title."

—Carmen Cozza

YALE'S LONGEST RIVALRY

Although the Yale-Harvard game is the biggest football event each year for Yale and Harvard alums, the Yale-Princeton rivalry has deeper roots. The schools are two of college football's earliest apostles. The annual meeting between the Bulldogs and the Tigers is the second most often-played series in all of college football. Only Lehigh and Lafayette, which sometimes met three times in a year, have played more often.

Yale has faced Princeton 136 times (entering the 2014 season) and leads in the series, 74-52-10. The first game was played on November 15, 1873, when Princeton beat Yale 3 goals to 0 at Hamilton Park. The game ball was stuffed instead of being inflated by a bladder. In a scene straight out of *America's Funniest Home Videos,* opposing players kicked the ball at the same moment and the ball exploded, scattering stuffing across the field. The game was delayed for half an hour until another ball could be located. Fifty-three years later, George M. Gunn, the Yale player involved in the play, turned the relic football over to Princeton University because the Tigers had won the game, reported the *New York Times.*

From 1876 to 1879 the games were played in Hoboken, New Jersey. The teams played in New York from 1880 to 1896, mostly at the Polo Grounds or Manhattan Field. Those settings were a jinx for the men in blue. Twice, in 1889 and 1893 the Tigers ended Yale's thirty-seven-game winning streak on a New York field. Several of these games were played on Thanksgiving Day.

The two schools made history on November 14, 1903, when Thomas Edison reportedly filmed the Yale-Princeton game in New Haven using a Kintegraph motion picture camera. The 11-6 game won by the Tigers was the first football game ever filmed. (The Edison films of the early 1900s have been preserved through the years at the Library of Congress.)

Yale and Harvard normally meet at the close of their respective schedules, but Harvard has not always been Yale's final opponent. Between 1877 and 1899, Princeton filled that role eighteen times. And from 1930 to 1936, Yale alternated its final game between Princeton and Harvard. The last time Yale closed its season against Princeton was in 1943, when Harvard was playing an informal schedule because of World War II.

Notable Games

One of the oddest games in Eli history was played on November 18, 1911, when Yale and Princeton set a record that may stand forever: the teams punted a combined sixty-four times. The Tigers, featuring Hobey Baker, "The blond Adonis of the gridiron," won 6-3 in a downpour at Yale Field II.

The Bulldogs and Tigers played to a 6-6 tie in New Jersey the following year. With Yale trailing 6-3 and one minute remaining, Yale's Hal Pumpelly, a substitute, drop-kicked the tying 49-yard field goal.

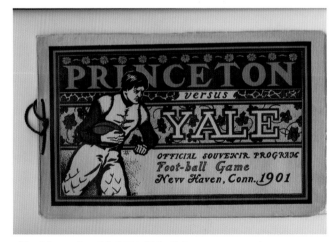

The November 16, 1901, Yale-Princeton game day program (YALE ATHLETICS)

"Pump," who always insisted the ball traveled 52 yards and 3 inches, was immortalized in print by the estimable Grantland Rice:

When you read some impossible story
Of a sub who was jammed in the game,
With one minute left where his glory
Companions were beaten in fame —
"He met the last hope like a fighter,
A full fifty yards without fail" —
Ere you start in to pan the poor writer
Shake hands with Pumpelly of Yale.

PUMPELLY'S **FEAT** **PALED** in comparison to the boot by Princeton's James Haxall, who drop-kicked a school-record 65-yard field goal in the 1882 Tigers' win over Yale at the Polo Grounds, then situated at Fifth Avenue and 110th Street.

Another startling moment occurred in the 1915 Y-P game when Yale's Otis Guernsey drop-kicked a 54-yard field goal, one of his two in the game to help Yale beat heavily favored Princeton 13-7 in front of 50,000 at the Bowl. The *New York Times* reported, "… Princeton came here today to take part in the obsequies of Yale's misfortune, but the flowers and condolences were wasted, for there was no Yale funeral."

Otis Guernsey.

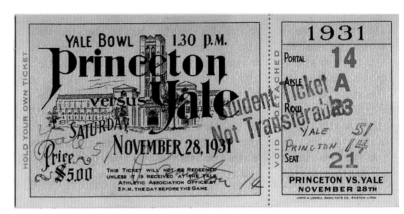

A ticket from the November 28, 1931, Yale-Princeton game. The Bulldogs closed the season with a 51-14 win over the Tigers.

In what may have been a first-of-its-kind-event in major college football history, and one that hasn't been repeated, two brothers served as opposing captains when Tim Callahan (Yale) and Mike Callahan (Princeton) did battle at Palmer Stadium on November 13, 1920. The previous year the two played opposite each other at center in the Bowl. Oddly, each was elected captain on the same day (December 3, 1919), 112 miles apart. The Tigers won both games.

In the 1930 contest the Elis, led by Freddie Linehan and Fred Loesser, made a famous goal line stand to beat Princeton, 10-7, at Palmer Stadium. For the first time in the history of the series the bands of the two universities combined on the field and together played Yale and Princeton songs. Another novelty was that the Yale band formed the letter "P" while the Princeton band lined up in a "Y."

Yale's Iron Men

From 1933 to 1935 Princeton lost only one game, the 1934 game against Yale. That day Yale played the same eleven players the entire game and pulled off a stunning upset in their 7-0 win over the highly touted Tigers. Princeton, coached by Fritz Crisler, was in the middle of a 15-game winning streak and was a candidate for the Rose Bowl while Yale entered the contest a mediocre 3-3.

WILLIAM WALLACE

William Wallace ('45 W, '49) was a *New York Times* sportswriter and author of *Yale's Ironmen: A Story of Football & Lives in the Decade of the Depression & Beyond*," which includes a detailed account of the 1934 Yale-Princeton game. Wallace contributed the following story prior to his death in 2012 at the age of eighty-eight.

"On November 17, 1934, my father took me to the Yale-Princeton game at Palmer Stadium. I was ten years old and was about to witness one of the most historic games in college football history when Yale played the same eleven players the entire game and defeated a heavily favored Princeton team.

"The drive from our home in Rye, New York, to Princeton, New Jersey, took four hours as we cruised along in our 1932 Ford Model A four-door sedan. A capacity crowd of 52,000 filled the stadium with all tickets priced at $3.50 in this era of the Great Depression.

"On the Friday morning before the game, the twenty-eight Yale players among the party of sixty-five left the Yale Station where the Yale Band gave them a spirited sendoff. At 10:00 a.m. the team departed the New Haven Railroad Station on the No. 7 train and arrived at Princeton about 1:30 p.m. The players then walked to the McCormick Field House and dressed for a 90-minute practice under head coach 'Ducky' Pond.

"The eleven players, who played the entire game totaling 138 plays, emerged as *Yale's Ironmen*, the title of the book I wrote in 2005 in their honor. The seniors included Clare Curtin,

the captain and left guard; Stan Fuller (left halfback) and Jim DeAngelis (center).

"The juniors were Jerry Roscoe (quarterback), Robert "Choo Choo" Train (left end), and Jim Whitehead (fullback). Whitehead was the primary ball carrier in the single wing offense.

"The sophomores included 1936 Heisman Trophy winner Larry Kelley (right end), Meredith Scott (left tackle), and Jack Wright (right tackle).

"There was no score until three minutes remained in the first quarter when Yale had a third and 13 on the Princeton 49 and pulled off a fake punt-pass play. Fuller was in punt formation but DeAngelis snapped the ball to Roscoe who fired a pass to Kelley. The talented receiver leaped high in the air, snared it and ran for a touchdown. Curtin then kicked the extra point and Yale led, 7-0, which proved to be the final score.

"In the third quarter 'Choo Choo' Train gave Princeton's Gary Levan a good lick on a punt return. Pond looked Train over and said, 'We better get him out of there.' 'Let him go,' said assistant coach Earl 'Greasy' Neale. 'The hell with it. Let eleven men beat them.' They did.

"Princeton outgained Yale 185-71 but 133 of those yards came on two long scoreless drives. The Tigers won the battle of the statistics but the exhausted Bulldogs won the war.

"The game was played in the dark ages of sports science... Yale trainer Frank 'Major' Wandle was leery of water for his athletes and did not proffer it in the halftime room. Instead he had Lou Walker, the assistant manager, soak sugar cubes with a handy bottle of rum and hand them out.

The Ironmen posed on their practice field 4 days after playing the entire game against Princeton: L-R (front) Larry Kelley, (RE), Henry Wright (RT), Paul Grosscup Jr. (RG) Jimmy DeAngelis (C), Captain Francis Curtin (LG), Meredith Scott (LT), Robert Train (LE) Curtin and Wright changed on the defense. L-R (top): Strat Morton (HB), Kim Whitehead (FB), Jerry Roscoe (QB), and Stan Fuller (HB). (YALE ATHLETICS)

"Two former Yale players now junior varsity assistant coaches, Walter Levering and Century Milstead, were at Harvard Stadium, scouting the Crimson in its 47-3 win over New Hampshire. When the Yale-Princeton score was announced, Levering, a 5-foot-9, 160-pound halfback, turned to Milstead, a robust 6-2, 220 and lifted Century off his seat.

"That evening the Yale team stayed overnight at the Hotel New Yorker across the street from the Pennsylvania Station in New York City. They went to the theater to see the musical comedy *Life begins at 8:40*, starring Ray Bolger and Bert Lahr. According to Roscoe, it was prearranged with the thought the team would need something to cheer them up after taking a beating from a strong Princeton team, who went on to win their next twelve games.

"I could never let go of the 'Ironmen.' For me that 1934 setting was like looking at a stunning portrait by John Singer Sargent and craving

to know more of the silent subjects. I followed the lifetime journeys of those 11 Yale subjects. Jimmy DeAngelis was the last surviving member until his death at age 97 on December 28, 2007."

The Uncanny 1936 and 1953 Games

Two of the more thrilling Yale-Princeton contests took place seventeen years apart at Palmer Stadium. The parallel between the 1936 and 1953 Yale-Princeton games is uncanny.

In 1936, when the Blue returned to Palmer Stadium for the first time since the "Iron Men" game, Wandle posted a sign that read, "It was done in 1934. It can be done in 1936."

Princeton took a 16-0 lead and was in front 16-7 at the half. Yale, featuring Kelley at end and its 1937 Heisman winner, Clint Frank, at tailback, stormed ahead 20-16 in the third quarter. The Orange and Black regained the lead in the fourth, but Yale drove 81 yards and Frank scored for a 26-23 victory.

Reunion of 1934 Ironmen: L-R: Larry Kelley, Jimmy DeAngelis, Jerry Roscoe, Earl "Greasy" Neale (asst. coach), "Ducky" Pond (head coach), and Bob Train.
(YALE ATHLETICS)

November 17, 1934, Yale–Princeton game day program.
(PRINCETON UNIVERSITY)

In '53, the Elis recovered from a 17-0 halftime deficit to take a 20-17 lead. Like the '36 Tigers, Princeton went ahead early in the fourth quarter, but Yale prevailed 26-24.

YALE-HARVARD

Before Army vs. Navy, USC vs. Notre Dame or Alabama vs. Auburn, there was Yale vs. Harvard. The Yale-Harvard rivalry that began in 1875 is older than the Statue of Liberty and has been hailed as one of the best in sports. Both schools are islands of academic excellence. AP reporter Hugh A. Mulligan, who covered the games until his death in 2008, called the two schools, "twin crucibles of American culture."

Former Yale President A. Bartlett Giamatti once said, "'The Game' was the country's last great 19th century pageant." For many, "The Game" transcends college football. Some view it as the "Corporate Bowl" since many graduates of both schools land jobs on Wall Street. For old Blues and Harvards it's a mystic renewal when alums convene and converse in the spirit of sportsmanship and reminisce about gridiron exploits of another time. High-spirited play, elaborate tailgate parties, pranks, excitement and tomfoolery are part of this unique football gathering.

The origin of the appellation "The Game" is not clear. Some credit *New York Times* writer Joseph M. Sheehan. His piece covering the 1952 Yale-Harvard game reads, "Jordan Olivar's [Yale's coach at the time] smartly drilled charges did proudly by their first year coach, who certainly must return after adding a victory in 'The Game' to six other triumphs."

In the November 20, 1953, edition of the *New York Times,* Arthur Daley referred to the next day's Yale-Harvard contest as "The Game." He further added, "or maybe it should be more properly described as THE GAME."

Harvard won the initial meeting between the two teams four goals to none. "In football's early days, touchdowns did not count in the scoring," said historian Bob Barton. "A team that touched the ball down behind its opponents' goal line was simply awarded a free kick for a goal. The spot where the ball was touched down dictated the spot for the kick, which sometimes was close to the sideline."

Entering the 2014 season, Yale and Harvard have met 130 times. Yale leads the series, 65-57-8, but in recent years Harvard has been the hammer and Yale the nail. "The Game" has become an exercise in canine cruelty, with Harvard winning 7 straight

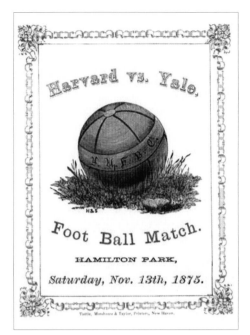

The game day program from the first game between the ancient rivals in 1875. Yale-Harvard game day programs carry a significant value. The program from the 1879 tilt recently sold for nearly $1,500. (YALE ATHLETICS)

and 12 of the last 13. In hubristic Harvard fashion, a T-shirt at the 2012 tailgates outside Harvard Stadium read, "KEEP CALM, IT'S ONLY YALE."

This is not the only era when Harvard has dominated the rivalry. Yale scored only one touchdown against Harvard in the 13 games played from 1908 through 1922.

Home field has not been a particular advantage for either team. The Bulldogs are 22-26-1 in the Yale Bowl, whereas at Harvard Stadium they are 25-25-3. Overall Yale stands at 30-30-3 in New Haven, while in Boston or Cambridge the Blue is 28-26-5. At neutral sites Yale is 7-1-0.

When Harvard Stadium opened on November 21, 1903, Yale spoiled the party by winning 16-0. Eleven years later to the day, Harvard returned the favor and smoked the Elis 36-0 in the Bowl's opening game.

Yale has been Harvard's last opponent every year since 1898, except for the war years ('18, '43, '44) and 1919, when Harvard went to the Rose Bowl.

But in 1876, the Elis opened the season on November 18th against the Crimson and finished its three-game schedule against Columbia on December 9, the latest date Yale ever played a football game.

The 1894 game, won 12-4 by Yale, was played in Springfield, Massachusetts. The game was so violent it became known as the "Springfield Massacre." Seven players, news accounts said, were carried off the field in "dying" condition. Boston columnist

George Sullivan wrote, "So savage was combat on a neutral Springfield gridiron ... that newspapers printed a casualty summary similar to those listing victims of a disaster..."

Because of the 1894 bloodbath, the schools did not meet in football for the next two years. The baseball, crew, and track and field teams avoided each other for one.

On November 22, 1902, Yale broke Harvard's twenty-three-game winning streak with a 23-0 victory at Yale Field II. It was Harvard's first loss since Yale beat the Crimson 28-0 in 1900.

"One of my vintage collectibles is a Yale press pass for the November 22, 1902, Yale-Harvard game played at Yale Field," said vintage collector Dan Riccio. "My grandfather, Ascanio J. Riccio, who worked at Yale as a foreman, gave it to me. He was an architectural engineer and designer who helped design the Yale Bowl and the Yale Divinity School."

"The Game" has generated peculiar behavior over the years but none matches the conduct of Harvard coach Percy Haughton who allegedly once tied a Bulldog doll to his car bumper and then happily motored around town for a few hours. Legend has it that in 1908 Haughton exhorted his players by choking a live bulldog before the game at Yale Field, a game won by Harvard, 4-0. When informed of the final score, President Theodore Roosevelt, a Harvard alumnus, interrupted a doubles tennis match with the French ambassador at the White House and danced an impromptu jig.

The 1909 contest was billed as the "Battle of the Giants." Yale had not allowed a point the entire season and Harvard had outscored its opponents 103-9 and was enjoying an eighteen-game unbeaten streak. Yale got on the board when center Carroll Cooney blocked a punt for a safety. Ted Coy, an outstanding drop-kicker and punter, then added two field

November 24, 1894, Yale-Harvard ticket
(YALE ATHLETICS)

goals for an 8-0 win and a national championship.

The on-campus spirit of this era was intense. In 1912 there was a school–wide march by Yale students to the football field for the last practice before the Harvard-Yale game. The crowd engaged in an impromptu rehearsal of songs and cheers for game day.

In the 1913 game, Harvard's Charles Brickley, who has been called the "da Vinci of the drop-kick," booted five field goals in the Crimson's 15-5 win at Harvard Stadium. The Yale scores came on a safety and a 36-yard Guernsey field goal. Harvard won the 1919 game in Boston, 10-3, but Yale's Jim Braden drop-kicked a 53-yard FG, the longest field goal in the history of the series.

Harvard's Eddie Mahan rushed for a series individual record 4 TDs in the 1915 game won by Harvard, 41-0. The mark endured for 98 years when Harvard's Paul Stanton scored four TDs, two rushing and two catches in the 2013 game won by the Crimson, 34-7.

Long before the 1934 Yale "Ironmen," the Elis pulled off a similar feat when Yale coach Tad Jones played a total of twelve men when they beat Harvard 6-3 in 1916 before an estimated crowd of 77,000 in the Bowl. Heylinger Church substituted for All-American George Moseley at right end. Joe Neville scored the only touchdown of the game on a one-yard plunge. It was the first touchdown that Yale had scored against Harvard in nine years.

More than 80,000 fans attended the November 20, 1920, game, which Harvard won 9-0. The crowd was the largest ever for an American sporting event at the time.

In the game Yale quarterback Fido Kempton and Harvard end John Gaston got into a fist fight and were ejected. Everett J. Lake, the Governor-elect of Connecticut, was in attendance "with the Crimson on his sleeve and a Harvard flag in his hand," as reported by the *New York Times*. It seems that after they had helped elect him to the Governor's chair, Yale men discovered Lake was a brilliant halfback on the Harvard team of 1890 that beat Yale. The *Times* noted that the 1920 game was the first time in the history of Connecticut that its Governor had rooted for Harvard, and "Yale feels that something ought to be done about it."

The 1923 Harvard game in Boston completed a perfect 8-0 season for the Elis. The contest was played in a torrent of rain turning the field into a quagmire. Yale fumbled eleven times, recovering ten of them. Harvard fumbled fourteen times and also recovered ten. Yale punted twenty-eight times, Harvard twenty-six. Yale scored first late in the first quarter when Raymond Pond picked up a fumbled punt by Marion Cheek and raced 68 yards for a touchdown "on a field that resembled seventeen lakes, five quagmires and a water hazard," wrote Grantland Rice, who christened Pond with the moniker "Ducky." Bill Mallory added the extra point and then kicked two field goals to make the final score 13-0. It was the first time the Elis had defeated the Crimson since 1916.

It is generally accepted that prior to the 1923 game in Boston, Yale coach Tad Jones made his enduring statement in a pregame pep talk, "Gentlemen, you are now going out to play football against Harvard. Never again in your whole life will you do anything so important."

Former Yale lineman Bill Lovejoy believes Jones's words have been misinterpreted. He said, "*Time* Magazine did a story on that statement and asked many players what Jones meant." He added, "My father, who was a center on that team, said people were being too literal. He said that the statement has been misinterpreted and Jones has received unjust criticism over the years. According to my father, Jones did not think that a football game would be the most important thing in a Yale player's life. Instead, what he meant was that you treat today's challenge as the most important thing and then you move on."

The Elis met the challenge, winning 13-0.

Yale won the 1926 game played in the Bowl, 12-7. Harvard's only touchdown resulted from a 35-yard pass from Henry Chauncey to Bill Saltonstall. Chauncey, a superb drop kicker, booted the extra point. Chauncey's son, Henry "Sam" Chauncey Jr., served as Yale's Vice President and Secretary from 1971-1981.

Starting in 1929, Yale's Albie Booth had a series of legendary encounters with his Harvard counterpart, Barry Wood. Not only did each run, pass, and kick; they also were rival shortstops in baseball. Wood, an All-America quarterback and Phi Beta Kappa student, led the Crimson to victory in 1929 and 1930. Booth's lone football win of the series came in '31, when his 26-yard field goal in Harvard Stadium was the only score of the game.

For several weeks after that game, Booth was in a hospital with an undisclosed respiratory ailment, and when he returned to class, he was kept out of sports competition. He rejoined the baseball team in mid-May. In his last home game for Yale, on June 21, 1932, his full-count bases-loaded home run in the first inning gave Yale a 4-2 decision over Harvard at Yale Field in front of an overflow commencement crowd of 7,500 for the annual commencement game. When Booth died prematurely in 1959, Wood, then a prominent physician, attended his memorial service.

Raymond "Ducky" Pond
(Yale Athletics)

Led by quarterback Barry Wood, who tossed two touchdown passes to Art Huguley, Harvard blanked the Elis 13-0 in the 1930 game. Mike Patricelli, who sold souvenirs, worked as an usher, and later supervised the sideline chain crew at the Bowl, was part of a unique exchange after the game.

"My cousin, Mike Patricelli, whom we all called 'Uncle Mickey,' had a piece of the goal post from the 1930 Yale-Harvard game," said John D'Antona. "He said that he had a bigger piece but traded a chunk to Harvard captain Ben Ticknor in the locker room in exchange for his jersey.

The Bulldogs won the 1935 game 14-7 in Boston. The winning touchdown was scored by Al Hessberg, also known as "The Albany Express." Hessberg was an outstanding running back and punter who played from 1935 to 1937. He was also a very good track athlete. Vin Brozek, who would one day wear the Yale blue, recalled Hessberg.

"When I was in high school I worked at the El Dorado Pharmacy behind the counter as a soda jerk. It was located on Chapel Street next to the Hotel Duncan. We had a liquor license and Yale students would often call and order beer. I would deliver the beer to the rooms and make 25 cents. One time I delivered beer to Al Hessberg's room."

Two-time All-American Clint Frank had his moments against Harvard. In the '36 game he tossed a 42-yard touchdown pass to Larry Kelley and made a bevy of tackles from his defensive halfback position in leading Yale to a 14-13 victory. After the game,

Albie Booth holds a football used in Yale's 1931 victory over Harvard. Yale wore white leather helmets such as the one on the table.

Harvard coach Dick Harlow visited the Elis' locker room. He congratulated Frank and said, "You are the greatest back I've ever seen." A year later Frank made an estimated fifty tackles and scored Yale's only TD in Harvard's 13-6 win.

Tailgating at The Game

For Old Blues, students, and fans of Yale Football, pregame tailgating is a long-standing tradition. Tailgate gatherings for the Yale-Harvard game attract the upper crust dressed lavishly in their tweeds and tartans. One might see anything from candelabrum style settings to campers with dining rooms. *New York Times* writer Gerald Eskenazi described a Y-H tailgate as "being filled with Jaguars and plaid-jacketed alumni lathering pate on toast triangles."

The festive pregame atmosphere was marred by tragedy in 2011, when a U-Haul truck carrying beer kegs to a fraternity party accelerated into a crowd. A young woman was killed and two others were injured. The driver of the truck, a Yale student, reached a plea bargain agreement in February 2013 and avoided prison.

Field Artwork

The Bowl turf has always had a pristine appearance. For many years a "P" and an "H" were added to the "Y" for the rival games. The Harvard game was special.

"Delaney Kiphuth, the athletic director, instructed me to cover the field every night with our five tarps so it would be dry for the game," recalled Rich

Albie Booth and Barry Wood were football and baseball rivals.

Schyner, a former superintendent of Yale Fields. "We had to make sure the grass got enough sunlight during the week, so I used to rotate the tarps, always keeping some of the field exposed to the sunlight."

Schyner's successor Tom Pepe added, "I always enjoyed getting the field ready and the artwork that went with it. For the "YALE" in the end zones, we had a stencil in house. The large "Y" and the "H" or "P" [for Princeton] had to be measured out with a measuring tape and strings. Each letter was sixty feet tall and sixty feet wide. This box was then squared off, using four pins (one in each corner). A string was then attached from pin to pin. Then, with measuring tape and string, each letter was outlined and marked with a marking machine.

"The paint used on the athletic fields is a latex paint, usually cut 50-50 with water. Usually two coats are needed. A side note: The grass is painted on the top side only. This allows the grass plant to continue to grow. If the leaf blade were totally covered, the plant would die."

Time has dimmed the national importance of the "Big Three" games. But for students, alums and fans, the fire still burns. The games are played with high intensity and spirit. And the tailgating tradition has never waned.

Clint Frank was one of the all-time Yale greats.
(YALE ATHLETICS)

Robert Lewis (center) is flanked by son, Tony, and wife, Janet, in the F-Special lot. The Lewis family has the longest standing tailgate spot outside the Bowl.
(RICH MARAZZI)

Yale alum and former Connecticut Governor Lowell Weicker (with trumpet) at a 1993 Yale-Harvard tailgate party with the Clam Diggers band.
(BILL O'BRIEN)

Tom Pepe, Yale's Sports Turf Supervisor.
(YALE ATHLETICS)

PART III

Yale Football

The Second Half (1941-2013)

YALE—COLUMBIA

(Yale Athletics)

CHAPTER 11

WARTIME YALE (1941-1945)

"Close if you must them classroom doors, but get a football team what scores."

—Polly Stone Buck

On December 6, 1941, the day before the Japanese attack at Pearl Harbor, a team from New York's Fort Terry artillery defeated Camp Edwards, from southeastern Massachusetts, 7-0 in the Bowl before a free admission crowd of 15,000. The game was billed as the Army's New England football championship even though Fort Terry was on Plum Island, just off Orient Point, New York. The military atmosphere was a harbinger of things to come.

THE NAVY'S V-12 PROGRAM

"Mother Yale" underwent the biggest transformation in her history during the war years as several branches of the military had a noticeable presence on campus. A total of 20,000 trainees in the armed forces studied at Yale during this time.

About 350 colleges, including Harvard and Princeton, dropped their varsity football programs for a season or more because of a shortage of players. College football survived in large part because of the U.S. Navy's V-12 program, begun on July 1, 1943, and based on 131 campuses in 43 states. One of those campuses was Yale.

Frank Santoro, leaving the field, played for Camp Edwards.
(DAN SANTORO)

The purpose of the V-12 program was to give prospective Navy, Marine, and Coast Guard officers a college education in areas the Navy most required, and to offer this course of instruction on an accelerated schedule

The NCAA welcomed the V-12 program which proved to be the engine that kept college football breathing. NCAA eligibility rules were relaxed to accommodate V-12 players. Because college campuses were denuded by the war, the NCAA permitted freshmen to play on varsity teams for the first time since 1905. Bob Pickett, a 205-pound fullback, and Stan Weiner were frosh standouts for the Bulldogs in 1942. Freshmen were allowed to compete on the varsity at Yale from 1942 to 1946.

Marines could play varsity football because they were under the Department of the Navy. Army soldiers, who were placed in Yale's Berkeley College, were allowed to participate only in intramural sports. Army Air Forces personnel used Yale facilities but were not formally affiliated with Yale and thus could not engage in varsity sports.

1942 EASTERN ALL-ARMY TEAM

Yale University served as the site of the training grounds for the Eastern division of the all-Army football team in 1942. The soldier team composed of skilled college players was quartered at the Ray Tompkins House for about one month beginning in early August and practiced at the DeWitt Cuyler Field adjacent to the baseball field.

Perhaps the most noteworthy player was former Stanford fullback Norm Standlee, who also had a distinguished career in the NFL. Al Kelley, whose son Dave would one day coach Yale's defensive line under Carm Cozza, also played for the All-Stars.

They were coached by Col. Robert Neyland, the legendary Tennessee Vols coach. His assistants included future Yale head coach Herman Hickman; 1st Lt. Bob Woodruff, who would go on to coach Baylor and Florida; and Murray Warmath, later head coach at Mississippi State and Minnesota.

The All-Stars played three games starting on September 12th with the proceeds going to the Army Emergency Relief Fund. They beat the New York Giants 16-0 at the Polo Grounds in New York, defeated the Brooklyn Dodgers 16-7 in Baltimore and lost 13-7 to the Chicago Bears in Boston.

Many military base teams were very strong. In '43 the Great Lakes Naval Training Station in Illinois, coached by Paul Brown, beat national champion Notre Dame. In 1944, Navy Lt. Raymond "Ducky" Pond, the former Yale player and coach, piloted the Georgia Pre-Flight Skycrackers.

Revolving Door of Coaches

Yale had a different head football coach each year from 1940 through 1942 as the winds of war swept the campus. The coaches, respectively, were "Ducky" Pond, who finished his seven-year tenure in 1940, Emerson "Spike" Nelson, and Howie Odell, who was a sweeping success. From 1938-41 the Elis were an ignoble 7-24-1. Pond's 1940 eleven won only one game; ditto for Nelson's only team in '41 during this ice age of Yale football. Tim Cohane wrote in *The Yale Football Story*, "Yale once King of the Conquered East, had hit the river bed."

Nelson's squad upset a strong University of Virginia team in the Bowl in his maiden game. Trailing 19-0 at the half, the Elis came roaring back to earn a gripping 21-19 win in one of the greatest comebacks in Yale football history.

World War II was already raging in Europe. In keeping with the strong patriotic mood in the country, the national anthem was sung for the first time in the Bowl before the Virginia game on October 4.

The Elis went winless the rest of the season while the Cavaliers didn't lose another game. Though suffering its fourth straight losing season in '41, Yale continued to embrace new ideas in the college game. Long before the rules mandated the practice, Yale numbered its players by position: ends (80s), tackles (70s), guards (60s), centers (50s), and backs (1-49).

Howie Odell replaced Nelson in 1942 and turned Yale's football fortunes around, restoring the program to the prominence it had in the mid-1930s. He broke away from the old single wing offense in favor of the more modern T-formation in 1944. At age thirty-one, Odell, a former running back and punter at the University of Pittsburgh, was the youngest major-college football coach in the country. Before coming to Yale, the Iowa farm boy was the backfield coach at Wisconsin. Under Odell, Yale football enjoyed a rebirth going 35-15-2 during his six-year term from 1942-47. Three times Yale won the "Big Three" title. His teams were 4-0 vs. Harvard and 4-1 against Princeton. Yale's '46 squad, a band of grizzly operatives that included many returning veterans, went 7-1-1 and was ranked 12th in the final AP poll.

Coach Emerson "Spike" Nelson and 1941 captain Alan Bartholemy
(Yale Athletics)

Howie Odell
(YALE ATHLETICS)

Westi Hansen and John Prchlik
(YALE ATHLETICS)

With eligibility rules eased, V-12 athletes whom the Navy transferred were immediately eligible to play wherever they moved. Their length of stay was undetermined, and they could be transferred on a moment's notice if a school offered a course the Navy felt they needed. In some circles they were referred to as "Lend-Lease players."

Odell had to constantly adjust, dealing with a revolving door of personnel. Tackle Westi Hansen, a native of Denmark, began college at Yale, then was kicked around like a soccer ball. He was shifted to Baldwin-Wallace, then to Northwestern, where he played in '45 before returning to Yale for his last two years. Tackle John Prchlik (pronounced PERCH-lik), who would play in the NFL for the Detroit Lions, left Yale for military duty after the Cornell game on October 7, 1944.

November 7, 1942, Yale-Cornell game day program reflects the wartime era.
(YALE ATHLETICS)

WAYNE JOHNSON, TWICE THE LETTERMAN

One transfer of note involved Harvard fullback Wayne Johnson, who played against Yale in 1942 and dropped a critical pass in Yale's 7-3 win. Soon after, he joined the Marines and was transferred to Yale where he continued his studies while preparing for a commission. Wearing Yale blue in '43, he broke his neck in the first quarter of Yale's opening 13-6 win against Muhlenberg and never played again, but he was awarded a letter nonetheless. Johnson has the distinction of being the only athlete to win varsity football letters from both Yale and Harvard. That season Yale athletic director Ogden D. Miller attempted to schedule twelve games. The aim was to load the schedule with several September encounters so that captain Townsend "Timmy" Hoopes and several others could play a few games before being graduated in October. Hoopes, who was a member of the United States Marine

Wayne Johnson is the only man to earn a varsity football letter from Yale and Harvard.
(YALE ATHLETICS)

September 18, 1943, Yale-Rochester game day program. Yale captain Townsend Hoopes is photographed with James A. Verinas, a New Haven native and decorated bomber pilot, who took part in twenty-five bombing raids over Germany. His dog, Stuka, an Aberdeen Scotty, was on board for all of his raids.
(YALE ATHLETICS)

Corps Reserve, played his last game on Oct. 23, 1943, against Army who featured future three time All-American running back Glenn Davis.

On October 28, 1944, Arnold Whitler played for Rochester in its 32-0 loss to Yale in the Bowl. After the game he took his sea bag to the Yale locker room to join the Yale squad. That same day Nick Fusilli was a starting guard for Dartmouth in its 14-13 win over Brown. The following week he wore Yale blue in the Elis' 6-0 victory over Dartmouth. Big Green coach Earl Brown cursed the

Marine Corps for giving him to Yale. In the game day program Fusilli appeared in the Dartmouth team photo but strangely was listed on the Yale roster.

The buses that formerly transported the players directly from the gym to the playing fields for practice were discontinued for lack of gasoline, and tires that were needed for the war effort. Because of gasoline rationing, only 13,000 showed up for the '43 Yale-Princeton contest in the Bowl that pitted twin brothers. Walter Brown, Yale's left end opposed his brother, Charlie, the center for the Tigers. Walter walked away smiling as Yale ended their season with a 27-6 win. Future Yale All-American Paul Walker (end), a Navy Trainee, and his brother Blake (QB), were teammates on that Bulldog squad.

THE UNDEFEATED 1944 BULLDOGS

In 1944, classes began in July to expedite the officer-training process. There were seventeen-year-old players on the Yale team who had less than a

In the November 4, 1944, Yale-Dartmouth game day program, Nick Fusilli (61) seated in the first row far left, played for Yale that game but is pictured in a Dartmouth uniform.
(YALE ATHLETICS)

1944 Yale backfield. The snapper is Jim Blanning, QB is George Loh, Bill Sadowski (12) Marlin "Buzzy" Gher (42). No. 14 is unidentified.
(YALE ATHLETICS)

week's vacation between high school graduation and their start at Yale. Roger "The Dodger" Barksdale and Vandy Kirk, both 17, were stars on an undefeated (7-0-1) team captained by Macauley Whiting. Kirk, a talented halfback, became the first Yale football player in the modern era to letter four straight years.

The only blemish for Odell's 1944 squad was the 6-6 tie game against Virginia on the final day of the season. Due to the war, Yale did not play Princeton and Harvard that year.

Although Yale did not play Penn from 1944 to 1955, the Elis had a player named William Penn in 1944 and 1945!

FROM PRISONERS OF WAR TO THE YALE BOWL

The pressures of playing football paled in comparison to the experiences of war. This was Tom Brokaw's "Greatest Generation." Four members of Yale's 1945

team—Martin Dwyer, Fritz Barzilauskas, Valleau Wilkie, and Bill Schuler—were all lieutenants in the Army Air Corps and all had been shot down while on aerial missions over German-held territory. All were Nazi war prisoners until freed by advancing American troops and all returned to play football at Yale. At twenty-five, Barzilauskas, a future NFL guard with the Boston Yanks and New York Giants, was the oldest player on the '45 team that went 6-3.

Barzilauskas had distinguished company. The Navy transferred Notre Dame running back Art Fitzgerald to Yale. Harvard paid the price as Fitzgerald scored three touchdowns in a 28-0 victory against the Crimson in the Bowl on December 1st. (An interesting footnote to the game is that this was the first time since 1875 that the Yale-Harvard game was played in New Haven in an odd-numbered year, a tradition that remains to this day. Prior to 1945, Yale hosted games in even-numbered years.)

Quentin "Monk" Meyer never returned.
(Yale Athletics)

"meritorious achievement" as turret gunner of a torpedo bomber during a strike against Japanese ships in Sampson Harbor, Rabaul, on November 11, 1943. Bolt Elwell, a tackle on the 1942 team, returned in '45 a first lieutenant. The press box in the Yale Bowl was subsequently named in his honor. Sportscaster Bill Brandt chose an "All-Purple Heart Collegiate All-America" team. Among his selections was Yale tackle Bill Schuler, who would play for the New York Giants in 1947 and 1948.

War claimed the lives of several Yale lettermen including 1940 captain Hovey Seymour, Frank Gallagher, Strat Morton, Quentin "Monk" Meyer, Gene Constantin, Bert Martin, Bill Knapp, Kay Todd Jr., Webster M. Bull, Kevin Rafferty, Cyrus R. Taylor, and "Memphis Bill" Mallory, captain of the undefeated 1923 team. Mallory, who joined the U.S. Army Air Forces as an intelligence officer, did not die in combat. On his return home for discharge in 1945, he was aboard a transport plane that crashed in Italy.

George Mead, the manager of the 1940 team, also lost his life. It would be impossible to determine how many others died as a result of various effects of the war.

The '45 team was composed of twenty-three civilian students and twenty candidates enrolled in the V-12 program. The mix of students hardly fit the Ivy League stereotype.

Yet this unusual blend of student-athletes helped Yale mark a football milestone. The Bulldogs' 41-6 win over the Coast Guard Academy, on November 17th, was the school's 500th football victory.

Heroes Who Returned ... And Those Who Did Not

Many players returned from the war with a chest full of decorations. Marlin "Buzzy" Gher, a running back, had been awarded the Air Medal for

Other Notables Who Served

Many prominent current and former Yale players served their country. They included wartime All-American center and linebacker Spencer Moseley (1942) and end Paul Walker (1943-45). Walker, a consensus All-American in '44 and third team in '45, went on to play in the NFL with the New York Giants. Moseley, who captained the '42 team, was

Spencer Moseley
(Yale Athletics)

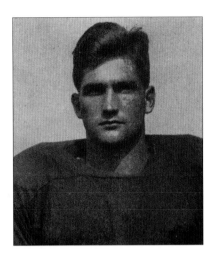

Paul Walker
(YALE ATHLETICS)

the son of George Moseley, the 1916 All-America Yale end. He became a Marine pursuit pilot in WW II and flew as a Marine reservist in the Korean War.

John Reed Kilpatrick, Yale's 1910 All-America end who had been a colonel in World War I, served in World War II as a brigadier general. Yale's 1937 Heisman winner Clint Frank was a lieutenant colonel in the Army Air Corps, serving as an aide to Gen. Jimmy Doolittle in North Africa, Italy and England.

GLENN MILLER COMES TO NEW HAVEN

Glenn Miller, one of the bestselling Big Band recording artists of this era, led the 418th Army Air Forces band, part of the Technical Training Command school headquartered in New Haven from March 1943 to June 1944. Major Miller lived in the Hotel Taft. His swing band was made up of servicemen who had been musicians in civilian life. In New Haven, Miller's band was multi-dimensional, serving as a marching band, dance band, and concert band. They played at enlisted men's dances at Yale, where couples danced to his classic tunes *Moonlight Serenade* and *In the Mood*. He also conducted a recruitment radio show from Woolsey Hall, titled "I Sustain the Wings." He made personal appearances for War Bond drives at the Yale Bowl, on the New Haven Green, and in local theaters. In July 1943 the Bowl was the site of a rally to sell war bonds that attracted an estimated 37,000 and raised

$2.5 million. Entertainers including Miller's band performed.

Miller subsequently took his show to England. On December 15, 1944, his plane disappeared over the English Channel en route to France to entertain U.S. troops. A memorial in his honor financed by Peter Cofrancesco sits at the Grove Street Cemetery in New Haven.

THE PLAYERS

Patrick Westfeldt (guard) '40, '41

ATTORNEY
DENVER, COLORADO

"I'm still haunted by the tragedy of witnessing Hovey Seymour, a former Yale teammate, lose his life. Hovey was an excellent halfback and a Grade A person. He became a torpedo bomber pilot during

Patrick Westfeldt
(YALE ATHLETICS)

the war and was killed flying a training mission in San Diego in 1944 when his plane missed the runway of an aircraft carrier that I was on. I saw his plane hit the port side and fall into the water.

"Hovey, who played from 1939 to '41, scored a big touchdown against Harvard in the '39 game that Yale won 20-7.

"I played for Emerson 'Spike' Nelson in '41. He was a good guy, a real straight shooter but gone after one year. I guess his 1-7 record didn't help, but the fact that he was the first non-Yale alumnus to coach the team might have contributed. In 1938 Spike was the head coach at Mississippi State College, which is now Mississippi State University. He was a lineman for the Iowa Hawkeyes in the mid-'20s.

"I started at guard for about half the season before a sophomore named George Ruebel beat me out. I recall playing against Bud Wade, a former classmate at Taft. Bud went to Princeton and we went head-to-head. By current standards of writing, one might say that it was war in the trenches that day. But those who loosely use the word 'war' in sports don't really understand what war is all about."

Nelson Talbott Jr. (halfback) '40, '41, '42

INVESTOR-BANKER
CLEVELAND, OHIO

"Because my father had captained the 1914 team, I knew all the Yale songs by the time I was nine years old, and Yale was the only school I ever considered attending. My two sons also went to Yale but did not play football.

"At Yale I played for 'Ducky' Pond, Spike Nelson, and Howie Odell. Nelson liked to recite a famous poem written in 1895 by English poet Rudyard Kipling, titled If. A popular line reads, *If you can meet with triumph and disaster and treat those two impostors just the same …* He did this for motivational purposes, but I guess it didn't help, since we went 1-7 in '41."

Ensign Hovey Seymour lost his life on March 2, 1944, during training on the *USS Altamaha*.
(YALE ATHLETICS)

Nelson Talbot Jr. was a high speed runner.
(YALE ATHLETICS)

Hugh Wallace (halfback) '41

INVESTMENT COUNSELOR
WILMINGTON, DELAWARE

"I only played my freshman and sophomore years because I went into the Air Forces during the war. In '41, when we beat Virginia 21-19, Fred Dent, who became the U.S. commerce secretary, kicked one of the extra points. That was a big deal. I think the first time I ever carried the ball was in that game and I ran for 18 yards."

Hugh Wallace
(YALE ATHLETICS)

Fred Dent (end/kicker) '40, '41,'42

PRESIDENT OF A TEXTILE MANUFACTURING COMPANY
U.S. SECRETARY OF COMMERCE 1973-1975
SPARTANBURG, SOUTH CAROLINA

"I was raised in Greenwich, Connecticut, and my father and other relatives would take me to the Yale Bowl. Seeing the Bowl and the players with the blue shirts impressed me—set the fires burning for my desire to someday attend and play for Yale. I was at the Bowl in '31 when Cadet Richard Sheridan from Army broke his neck making a tackle, resulting in his death.

"In '41, we went up to West Point for a preseason scrimmage. After the scrimmage we were invited to eat with the cadets, and for the first time I saw people eating square meals. Every cadet had to sit straight up in his chair, put his fork over the dish, bring it straight up so it would be level with his mouth and then bring it toward his mouth. It was the damnedest thing I ever saw.

"In preparation for the '41 and '42 seasons we would spend a week to 10 days at The Gunnery, a school in Washington, Connecticut. It gave us a chance to bond and get in shape.

"Ivy Williamson, who captained the 1932 national champion University of Michigan football team, coached the ends and had a good game plan when we beat Virginia in '41. Williamson was petrified of the speed of 'Bullet Bill' Dudley and C. Edgar Bryant, their outstanding backs, so on punts we were instructed to stay wide in order to turn Dudley and Bryant toward the middle. The game plan was not to allow them to get to the outside. On a punt to

Fred Dent
(YALE ATHLETICS)

Bryant, I went straight down the field and managed to turn him in where I dove and caught his heel. It felt good to come through on a planned situation.

"In '42 we scrimmaged the Army All-Stars on the Anthony Thompson Field and held them scoreless while we scored one touchdown. I remember seeing Norm Standlee. I marveled at his size (6-2, 238 pounds) and the size of many of his teammates. They couldn't believe how small we were. One guy commented, 'We had kids bigger than this in high school.'

"When we beat Harvard 7-3 in '42, Tim Hoopes scored the only touchdown and I kicked the extra point. Tim became the assistant secretary of the Air Force in the Lyndon Johnson administration and authored a number of books.

"As for some of my teammates, I have fond memories of players like Hovey Seymour, George Greene, and Jim Potts, an outstanding human being. Potts was a fullback who became a member of the CIA, and Greene, my rival for the end position, married a girl who was my wife's roommate in high school."

Richard Cooley (end) '41-'42

COMMERCIAL BANKER
SEATTLE, WASHINGTON

"A dropped pass was one of the highlights of my career? Let me explain.

"In '42 we played Harvard in the Bowl in front of 23,500, the smallest crowd to ever witness a Yale-Harvard game in the modern era. It was a wet, rainy day, the war was in progress, and there was gasoline rationing, all factors that I think contributed to the low attendance.

"Harvard scored first on a field goal by Bob Fisher. They later had a 70-yard punt return touchdown called back because of a penalty. We scored

Richard Cooley's WWII injury ended his football career.
(RICHARD COOLEY)

our touchdown in the fourth quarter on a 61-yard pass play from Hugh Knowlton to Tim Hoopes. Fred Dent then kicked the extra point.

"We ran out of the single wing. Sam Scovil was our quarterback, but he was used as a blocker.

"Late in the fourth quarter, Harvard sustained a tremendous drive, maybe 90 yards. The excitement in the final minutes was unbelievable. On the last play of the game Harvard was on our 7-yard line when they pulled off a play that fooled us. Wayne Johnson, one of their receivers, ended up by himself near the goal line and he dropped a pass that hit his waist. The game was over and we won, 7-3. It was so exciting. We didn't win the right way, but we won. And would you believe Johnson was transferred to Yale the following year and suffered a season-ending injury when he broke his neck in the first game of the year!

"Because we won the Big Three title, at the end of the season we all got little gold footballs with the Princeton and Harvard scores on top of the football.

"I went into the Army in March of '43. I was a P-38 fighter pilot and was stationed in Belgium. One day on a test hop I crashed and lost an arm. I was never able to play football again when I returned, but I did get my degree in the summer of '45.

"Because of the V-12 program, there were a lot of people at Yale during the war that were not really Yale people. The whole scene changed after the war.

"I've had some interesting moments, but I'll never forget that dropped pass."

Willard Overlock
(YALE ATHLETICS)

Willard Overlock (center, linebacker) '41, '42, '45

ATTORNEY
REDDING, CONNECTICUT

"During my freshman year the coaches selected seven teams on the depth chart. There were seven players left and I was one of them. One of the coaches threw us a football and assigned us to a certain area. This was not the best start to my Yale career. However, as the year went on, I managed to move up the ladder.

"I went into the service and came back from the war in October '45. I went down to register for classes, then went over to watch the team practice. When head coach Howard Odell spotted me, he told me to get up and get into a uniform.

"I had just one week of practice before I was put into a game. Our starting center got hurt and Odell looked in my direction and yelled for me to get into the game. I really didn't know the plays that well but managed to get by. I played at 6- feet, 170 pounds.

"I have attended many Yale-Harvard games in the Bowl. I owned a '32 Packard with a rumble seat and would drive down from New Canaan, Connecticut."

Willard Overlock died on December 22, 2011, at age eighty-nine. He was a bombardier in the US Army 8th Air Force.

Vin Brozek (JV quarterback) '45

EXECUTIVE VICE PRESIDENT OF CONNECTICUT WHEEL RIM
BRANFORD, CONNECTICUT

"I joined the Navy in '42, and a couple of years later I went to Wesleyan on the V-12 program and was the first T-formation quarterback there under

coach Norm Daniels. In '45 we beat the Yale JV team 20-7 and I scored one of the touchdowns. Strange as it may seem, I found myself wearing a Yale uniform a few weeks later because the V-12 program closed down at Wesleyan and I transferred into the ROTC program at Yale with essentially the same courses.

The Bush Family

"I reported to football practice on November 1, 1945, along with future President George H.W. Bush. We used to kid around a lot with George, but for some reason he only stayed on the football team a few days. He would captain the '48 baseball team and play in the College World Series in '47 and '48. His brother, Jonathan, who lettered in 1950, kicked the winning extra point in Yale's 14-13 win over Holy Cross in 1950.

"I played on the JV team under coach Albie Booth, who was quiet and subdued. My job was to run the opponents' plays against the varsity. A few transfers like Frank DeNezzo made the varsity. He intercepted 10 passes in his two-year ('45, '46) Yale career and still ranks in the top ten in that category.

"Practices were interesting. The field conditions were horrible, as I remember it being muddy and cold. I recall throwing often to Paul Walker, the great end.

"Head coach Howie Odell was a tough guy. One day Art Dakos, the first-string quarterback in '45, was having trouble taking the snap and executing the short backward pass. Odell got so damn mad he said, 'I could kick it over there better than you can throw it over there.'

"I stayed two semesters at Yale before returning to Wesleyan, where I graduated in 1947."

A Popular Opponent

Fran Lee (halfback/safety)
Harvard '39, '40, '41 (captain)

Interstate Commerce Commission/Dept. of social
services in Connecticut
Branford, Connecticut

Fran Lee died on March 29, 2012, at the age of ninety-three, shortly after he was interviewed. At the time, he was the oldest living football captain of either Harvard or Yale. In 1941 Harvard coach Dick Harlow said that Lee was the best defensive back in the nation. Lee, who is a member of the Harvard Hall of Fame, was the recipient of the National Football Foundation Merit Award.

"I was the first son of a Yale alumnus to captain the Harvard football team? I was born in 1918 and grew up at 1985 Chapel St., not too far from the Yale Bowl. When I was a kid we used to sneak into the Bowl and play football games, and I also used to park cars in our driveway on game day. I played for Chick Bowen at Hillhouse before going to Choate.

Harvard recruited heavily at Choate, which is why I went there instead of Yale.

"In the three years I played against Yale, we beat them twice. We shut them out in '40 (28-0) and '41 (14-0). It was a thrill to come back and play in the Bowl with a delegation of family and friends on hand. In the '40 game we were winning 14-0 in the last quarter when I received a punt on our 22 yard-line. I faked a handoff and ran 78 yards for a touchdown. It remains the longest punt return for a touchdown in the history of the Yale-Harvard series. Charley Spreyer, who was also from New Haven, scored our last touchdown. I also had an 88-yard touchdown run against Princeton which remains the fourth longest in team history. And I once had an 82-yard punt return against Dartmouth.

"After graduation in '42 I enlisted in the Army and served as an intelligence officer in the European theater through the end of the war."

Ticket prices for the '40 Y-H game were $3.85 for reserved seats and $2.20 for general admission.

THEY REMEMBER THE WAR YEARS

DR. LEN FASANO (GUARD) '47, '48, '49

"The first game I ever saw in the Bowl was the opening game of the '41 season on Oct. 4th when Yale beat Virginia. I was fourteen years old. I used to buy Yale feathers wholesale and sell them outside the Bowl before games. And with my profits, I would buy a ticket to get into the game."

STAN CELMER

"Yale wore a much lighter blue jersey in the early '40s. They went to the darker blue after the war. And for a period during the war years they wore

white jerseys for home games. In the early '40s Yale wore helmets with a design like Michigan's, without the stripes. They subsequently wore leather helmets without the crest in front.

"When Army came to New Haven, the cadet corps would travel by train. They would march from the New Haven railroad station to the Green and from there to the Bowl. It was an impressive sight.

"I recall being at the Yale-Army game on October 23, 1943, when Army beat Yale 39-7. Glenn Davis, the great Army running back, was very fast, but Yale's 'Scooter' Scussel caught him on one play from behind. Yale held Davis to

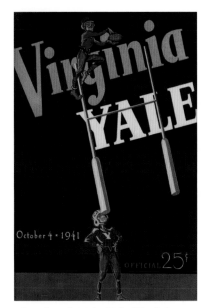

October 4, 1941, Yale-Virginia
game day program
(YALE ATHLETICS)

22 yards in 10 carries and no touchdowns, although he threw for two touchdowns. 'Scooter,' who was a Marine transfer from UConn, had a 72-yard run before he was tackled by Davis.

"Against Princeton that year 'Scooter' scored three touchdowns and threw a pass to Paul Walker for another in Yale's 27-6 win. Scussel, who later signed with the Los Angeles Dons of the All-American Football Conference, probably ran the 40 in 4.2 or 4.3. I have a picture of him riding a scooter.

"My all-time favorite Yale player was Spencer Moseley who played center and linebacker and captained the '42 team. At 173 pounds, he wasn't very big, but he was tough. In '41 he played with a broken jaw that was wired up in a leather case.

"Spencer was known for getting into bar fights. Apparently, before the start of the '42 season he went to the aid of a friend at Basil's bar near State and Edwards. His face was messed up pretty good. He told coach Howie Odell that he fell out of the front seat of his friend's car. When I heard that, I laughed."

DAN SANTORO

"My father, Frank Santoro, played in the Yale Bowl on December 6, 1941, the day before the Pearl Harbor attack. He played for the Camp Edwards team from New Bedford, Mass. against Fort Terry. Fort Terry won the game 7-0 when Eddie Kriz of Stratford threw a 28-yard touchdown pass to Angelo Cuseo of Westport. Dan Mulvey of the *New Haven Register* quipped, 'It was the finest play uncorked in the Yale Bowl this season.' Frank Skerlick of Ansonia intercepted a Kriz pass. Each team brought its own band and after the game the Fort Terry team had a party in Bridgeport, where it received its trophy."

ROCKY GILLIS

"My dad, Frank Gillis, who helped start the Walter Camp Foundation, played his freshman year at Harvard before he transferred to Yale because of the military program he was in. At Yale he played in '43, '44 and '46 as a halfback, punter and linebacker. Those were the days they wore leather helmets. In '45 he was scheduled to go to Japan as part of a Marine invasion force but never went because of the atomic bombs that were dropped. He was always proud of the 1944 team that went 7-0-1."

AL OSTERMANN

"I caught my break when Odell coached. I used to plow the victory gardens during the war down near the Bowl. They used to say if it wasn't for me, there would have been no football at Yale during the Second World War. Because I had a tractor and a telephone truck, I was able to get a lot of gasoline stamps. I would donate a great deal to the Yale football people to be used for transportation purposes."

SAM BURRELL

"I grew up in New Haven and the first game I ever saw in the Yale Bowl was October 31,

1942, when Yale beat Brown, 27-0. I was ten years old and went with a group from the Dixwell Community House. That year, Yale had players like Spencer Moseley, Bolt Elwell, Tim Hoopes, Hugh Knowlton and Endicott Davison. Ironically, my son Abbott, has been an assistant football coach at Brown since 1994."

FRANCIS T. "FAY" VINCENT JR.

"My first game in the Yale Bowl was in 1945. I remember seeing Yale captain Paul Walker, who played with the Giants in '48.

"When I was a kid, my father, who captained the 1930 team, got me a job in the Bowl and it was part of my life. I worked outside Portal 12, which was the field headquarters. I worked for Joe Festa, a telephone company employee who had gone to Yale and was in charge of game-day operations in the Bowl. I did errands like carrying messages up and down from the press box."

Joe Festa, a 1927 Yale graduate, was a Yale Bowl fixture from 1933 to 1979 as the supervisor of attendants. He also worked other major Yale athletic events. Festa oversaw 500 to 900 workers and volunteers to help crowd-control security. He also supervised the ushers, ticket takers and Bowl communications. Festa was described as "the central nervous system of the Bowl."

FRANK CARRANO

"I well remember the World War II years as a kid living in New Haven. Every Friday night the Glenn Miller Air Forces band would march down to the New Haven Green where the World War I monument was. There were several guys from New Haven in the band. They would have retreat at the Green and take the colors down. They also had an anti-aircraft barrage balloon.

"My dad took me to a Yale game in the '40s on a cold, rainy, snowy day. As we entered the Bowl, vendors were selling olive drab protective garments, like one-piece ponchos. The fans bought newspapers and put them over their heads to serve as protection against the elements. They then rolled the soaked papers into balls and threw them at each other. When we got home, my mother gave my father hell for taking me out in the rain and snow."

FOLLOWING THE WAR, normalcy was returned to the Yale campus. The Odell years were about to come to an end but the arrival of exciting running back Levi Jackson created promise for the future along with the hiring of coach Herman Hickman, one of the more colorful figures in the history of Yale football.

(Yale Athletics)

CHAPTER 12

THE POST-WAR YEARS (1946-1949)

*"To let down is human. Don't let Yale
be human on Saturday."*

—Amos Alonzo Stagg to the 1947 Yale
football team before the Elis played Harvard

In 1946, Yale was bursting at the seams with returning GIs and a record freshman class of 1,800 students. The university's normal enrollment of 5,200 had ballooned to 8,500.

Howie Odell's 1946 team, which went 7-1-1, was a mix of older returning GIs and fledgling hopefuls. Interior linemen John Prchlik, Westi Hansen, and Endicott Davison were military tested. Other former servicemen on the team were Dick Jenkins, Fritz Barzilauskas, Bolt Elwell, Bull Montano, and Swede Larson, whose ages ranged from twenty-three to twenty-six—graybeards for college students. The team was captained by Dick Hollingshead, a rugged 205-pound tackle, and buttressed by a talented group of freshmen, including guard Vic Frank, quarterback Tex Furse, and running backs Ferd "The Bull" Nadherny and the highly touted Levi Jackson. "The Bull" carried the load inside while Jackson dazzled outside with his "shake and bake" moves.

Dick Hollingshead captained Yale's first post WWII team.
(YALE ATHLETICS)

Yale's only loss of the '46 season came at the hands of No. 11 ranked Columbia. Led by the passing of Don Kasprzak and the receiving skills of end Bill Swiacki, the Lions overcame a 20-6 deficit to beat the No. 15 ranked Bulldogs, 28-20, in a game played in the rain at the Bowl.

In 1947, Tex Furse scored three times, leading Yale to a 31-21 win over Harvard in the Bowl before 70,388 chilled fans. That year the Bulldogs averaged 47,560 fans per game, a Bowl record for a single season. In attendance was the legendary Amos Alonzo Stagg, who last witnessed a Yale-Harvard game in 1898. Two days before the game, he attended the Yale practice and said to the team, "To let down is human. Don't let Yale be human on Saturday."

Robert F. Kennedy, the future attorney general of the United States and senator, was an end on that Harvard team. Wearing number 86, he saw limited action because of a leg injury. RFK reportedly "hobbled down the sidelines on a kickoff with his leg encased in a special brace."

According to Tim Cohane, Howie Odell did not see a promising future for the Yale program he had resurrected. Instead of rebooting, he relocated—3,000 miles away. After the '47 season, in which Yale went 6-3, Odell headed west to the University of Washington.

Future U.S Senator and Attorney General Robert Kennedy was pictured in the November 22, 1947, Yale-Harvard game day program.
(YALE ATHLETICS)

HERMAN HICKMAN

In 1948, Yale hired the colorful Herman Hickman, a hefty, jocular man with scholarly wit, to be the Bulldogs' head coach. He was as comfortable talking Kipling and Shakespeare as he was football. Writer Hugh A. Mulligan referred to Hickman as "Yale's Falstaff with a football under his arm." Before the 1948 Harvard game he recited, in toto, "Spartacus to the Gladiators" in an attempt to motivate his team. He ended the monologue with this spirited exhortation: "If we must die, let it be under the clear sky, by the bright waters, in noble, honorable battle!" Unfortunately, Yale took the first part of the challenge to heart (figuratively), losing the game 20-7.

Hickman was an avid cigar smoker, enjoyed entertaining his players at his Woodbridge home with his wife, Helen, and Handsome Dan VII, the Yale bulldog mascot that Yale had donated to him.

Hickman arrived in New Haven with an attractive portfolio. An All-America guard at the University of Tennessee, he also played for the NFL's Brooklyn Dodgers (1932-34) and was a professional wrestler known as "the Tennessee Terror." He was an assistant at West Point under Earl Blaik. Success, however, did not follow Hickman to the ivy walls of Yale. His teams compiled a disappointing 16-17-2 record over four years but his '48 edition did upset Wisconsin on the road. The Elis did not beat a strong Badger team but they did humble a Big Ten team at a time the hegemony of college football had shifted from the east to other parts of the country.

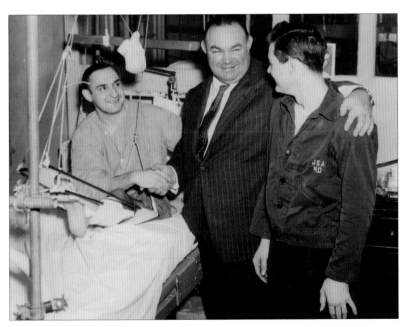

Herman Hickman visits private first class Joe DeCrosta in the Waltham Medical Hospital in Waltham, Massachusetts, in 1951. DeCrosta, a huge Yale fan, was injured in the Korean War.
(Joe DeCrosta Jr.)

The laureate of the locker room was driven to beat Princeton, a power during this era led by All-American running back and Heisman winner Dick Kazmaier. But he never did.

Hickman was notably absent from the '48 King's Point game and the '49 Brown game because he was scouting the Princeton-Harvard game both years. The Bulldogs lost the Brown game, 14-0. Although a coach's missing a game for reasons other than an inexcusable absence would be unacceptable today, it was apparently a practice among college head coaches in football's pre-modern era. Even Notre Dame's iconic coach Knute Rockne delegated his sideline responsibilities on at least one occasion. In 1926 Rockne put an assistant coach in charge against Carnegie Tech, a team the Irish were expected to beat, while he went to the Army-Navy game to do some publicity work and scout the Midshipmen for the following season. Carnegie Tech shocked Notre Dame, 19-0, ruining their bid for an undefeated season. One can only speculate the thunder that would generate among alumni and fans in today's high octane, intense sports climate.

Hickman, who coached the North team for three years in the annual North-South game, developed into a TV personality in the early '50s. Under apparent pressure to either coach or remain in TV, he chose the latter despite being under a ten-year contract at Yale. He also wrote a football column for *Sports Illustrated* called "Hickman's Hunches." Hickman, who kept his Woodbridge residence after he left Yale, died in 1958 at age forty-six in Washington, D.C. of complications following gastric ulcer surgery.

A Talented Toe

One diminutive standout of the post-war era was Billy "Boola-Boola" Booe, who stood 5-6 and weighed 146 pounds. Booe lettered four years and

Billy Booe
(YALE ATHLETICS)

was one of Yale's all-time sure-footed place-kickers. (He was also the first Yale graduate to become a professional golfer.) On November 8, 1947, Brown, with Joe Paterno as its No. 2 quarterback, beat Yale 20-14 in the Bowl. The game was played in a 55-mph gale and a lashing rain. Booe, who began a string of 28 consecutive extra points in that game, was 22 for 22 for the '48 season. His record was surpassed by John Troost, who made 39 straight from 2001-2003.

On October 2, 1948, Yale beat the University of Connecticut 7-0 in the schools' first meeting with Levi Jackson scoring the lone touchdown. It was the start of a series that culminated in 1998. The week after the '48 UConn game, Columbia beat Yale 34-28 before 55,000 in the first game ever televised from the Bowl. Under head coach Lou Little, the Lions were led by quarterback Gene Rossides and halfback Lou Kusserow.

THE PLAYERS

Bill Conway (center/linebacker) '45, '46, '47, '48 (captain)

MINING BUSINESS (SALES)
CLEVELAND, OHIO

Bill Conway is the oldest living Yale captain. His 83-yard interception return in 1948 vs. Dartmouth is the second longest in Yale football history.

"In those post war years with a lot of returning vets there wasn't a lot of emotional pep talks from the coaches but quite a bit of colorful references to some of our opponents by teammates. One pep talk

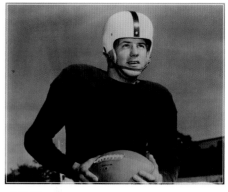

Bill Conway
(YALE ATHLETICS)

however from Clint "Cupie" Black, the 1916 captain, is memorable. In telling us how important winning the Harvard game was for Yale he said we should relish being able to meet our opponents in later years on the streets of New York and be able to say, 'I beat you, you Son of a Bitch!'

"Beating the University of Wisconsin 17-7 in Madison in '48 was obviously the high point of our season especially when the chant came up "Good bye Harry" in reference to Harry Stuhldreher, the Wisconsin coach and one of Notre Dame's Four Horsemen in the Knute Rockne era. He was gone shortly after. I was limited to snapping for kicks as I hurt my knee against Vanderbilt but felt I had a role as we kept them on their heels and Billy Booe iced it with a field goal.

"Bob (Jabbo) Jablonski, a tough but short guard from the Chicago area, faced a new opponent in the third quarter who mouthed off to him about Yale and his abilities. Jabbo was reported to reply, 'Why you jerk (more likely 'bastard') if you were any good you would have been in here a lot sooner.' Jabbo had no trouble handling him physically either.

"I graduated from the University School in Cleveland which has produced five Yale captains, one behind Andover. I claim we are tied since Hank Higdon left us for Andover after his sophomore year. So it's 5 1/2 to 5 1/2."

Dr. Len Fasano (guard) '47, '48, '49

INTERNIST AND GENERAL PRACTITIONER
NEW HAVEN, CONNECTICUT

"Reggie Root was my high school coach at Hillhouse High School in New Haven, where I played with

Levi Jackson and Joe Finnegan. I was an all-state guard. Coach Root taught me the fundamentals of blocking and how to head fake, which saved my life all the time. I would get the defensive player to go in one direction with my head fake, then come back and hit him with my shoulder.

"I'll never forget a game at Columbia when I suffered a concussion. One of the officials asked me if I was OK. I said, 'Yes. Why do you ask?' He said, 'Because you're in the Columbia huddle.' And speaking of Columbia, I played in that great game in the Bowl in '48 when they beat us 34-28. Their quarterback, Gene Rossides, was so fast you couldn't catch him.

"The most exciting game I ever played in was the '49 Princeton game. It was the most disappointing and most thrilling game for me at the same time. I remember intimidating the Princeton guards, as I was able to move them around. There was one play we called and I was supposed to pull and hit the tackle. As I tried to get through, I had to run between our quarterback and the center. Stuart Tisdale, our quarterback, got in the way. I complained bitterly about this to our coaches. Our line coach took me out of the game. He hated my guts because he thought I

was too small to play and did everything for me not to play. We lost the game 21-13 because of that play. But it was a thrill to me because I was able to beat the guard I was playing against. I actually had him fall in front of me. He didn't even try to resist me.

Dr. Fasano died on July 31, 2011, at age eighty-four shortly after this interview.

Ferd Nadherny (halfback) '46, '47, '48, '49

PRESIDENT AND SEARCH CONSULTANT
RUSSELL REYNOLDS ASSOCIATES
LAKE FOREST, ILLINOIS

"During my years at Yale I had the privilege of playing football in the Yale Bowl and basketball at Madison Square Garden when we played in the NCAA tournament in '49. I began my college career at the University of Wisconsin, where I played just three weeks before I got drafted into the Navy. While in the service, I played for Paul Brown at the Great Lakes Naval Training Station. We had a great team—even beat Notre Dame. Pro football Hall of Famer Marion Motley was our first-string fullback, and I was his

L-R: Len Fasano and Joe Finnegan
(YALE ATHLETICS)

Ferd "The Bull" Nadherny
(YALE ATHLETICS)

understudy. We also had Frank Aschenbrenner, the All-American from Northwestern, future Minnesota Vikings coach Bud Grant, plus Zeke O'Connor and Marty Wendell from Notre Dame.

"I never returned to Wisconsin. After being encouraged by some businessmen in Chicago, I decided to go to Yale, where I was able to play four years of varsity football and basketball because I had been in the military. They called me 'Ferdinad The Bull' because I carried the ball through the line. I was listed as 6 feet 1 and weighed 192.

"One of my biggest thrills came as a freshman in '46 when we beat Harvard 27-14 after trailing 14-0 at the end of the first quarter. I scored two touchdowns that game on 9- and 5-yard runs.

"Another big thrill was beating Wisconsin in '48 in Madison after losing 9-0 the year before in the Bowl. The stadium was full and I scored a touchdown with my family at the game."

Ferd Nadherny died on March 12, 2013, at age eighty-six, two years after he was interviewed for this book.

Bobby Raines (halfback) '47, '48, '49

MINISTER
UNITED CHURCH OF CHRIST CONGREGATIONAL
GUILFORD, CONNECTICUT

"I had the privilege of playing in the same backfield with Ferd 'The Bull' Nadherny, who ran through the line like thunder, and Levi Jackson, who was lightning quick and made startling, rapid cuts. A writer from the *New Haven Register* called us 'The weather report backfield—thunder, lightning and Raines.'

"I guess my moment of glory on the field was when we beat Wisconsin in '48 at Camp Randall Stadium. We had just come off a tough 34-28 loss to Columbia and entered the Wisconsin game with a 2-1 record. Ferd scored the first touchdown and then I ran for 49 yards to the 21-yard line before I was tackled by Clarence Self. That was a time in my life I would have liked to have been 'Selfless.' Levi eventually ran it in from the 2. Billy Booe kicked a field goal that game and kicked two extra points. Ironically, I caught Self that game from behind when I was playing halfback on defense.

A Heroes' Welcome

"When we returned to New Haven the following night, a crowd of about 1,000 students and fans greeted us at the New Haven railroad station. The Yale band was there, as were Mayor William Celentano and several city officials. We rode in a motorcade back to campus and many marched back. Coach Herman Hickman rode in the mayor's car and Jackson, Nadherny, Conway, and I rode in a bright yellow Cadillac through the streets of New Haven. The parade went to the Old Campus where Hickman, who was carried on the shoulders of students, gave a brief speech in front of Wright Hall. He said, 'If the team keeps on showing the old Yale fight they had at Madison, we ain't gonna lose many games.'

"The following week Vanderbilt beat us 35-0 in the Bowl, and we finished the season losing four out of our last five games.

"In '49, Cornell beat us 48-14. Just before the half I ran a kickoff back for 81-yards down to the 8-yard line. We scored a couple of plays later. We finished a mediocre 4-4 but we did beat Harvard 29-6.

Polio Scare

"In '49 we only played eight games (4-4) because the Fordham game, scheduled for October 1, was canceled. Dale Liechty, whom I roomed with for

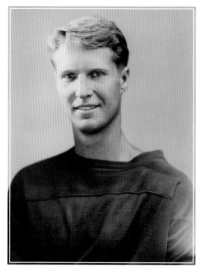

Bobby Raines
(YALE ATHLETICS)

three years at Calhoun, came down with polio, and the administration wasn't sure whether this was an isolated case or an epidemic. So the Fordham game was canceled because they did not think it was wise to have so many people assembled together in the Bowl. Dale, who was a funny guy, made a pretty good recovery and got into a play or two at the end of the Harvard game so he could get his letter. The polio left him with a slight limp.

The fullback who conquered polio died in 2013. Liechty, who had a successful career in medicine, was a professor of endocrine surgery at the University of Iowa and the University of Colorado.

Son of a Bishop

"Before coming to Yale I served in the Navy in the Pacific and was a radar technician and seaman first class. At Yale I was an undergraduate deacon.

"My father was a Methodist bishop. [*New York Times* sportswriter] Red Smith wrote a piece about the '49 Harvard game that we won, 29-6 win. I had nine carries for 99 yards, leading all backs in rushing yardage. Smith referred to me as a reserve back and wrote, 'Bobby Raines was the hottest son of a bishop in the state of Connecticut.'

"We had our share of parties. The girls would stay at the local hotels or at the homes of various Yale faculty members. They weren't allowed in our rooms in those days."

Dale Liechty
(YALE ATHLETICS)

Motorcade celebrating Yale's win over Wisconsin in 1948. Back seat L-R: Ferd Nadherny, Levi Jackson, Bill Conway, and Bobby Raines.
(YALE ATHLETICS)

1949 team: *Bottom row* L-R: Dave Grimes (81), John Anderson (79), Len Fasano (68), Emery "Swede" Larson (55), Bob DeVitt (62), Vic Frank (61), Joe Finnegan (76) and John Setear (89). *Top Row* L-R: Ferd Nadherny (14), Dale Liechty (43), Don Wagster (35), Stu Tisdale (20), Levi Jackson (40), Bobby Raines (41).
(YALE ATHLETICS)

THEY REMEMBER THE POST WAR YEARS

RAY PEACH

"It was kind of strange how I met Fritz Barzilauskas.

"I spent my professional career in the banking business. One day in 1975 Fritz's wife came into my office to ask about a client. I asked her if she was related to Fritz and she said, 'Yes. That's my husband.' That really pumped me up. I gave her the scores of all nine Yale games in '46.

"Mrs. Barzilauskas went home and told her husband about me. The next day I got a phone call from Fritz, and he asked if he could come to my office to see me. Of course I obliged, and we spent two hours talking Yale football. Fritz loved Yale. He was an assistant coach at Yale for many years and also served as director of Yale's intramural sports program from 1962 to 1977.

"In the early '80s, I was on a customer call to the Crabtree-Haas automobile dealership in Shelton, Connecticut. I met with the owner, Bob Crabtree Sr., and he had a plaque in his office from King's Point. He told me that he was on the '47 team. I said to him, 'I remember a kid from King's Point who intercepted a Yale pass and ran it in for a touchdown just before the half.' He replied, 'That was me.' Yale won that game 34-13."

JOEL ALDERMAN ('51)

"The atmosphere in the Bowl when I was a student at Yale from 1947-51 was great. There was a section that was reserved for Yale students who actively supported the cheerleaders. The cheerleaders were dressed in white with megaphones who would yell out certain cheers and the section of students would respond. To sit in this section you had to be a Yale student or a guest of one.

"In those days the Yale band would be on the field and could be seen during the game. For the Harvard game the two bands would go to the

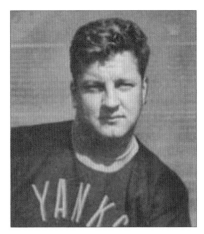

Guard Fritz Barzilauskas, a former prisoner of war, was a first round draft pick in 1947 for the NFL Boston Yanks.
(YALE ATHLETICS)

center of the field where the Yale band would form a "Y" and the Harvard band an "H." Then together they would play the National Anthem. What a great sight that was. I could never understand why these two universities stopped doing this.

Over the years the Yale Precision Marching Band has transitioned from an assemblage of serious minded musicians and conventional marching routines to shows that have been politically charged and risqué. In the '70s and '80s it was a tradition for the band to play "The Stripper" at the end of the third quarter while a Yale student/students would partially disrobe to the encouragement of their nearby peers.

TOM HACKETT ('50)

"I was discharged from the Navy in August 1946 and entered Yale. I lived home my first two

Coach Herman Hickman runs his '49 team through a practice at the Bowl. Levi Jackson is No. 40.
(YALE ATHLETICS)

years because the conditions were so crowded with students returning from the service. Kids were living in the gym, the Quonset huts, the dorms etc. Our class ('50) was the largest ever at Yale. My junior year I moved into [Room] 1188 Trumbull. Lenny Fasano, a pre-med student and a guard on the football team, would often show up at parties with the other pre-med students."

Note: *In 1950 Yale conferred Bachelor degrees on 1,653 students.*

THE PLAYERS REMEMBER HICKMAN

BILL CONWAY

"My participation as captain-elect in the search for a replacement for Howie Odell as head coach was interesting. I was involved in meeting and interviewing candidates in New York and Fairfield County with the then powers, Ted Blair, Bob Hall, Walt Levering, and others. To my later regret we were all taken in by the humor and theatrics of Herman Hickman rather than the football brains of the likes of Columbia coach Lou Little. Herman

was entertaining but not a good coach as his record showed."

BOBBY RAINES

"One of the great stories is the time Herman sent in a play and it didn't work. One of the players said, 'What do we do now?' Herman sent in another play and it didn't work. The same player asked, 'What do we do now?' Herman gathered us all in prayer and said, 'Our father who art in heaven...' He recited the Lord's Prayer, asking for divine intervention."

FERD NADHERNY

"I wasn't a big fan of Hickman. As far as I was concerned, he was out for Herman Hickman. He was a showman, a jovial guy. When he recited *Spartacus* before the '48 Harvard game, it didn't go over well with me. It was showing off. He thought we were going to jump up and down and run through the door.

"Hickman had a television show covering the college games that were scheduled on Saturday. He used to have a couple of our players go to the library and do some research about the topics he was going to cover."

LEN FASANO

"I played for Howie Odell and Herman Hickman. Herman was a more personable guy. He was very bright.

"Herman called me 'Little Len.' They had me listed at 184 pounds but I never weighed 184 pounds. I only weighed 164 pounds. To elevate my weight I stuffed my cleats, helmet, shoulder pads, etc. into my pants. That made me 184 pounds. When the guy taking the weights yelled, 'Lenny Fasano 184,' Hickman said, 'Like hell.' Hickman ordered me to take off the pants. When I did that I had to remove all the equipment. If you look in the September 24, 1949, game day program when we played UConn, I was listed at 5-7 ½, 182 pounds.

"Hickman described our undersized line that year as 'the seven dwarfs.' We were not very big, but overall our small but gritty line played good ball. I'll never forget guys like Bob Jablonski, Walt Clemens, Brad Quackenbush, the '50 captain, Ed Emerson, Vic Frank, Bud Philipp, Win Lovejoy, John Setear, and Ray Albright.

"I played my last game in '49, when we beat Harvard in the Bowl 29-6. I had infectious mononucleosis and told Hickman that I didn't know how long I would last. He assured me that he would put in a replacement if we got a one- or two-touchdown lead. He never did. When the game was over, I was so exhausted they had to carry me out of the Bowl to the infirmary, where I stayed for about five days."

ED WOODSUM (OFFENSIVE END) '50, '51, '52

"I played for Herman Hickman and Jordan Olivar, and the two were quite different. I thought Hickman tried to give us too many different plays. This was not a good idea, because several players had limited practice time because of science labs. Hickman had outside interests. He was on a General Electric panel TV show, and I think he was given the choice of coaching football at Yale or going into television. He took the latter.

"When Olivar came in '52, it was a welcomed change after going 2-5-2 in '51. He was focused and there was more excitement on the team. But like Hickman, he had outside interests (insurance business) and after the '62 season was given the same choice as Hickman. Olivar chose to devote full time to his insurance business in California."

BOB BRINK (QUARTERBACK) '53, '54

"Hickman was a great storyteller. When he recruited me, he invited my father and me to lunch at Mory's. On Thanksgiving in '51, he had a number of us freshmen to his house for dinner and regaled us with stories about his days working with (Earl) Blaik at West Point.

"Hickman had the reputation of being a great defensive line coach when he was at West Point under Blaik. Hickman and New York Giants football coach Steve Owens devised a system in the hope of beating Princeton in '51.

"About 99 percent of the time, Princeton ran the single wing off tackle. Yale's game plan was to open a hole on defense and have Bob Spears close the hole and nail All-American running back Dick Kazmaier on the first play of the game. I think if he could have put Kazmaier out of the game he would have. But the plan failed. Kazmaier started to his right, stepped toward the line, then threw a 67-yard touchdown pass to Leonard Lyons. Princeton won the game, 27-0.

"Herman rubbed a lot of the old alumni the wrong way. Their idea of Yale football and Herman's were quite different, including his style of recruiting. His line coach was 'Peahead' Walker, who was of the Southern mode. For 'Peahead,' football came before studies. People will tell you that Herman was given the choice to either coach football at Yale or do his television show in New York. I don't believe it. My understanding is that Herman was asked to resign. He had a 10-year contract and they bought out the contract."

BYRON CAMPBELL (END) '53, '54

"Herman Hickman was a most likable extrovert who obviously loved life and loved to eat. Jordan Olivar was almost the opposite. He was rather austere and a very private person—no glad-handing that I remember."

CONNIE CORELLI (FULLBACK) '52, '53, '54

"Hickman was obsessed with beating Princeton. During my freshman year in '51, we played

Princeton's single-wing offense the entire season under coach Gib Holgate to help prepare the varsity for the Princeton game.

"Yale had a bye week between the Dartmouth and Princeton games which gave the varsity two weeks to prepare for the game. I was one of the thirteen freshman players who scrimmaged the varsity the two weeks prior to the game. Three different players played the role of Heisman winner Dick Kazmaier, and we even wore Princeton jerseys.

"The varsity players, in an attempt to intimidate us, would yell, 'Raw meat, raw meat,' like they were going to chew us up. Overall we held our own. We scrimmaged under the lights, and the practices would run so long we would miss the chow line back on campus. But that was not a problem, because Herman would take the freshmen out to a local Italian restaurant that he had an interest in."

Gib Holgate was a wingback on the 1943 Big Ten champion University of Michigan football team. A Marine Corps officer during World War II, Holgate came to Yale in 1949 as an assistant coach on Hickman's staff. In 1951 he became the head freshman football coach and led the Bullpups to a 14-year record of 52-26-7. His 1953, 1954 and 1959 teams were unbeaten. He was appointed assistant athletic director at Yale in 1961, then associate athletic director in 1967.

ED MOLLOY (QUARTERBACK) '51, '52, '53

"As the story goes, coach Herman Hickman said to me late in the '51 Harvard game, 'You start pitching and I'll start walking.' When the game ended he walked out of the Bowl for the last time as the Yale head football coach."

DON SCHARF ('55)

"Bob Hall, the athletic director, and some alumni worked behind the scenes to make the TV gig more attractive for Hickman. They wanted a coach that was going to be here. Herman was only at practice one or two days a week the last couple of years. Gib Holgate ran the freshmen team as well as the varsity. Hickman didn't even know who the Yale captain was in '51 (Bob Spears). He had to ask Holgate."

RAY PEACH

"Hickman shopped for his meats at 'Steve's Quality Market' on 1089 Whalley Avenue in New Haven. One day Herman came in and bought some steaks. In his car waiting were Yogi Berra and Phil Rizzuto, two future Yankee Hall of Famers. They then went to Herman's house for dinner. He knew a lot of people."

DAN MULVEY JR.

"Because my father was the sports editor of the *New Haven Register,* I once attended a dinner at a Savin Rock restaurant in West Haven where Hickman was speaking. My father told me that Herman ate three dinners that night."

JOEL E. SMILOW '54

"When as a freshman first I came to Yale, Herman Hickman was the Yale football coach. He was referred to by the press as "the Poet Laureate of the Smokies." I never met him, but got a kick out of it when he once was asked by a reporter if he felt a lot of pressure from alumni to win games. He answered, 'I have a philosophy, which is to win enough games so that they'll be sullen but never mutinous.' "

DAVE KELLEY (DEFENSIVE LINE COACH 1973-96)

"My dad, Al Kelley, was an assistant coach under Hickman at Yale in '50 and '51 before becoming the head football coach at Colgate and Brown. Dad was the 'other' end on the Cornell football team opposite All-American Brud Holland in 1938. Dad would often pick Herman up in the morning and take him to work. He would bring Herman to the dining hall on the lower floor of the Ray Tompkins House. Herman had a voracious appetite."

HERMAN HICKMAN'S CHARISMATIC personality played well with the press but his mediocre record was not harmonious with old Blues who had experienced the taste of winning under the leadership of Howie Odell.

But other aspects of the Hickman tenure stood out. Levi Jackson, the first African American football player ever at Yale, was never referred to in terms of a "Great Experiment," as had been true of Jackie Robinson, who broke the color line in major league baseball one year after Jackson entered Yale. But Levi Jackson proved to be a symbol of racial progress nonetheless. His ascendency to the football captaincy in 1949, in a predominately white, upper crust Ivy League school, was national news. Some have compared Jackson's achievements to those of Jack Roosevelt Robinson.

CHAPTER 13

A TRIBUTE TO LEVI

"Certainly he is a credit to his race—the human race."

—Charles Loftus, Yale's former sports
information director, on Levi Jackson

Levi Jackson
(YALE ATHLETICS)

on a white football team in a white university, and later in a corporate world that was largely white. At Yale he was one of three black students in a student body of 8,500.

Jackson was the youngest of six children. He came from a home with no economic advantages. His family moved from Branford, Connecticut, to New Haven in the fall of '43 when his father, George Washington Jackson, took a job at the Winchester Repeating Arms plant. A butler for prominent New Haven families, the elder Jackson would become a master steward and chef in Yale's Pierson College.

Levi played his junior and senior years at Hill-house High, then officially known as New Haven High School. Twice he earned all-state honors in football, leading the Academics to 7-0 and 7-1 records respectively. He also starred in basketball and baseball and found time to run track in between, winning state championships in the 100-yard dash and discus.

Y ALE UNIVERSITY WAS founded in 1701. Recent evidence has come to light casting doubt on the first African American to graduate from Yale College. Some contend that it was Richard Henry Green in 1857 while other sources indicate that it was a man named Moses Simon as far back as 1809.

One thing is certain: Levi Jackson was *not* the first African American to attend Yale, and he was not the first of his color to play in the Yale Bowl. That honor goes to Brown's Fritz Pollard, who played in the Bowl in 1915. But Jackson was the first to play football for Yale and the first to captain any varsity sport at the university. He made his mark in a white man's world,

Levi Jackson scores one of his six touchdowns in the 1943 Hillhouse-West Haven game. Roy Carlson (44) pursues Jackson.
(NEW HAVEN REGISTER)

Jackson was no stranger to the Bowl. In the 1943 Hillhouse-West Haven Thanksgiving Day game, he rushed for 272 yards, scored six touchdowns, and converted four extra points in Hillhouse's 52-6 victory.

After high school, Jackson served in the Army in 1945 and played for the Camp Lee, Virginia, football team before entering Yale. Camp Lee played an exhibition game against the New York Giants in Newark when Jackson sprinted for an 80-yard touchdown in his team's 7-0 win over the Giants. According to his longtime teammate and Army buddy Len Fasano, the Giants were so impressed by Jackson's performance that they offered him $10,000—enough then to pay for four years of college tuition and more—if he'd join them after his Army hitch. Instead Jackson, aided by the GI Bill of Rights, enrolled at Yale in the fall of 1946 with the encouragement of his high school coach, Reggie Root, a former Yale tackle who had been Yale's head football coach in 1933.

Levi's mother wanted him to go to Yale and become a lawyer. It was an unlikely scenario—a black kid from a public high school mixing with students from blue blooded academies like Choate, Taft, Exeter, and Loomis. "Those guys were real rich and real intelligent and I didn't think I was," Jackson told the *New Haven Register* in 1999. "I worked hard and it paid off. I never thought I could make it there, but I did."

Jackson not only succeeded, he was tapped for Skull and Bones, a prestigious Yale secret society that is famously cloaked in mystery. For many years membership was almost exclusively limited to white Protestant males. Apparently not impressed, Levi turned down the invitation.

Jackson was box office from the start. He showed his brilliance in his Yale debut on September 28,

1946, scoring two touchdowns in Yale's 33-0 win over the Merchant Marine Academy (King's Point). He ran with swivel-hipped deceptiveness—sidestepping, shifting speeds, pivoting, and spinning. His performance was a harbinger of things to come. In the 28-20 loss to Columbia that year, he took a kickoff and ran 86 yards, weaving and twisting his way through a bevy of tacklers. Yale's linchpin was fifth in the nation in rushing—ahead of Heisman Trophy winner Glenn Davis of Army and earned third team All-America honors. As *New York Times* sportswriter William Wallace put it, Jackson's "darting speed brought crowds of 60,000 or more to the Yale Bowl." Jackson was never the same after suffering a preseason leg injury in 1947 in a scrimmage at West Point.

Jackson rushed for 2,049 yards in his Yale career. When it ended in 1949, he owned thirteen Yale records in rushing, total offense, scoring, kickoff returns, and punting.

A VICTORY FOR RACIAL TOLERANCE

Levi's Yale teammates embraced him and elected him captain of the 1949 team. His election, which took place nineteen months after Jackie Robinson had broken the color line in major-league baseball, was another milestone. It was a victory for racial tolerance, achieved not through force but through the respect his teammates felt for him. His election was national news. William Wallace was an undergraduate assistant in Yale's sports information office at the time. He described the atmosphere after the

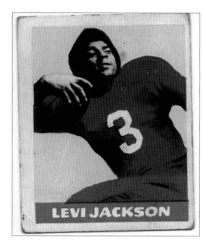

1948 Levi Jackson Leaf card
(THE TOPPS COMPANY, INC.)

announcement this way: "The day following the announcement of Jackson's election was a busy one in Yale's sports information office at the Ray Tompkins House. The telephones rang and rang. Charles Loftus, the deft director, fielded one call after another from a wide variety of newspapers and magazines, several outside the mainstream of sports."

Jackson's captaincy was significant, but it did not lead to an immediate increase in Yale's recruitment of black athletes. Not until 1955 would another African American wear the Yale blue in football. That was Ellsworth Morgan, who like Levi was a running back, wore No. 40, and played some varsity basketball. The parallels stopped there as Morgan never was a key player. The only other black captains in Yale football history are Rudy Green (1974), Jordan Haynes (2011), and Deon Randall (2014).

Jackson was also a member of the 1948-49 basketball team that lost to Illinois in the NCAA tournament. It was while a member of the basketball team that he experienced racial indignity as a Yale athlete. On a trip to Stanford, the team had a layover in Dallas. A restaurant manager told Jackson he couldn't serve him in the dining room. His teammates protested, and so the team ate together in an alternate location: the manager's office.

JACKSON'S CORPORATE CAREER

After graduating from Yale Jackson joined the Ford Motor Company where he rose to the corporation's urban affairs manager and a member of the task force working to revive Detroit after the 1967 race riots. He retired in 1983 as one of the company's top-ranking executives and died in 2000.

Currently, high school football coaches from the Southern Connecticut Conference schools in New Haven and adjoining towns select a Levi Jackson All-Star team in memory of the former Yale great. The team is honored by the New Haven Gridiron Club at its annual awards dinner.

THE PLAYERS REMEMBER LEVI

DR. LEN FASANO (GUARD)
'47, '48, '49

"Levi Jackson was my best friend. We played together in high school, studied together, and took exams together. He was just the nicest gentleman you ever met. I loved him and we were like brothers. We knew one another so well that when a situation occurred on the field, he knew exactly where I was so I could block for him. You could not catch Levi from the front. So my idea was to knock anybody off behind him without clipping.

Levi and Jim Crow

"At Yale he was accepted like anyone else. But when we were in the Army at Camp Lee in Virginia that was not the case. One day we were in Richmond and I said, 'Let's go out for lunch.' He said, 'I can't have lunch with you, but let's take a ride.'

"We got on a bus and there was a black line marked on the bus. The law was that blacks had to sit behind the line. I put Levi in the front with me but the bus driver said that Levi must sit behind the line. I said, 'If that's the law, that's the law.' So I sat behind the line with Levi and the bus driver said, 'You're not allowed to sit behind that line.' I said, 'Why not? I'm not moving.' We had a little tussle and all of a sudden two black men got on the bus and whispered into Levi's ear and said to me, 'You're in trouble.'

"They took me off the bus and put me on the floor in the back of a taxi cab that was for blacks only. They put a blanket over me and sat in the back seat with their feet on top of me while Levi sat in front with the driver as he sped away.

"I got out of Richmond. Referring to my Italian ancestry, they were all looking for the 'Dago' who was with the black boy. They wanted to string me up. After that we asked for our discharge and got it because we were both going to go to Yale.

Vote for Captain

"Levi was beloved by his teammates. Late in November in '48 we voted for captain for the '49 season. It was a secret vote held on the second floor of the Ray Tompkins House. No one was allowed to discuss whose name he was going to write on the paper ballot. The vote was 49-1 for Levi, who was a great fullback and punter.

"I couldn't believe anyone voted for someone else. After the vote was announced, I said to Levi, 'I've got to find out who voted for the other guy.' He said, 'I did, Lenny. I wouldn't vote for myself.'

"Levi was the first of his race to be chosen for the prestigious honor in the history of Yale football. It made national news.

"I maintained a relationship with Levi throughout life. I even tended to him as a doctor because I loved him so much. I went to his funeral in Detroit and, sad to say, I was his only Yale teammate there."

BOBBY RAINES (HALFBACK) '47, '48, '49

"It was sensational news when Levi was elected captain of the '49 team, and it was not symptomatic of any change in Yale policy about admitting blacks. At the time there were about a half dozen Negroes on campus. In '47, Endicott Peabody 'Cotton' Davison was the Yale captain, and he was from a prominent Episcopal family. Bill Conway, who came from a Catholic family in Cleveland, captained the '48 team, and then came Levi, a black kid who was originally from Branford, Connecticut, before he moved to New Haven. He was an anomaly. At the time there were alumni that were angry that a black man was playing football for Yale, never mind being elected captain. When we elected Levi captain we drank our traditional glass of champagne and threw our glasses into the fireplace.

The Seven Dwarfs

"When [Yale coach] Herman Hickman saw our undersized linemen in '48, he labeled them 'the Seven Dwarfs.' The next day we practiced at Anthony Thompson Field, and the linemen showed up wearing strips of adhesive tape on their chests with the names of the Dwarfs: 'Bashful,' 'Doc,' 'Dopey,' 'Grumpy,' 'Happy,' 'Sleepy' and 'Sneezy.' And would you believe, Levi, displaying his wonderful sense of humor, wore a strip lettered, 'Snow White.'

"One time a writer asked Levi, 'How long have you been a black halfback?' Levi answered, 'I've been a halfback for three years and black all of my life.' The story has *veritas* because it showed that Levi had a wonderful sense of self-mockery.

"Levi died on December 7, 2000, in Detroit at age 74. Shortly after his death we had a memorial service for him in Battell Chapel at Yale. I participated in the service. It was an honor."

FERD NADHERNY (HALFBACK) '46,'47,'48,'49

Tapped for Skull and Bones

"Every April, fifteen men in their junior year were chosen to each of the six secret societies at Yale. The ritual is known as 'Tap Day.' We were standing in the courtyard at Branford College under the Harkness Tower when Levi was 'tapped' on the shoulder by a member of Skull and Bones. Levi said, 'No.' Levi and I subsequently joined Berzelius, another secret society at Yale.

"I couldn't believe that Levi turned down Skull and Bones, a very prominent secret society that included names like former President and Supreme Court Justice Howard William Taft,

L-R: Art Fitzgerald, Ferd Nadherny, Tex Furse, and Levi Jackson talk Yale Football.
(YALE ATHLETICS)

President George H.W. Bush, his son President George W. Bush, Supreme Court Justice Potter Stewart and many others.

"Levi was my most unforgettable teammate, but he played a part in my biggest disappointment at Yale, which was not being elected captain of the football team my senior year. Levi was chosen, and he deserved it."

BILL CONWAY (CENTER/LINEBACKER) '45, '46, '47, '48 (CAPTAIN)

"After we beat Wisconsin in '48, Levi had asked to join my dad and me for a steak at the Blackstone Hotel in Chicago during our wait for the return train trip to New Haven. My dad walked up to the dining room maitre d' and simply said my son and his teammate just beat Wisconsin and we are here for a meal to celebrate. The fellow to his credit seated us in the crowded room without a fuss although Levi may have been the first black ever served in that hotel dining room."

JOHN DOWNEY (GUARD) '50

"I went out for football in the middle of preseason practice my sophomore year in '48. I didn't realize that football players didn't wear eyeglasses under their helmets, so I put my glasses on so I could find my way to the practice field. I looked like a real doofus. The players looked at me weird. But Levi Jackson, who was a junior at the time, Len Fasano, and our captain, Bill Conway, welcomed me. It made me feel good. Levi was a great football player, but he was even a greater person. He dealt with a complicated situation and handled it well."

HERB HALLAS (HALFBACK/SAFETY) '56, '57, '58

"Playing for Yale was a childhood dream come true. I grew up in Windsor, Connecticut, and my parents would take me to Yale games, the first being the '48 Brown game when the legendary Levi Jackson led Yale to a 28-13 win. Wearing No. 40, he dashed all over the field and ran for about 174 yards. I was so impressed with Levi, that I decided then and there that I wanted to go to Yale and be like Levi Jackson. In '56 I got my first varsity uniform and when the equipment manager gave me No. 40, I was thrilled."

THEY REMEMBER LEVI

RAY PEACH

"My favorite Levi Jackson story revolves around a practice session the week of the Yale-Harvard game. The team wasn't executing a play to Hickman's satisfaction and it was getting dark. Hickman barked, 'I'm going to run this play all night and push your faces in the dirt until you're black.' Levi, who had a good sense of humor nonchalantly quipped, 'Can I leave now, coach?'"

SAM BURRELL, YALE ASSISTANT COACH

"I remember seeing Levi Jackson's first game against the Merchant Marine Academy. I knew Levi well. His girlfriend, Virginia Moore, who later became his wife, lived next door to me. I recall watching Levi play in the 1947 Wisconsin game when the Badgers beat the Bulldogs in the Bowl, 9-0."

TOM HACKETT ('50)

"My first couple of times in the Yale Bowl was when I was a student at West Haven High School in the early '40s. Every Thanksgiving we played Hillhouse in the Bowl and I'll never forget Levi running all over us. Who would think that in a few years, Levi and I would be classmates at Yale?

"In 2000, our class had a 50-year reunion. Levi was there and we all got our picture taken with him. About half of his high school team showed up, even though they didn't go to Yale. He was not well and couldn't stand very long. He passed not long after that. "

DON NIELSEN

"In 1944 I had the opportunity to play in the Bowl as a sophomore for West Haven High School against Hillhouse on Thanksgiving Day. What a thrill it was. I tackled the great Levi Jackson twice which is how I got my letter."

BILL O'BRIEN

"In 1987 Levi was honored as 'The Man of the Year' by the Walter Camp Foundation. It was important for us to recognize Levi in his hometown of Branford, Connecticut, where he was raised before moving to New Haven. Judy Gott, the first selectperson at the time,

Levi Jackson accepts his Walter Camp Man of the Year Award in 1987.
(BILL O'BRIEN)

took him to his old neighborhood on Harbor Street. We knocked on the door of his old home, a beautiful house on the Branford River, and a very nice lady greeted us at the door. I explained who Levi was and that he was raised in this house. I asked if it would be possible for him and his sisters to come in and relive some old memories. She obliged and invited them in. Levi came out and said, 'I remember this house like it was yesterday.'"

GEORGE GRANDE

"My mother, Mary, was the director of physical education for the City of New Haven, the founder of the Harvest Festival and the first secretary for the Walter Camp Football Foundation. She ran the summer school playground program and used to give jobs to underprivileged and troubled kids. One of them was Floyd Little, the former Hillhouse High School football star, who went on to have a great career at Syracuse University before becoming an NFL Hall of Fame player for the Denver Broncos. At the time, Levi was trying to get Floyd into Yale, but he just didn't have the grades. Levi said, 'Of all the guys I wanted to see go to Yale, it was Floyd, but it just didn't work out.'"

presented him with the Key to the Town in a ceremony at the Branford Intermediate School. Levi addressed the student body of the school, as well as members of the high school football team who also were in attendance. We then

L EVI JACKSON RANKS as one of the great running backs in Yale football's storied history. But his most significant achievement under the elms was perhaps that of a trailblazer for future genera-

tions of men and women of color who have earned Yale diplomas. The university's contemporary multi-diversity student population can trace its roots to Levi Alexander Jackson. He should always be remembered.

CHAPTER 14

THE 1950S—THE OLIVAR ERA

"Yale had the same kind of spirit which was found on the beaches of Dunkirk and in the Battle of Britain."

—Charley Kellogg, *New Haven Register*, after Yale upset Army 14-12 in 1955.

WHILE THE KOREAN War raged on, Jordan Olivar (born Giordano Olivari)—a tall, gracious, long-chinned man who had been hired as an assistant coach in the spring of 1952—succeeded Herman Hickman as head coach the following fall. He was a proponent of the Belly-T offense, a variant of the popular Split-T. The Belly-T gave the quarterback the option of handing off to the fullback, after placing the ball near the back's midsection, or keeping it himself, in which case he would run with the ball or pitch out.

Olivar had good results with the Belly-T. During his eleven-year coaching career at Yale, he compiled a 61-32-6 record and won two Ivy League championships. He had a personal first as well: Olivar was (and is) the only head Yale football coach to have coached his son. Harry Olivar earned letters as a tackle from 1957 through 1959.

Olivar coached in an era when the NCAA sent mixed messages when it came to player safety. As early as 1951 the NCAA adopted restrictions on face masks, mandating that they be made of non-breakable, molded plastic with rounded edges. By the mid-1950s face masks were widely worn by players throughout the country on all levels of play. Conversely, the NCAA established "iron man" football when it set new substitution rules in 1953. The rules prohibited a player from returning to a game in the same quarter in which he was taken out, except in the last four minutes of each half. The idea was to reduce the financial burden on small schools that could not afford the large rosters demanded by the platoon system that became popular after the war. The convoluted "iron man" rules, however, resulted in players playing both ways and remaining on the field for long periods of time.

Olivar's 1953 team was the first to make an airplane trip for a football game; the Bulldogs flew to Ithaca, New York, where it played a scoreless tie with Cornell. Four weeks later the Elis were on the road again, beating Princeton 26-24 in a dramatic comeback at Palmer Stadium. Prior to that, Princeton had defeated Yale six consecutive years as it dominated Ivy League foes with the help of 1951 Heisman winner Dick Kazmaier.

Army, ranked No. 6 (UPI) and No. 7 (AP), demolished the Elis in 1954 by a score of 48-7 in front of 73,600 spectators in the Bowl. But the following year, the Bulldogs, a nineteen-point underdog, rebounded, pulling off one of the most stunning victories in the history of the program when they defeated the 19th ranked Cadets, 14-12.

The '55 Harvard game, played on a snowy day in New Haven, saw the Elis win 21-7. Yale's Gene Coker ran for 105 yards. Harvard's only touchdown was scored by future United States Senator, Ted Kennedy (No. 88) with his father, Joe, and brothers Jack and Bobby in attendance. A wide receiver, Kennedy caught a touchdown to cap a 92-yard drive.

The '56 squad led by the talented running tandem of Dennis McGill and Al Ward, won the first formal Ivy League championship, their only blemish, a 14-6 loss to Colgate. There was a measure of parity as a different team won the title in each of the Ivy's first four seasons.

The Space Age began in 1957 when the Soviet Union launched Sputnik I. On November 23, 1957, Yale sent Harvard into orbit in a 54-0 uprising in the Bowl, the Blue's largest margin of victory over its traditional rival. But the euphoria of that meeting was short lived. In 1958 and 1959, the Bulldogs sputtered, going 2-7 and 6-3. In '59 the Elis got off to a fast start: they were undefeated and unscored upon after the first five games and ranked 15th in the nation, tied with Oklahoma. However, they dropped three of their last four games.

THE PLAYERS

John Downey (guard) '50

SUPERIOR COURT JUDGE, STATE OF CONNECTICUT
NEW HAVEN, CONNECTICUT

John Downey was a prisoner of war for twenty-one years. His endurance and support from the Yale family pushed him to the finish line.

John Downey
(YALE ATHLETICS)

"I played my last football game for Yale on November 25, 1950, when we beat Harvard away. Almost two years to the day from that game, I was a prisoner of war in China, living in very spartan conditions.

"Soon after I graduated from Yale in '51, I joined the Central Intelligence Agency. This was during the Korean War, when China was an ally of North Korea against the U.S.-backed South Koreans. It was our war and it was something we had to deal with. On November 29, 1952, I was on a mission to pick up an anti-communist Chinese agent in a low-flying aerial snatch maneuver. We were flying in a C-47, and just as we were about to hit the target in Manchuria, all hell broke loose. We were being fired on from all angles. Our pilots, Robert Snoddy and Norman Schwartz, flew the plane through treetops and we bounced around in the back of the plane like peas in a tin can. The pilots lost their lives after the plane went up in flames. But my partner in the mission, Richard Fecteau, and I, who were both paramilitary officers, survived the crash and were captured by the Chinese. We were taken to Shenyang, where we were placed in solitary confinement.

"The first eleven months we were put in small basement cells and shackled in ankle chains. Later we were transferred to Beijing. We were brought to trial in '54 for engaging to overthrow the Chinese government and sentenced. The trial lasted one day. Fecteau was given twenty years and I got life.

"Our families were not aware that we were alive for quite some time. The first three years were miserable. One day I began shaking uncontrollably and thought I was having a breakdown. Down the road, our mothers were allowed to visit us, and what a wonderful feeling that was.

"While in prison we were exposed to a daily program of political re-education. It proved to be a positive, since it was a diversion from the monotony of being incarcerated in a 5 x 8 prison cell. I was able to watch television, but the only television we saw was Chinese TV.

"But despite all of this, I was never too far from Yale football. Charley Loftus, the sports information director at Yale, used to send me programs

Ed Senay, nursing an ankle injury, led Yale in rushing in 1950 (706 yards). Barry Baldwin and Skip Hill look on.
(YALE ATHLETICS)

and newsletters to keep me updated on Yale football news. And while I was imprisoned, I did a lot of reminiscing about my teammates at Yale, the practices, the games and the general camaraderie we enjoyed together in the field house. I read Tim Cohane's wonderful book, *The Yale Football Story,* and I would think about the practices during the week of the Harvard game, when Yale football legends like Pudge Heffelfinger and 'Cupie' Black, who captained the 1916 team, would visit with us and give us pointers. Heffelfinger was a firm believer in the two-point stance. Boy, was he tough.

The '68 Yale-Harvard game

"My mother had a good friend, Grace Pactor, who went to the Yale-Harvard game in '68. She left the game early and sent me a postcard, which I received about three weeks later, informing me that Yale had won the game 29-13. I was very pleased about that. Well, on Christmas Eve I received a package from Charley with updated football news and read that the game ended in a 29-29 tie. Of anyone in the world who cared who won the Yale-Harvard game that year, I was probably the last to learn the results. Fecteau, who had played tackle for Boston University, really broke it off on me.

Freedom

"Fecteau was released from prison in '71 and I was released in '73. We're still good friends. When Richard Nixon became president, his ground-breaking visit to the People's Republic of China in 1972 and the efforts of Henry Kissinger opened diplomatic relations between the United States and China, and it certainly helped me gain my freedom. My sentence was changed from life to five more years, but I was released early because my mother had a series of strokes and I was allowed to see her.

"Both Fecteau and I were later awarded the Director's Medal from the CIA and were offered positions in the CIA. I politely declined, saying, 'I don't think I'm cut out for this type of work.' I eventually went to Harvard Law School, and Fecteau became an assistant athletic director at Boston University. Ironically, I married a Chinese-American woman who grew up in the province of Manchuria, but I met her in New Haven.

"Some people say that my life is deserving of a movie. I say my life is 500 blank pages, just living in a cell 9,000 miles from the Yale Bowl."

Note: In 2013, Downey and Fecteau were given the Distinguished Intelligence Cross, the Central Intelligence Agency's highest honor for valor. For more on the Downey-Fecteau incarceration in China, see a documentary on YouTube titled "Extraordinary Fidelity."

Charlie Yeager (student manager/end) '52

President of a local insurance agency
Buffalo, New York

A Student Manager Scores a Point

"I was the Yale student manager in '52. Former Notre Dame quarterback Angelo Bertelli, the 1943 Heisman winner, was hired as an assistant coach under Jordan Olivar as was 'Bullet Bill' Dudley, a former All-America running back at the University of Virginia who is in the NFL Hall of Fame. Bertelli had quite an arm and I used to like to have him throw me passes. I would say, 'Bert, throw me a pass.'

"One day after one of the preseason practices, Olivar and Jerry Neri, one of his assistants, called me in and said that they were impressed at the way I attempted to catch Bertelli's passes and if Yale had

Yale student manager Charlie Yeager scored a point in the 1952 Harvard game.
(YALE ATHLETICS)

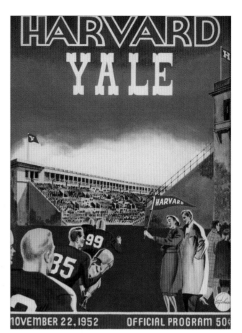

November 22, 1952, Yale-Harvard game day program
(VIC JOHNSON/ HARVARD UNIVERSITY)

a comfortable lead in the Harvard game, they were going to put me in to catch the extra point that counted for one point then.

"The day before the Harvard game we practiced in New Haven before we took the train to Boston. At that final practice of the season, we ran through the play twice. I would line up at right end next to right tackle Peter Radulovic and run a square out to the right.

"Game day was a gray, overcast day at Harvard Stadium. In the first half I was on the sideline in civilian clothes, conducting my manager's duties. At halftime we had a commanding 27-7 lead so, without even being instructed, I got into my Yale football uniform, No. 99, since I knew there was a good chance that I would get the call. Why No. 99? Simply because it was available and was the smallest jersey.

"In the third quarter we scored on a 26-yard pass from Ed Molloy to Ed Woodsum. After Bob Parcells kicked the extra point to make the score 34-7, Olivar said to me, 'The next time we score, you go in.'

"Molloy connected on a 58-yard touchdown pass to Woodsum with 4:11 left in the third quarter. I immediately ran onto the field and headed toward the goal line to the left of the Yale bench. I was ready for my 15 seconds of fame.

"The players on the field started laughing. It had to be a spectacle for the fans as well to see a 5-foot 5, 145-pound end run onto the field. In the huddle Molloy called, 'Fake extra point-pass to Yeager.'

"When we broke the huddle I lined up next to Radulovic, ready to run my square-out. I wanted to get into the end zone and go down and out. Molloy was the holder and Parcells was the kicker.

"I got off slow on the snap, and as I left the line of scrimmage I was hit hard by a Harvard defensive back who was coming in, trying to block the apparent kick. I bumped off Radulovic who proceeded to get my momentum going by pushing me into the end zone. Molloy, who had taken the snap, got up in a pass mode but couldn't see me as I was being bounced around in the area of the line of scrimmage like a pinball machine. So he started to run toward the goal line and when he saw a blue jersey, he lobbed the ball, which fell softly into my arms. Ed later told me that he didn't know it was me he was throwing to. He could have run in and scored himself if he wanted to.

"After I caught the ball I kept running about 5 yards beyond the end zone to make sure I didn't get hit. We were now up 41-7 and I ran back to the bench, where I received some congratulations.

"The press box wasn't sure what happened. Stan Venoit, the assistant public relations director under Charley Loftus, came down to the field and was astonished as to what had happened. He said, 'If I didn't see it with my own eyes, I wouldn't have believed it.'

"There's no doubt that my appearance in the game was strange, almost fictional. I find it bizarre that the front cover of the game-day Yale-Harvard program had a portrait by artist Vic Johnson of three imaginary Yale players coming onto the field heading toward the open end of the stadium, led by No. 99, which is the number I wore. It was incredibly prophetic. The following day someone wrote in the *Boston Herald,* 'Program foretells surprise Yale score.'

"Initially there was some grumbling from the Harvard side. Some looked at my appearance as the ultimate insult: that Yale would not only shellac Harvard 41-14 but would allow their student manager to play.

"But over the years the Harvards have been very gracious. About a month after the game, I was invited to speak in Syracuse to the Harvard Club, and I was presented with a Harvard chair.

"Hey, it was a fun ride. I guess you can say that Notre Dame had its 'Rudy' and Yale had its 'Charlie.'"

Ed Molloy (quarterback) '51, '52, '53

SALES AND SALES MANAGEMENT IN THE LIFE INSURANCE AND REAL ESTATE FIELDS
YARMOUTH, MAINE

"I was well aware of the great Yale football tradition long before I enrolled at Yale. My uncle Frank Gallagher, the son of Irish immigrants, played center for Yale in the Kelley-Frank era. He lost his life in World War II while in the Navy.

"I think my biggest thrill was the Harvard game my sophomore year in '51. We were trailing 21-14 late in the fourth quarter when I replaced Jim Ryan, who was injured, and sparked a 65-yard drive to tie the game, 21-21. I connected with Ray Bright for a 14-yard touchdown. After the game I went back to Branford College and since I didn't have a date, I went down to the basement to shoot pool and hang out. One of my good friends, thinking we had lost

Ed Molloy is the only Yale quarterback to throw four touchdown passes in a game against Harvard.
(YALE ATHLETICS)

the game, tried to console me. He said, 'Tough luck, Eddie.' You should have seen his face when I told him the outcome.

"Most of my playing time occurred during my junior year in '52 because I tore an ACL in a preseason scrimmage against Boston University my senior year. The '52 Harvard game when I threw four touchdown passes, three to Ed Woodsum and one to Hub Pruett, was a great thrill. That's a record that I'm very proud of. My favorite target was Woodsum who was a fabulous receiver. If you threw the ball anywhere near him, he would catch it. If he couldn't catch it, he made sure the defender didn't intercept it."

Dad to the Sidelines

"In '52 we beat Dartmouth, 21-7. In that game one of the Dartmouth tackles broke my nose. They took me over to the sidelines and had me lying flat on the ground on my back. While they were stuffing my nose, my father came down to the field from his seat to check on my condition. Among other things he said, 'Thank God they didn't get your teeth.'

"He returned to his seat and I went back in the game. There were two young guys sitting next to him, drinking whiskey. They asked, 'Who is that guy going into the game?' My father proudly answered, 'That's my son.' They then offered dad a well-deserved shot. Of course he obliged!"

Ed Woodsum (offensive end) '50, '51, '52

ATTORNEY/ YALE ATHLETIC DIRECTOR (1988-94)
CAPE ELIZABETH, MAINE

Ed Woodsum is the only Yale receiver to twice score three touchdowns in a game on pass receptions. His 15 TD receptions ties him for fourth spot on the Yale career list with Ron Benigno. Only Eric Johnson (23), Curt Grieve (20) and Ralph Plumb (16) have more.

"Because it was the last game I ever played, there's no doubt that the highlight of my career was the '52

Ed Woodsum was Ed Molloy's favorite target.
(YALE ATHLETICS)

Dick Kazmaier was the Heisman Trophy winner in '51 and one of Princeton's all-time great backs.
(YALE ATHLETICS)

Harvard game, when we won 41-14 and I scored three touchdowns on passes from Ed Molloy of 4, 26, and 58 yards. The 4-yard pass, which resulted in our first touchdown, was the toughest as I recall. The route was a sharp cut across the middle, and since we were so close to the goal line, it was crowded back there. The only chance Ed had was a pass high enough to avoid the heads and arms of everyone except me. And by gosh, he did it—perfect timing and perfect height.

"Of course, that's the game when Jordan Olivar put in our student manager, Charlie Yeager, to catch a pass for an extra point.

"At the time I didn't think much of it, but the next day I reflected on the idea and said, 'Oh God, what have we done?' It looked like we were rubbing it in. With the benefit of hindsight, I guess I wouldn't have done it if it were my call. The only plus was that it was a huge thrill for a young man who loved football but did not have the size or skill necessary to play on a college team. I don't think that play overshadowed what we accomplished as a team that day, beating Harvard like we did.

Four TDs vs. Brown

"The '52 season was certainly memorable. I caught around 40 passes, which was unusual at the time because the passing game in college football was not what it is today. In the Brown game, I scored all four touchdowns in our 28-0 win. I caught three passes and pounced on a ball in the end zone that a Brown punt receiver fumbled. One of my roommates at Calhoun, Charlie Deen, was right alongside me, and he could have fallen on the ball just as easily. He quipped, 'You're a hog. Isn't three touchdowns in a game enough for you?' Another one of my roommates, Bob Parcells, kicked all the extra points that game. If I had let Deen fall on the ball, that would have been some trifecta—three roommates scoring all the points in a Yale game.

The Great Kazmaier

"Princeton beat us in '51, 27-0. They were ranked fifth in the country, and they had the great Heisman winner, Dick Kazmaier, (who accounted for 1,827 yards rushing and passing) that year. As we were entering the field at Palmer Stadium we walked by a vendor's stand and there were racks of *Time* Magazine with Kazmaier on the front cover. That gave me a strange feeling, since we were about to compete against him. The Tigers also had an All-America tackle in Holly Donan. Princeton had a great aggregation of talent, and the final score proved that. The next year we played them in the Bowl and I think we were good enough to beat them. They had beaten us the last five years and we were ready for a turnaround. Late in the first half we were on the Princeton 7-yard line and couldn't score. Homer Smith then ran 93 yards for a touchdown putting Princeton ahead 20-7 in a game we lost, 27-21."

Bob Brink (quarterback) '53, '54

EXECUTIVE VICE PRESIDENT OF THE HEARST CORPORATION
MAGAZINE DIVISION
CAREFREE, ARIZONA

"My father, who played at Northwestern in the old days, came to every one of my games in high school

Bob Brink
(YALE ATHLETICS)

and college at home and on the road. He would drive up from Manhasset, Long Island.

"The highlight of my career was beating Princeton in '53 at Palmer Stadium in what can be described as an epic game. My dad was there but unfortunately he left the stadium before the end of the game after Princeton took a late 24-20 lead and never saw our final touchdown.

"We were losing 17-0 at the half when our coaches made an adjustment and put us into a 'no-block' offense. Princeton's defense was set up where they reacted strongly to the pressure side of the block. If you tried to block them to the outside of the hole, they worked to close the hole. So our linemen were instructed to dummy block. If we wanted to run outside the tackle we would fake a block like we wanted to run inside the tackle. The Princeton defense would then scrape off the block and react to the inside. We thought the coaches were crazy, but it worked.

"I scored the first touchdown in the second half on a 7-yard run that culminated a 68-yard drive. Princeton then fumbled on the kickoff and it was recovered on the Tigers' 37 by Connie Corelli. Minutes later Pete Shears scored from the 2-yard line. We then kicked off and our sophomore tackle, Phil Tarasovic, forced a fumble from Art Pitts that was recovered by John Phillips on the Princeton 34. On the last play of the third quarter, Jimmy Lopez, who replaced me at quarterback, ran 25 yards for a TD.

"Hub Pruett, who had kicked the first two extra points, missed on the third try but we went ahead 20-17. Then on the third play of the fourth period Princeton's Royce Flippin ran 68 yards for a touchdown and Dick Martin kicked the extra point to give the Tigers a 24-20 lead. Flippin was always a thorn in our flesh.

"We had the ball on our 45 with 43 seconds remaining in the game. Lopez then fired the ball to Larry Reno, a sprinter on the track team, and Reno got it down to the Princeton 12. Reno was put on the team just a couple of weeks earlier because we lacked team speed. And with 24 seconds left, Lopez passed to Bobby Poole, who took the ball over his shoulder at the 3-yard line and wheeled into the end zone for the touchdown to give us a 26-24 lead, which was the final score. The extra point was blocked, but it didn't matter.

"This was the game of my life and I was ecstatic. But when I got to the clubhouse, I found my father in tears. He looked at me sadly and said, 'For Crissake, what a terrible loss.' Shortly after, the team presented him with the game film. The oddity of that game was that we ran forty-two consecutive offensive plays and Princeton did not run a play from scrimmage in the third quarter because of their fumbled kickoffs. I just wish my dad was there to see the end of the game.

Army Crushes Yale in '54

"The '54 Army game was sold out. We were undefeated at 5-0-1 entering the game, and our coaches wanted this one. They hated Army coach Earl "Red" Blaik because his Army team had defeated Olivar's Villanova team during the war years, 83-0.

"Army beat us, 48-7. After the game, Blaik saw Yale assistant coach Jerry Neri in the Lapham Field House, where the coaches and writers conducted their postgame interviews. Blaik yelled down to Neri, 'If you haven't got the fuckin' horses, you shouldn't be on the field.'"

Connie Corelli (fullback) '52, '53, '54

SILK FLOWER BUSINESS
SANDY HOOK, CONNECTICUT

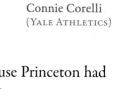

Connie Corelli
(YALE ATHLETICS)

"Our 26-24 win over Princeton in '53 was exciting. The game program that day had an illustration of six Yale babies crying because Princeton had beaten Yale six years in a row. But I guess you can say that on that day we were Princeton's daddy!

Death of a Roommate

"Not all days were happy ones. My sophomore year I roomed with Demetre Homer, a lineman who died (September 28, 1952) a couple of days after playing in a J.V. game against New Britain Teachers. He got into a couple of plays and was treated afterward for a mouth cut. He returned to his room at Saybrook College where he later complained of not feeling well. He was rushed to the hospital and died two days later. When he was a youngster he fell off a truck and suffered a serious head injury. I believe his death resulted from complications of his childhood injury. I don't think the Yale people were aware of his childhood accident. [Contemporary news accounts reported that Homer died as the result of a head injury.]

"I went to his funeral in White Plains, New York. Sadly, I was his only teammate who attended."

Byron Campbell (end) '53, '54

PRESIDENT AND PUBLISHER OF SEVERAL DAILY NEWSPAPERS,
INCLUDING TWO OWNED BY THE CHICAGO TRIBUNE
HILLSBORO BEACH, FLORIDA

"Early in games Jordan Olivar used to have me go down in the secondary, do a fake roll block, then

Byron Campbell
(YALE ATHLETICS)

Bill Lovejoy
(YALE ATHLETICS)

get up and receive a pass. It was pretty effective. We did it in the '54 Harvard game on the first play or very early in Yale's first offensive drive. I caught the pass and ran it to somewhere between the Harvard 20-and 30-yard lines. That game, albeit a loss, was the high point in my football career. I scored a touchdown on a pass from Bob Brink and a safety when I tackled Matt Botsford after he intercepted a pass and his momentum took him into the end zone."

Bill Lovejoy (offensive and defensive tackle) '54, '55

CARDIOLOGIST
UPPER MONTCLAIR, NEW JERSEY

"I was brought up with a God-like image of my father, Winslow, who lettered from 1922 through 1924. He was on the great undefeated, untied '23 team and was the captain and All-America center on Yale's undefeated 1924 team that went 6-0-2. There was a player piano in my grandmother's house, and when I was a little kid I used to play all the Yale songs. I would also read about my dad's football career from programs and magazine articles.

"It was not easy being the son of a Yale legend. The expectations for me were high, and I was always compared to my father. He was a 5-foot-10, 185-pound center and linebacker, and I was a 6-2, 220-pound tackle. When I won the Bill Mallory Award at the 1956 graduation ceremonies, Yale President A. Whitney Griswold still introduced me as Win Lovejoy's son. A close friend and teammate was upset that I was still being introduced that way, but I was proud of it.

"My late older brother, Win Jr., who played for Yale in '48 and '49, was plagued by hamstring problems.

Traffic Jam

"In '54 we were 5-0-1 entering the Army game, our one tie (13-13) coming at the hands of Colgate. On the way to a sold-out Yale Bowl for the Army game I was in a car with three seniors: captain Thorne Shugart (guard), Jim Doughan (center), and Bob Gallaway (tackle). The police would not let us on Derby Avenue. Talk about a distraction. We were going crazy. Shugart, who was a tough, tempestuous guy, was really angry. He was going off the wall. But finally they let us in.

Life Magazine Photos

"During the '54 and '55 seasons, a Yale student photographer was taking pictures of the football team all over the place. He never talked to us, and nobody knew who he was. He would take candid photos of the players in the locker room, training table, pool room, gym etc. It was annoying, especially when he would take pictures of us in the locker room just before a game when there was a great deal of tension. We were surprised when the photographs appeared on page 70 of the October 31, 1955, edition of *Life* Magazine under the title, "A Dangerous Silence." The meaning of it was that we were about to go to war on the football field.

Nasty Alumni Letters

"In '55 we achieved a wonderful payback win over Army and were heavy favorites to beat Princeton the following week but lost, 13-0. We were banged up after the Army game. I was a one-legged tackle because I injured my knee, and Loucks was coming off a concussion.

"Word leaked out that Dick Winterbauer, our very good second-string quarterback, had viral hepatitis and wasn't going to play. So Princeton coach Charlie Caldwell forced Dean to run, knowing he did not have Winterbauer as a backup. He fumbled a couple of times and threw an interception. But in my opinion he played one of the best games of his life. Some of our 'supportive' alumni wrote him nasty letters, which was outrageous.

Lovejoy was a recipient of the William Neely Mallory Award that is named in honor of Yale's 1923 football captain. It is given to the senior man who, on the field of play and in his life at Yale, best represents the highest ideals of American sportsmanship and Yale tradition.

Dean Loucks (quarterback/ safety) '54, '55, '56

EMPLOYMENT/REAL ESTATE
WHITE PLAINS, NEW YORK

Dean Loucks
(YALE ATHLETICS)

"I played quarterback and linebacker for my father, Glenn Loucks, at White Plains High School in New York. He had a legendary reputation and was very influential in my life. College coaches from all over the country, including Jordan Olivar, would visit our house to learn his Split-T offense.

"At Yale I called the plays just before the snap at the line of scrimmage, and

Edward M. Kennedy (right) with Harvard teammates.
(JOHN F. KENNEDY PRESIDENTIAL LIBRARY AND MUSEUM)

nobody ever picked it up. Our offense was a combination of the Split-T and the Belly-T. I would fake to either Denny McGill, Al Ward, or Steve Ackerman and keep the ball. McGill and Ward were amazing players, and Ackerman was the straight-ahead guy who held the linebacker in place. If I rolled left I would on occasion pass with my left hand because I was ambidextrous. When I dropped back, coach Jerry Neri insisted that I throw with my right hand.

Bonding with the Harvards

"In the winter of '55, it was arranged that four Harvard players and four Yale players would go to a Broadway play together to promote good sportsmanship. I was one of the Yale players and Ted Kennedy was one of the Harvard players chosen for the trip. There was a competitive feeling among us. We ended up beating Harvard (21-7) in '55 in a swirling snowstorm and Kennedy scored Harvard's only touchdown. Trailing 14-0, Harvard quarterback Walt Stahura threw a pass into the end zone intended for Dexter Lewis. The ball deflected off Lewis and fell into the hands of Kennedy."

Paul Lopata was one of Yale's all-time great ends.
(YALE ATHLETICS)

Paul Lopata (offensive & defensive end) '54, '55, '56

MEDICAL MARKETING
TEMPE, ARIZONA

Paul Lopata was a first-team All-Ivy, All-East, All-New England and third team AP All-American in 1956. In 1960 he was chosen for the All-Ivy first team for the decade of the 1950s.

"Before enrolling at Yale, I spent a week at Michigan State, where I was heavily recruited by head coach Duffy Daughtery and graduate assistant Frank Kush. Penn State was also interested in me. Joe Paterno, who was an assistant to head coach Rip Engle, came to my house to recruit me.

"The low point of my career was our 14-6 loss to Colgate in '56, our only loss of the year. Colgate was led by their excellent quarterback, Guy Martin, and they had a great back in Walt Betts. We could have been the first undefeated, untied team since the great 1923 squad.

"Colgate also beat us in '55 (7-0). It was one of three games that I was voted the outstanding player of the game. I'm flattered and proud of the wonderful comments I have received from my coaches. After that Colgate game, coach Jordan Olivar said, 'If we had 11 Lopatas, we could play and defeat any team in the nation.' The following year our ends coach, Harry Jacunski, said that I was the best all-around end he ever coached, and that included the years he coached at Notre Dame and Harvard. That was high praise coming from a guy who played in the NFL.

"During my era teams didn't throw the ball like they do today. I was the leading receiver in each of my three years and caught a total of 43 passes,

with my high being 16 in '55. Because teams didn't throw often, it limited the number of sacks I had on defense. However, I did make many tackles for losses.

A One Day Broadcaster

"Although I never went into broadcasting, I did have one interesting experience. Jack Castle, who played at Yale with Clint Frank and Larry Kelley, invited me to the Rochester (N.Y.) Country Club to be a commentator for the 1957 Yale-Harvard game. Yale won 54-0. That was fun!"

Vernon Loucks (offensive & defensive end, kicker) '54, '55

CEO IN THE HEALTH CARE BUSINESS
LAKE FOREST, ILLINOIS

"Although many may have wondered, Dean Loucks and I are not related. Our fathers both came from upstate New York, however, and became very good friends. I was on the receiving end of many of Dean's passes, and I guess Loucks to Loucks was an unusual attention-getter. Paul Lopata, who was really outstanding, was our left end and I was on the right. In the '55 Harvard game, I scored Yale's first touchdown in the second quarter when I caught a 7-yard pass from Dean to give us a 7-0 lead. I added all three extra points. How can I forget a day like that!

"My biggest thrill at Yale was winning the first formal Ivy League championship in '56.

Vernon Loucks
(YALE ATHLETICS)

A Humanitarian Mission

"The final game of my career we beat Harvard in Boston 42-14 in 1956. They had a running back named John Simourian who scored one of their two touchdowns. Though we were on opposite sides of the football field, we got to know each other rather well over the years.

"In fact, our football relationship gave John and me the opportunity to connect in a very important humanitarian mission. In 1988 there was a serious earthquake in Armenia in the Soviet Union. The city of Spitak was destroyed, including many of the hospitals. The Armenian government let in foreign aid and workers to help in the recovery. John, who owned a transportation company, called me at Baxter International, where I was the CEO, and asked if I could help with medical products. We sent a couple of planeloads of medical supplies, including IV solutions, heart-lung bypass equipment and dialysis machines.

"Subsequently, I was honored one night in New York City for a totally unrelated issue and John was on the program. To my surprise, he presented me with the No. 83 Harvard jersey, which was my number at Yale. Both jerseys still hang in my closet."

Denny McGill (right halfback) '54, '55, '56

FORMER CHIEF MUNICIPAL JUDGE IN JERSEY CITY, NEW JERSEY, AND PRESIDING JUDGE OF HUDSON COUNTY KIAWAH ISLAND, SOUTH CAROLINA

Dennis McGill and Al Ward epitomized the balanced attack in the Belly-T system. Their career statistics (1954-56) are remarkably similar: McGill 264 carries for 1,692 yards and 21 TDs; Ward 258 carries for 1,284 yards, 19 TDs. Both were selected to the All-Ivy First Team in 1956 along with Lopata and guard Mike Owseichik. In 1956 McGill won the George Bulger Lowe Award as the outstanding football player in New England and was an honorable mention All-American. His 93-yard run vs. Dartmouth in '56 remained a school record until broken in 2013 by Kahlil Keys's 94-yard run vs. Columbia.

Dennis McGill
(YALE ATHLETICS)

"My nickname was 'Dennis the Menace.' Hank Ketcham, the creator of the *Dennis the Menace* comic strip, once gave me an original comic strip of the character. Apparently I attracted sports cartoonists. We beat Columbia 13-7 at Baker Field my sophomore year in '54 and Willard Mullin, the dean of sports cartoonists, did a caricature of me after that game. He must have been inspired by a 56-yard run I made. The following year we beat Army, and Mel Graff did a caricature of me and inscribed it, 'To Dennis McGill, in fond memory of the Army-Yale game.'

Memorable Games

"We led 14-7 going into the last quarter of the '55 Harvard game. On the first play of the fourth quarter I intercepted a pass and ran for 39 yards down the right sideline for a touchdown. Vern Loucks caught a pass from Dean Loucks for our first score and Al Ward scored on a 1-yard run. We won 21-7. Great day!

"The following year we beat Princeton 42-20. It was the last game I ever played in the Bowl and one of the most memorable. Loucks hit me with a pass to put us on the board. Princeton came back and tied it. Ward then ran 68 yards before he was brought down. I then carried the ball down to the one and Al took it in. I recall we blocked a punt that game and Steve Ackerman picked up the ball and ran to the end zone. I scored two touchdowns and threw a touchdown pass to Jack Pendexter. It was the only pass I threw in my varsity career.

L-R: Gene Coker (35), Dennis McGill (24), Dean Loucks (11), and Al Ward (48)
(Yale Athletics)

"In '56 we were ranked third in the country in a preseason poll and finished 17th. To help prepare for that season and the Belly-T offense, which I believe coach Jerry Neri brought over from the Washington Redskins, Loucks invited Ward, Ackerman and me to White Plains, New York, where his father was the football coach at the high school. The four of us practiced together daily for about one week in August before our preseason practice began.

"From an individual standpoint I can't forget our 19-0 win over Dartmouth in '56 when I ran 93 yards for a touchdown. We were on our own 7-yard line and facing the scoreboard at the north end of the Bowl when I went wide of our left tackle and ran up the sideline. I shed one tackler by giving him a forearm. That was a technique I often used as a runner.

Jocko

"While at Yale I was befriended by Jocko Sullivan, who ran a popular restaurant on Chapel Street. It was like the Toots Shor's of New Haven. Jocko became my father away from home. I often went there for dinner after games. When we beat Army

in '55 that night I went there with my parents and girlfriend, Irene Bogacz, whom I would marry. Sometimes Jocko would call my dorm at Pierson College and invite me over for a roast beef sandwich. He would get me many speaking engagements on the rubber-chicken circuit in the New Haven area. One night I was on the dais with New York Giants football stars Frank Gifford and Kyle Rote. They got paid but I didn't.

"Jocko had a large mural of me scoring my first of two touchdowns against Princeton in '56. I understand Sullivan's restaurant, under a different ownership, underwent renovations in recent years, and the mural was covered by sheet rock. What can I say? It was up over 50 years which I consider an accolade in itself.

"Over the years, local families have unofficially adopted Yale players. My family was Walt and Belle Fogarty. After a game, if I didn't go to Jocko's, I went to the Fogartys' for dinner. I had a good experience outside the Yale community in New Haven, thanks to Jocko, Walt, and Belle.

Al Ward

"Al and I were very close and were in each other's wedding parties. I'm a Roman Catholic and went to Mass before every game. He was Episcopalian, but he attended Mass with me. There are some football-related parallels in our lives. Our senior year we each rushed for exactly 639 yards. Al turned down an offer to play with the Chicago Bears after graduation, and I did likewise with the Philadelphia Eagles.

Al Ward
(YALE ATHLETICS)

"Later in life Al was into biking. On September 11, 2003, he went over the top of a hill, not expecting anything on the other side, when he ran into a parked gardening truck. He broke his neck and died. After he passed away I sent a DVD narrated by Jordan Olivar to all of my varsity teammates in memory of Al and any teammates who had passed. The disk contained all of our Ivy League games between '54 and '56 and included the '55 Army game."

Dick Winterbauer (quarterback/safety) '55, '56, '57

PULMONARY AND CRITICAL CARE PHYSICIAN
MERCER ISLAND, WASHINGTON

Dick Winterbauer was a first-team All-Ivy selection and an honorable mention All-American in 1957. He threw 20 touchdown passes in his career, a Yale record at the time. In passing efficiency—a metric developed by the NCAA long after he graduated—Winterbauer outranks every quarterback in Yale's history except Brian Dowling.

"After playing Army I developed viral hepatitis and didn't play against either Princeton or Harvard in '55. I was in the Yale infirmary when we played Princeton and listened on the radio. The Sunday after, my attending physician came in with the vital signs sheet and told me he had been called at home because during the game my pulse went up to 110-120 and no one could figure out why. I was on the field but in street clothes for the Harvard game. "I competed with Dean Loucks, who was a year ahead of me, for the quarterback position. Dean was a very good player. The first time I met him he was as nice and gracious as can be. He extended a great sense of welcome despite the

fact we were competing. My sophomore and junior years I rotated with Dean. He would play the first and third quarters and I would play the second and fourth quarters. I found that very difficult because I could not get into a rhythm. Dean was the better defensive player, and perhaps I had an edge on offense.

"Although we lost a lot of talent from our '56 Ivy League championship team, we had a lot more talent in '57 than people gave us credit for. Herb Hallas and Rich Winkler did an amazing job replacing McGill and Ward. The three people I relied on heavily were Gene Coker, (Captain) Jack Embersits and Mike Cavallon. Coker followed Ackerman at fullback. Gene was from

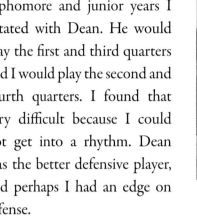

Dick Winterbauer
(YALE ATHLETICS)

1957 captain Jack Embersits (left) with back-up quarterback Oliver "Pudge" Henkel (right). Embersits, who died in 2009, was the recipient of the George H.W. Bush Lifetime Leadership Award in 2011. Henkel managed Gary Hart's 1984 presidential campaign.
(YALE ATHLETICS)

Texas and I could still hear him say, 'Golly' in his deep Texas drawl. Cavallon filled the void left by Lopata at end. Cavallon was terrific. He didn't have blazing speed, but he ran exceptional routes and he could catch the ball in a crowd. Then there was Embersits, who personified toughness. They called him the 'watch-charm guard' because he was undersized. I used to room with Pendexter, a very good defensive end.

"Our toughest loss came at the hands of Penn at Franklin Field. Penn was winless (0-6), and as a team we were looking past Penn to Princeton, our opponent the following week. Penn beat us 33-20, the biggest disappointment of my Yale career. Our other loss came earlier in the season against Brown, 21-20.

A Telegram for Jordan Olivar

In our 54-0 rout over Harvard in '57, everything came together. In the first half I threw touchdown passes of 27 and 9 yards to Cavallon and Hallas made a 58-yard touchdown grab. We were ahead 34-0 at the half. Just before the start of the second half, a guy came on the field with a Western Union telegram for coach Jordan Olivar. It was from one of the Harvard classes. It simply read, 'Please!' They were hoping that Jordan would show mercy.

L-R: Eddie O'Donnell (trainer), Bill Dudley, Jack Prendergast, Stu Clancy, Jerry Neri, Jordan Olivar (head coach), Harry Jacunski, Bill Simon and Gib Holgate
(Yale Athletics)

"I was one of the many players recruited from the Chicago area by Bob Anderson. I know I made the right choice when I chose Yale because I was treated as a student athlete. I can't say enough how well I was treated by the Yale coaching staff."

Mike Cavallon (offensive and defensive end) '55,'56,'57

INTERNATIONAL BANKER
CHADDS FORD, PENNSYLVANIA

Mike Cavallon was an All-Ivy First Team end and an honorable mention All-American in 1957 and led the league in receptions and receiving yardage.

"What does one do when you reach the pinnacle of life at age twenty? That's a question I asked myself at the end of my Yale football journey.

"When I reflect on my football days, I recall that during the preseason training practices, two a day in the August heat and dust before anyone else was even back from vacation, some brilliant thinker decided we should not drink water after each practice, for fear of filling up and not having room for the wonderful (no joke) training table fare. As if! So we were given about six ounces of Coke and told not to drink water. What would they say about that today?

"Another thing that amused me, being a Midwesterner from New Trier High School in Chicago where the football team was pretty animal-like, was the rest time during those preseason days. It seemed that the favorite pastime when we were 'relaxing' was the number of bridge games that went on.

"When I think of the Harvard games, I think of the poor weather conditions we played in. In '56 at Harvard, the field was like a plowed field that froze hard in the cold. Shortly into the game we put on sneakers to help our footing. It must have been a good idea since we won, 42-14.

Mike Cavallon
(YALE ATHLETICS)

"After playing Harvard in poor weather and field conditions for three years, the '57 Harvard game in the Bowl, however, was on a warm late November day. We won the game 54-0 and Dick Winterbauer threw two touchdown passes to me. We got into a great routine together, and the timing of his passes was flawless. If we'd played one more season together, we would have been deadly. Dick was really the most important individual on the team. And he played safety on defense.

"In the second quarter I caught a pass from Winterbauer on the goal line and scored, giving us a 26-0 lead before Winterbauer kicked the extra point. John Pendexter helped by keeping Harvard's Chet Boulris from getting to me. Boulris turned around and in frustration, right in front of a referee, took a swing at Pendexter and was thrown out of the game. That may have been a factor in Harvard's collapse.

"I think that the 1957 football team (6-2-1) was exceptional in a number of ways, not just because I was on it. Unfortunately, we found that many of the best players from the class behind us, and even from our own class, had dropped out, the reason being that there was so much talent ahead of them, there was not much playing time for them.

Yale 20 Princeton 13

"Winterbauer, who became a doctor, threw with surgical precision. He made me a hero in the '57 Princeton game by throwing me two touchdown passes, and Coker, our fullback, tossed one to me. It was the only pass Coker threw in a game all season.

"I did play some good defense, too. Princeton had the ball when the game ended. Hewes Agnew carried

on the final play and was tackled; you guessed it, by our captain, Jack Embersits, and Cavallon.

"Embersits was hit pretty hard in the head early in the second half and never could remember the rest of the game. We were so short of players that both he and I played the whole game, every play. Of course we were taught to play both offense and defense because of the NCAA substitution rules.

"We had a great bunch of guys, and we have stayed in touch over all the years. Sadly, we lost Embersits, the '57 captain, and Pendexter. I guess we are getting old, but I do have golden memories.

"As I said, it's not easy to reach the pinnacle of your life at age twenty. There is no way to go but ...?"

Alvin Puryear (offensive & defensive tackle) '57, '58

COLLEGE PROFESSOR AND MANAGEMENT CONSULTANT
WILLIAMSBURG, VIRGINIA

"One of my fondest memories was beating Princeton and Harvard in 1957. Because Yale lost at least nine two-way starters from the '56 Ivy League championship team, we were not sure what to expect in '57. We were 4-1 entering the Dartmouth game, our only loss coming against Brown. Dartmouth, coached by Bob Blackman, was undefeated when they came into the Bowl with a very good team and a fine young sophomore quarterback in Bill Gundy. Because a version of the Asian flu hit our team and several players were sick, I had to play about 57 minutes in that game. We were winning 14-7 late in the game when Jordan Olivar put

Al Puryear

in several fresh players to rush the passer. Unfortunately, Dartmouth was able to score a touchdown and the game ended in a tie.

"The next week we were scheduled to play a winless Penn team, followed by Princeton. I think that the coaches and players may have been looking past Penn to Princeton, which was undefeated in the league. Penn ended up beating us. Even though we beat Princeton and Harvard, our two losses in the Ivy League kept us from the championship. Princeton beat Dartmouth on the final day of the season, 34-14, to win the Ivy title.

"I have been told that I was the first African American to be a starter at Yale after Levi Jackson. In the 1950s only four or five African Americans attended Yale College each year. I had attended a racially segregated high school in Hampton, Virginia. Although I had been accepted at Yale, I decided to attend Hampton Institute, where I played varsity football for one year. I entered Yale as a freshman in 1956. As a transfer, I was ineligible to play my senior year, so I served as a 'graduate assistant' for the Yale freshman team. That experience led to my joining the coaching staff at Riverdale Country School in New York City, which had a 51-game undefeated streak during my five years on the staff. One of our outstanding players was Calvin Hill, who was an All-Ivy running back at Yale and a first-round draft choice of the Dallas Cowboys in 1969."

Herb Hallas (left halfback/ safety) '56, '57, '58

Teacher/attorney
Farmingdale, New York

A Record Punt Return

"In '58 I returned a punt against Penn for 94 yards, which is still a Yale and Ivy League record for the longest punt return. I received the ball on our

6-yard line facing the scoreboard. I knew that Penn's David Coffin was very fast. Coffin and I were probably two of the fastest runners in the Ivy League. I initially got two great blocks from Rich Winkler and Matt Freeman. The rest of the team blocked very well in our designed play, knocking Penn guys down all over the place. I ran up the right sideline behind a wall of blockers and was around midfield in front of the Penn bench when I saw

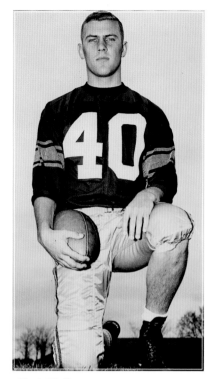

Herb Hallas
(Yale Athletics)

Coffin from the corner of my eye, approaching me at the end of the wall. I could hear the crowd—it was a swelling roar as I ran down the sideline. As I continued running I could hear footsteps behind me, getting louder and closer.

"I knew it had to be Coffin, and I ran faster and faster. Would I make it to the goal line? When I finally crossed the goal line, I turned around to see who had been trying to run me down—but no one was there. The footsteps must have been all in my head. If those footsteps I thought I heard were his, he was not the fleetest back in the Ivy that day. It was the only touchdown we scored that game, losing 30-6.

"I've been asked if I ever want to see my 94-yard punt return record broken. Let's put it this way: I would be very happy for the player, because records are made to be broken, but I have to admit, I am very conscious on what yard line the receiver catches the ball before making his punt return.

"We had a tough year, going 2-7 in '58, losing all seven Ivy League games. The season might have been different if two great linemen who had been starters on our 1956 Ivy championship team had not left school after their sophomore year—Alex Kroll and Charlie Griffith. Kroll was later an All-American at Rutgers and played for the New York Titans in the old American Football league in 1962.

Beating a Harvard Defender

"In '57 we beat Harvard 54-0. I scored three touchdowns, two on short runs and the other on a 58-yard pass from Winterbauer, who had called a Z-out pattern pass play. I ran at the safety at three-quarter speed, then continued at the same speed to the right and broke to the left at full speed, leaving the defender in his tracks. When I broke to the left and shifted gears, I could hear the Harvard safety yell, 'Oh shit!' From then on, for many years, whenever I heard that expression, I thought of Harvard. I occasionally still do.

"My brother Hank, who lettered from1960 to '62, and I both scored touchdowns in the Yale Bowl. That's something not many brothers have done."

Unofficially, the only brothers to score touchdowns for Yale in the Bowl are the Hallases and Dave and Dan Iwan (1993 and 1994).

Richard Sigal (halfback) '57, '58

Attorney
New York, New York

"Jerry Neri, the backfield coach, used to teach a blocking technique that was termed the Neri knee drive. You would drive your right knee right through the legs of the man you were blocking and turn to lay the guy out. My sophomore year I was blocking Mike Cavallon, the great end who was a senior and I

was a sophomore preparing the first string for the upcoming game. I found myself sitting on top of him. Neri comes over and says, 'Richard, that wasn't the way to do the knee drive.'"

Sigal's brother, Robert, was a running back who lettered in '55 and '56.

Richard Sigal
(Yale Athletics)

Jim Little (halfback) '59 freshman

CORPORATE ATTORNEY, BANKER
Edgewater, Maryland

"Playing for Glen Ridge High School in New Jersey in '58, I became the second highest scorer in the state as a wide receiver and running back. College football programs mistakenly thought I was good but what they didn't realize was that my quarterback was the best passer in the state. I was the valedictorian of my class and was recruited by Yale, Harvard, Princeton, and a number of other schools.

Jim Little
(Yale Athletics)

"Unfortunately, my dad died suddenly in the summer before my sophomore year. His death took a lot out of me. I lost my spirit to play and I left the team before the first game."

When Yale upset Army 14-12 in 1955, it proved to be one of the greatest wins in the annals of Yale football. The Cadets won the battle of the stats out rushing (176-120) and out passing (77-40) the Elis but Yale won the war. The proud men who wore the Yale blue that day, recall the game.

THE PLAYERS

DEAN LOUCKS

Dinner with Lombardi

"In the winter after my senior season in high school, Vince Lombardi, who was an assistant at West Point, tried to recruit me. He took me to Parise's Steak House for dinner. I loved steak and ordered a big steak for my meal. When the waiter brought it to the table it was very rare. Lombardi said, 'Look at all that blood.' I looked and fainted. That's right; I actually fainted in front of Lombardi. The same thing happened to me years later when I coached high school football. I haven't had steak since 1994.

"At Yale, I played with a special group of players and for a great coaching staff. I never could focus on myself. My biggest disappointment was losing to Army in '54, my sophomore year. Up until that time I had never lost a football game, as my high school and Yale freshman teams went undefeated.

"The following year we beat Army in the Bowl, 14-12. Although not many know this, I played almost the entire game both ways with a concussion. From our scouting report we knew that if their center blocked the guard to his right or left, it was going to be a pass play. I played safety on defense, and my job was to shoot through the middle and bring the quarterback down if I saw the center block to his right or left. On one play I blitzed their quarterback, Don Holleder, and suffered a concussion.

"I sat on the bench and had no memory. My father, who knew Jordan Olivar well, rushed down to the field from the stands to check on my condition. The doctor asked me a series of questions, but I kept telling him that I was all right because I wanted to play. So they put me back into the game.

"We trailed 6-0 in the second quarter and had the ball close to the Army bench facing the end zone opposite the scoreboard. Our great end, Paul Lopata, split wide to the left and I threw him a hook pass that was almost intercepted. Keep in mind that I was not playing at 100 percent because of the concussion. I was numb and nobody knew it. Then one of the strangest things happened. As Lopata was running back he overheard one of their coaches tell a defensive back to keep backpedaling but be prepared for the square-out. Lopata told me this and said, 'Throw it deep.' I did and he caught it for a touchdown. Paul made the call and he deserves the credit. Al Ward scored in the last quarter and we won.

"After we beat Army, I received a letter from Lombardi. Recalling the night I fainted, he joked, 'I should have taken you out for dinner before the Yale-Army game.'"

PAUL LOPATA

Paul Lopata awaits a Dean Loucks pass in the 1955 Army game. They connected on a 15-yard play for Yale's first touchdown in a 14-12 victory.
(John Well)

"There's no doubt that beating Army in '55 was the highlight of my Yale career. That year Army moved All-America end Don Holleder to quarterback and shifted All-America lineman Ralph Chesnauskas to the end position. We went head-to-head all afternoon and went at it pretty good. We did some trash talking to each other throughout the game, which was unusual for that era. There was one play when he dropped a pass he probably should have caught and I wisecracked, 'Nice going, Ralphie.'

"The 15-yard touchdown pass I caught in the second quarter was set up from the play before. I ran a square-in pattern and the ball was thrown behind me. I came back to the huddle and told Dean Loucks that I thought I could beat the defensive back to the outside because he was playing in and close. The next play I ran a square-out. I took a couple of steps deeper and got behind him. I caught the pass around the 4- or 5-yard line, turned and put my head down as I went into the end zone."

VERNON LOUCKS

"How do I explain the unlikely turnaround from '54 to '55? I think humility had a lot to do with it. We had never played a "Red" Blaik-coached team before 1954. We were well coached but not prepared physically. They were well coached and in fabulous condition. In '55 we got a new trainer, Bill Dayton, from Texas. He put us through a set of rigorous exercises in preparation to play at a higher level. He also handled injuries differently. I had a knee problem, and prior to Dayton's arriving they used to tape my knee. He put me on a weight-training program over the summer to strengthen the knee and used no tape during the season. Dayton was a major factor in our turnaround. When we went on the field in the '55 Army game, we expected to win."

DENNY MCGILL

"Beating Army in '55 and defeating Princeton in '56 were my biggest thrills. It was outlandish how Army had beaten us the year before. In the '55 game, Al Ward's four-yard plunge at the goal line resulted in the winning score in the middle of the fourth quarter. Don Holleder made a tackle on me that prevented me from scoring but I returned the favor by intercepting a Holleder pass and breaking up another one. Felix 'Doc' Blanchard, Army's 1945 Heisman Trophy winner, was on Army's coaching staff. Ironically, I idolized him when I was a kid, but on that day I helped Yale beat his team.

"Before the season opened, captain Phil Tarasovic asked his father which game ball he would like. His dad said Army. We weren't expected to beat Army, especially after losing 48-7 the year before, and family members tried to talk papa Tarasovic out of his decision but he insisted on Army. Immediately following our great victory against Army in '55, Phil grabbed the ball and raced into the Yale Bowl stands to hand the ball to his dad. It was like a movie."

MIKE CAVALLON

"In Army's last several games against Ivy opponents, Army had rolled up 408 points while giving up eighty. Willard Mullin, the great sports cartoonist from the *New York World Telegram and Sun*, depicted a huge Army player leaning on a wall of ivy, standing over a Yale bulldog. The Army player, beaming with overconfidence, said, 'Thou are crumbling to the dust, old pile! Thou art hastening to the fall. And around thee in thy loneliness, Clings the ivy to thy wall.'

"The angered bulldog answered, 'Don't lean on that, you big gorilla! Th' whole thing will fall down!'

"Following our upset win, Mullin ate some humble pie and created another cartoon. This one had the Yale bulldog atop a pile of crumbling bricks from the collapsing wall of Army dominance. On the bottom of the rubble lay the Army player crushed from defeat. The bulldog bantered, 'I told yez, yez shouldn't not oughta lean on them there crumbly ivy crusted walls.'"

DICK WINTERBAUER

"In the '55 Army game I kicked the two extra points in our upset win. One of the things I recall about that game was the size of the Army players. At West Point there were height and weight restrictions. Walking up to the line of scrimmage they all looked like they were the same height and weight. They were very quick and physically fit. But I think we were better prepared physically to face Army than the '54 team was, and that was an important factor in our win.

"To add a bit of levity, my parents used to stay at the Hotel Taft in New Haven when they came to see me play. They were in the lobby the weekend of the '55 Army game when my mother said to my father, 'Hank, I just saw one of the boys from the Army team. He's the biggest, ugliest player I've ever seen.'

"She didn't realize it, but the guy she was talking about was our captain, Phil Tarasovic."

REMEMBERING TRAINER DAN CASMAN AND THE "ALL-UGLY SQUAD"

Dan Casman, the pug nose Yale trainer from 1944-65, was known for his "All-Ugly Squad" creation. The Dan Casman Award is presented to the Men's Lacrosse underclassman who, in the judgment of the trainer, through his spirit and attitude has contributed the most to team spirit and morale.

CONNIE CORELLI (FULLBACK) '52, '53, '54

"In our era, face masks on helmets were not

mandatory. I broke my nose in '52 and wore a single-bar mask. Because our faces weren't that well protected, a player could get pretty ugly after taking enough shots to the face. Dan Casman, one of our trainers, picked up on this and established an 'All-Ugly squad' to add a little levity. As guys would get hit, he would assign them to the 'All-Ugly squad.' My face was so marked up in '54 that I was chosen the 'All-Ugly' captain. Phil Tarasovic, captain of the '55 team, was also captain of the 'All-Ugly Squad' his senior year."

L-R: 1955 captain Phil Tarasovic, Dan Casman, and Connie Corelli
(YALE ATHLETICS)

KEN WOLFE (HALFBACK/ DEFENSIVE BACK) '58, '59, '60

"Dan would often target the sophomores. During the '58 season he said that Lou Muller and I were the two ugliest guys on the team. I lost my front teeth playing high school football and had a partial plate. When I played at Yale, I removed the plate and must have looked scary. Casman would bet you that he could walk up a flight of stairs on his hands. One day I took him up on it and lost the wager."

IAN ROBERTSON (END) '60, '61, '62

"Casman was one of those unforgettable characters. He was the bestower of names. An ex-fighter, he was not classically handsome, had a flat nose without cartilage and breathed like a bulldog."

TED LIVINGSTON (TACKLE) '65, '67, '68

"Dan had nicknames for many of the players. He would call Lew Roney, 'Macaroni.'"

AL BATTIPAGLIA, YALE TRAINER (1956-1992)

"I continued the 'All-Ugly Squad' after Dan left. I would draw cartoons of the players who were on the 'All-Ugly Squad' and the players loved it.

"Dan was also a former boxer and a West Haven policeman. He gave me great advice. He said, 'Unlike the military, we are not under fire. We should always take our time with the athletes on the field.' He also said, 'It's important to know what you don't know.' When an athlete was injured on the field, if a trainer dropped his hat that was the signal for the team doctor to come on the field.

"I was in the Army Air Force Medics (1945-47) which led to my position as a Yale trainer. When I first arrived Eddie O'Donnell was the head trainer and he was very helpful.

"I worked with many great people like Joe Kearns, Frank Foley, Whitey Fitzsimmons, Rudy Schneider, Bill Dayton, Bill Kaminsky, Joe Canzanella and Dave Stanton. Billy K. had the magic touch with the tape. One of my favorites was Skip Ott who was on the equipment staff before he was switched to the training staff."

Al Battipaglia died on January 7, 2014, at age eighty-six.

STEVE COHEN

"My grandmother was trainer Dan Casman's sister. He now has a team award named after him. I named my son Dan after him."

DAVE KELLEY, YALE DEFENSIVE LINE COACH (1973-96)

"My father coached Jack Downey. While in prison to help maintain his mental well being, he would think about going through a full day of football practice at Yale with my father often in his mind. He once told me, 'Your father saved my life.' I get choked up every time I think about that."

FRANK STOLZENBERG ('53)

"My final game as a spotter was November 22, 1952, at Harvard Stadium where Yale beat Harvard 41-14. Before the game I went into the locker room to meet with coach Jordan Olivar as I always did. Olivar told me that Charlie Yeager, the student manager, might get into the game. I was shocked. I yelled, 'You can't do that.' But I did my job and was told that if Yeager played, he would be wearing uniform jersey No. 99.

"When Charlie went into the game I couldn't believe my eyes.

"When Charlie caught the pass, I thought he was going to run out of the stadium, like Tom Hanks in the 1994 movie *Forrest Gump*.

"Russ Hodges, the legendary announcer, looked to me for a name but I was afraid to tell him that it was the Yale manager because I thought that he would think it was a joke and would ask me who the real player was since the manager was not really a possibility. When he insisted, I pointed to No. 99 at the bottom of the chart. On the air Hodges said, 'According to my spotter, Frank Stolzenberg, it was Charlie Yeager, a student manager, who scored the extra point.'

"That's how I ended my career as a spotter."

DON SCHARF

"I competed for the student manager's job my sophomore year in '52. I came in third and only the first two get chosen. But I hung around the practice field and helped out. The following year ('53) I went to watch practice and they were short-handed. This was a sleepy era in Yale football. I started helping around when one day coach Jordan Olivar asked if I would stay on a permanent basis. So unofficially, I was a student manager in '53 and '54.

"You should have seen Charlie Yeager putting on the pads at halftime of the '52 Harvard game. The shoulder pads dwarfed his body. It was a hysterical scene. When he entered the game I was on the sidelines.

"The press was completely confused."

BOB CUMINGS

"I was a freshman at Yale when a classmate of mine fixed me up with a blind date for the '52 Yale-Harvard game. The idea of Charlie Yeager playing in that game made us Yalies excited because we really stuck it to Harvard.

"By the way, my date, Carolyn Fowler, was a junior at Newton High School. We fell in love and have been married for almost 60 years. It was quite a day!"

STAN CELMER

Bolting a Brother's Wedding

"I bleed Yale blue. I even pushed up my wedding date (September 12, 1953) so it wouldn't conflict with Yale's opener against UConn on the 26th.

"There was one wedding, however, that did conflict with my intense interest in Yale football. It was my brother's wedding, and I was the best man on a day that Yale was playing in the Bowl. I told him that he better hurry with the dinner, because I was going to leave and go to the Yale game. He said, 'The hell you are.' I said, 'I'm telling you, I'm going to the game.'

"I made the traditional toast at the reception and jumped in my car with another brother. We drove from Cheshire to the Yale Bowl and arrived in the second quarter and stayed for the rest of the game. We had to be a strange sight, sitting in the area of Portal 12 wearing tuxedos at a football game. I never returned to the reception. If I did my brother would have probably killed me."

STEVE MCGILL

Steve McGill is the son of former Yale running back Dennis McGill.

"I learned late in 2012 through a column in the *New Haven Register* by Randall Beach that the mural on the wall of Sullivan's restaurant in New Haven showing my dad's first of two touchdowns he scored in the '56 Princeton game had been covered by sheet rock due to renovations. The piece had endured through the ownership of Jocko's, then Kavanaughs and Sullivan's.

"This was a bit upsetting to me so I designed a framed montage for my father to commemorate that moment. Included is the actual picture from a newspaper clipping of him scoring the touchdown as well as the Yale-Princeton game day program cover (November 17, 1956) that I found on-line. There's also a family photo that was taken in front of the mural in 1997, the year of dad's 40th class reunion.

"There used to be a plaque with the original piece that was taken down when Kavanaugh's sold the restaurant. So I had a replica of the plaque made to go with the montage.

"The silver lining to the story is that a man named Kevin Driscoll, who read Beach's column, sent me my father's chin strap from the 1955 Army game. Kevin was a 12-year-old Boy Scout at the time and worked the game as a rope guard. After the game he asked dad for his chin strap. My father obliged and Kevin has had it for over 55 years. He sent me the chin strap with hopes of putting a smile on dad's face.

"He did!"

JOEL SMILOW ('54)

"I was a student at the Harvard Business School in '57 when Yale pummeled Harvard 54-0 in the Bowl. My wife and I were with another couple. The other guy was my B-School classmate, also Harvard '54. He bet me that Yale would never beat Harvard that badly again in 25 years. Twenty-five years went by, and Yale never duplicated a 54-point win. I had to pay off by hosting them at a very expensive New York City restaurant. I now have an annual recurring bet on 'The Game'—no points and no discussion— with three other Harvard friends. Having lost twelve of the last thirteen years (going into 2014), it feels like a reverse annuity."

RAY PEACH

"The '55 Yale-Army game was clouded with some controversy. It rained the night before and the Bowl turf was not covered. Army coach Earl "Red" Blaik saw this as an effort on the part of Yale to slow his runners and he was

L-R: Pete Riddle, Art LaVallie, Dick Winkler and Harry Olivar. Winkler captained the 1959 team. Olivar was the son of head coach Jordan Olivar.
(YALE ATHLETICS)

openly critical about it. When the game ended a fight broke out between several players and it stopped abruptly when the Army band played the *National Anthem*."

JOE CASTIGLIONE

"From 1954 to '63, I saw every Yale home game except the '58 Colgate contest, because that was the day I received the Roman Catholic sacrament of confirmation. I remember sitting in the end zone on the scoreboard side for the

'55 Harvard game on a snowy day when Ted Kennedy scored Harvard's only touchdown below where we were sitting."

ROBERT LEWIS

"We lived in Great Neck, Long Island, but had a summer home in the Stony Creek section of Branford. On Yale football weekends we would stay at our Branford home. The first game I recall seeing was Yale's 14-6 loss to Colgate in '56. Colgate intercepted a pass near the end of the game and ran the ball back for a touchdown. I could not believe how exciting McGill was. I became an instant Yale football fan because of McGill.

"In '57 my parents took me to the Penn game at Franklin Field, a 33-20 loss to the Quakers. I'm walking off the field when Nolan 'Lanny' Baird, a very dejected Yale lineman covered in blood, sees me and says, 'Tough game—would you like my chin strap?' An 8-year-old child never forgets a moment like that."

THE 1950S REPRESENTED a decade when a student manager scored an extra point for the Elis; when face masks were popularized on all levels; when Yale scored an historic win over Army; when Yale fans were treated to the running talents of two great backs.

For the Elis, the "era of good feelings," as the Eisenhower years were known, carried through to the 1960 season, when great things were in store for the Bulldogs.

YALE UNIVERSITY'S UNDEFEATED IVY LEAGUE CHAMPIONS 1960

Top row, left to right: Richard Stenzel, David Mawicke, David Keller, Sherman Cochran, Paul Bursiek, James Pappas, Robert Clark, Ruly Carpenter, Ian Robertson, William McCormick, Robert Jacunski, James Brewster, Matthew Black, Wolf Dietrich, John Bienvenue, Daniel Byrd, Jerome Kenney, Thomas Iezzi.

Third row: Richard Williams, Craig Zimmerman, Peter Kiernan, Richard Jacunski, Michael Halloran, Ted Hard, James Thompson, William Leckonby, Richard Wisner, Conrad Shimer, Gordon Kaake, Tim O'Connell, Erik Jensen, Henry Hallas, Frederick Andreae.

Second row: Robert Jones, Robert Hall, Wilford Welch, Dennis Landa, Henry Higdon, Jud Calkins, Wallace Grant, Chris Clark, Lee Marsh, Peter Truebner, William Kay, Stan Riveles, William Gengarelly, Manager Cotesworth Pinckney.

First row: James King, Lee Mallory, Benjamin Balme, Hardy Will, Robert Blanchard, Captain Michael Pyle, Thomas Singleton, Louis Muller, Ken Wolfe, Jack Kickam, John Hutcherson, John Stocking, George Lundstedt.

The undefeated, untied 1960 Yale Bulldogs
(YALE ATHLETICS)

CHAPTER 15

THE HISTORIC 1960 TEAM

"Our team's motto: 'the older we get,
the better we were.'"

—John Stocking, '61, an end on the 1960
Yale football team, *Yale Daily News*,
November 18, 2010

Ian Robertson
(YALE ATHLETICS)

FRANK BIRMINGHAM, THE sports editor of the *New Haven Journal-Courier* in 1960, met President John F. Kennedy at an event in New York in early 1963. As Birmingham extended his hand upon being introduced, the President asked, "Was Yale's undefeated 1960 team really as good as its record?"

Jordan Olivar's 1960 team is considered the gold standard of Yale football in the post-World War II era. The '60 team remains the last undefeated, untied Yale eleven. The Bulldogs capped off a perfect season that year with a 39-6 victory over Harvard. Led by Ivy League first-team selections Tom Singleton (QB), Bob Blanchard (FB), Mike Pyle (T), Ben Balme (G), and Hardy Will (C), the Bulldogs (9-0) shared the Lambert Trophy with Navy as the best team in the East, and the final Associated Press poll ranked Yale 14th in the country. The UPI poll had them 18th. At the time, Ivy League rules limited the season to nine games. With the exception of the Harvard contest, the Elis played all of their games in the Yale Bowl.

Forty-two members of the 1960 team were reunited and honored before the Princeton game on November 13, 2010, to help celebrate the 50th anniversary of their historic season. Fittingly, the Elis won that day, 14-13.

THE PLAYERS

Ian Robertson (end) '60, '61, '62
SERIAL ENTREPRENEUR
SANTA MONICA, CALIFORNIA

The "Fugahwees"

"They called me 'Pines' for 'Pineapple' because I went to high school in Hawaii. When I arrived in New Haven and put on the pads, I quickly realized that I was no longer in tropical paradise. This was especially true in 1960, my sophomore year, playing against that great '60 team in practice daily. They kicked the living shit out of us. To help them prepare for the Harvard game, we ran Harvard's plays. It was bitterly cold and the wind blew right through you. Practicing under the lights at night in late November made it seem colder. It hurt to hit, the ball stung your hands and the frozen mud skinned your knuckles as you took your stance.

The seniors ran all over us. Hitting and hurting, numb with cold, one night Erik Jensen, our center, said, 'Come on Fugahwees—Let's get in there and fight.' I queried, 'Who are the Fugahwees, an Indian tribe?' 'No,' he replied. 'What the Fug Ah We doing out here?'

"I asked myself that question many times.

Jacunski's Drill

"Coach Harry Jacunski had a drill where the veterans (juniors and seniors) would go to one side and the rookies (sophomores) would go to the other side. The sophomores were on offense and had to block a veteran, one on one. What the sophomores did not know is that upperclassmen knew how to deliver a forearm blow across the face.

"On the first day of practice I had to go against Jim Pappas, one of the toughest guys on the team. When he played football, the look on his face made Jack Nicholson in *The Shining* look like jolly old St. Nick. 'Poose,' as we called him, broke my nose with a stiff forearm. Harry just smiled and simply said, 'OK; once more on two.'

"During those torrid preseason practices, I was severely dehydrated and longed for a drink. But we were told that water gave you cramps, so we got none of that. At Choate I played for Jack Davison, who played on that great 1951 Princeton team, and we drank nothing. One day I lost seventeen pounds. At Yale we got salt pills and feasted on small orange wedges and teeny cups of Coke.

"Bruised, bloody, exhausted, and overwhelmed by the heat and the level of play in the morning session, we bused back to the Ray Tompkins House for lunch and a rest. The battle damage reports were the talk of the floor.

"Following lunch, we boarded the bus and headed back to hell. Awaiting me were my wet pads, wet dirty jersey, wet pants, and damp helmet that hung in my locker from the morning drills. I donned my battle gear and stumbled back into the fray.

"How would you like to spend part of your day doing punt-blocking drills? We were to cover the punter's foot with our hands, chest or face. One of the best punt blockers I ever saw was Bob Blanchard.

"By the last day of camp I was semi-ambulatory and quasi-comatose, but I was one of the survivors.

The "You Guys"

"I have the distinction of being the only Yale player to twice captain the 'You Guys,' as I proudly held this coveted position in my junior and senior years,

'61 and '62. Let me explain the background of the 'You Guys.'

"The varsity players, or first three units, were posted blue, red and gold, a.k.a. the 'Bulldogs,' the 'Apaches' and the 'Tomahawks,' and were assigned to individual coaches. Coach Olivar said to the rest of us, 'You guys go with coach (Bill) Simon.' The 'You Guys' were essentially the JV team and were coached during games by Stu Clancy. No doubt, we had our own identity that seems to swell with time. When we went up to Cambridge, we stayed in a separate hotel from the varsity, a bit down at the heel. But the Dallas Texans were in town for a game and they stayed there, so I guess it wasn't too bad.

"The 'You Guys' should have gone undefeated in '60, just like the varsity. The only game we lost was at West Point. We scored a touchdown that was called back because a whistle had blown. True, there was a whistle, but it was on another field.

"Speaking of the coaches, they are usually good for one-liners. One that gave me a chuckle involved Wolf Dietrich, a lineman of German ancestry. If he blew a blocking assignment, coach John Prendergast would say, 'Now I know why the Germans lost the war.'

The Sophomore Hero

"Wally Grant kicked the winning field goal against UConn in the opening game. In the second game, against Brown, Wally's field goal gave us a 3-0 lead. Jordan Olivar said, 'If this score holds up, Wally will be the most popular sophomore since Albie Booth.' We tacked on a touchdown and won 9-0.

"I'm not sure where our destiny would have led us without Wally. But at the end of the season he was not awarded a letter. Many, including Blanchard, Singleton and me found this appalling. Fifty years later I called Tom Beckett, Yale's director of athletics, and asked if there was a way he could arrange for Wally to get a letter. He replied that he could not do that. So we took the matter into our own hands. In 2010, at the 50-year reunion of the '60 team, we gave Wally his letter. My son photo-shopped my letter from 1962 and changed it from my name to Wally's."

Hank Hallas (wide receiver/defensive end) '60, '61, '62

FINANCIAL MANAGEMENT OPERATIONS IN BANKING AND INSURANCE
FORT MYERS, FLORIDA

Hank Hallas
(YALE ATHLETICS)

"Did you know that the 1960 team was never behind the entire season? They are the only Yale team to accomplish that feat since the great 1909 team. The '60 team is still the last Yale Division I team that was nationally ranked.

"Ian Robertson and I were teammates at Yale for four years as ends and in fact played against each other in both football and track in high school (Ian at Choate and Loomis for myself). We were eventually known at Yale as the 'Invisible Invincibles,' since both of us, being quite tall/skinny, couldn't be seen if we turned sideways. Ian is an ageless sophomore and I may have progressed—not sure."

Ed Kaake (kicker) '59, '60, '61

SECURITIES EXECUTIVE/EMPLOYEE BENEFITS BROKER
CARMEL, INDIANA

"My senior year at Flint Central High School in Michigan, I had a classic ACL tear with significant meniscus damage playing football. In the summer before my sophomore year, I played baseball in an industrial league and was paid weekly $25 cash and a case of Carling Black Label beer. Exactly one week before leaving for pre-season football, I was catching and the batter hit a swinging bunt. I jumped out to field the ball, planted my left leg and used it to pivot to the right to make the throw to first base. And 'pop'—out went the knee again. Thankfully the swelling was down when I reported for football practice. Then tragedy—the knee got hit two more times, again swelled up, and the docs said 'no more contact.' My Yale football experience vanished. I was devastated.

Ed Kaake
(YALE ATHLETICS)

"I remember leaving the medical center and walking to the Ray Tompkins House, where I broke into the coaches meeting to tell them. Coach Olivar asked, 'Which knee?' I said, 'Left knee.' He asked, 'Which leg do you kick with?' and I said, 'Right.' I went from utter despair to ultimate exhilaration. Jordan Olivar had saved my football career.

"Later in the season I kicked a 46-yard field goal against Princeton, which just missed center Mike Pyle's rear end by about a foot, but it set a Palmer Stadium record.

"My junior year (1960) we had a few guys who could place kick. One was sophomore Wally Grant. Again, I had the stronger leg and was regarded as the starting kicker. In our first game against Connecticut, nearing the end of the game, score tied, coach Olivar called me to get ready for a field goal. Our third-down play didn't get us the first down, and I am standing next to Ollie ready to go in. All of a sudden, Ollie calls for Wally to go in for the field goal. This surprised everyone, and Wally's successful field goal giving us the 11-8 win is another story.

"I was devastated, humiliated, wanted to die, to say the least. I think I was first in the locker room, first to shower. I wanted to get out and as far away as I could. I was done. As I turned to go, Ollie was coming directly toward me. He apologized, then explained that the coach who worked with the kickers was in the press box and thought I looked nervous so he called down to Ollie to use Wally. Nervous? I had a habit of standing on my left leg and shaking my right leg to make sure everything was loose and ready to go. This could have been mistaken for nervousness. I have never experienced nervousness when I played, regardless of the sport.

"Jordan said he knew how I must have felt and he asked me to stay with the team. I have tears falling from eyes as I tell this to you. That man loved us kids, knew what I was going through and he reached out. I've had and known many coaches in my athletic experience, none ever matched coach Jordan Olivar.

"Before the '60 Harvard game the locker room had a mystical atmosphere.

"We were up 14-0 moments before the half, and 'Ollie' calls me for a 33-yard field goal, an important score as it would put us up by three possessions. I made the kick and we went on to steam roll Harvard. Redemption at last!

"In retrospect, I felt like I was the sideshow freak for three years. I didn't get dirty, sweat much, get banged up, yet I enjoyed all the spiffs that go with football glory. And I always felt a little guilty—and not quite 'one of the guys.' Even though I made those field goals at Princeton and Harvard, I still didn't feel right. Specialist kickers just weren't 'the thing' in 1960.

"All of that, however, was erased when we were honored in 2010 on the field of the Yale Bowl, the 50th reunion of our undefeated team. The event was organized by Tom Beckett, Yale's director of athletics. I could never thank Tom enough.

"I now feel 'whole' and it feels good!"

Ruly Carpenter
(YALE ATHLETICS)

Ruly Carpenter (end) '60, '61

FORMER PRESIDENT OF THE
PHILADELPHIA PHILLIES
MONTCHANIN, DELAWARE

"My first few days of varsity practice in '59 as a sophomore was a rude awakening. I had some success as a receiver in high school. Well I ran a slant pattern over the middle and was wide open as I waited for the ball. Before you know it, I found myself on the ground. Mike Pyle gave me a shot like you wouldn't believe. While on the ground I said to myself, 'What am I doing here?' Pyle who went on to captain the Chicago Bears just stood over me drooling."

Mike Pyle (center, tackle) '58, '59, '60 (captain)

NFL PLAYER/STOCKBROKER
GLENVIEW, ILLINOIS

Mike Pyle, who embraced bruising collisions, was an All-Ivy first team selection and an honorable mention All-American in 1959 and 1960. He played center with the Chicago Bears for nine seasons (1961-1969), earning a Pro Bowl berth in 1963, a year the Bears won the NFL championship.

"My teammates called me 'Bungo' but I never knew why. The undefeated, untied 1960 team! I'm amazed that over 50 years later, that song is still alive. No doubt beating Harvard 39-6 to cap off a perfect season was the biggest thrill of my Yale career. That night we hung around the hotel and had quite a party. I think I got drunk.

"I had played center my entire career at Yale but volunteered to play tackle my senior year because we needed another tackle and that would be best for the team. I guess it worked out pretty good. Hardy Will, a teammate of mine at New Trier High School in

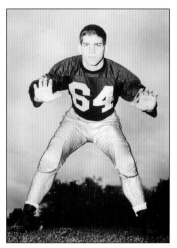

Hardy Will was an All-Ivy first team selection at center in 1960.
(Yale Athletics)

Chicago, played center. I believe that if I had remained at center, I would have been an All-American center that year.

"I also played high school ball with Tom Singleton. Ironically, he was the captain our senior year in high school and I was the captain our senior year at Yale. Both of us were also in Skull and Bones.

"I suffered two concussions during my football career. One was at Yale and the other was when I played with the Chicago Bears. Singleton had everyone in the huddle but me. He shouted, 'Pyle, come in the huddle.' Apparently I was in a daze, wandering around looking for my chin strap that was on top of my helmet.

"We used to call Bill Dayton, our trainer, 'the mild-mannered sadist' because before a game he used to tape ankles and knees so tight.

"Jim Pappas would have had a great senior year had he not graduated in three years to go to the Stanford Medical School. I recruited Jim to come to Yale.

Mike Pyle captained Yale and the Chicago Bears.
(Yale Athletics)

He was the best arm wrestler on our team. I think he could have played in the NFL.

"We had a lot of respect for Harvard quarterback Charlie 'Riverboat' Ravenel, the charming rebel from South Carolina. Not only did we invite him to be a speaker at our senior dinner in 1960, we invited him to our 50th year reunion in 2010.

The Bears

"I played in the 1961 College All-Star game as a member of the Chicago Bears against our great All-American guard, Ben Balme, who was trying out with the NFL champion Philadelphia Eagles. My rookie year I was nominated to be captain along with Mike Ditka, my roommate. Big Doug Atkins stood up and said, 'Mike Pyle will be the captain. He's from Yale.' You had to hear him emphasize the word 'Yale.'

"Would I want to see another Yale team have an undefeated, untied season? To be honest, no!"

At this writing Mike Pyle is a patient at the Silverado Memory Care Community in Highland Park, Illinois. Pyle, who suffers from dementia, has chronic traumatic encephalopathy, or CTE, a disease that has been linked to repetitive brain trauma. Silverado is a national chain that has an arrangement with the NFL to treat all former players with at least three years of service—and dementia—free of charge.

Bob Blanchard (fullback/ linebacker) '58,'59,'60

FINANCIAL ADVISOR AND INVESTMENT MANAGER
HAMDEN, CONNECTICUT

In 1960 Bob Blanchard was an All-Ivy first team selection and earned UP and AP honorable-mention All-America honors.

"I was born in Cambridge, Massachusetts, a long punt from Harvard Stadium (Soldiers Field), where I played my last football game to cap off an undefeated, untied 1960 season. Walking off the field with my teammates, coaches and a huge crowd of fans who had surged onto the field was the biggest thrill of my college football career. My uncle Carl found me and surprised me when he asked me for my helmet, which he quickly placed under his overcoat. He took it home and had it painted with a clear shellac to preserve all of

Bob Blanchard
(YALE ATHLETICS)

our opponents' colors which had marked it up during each game of the season. He gave it to me a month later as a very treasured Christmas gift.

99-Yard Interception Runback

"One of my best games came against Colgate in the Bowl when I intercepted a pass on our one-yard line and ran it back for a 99-yard touchdown, still a Yale record. Our defensive line put enormous pressure on their quarterback to force him to make an inadvisable pass. A short time earlier I had thrown a 37-yard touchdown pass to John Hutcherson. I threw the ball on a sweep to the right. Our coaches knew the defense would play for a run when I carried the ball on a sweep. 'Hutch' was wide open.

"During the game Uncle Carl, who normally attended every game, was in Florida on business. He phoned the Yale press box in the second quarter to see how I was doing. Charley Loftus, the sports information director, told him I had thrown a touchdown pass and run back a 99-yard interception. Uncle Carl snapped, 'Stop spoofing and tell me what is really happening.'

A Great Staff

"Not enough can be said about our coaching staff. They brought extensive football experience and

knowledge to the job. On one occasion, coach Jerry Neri replayed one offensive play 35 times to refine the steps, handoffs and timing of our backfield.

"We had very fine backs competing for fullback/ linebacker, my position. Ted Hard and Mike Halloran were two of them. They brought out the best in me, I feel. Unlike most jobs in the real world, on a football team there are four of five guys competing for a starting position.

Final Game in the Bowl

"The last game I played in the Bowl was in our 43-22 win against Princeton. Their running backs, Hugh 'Great' Scott and John 'Silky' Sullivan, were very talented, and Princeton was a formidable threat to spoil our march to a perfect season. The game drew over 62,000. A good friend of mine, a Yale grad, called me from New York City because he needed two tickets. I was able to help him out.

"Rallies were held Friday evenings on the Cross Campus before our home games. Coach Olivar and a few players would say a few words. The Yale marching band played fight songs and the cheerleaders led cheers for the hundreds of students and fans who attended. Needless to say, the energy filled the night and the campus in a huge way and pumped up our team for Saturday's contest."

Tom Singleton (quarterback/ defensive back) '58, '59, '60

CONSUMER PRODUCTS BUSINESS FOR FOUR DIFFERENT CORPORATIONS
GREENBRAE, CALIFORNIA

In 1960 Tom Singleton was an All-Ivy first team selection. He was also an honorable mention All-American and the winner of the Bulger Lowe Award as the outstanding player in New England.

Tom Singleton
(YALE ATHLETICS)

The Aerobic Dance Instructor

"In '58, my sophomore year, we went 2-7 and lost every Ivy League game, my biggest disappointment at Yale. Our only wins were against UConn and Colgate. We were plagued by injuries that year as both Mike Pyle and I suffered concussions. I was hit in the head by an unblocked tackle in the Columbia game. They knew I was in trouble when I lined up behind the guard to call signals. When I woke up I was on the bench.

"After the '58 season, assistant coach Jerry Neri queried Bob Kiphuth, the swimming coach, as to how the backs and receivers could improve their footwork. Kiphuth suggested an aerobic dance instructor from New Haven. This man volunteered his time and conducted classes for the backs and ends in the late afternoon during the winter in the Payne Whitney Gym. We would take this class three days a week. The coaching staff could not believe how our speed and agility improved for the '59 season.

"We were undefeated, untied and unscored on the first five games of the '59 season before Dartmouth beat us 12-8 in the Bowl on a rainy day. The Bowl was so saturated that both teams tried to run near the sidelines to get better footing. In my opinion the weather was a factor in our decline that year, when we lost three out of the last four games. We did beat Princeton.

Car Pool to the '60 Princeton Game

"The '60 Princeton game would be my last game in the Yale Bowl and, needless to say, I was excited. Several of us would car pool to the Bowl and about 10:30 that morning Bob Blanchard, Mike Pyle, Hardy Will and Ben Balme piled in my car and we headed out to the Bowl. Because of the large crowd of tailgaters that day, we couldn't get through a street because it was blocked off for half a mile. We tried telling this young policeman that we were Yale players and needed to get to the field house to get dressed. But he didn't believe us and wouldn't let us through the barricade. Finally Pyle, who was 6-3, 233, stepped out of the car and politely requested that we be allowed to get through. The young cop still refused. Pyle then got serious and said, 'If you don't take down that barricade, we're driving through.' Just around this time, the young policeman's sergeant drove up as things were really beginning to escalate. Luckily the sergeant recognized Pyle and let us through.

Ken Wolfe scores TD on pass from Tom Singleton in Yale's 43-22 win over Princeton in 1960.
(YALE ATHLETICS)

"*Sports Illustrated* sent out a reporter to write an article about the game, which gave us national exposure. I had a pretty good day. I threw three touchdown passes. But I want to credit coach Jerry Neri, who called two of them for Kenny Wolfe, our right halfback, on an out and up pattern. Neri saw that we could fool one of the Princeton defensive backs by running that pattern. Olivar was asked after the Princeton game if this Yale team was the best he had coached. He said, 'Wait until after the Harvard game.' Olivar eventually acknowledged in a video produced by Mike Pyle under 'Pudge Productions,' that the '60 team was his best team.

Yale's Built-In Scout

"Harvard now stood in the way of our perfect season. We were aware that the 1921 and 1937 Yale teams, led by Mac Aldrich and Clint Frank respectively, had undefeated seasons spoiled by Harvard. But it would not happen in '60 as we rolled Harvard 39-6. There is an interesting story behind the first touchdown we scored that game.

"Earlier in the season we played Penn. We ran the Belly-T, and on the first play from scrimmage I faked to Bob Blanchard up the middle, then handed off to Kenny Wolfe, who ran for a touchdown. It was Blanchard who made the play work because he did such a great acting job carrying out the fake, thus drawing the defense in on him. Left halfback Lou Muller's job was to block the safety, which he did.

"Teams were allowed to exchange two films, and the Penn game was not on Harvard's list. Because of our success with that play against Penn, our game plan was to run that play the first time we got the ball. We did, and Wolfe ran 41 yards for a touchdown on our first play from scrimmage.

"One of my former teammates, Brian Kenney, graduated in three years and was now enrolled in the Harvard Business School. Coach Harry Jacunski suggested that Brian could help us by attending Harvard games and stationing himself in the end zone to check the Harvard line splits. Although Brian was no longer playing with us, he was a factor in our win and was a part of that play."

Brian Kenney (fullback/ linebacker) '58, '59

INVESTMENT ADVISOR
HIGHLAND PARK, ILLINOIS

"I elected to graduate from Yale in three years so that I could attend Harvard Business School and spend only five years total between undergraduate and graduate school. I was thrilled when coach Harry Jacunski asked me to scout each of Harvard's home games in 1960.

"Under the one-platoon rules then in existence, a team was allowed only one substitution in the changeover from offense to defense. I noted that Harvard took out its gimpy-legged quarterback, Charlie Ravenel, and left in its center, who I felt was weak on defense. To take full advantage, I felt we should open the game by making a good fake to our fullback, Bob Blanchard, thus freezing Harvard's vulnerable player, and then hand off to the splendid halfback, Ken Wolfe. The play worked to perfection as Wolfe ran untouched for the TD. Ironically, Harvard should have

Brian Kenney
(YALE ATHLETICS)

known that I was scouting them because the player who was victimized was the college roommate of my closest friend from nearby Newton, Mass., with whom I was in constant contact."

Ken Wolfe (halfback/def. back) '58, '59, '60

Former chairman and CEO of the Hershey Company
Hershey, Pennsylvania

Ken Wolfe earned honorable mention All-America honors in 1960.

"It continues to amaze me how many people actually saw the touchdown I scored against Harvard in the 1960 game on our first play from scrimmage. The game was televised nationally and on the Armed Forces Network. The night before the tragic "9/11" attacks, I attended a banquet in New York City and was sitting with several guys including Yale graduate and then-New York Gov. George Pataki. I couldn't believe how many told me they watched the game when they were in Korea and Japan.

"I remember the late Jim McKay interviewing the Yale players before the game. Over the years, I've gotten a lot of credit for that touchdown, but the guy who made it work was Bob Blanchard, our powerful running fullback. We normally opened every game with Bob running into the line, but not that game. Blanchard made a great fake and the Harvard defense ignored me. I took off and nobody touched me.

The Wrong Side

"When Wally Grant kicked the field goal to give us a 3-0 lead over Brown in '60, I was the holder and lined up on the wrong side. Jim Kaake was the other kicker, and I thought that one of the two was a left-footed kicker and got confused. I got down on one knee and Wally cried, 'You're on the wrong side.' But

it was too late for me to change. That game I ran back the opening kickoff 100 yards for an apparent touchdown, but it was called back because of a penalty.

Ken Wolfe
(Yale Athletics)

Lost Contact Lens

"In the '60 game against Cornell, which we won, 22-6, I lost a contact lens when I was tackled early in the first quarter. The search party had abandoned hope when DuPont Guerry, IV, a managerial candidate with keen eyes, found it. It was fitting that his dad was an ophthalmologist.

"My biggest thrill at Yale? It was my teammates. We all got along extraordinarily well over the years and have remained close. Tom Singleton, Blanchard and the 'You Guys' have held the group together for over 50 years.

"During the 1990s I was asked to speak to the Yale football team at Ray Tompkins House. One player asked me to compare the great 1960 team and the one he currently played on. I said, 'Your team is bigger, more muscular and faster. But there's one difference—we didn't lose a game!'"

Jerry Kenney (halfback) '60, '61, '62

CEO Executive Management Committee, Merrill Lynch;
Vice chairman and member of Board of Directors,
Merrill Lynch
New York, New York

The Kenney Clan

"I'm the second of four brothers to play football for Yale. My older brother, Brian ('58, '59), preceded

1960 backfield L-R: Tom Singleton, Ken Wolfe, Bob Blanchard, and Lou Muller
(YALE ATHLETICS)

me, and I was followed by Robert ('64, '65, '66) and Rich ('68, '69). We are the only four-brother combo in Yale football history. And Robert's son, Jeff ('91 and '92) also played for Yale.

"When I was a freshman in '59, we had 1,100 students in our class, and between 100 and 150 went out for football. Playing on that undefeated 1960 team was special. The culture of Yale at the time drew the biggest crowds in the Northeast. If I recall, Yale was the national TV game of the week in consecutive weeks.

"A Monster"

"Off the field Ben Balme was a mild-mannered guy. But put him in pads on a football field and he turned into a monster. One day Balme and Pyle were coming off the field together when someone pushed Pyle into Balme. Ben yelled at Mike, 'Don't ever get knocked into me again.' And he was serious."

Jerry Kenney
(YALE ATHLETICS)

Ben Balme (offensive and defensive guard) '58, '60

ORTHOPEDIC SURGEON
PORTLAND, OREGON

Ben Balme was cut from granite. Some called him "The Em-Balmer." He was a first team AP All-American and first team All-Ivy selection in 1960.

"I followed my brother Jim to Yale who played for Herman Hickman and graduated in 1953. I mention my brother as I probably would have quit football after my freshman year in high school if it hadn't been for his advice. I was a fifth-team quarterback who weighed 120 pounds and stood 5 feet 5 inches. I was pretty discouraged after that freshman year. I remember my brother, in the summer before my sophomore year, taking me into the back yard and teaching me a good balanced lineman's stance allowing pulling and straight-ahead blocking and then of course suggesting that I give up the backfield for the line.

"I didn't play in '59 because I was on probation for being a part of a few pranks my sophomore year. I was ready to transfer back to the University of Oregon or Oregon State and play in the Pac-8, but of course returned to finish out at Yale.

"Yale was very good to me, helping me mature and realize that there are more important things than football. I played with many top-notch players, including Mike Pyle, later to become an All-Pro with the Chicago Bears. Tom Singleton could have played with the Green

Ben Balme is the last Yale first team AP All-American.
(YALE ATHLETICS)

Ben Balme throws block for Ted Hard in Yale's 22-6 victory over Cornell in 1960.
(YALE ATHLETICS)

Bay Packers. It was a terrific year, going undefeated and tying for the Lambert Trophy as the best team in the East.

"I was drafted by the defending NFL champion Philadelphia Eagles and was the 37th or 38th player left at the time of paring down to 36 players. I was released the week before the start of the '61 season despite the fact that Eagles coach Nick Skorich felt that my fundamentals were the best on the team. For that, I give all the credit to my brother and the instruction he provided me in the summer of '55. I could have played with the San Diego Chargers of the AFL or in Canada but decided to complete my medical school studies.

"I believe that I would have enjoyed playing a few years of pro ball, but medicine has been a good place for me and I'm where I belong."

Jim Thompson (center/ linebacker) '60, '61, '62

ATTORNEY
ROCKVILLE, MARYLAND

The Destroyer of Facemasks

"The linemen at Yale on the 1960 team had a preseason workout called the "Dive Drill." There we'd

Jim Thompson
(YALE ATHLETICS)

have the dive pit, a rectangular lined off area about 7 to 8 yards wide and perhaps 20 yards deep with tackling dummies on the boundaries. In the center of the pit you had a line of scrimmage with a center plus two offensive linemen split out on either side about three yards. Behind them, you had a full T formation backfield with the quarterback and two or three running backs who basically ran dives straight ahead in the seven yard area between the tackles. Across the line was the defense with a middle guard and two defensive linemen lined up nose to nose with the offensive linemen. Everyone was told that the snap count was on '2.' The defense was told to stop the play like a goal line stand and the offense was told to root them out and open holes for the backs to run through.

"When the QB called '2' all hell broke loose. For centers, like me, we had the task of blocking the middle guards and especially Ben Balme without even the slight advantage of knowing the secret snap count to get a head start. Each middle guard would take five turns in the pit and then be replaced by another. We had six to eight centers, and we'd take one snap and rotate. It didn't take us long to figure out that blocking Ben was worse than a car crash. So we all learned to count to five and rotate toward the back of the line as long as possible to avoid Ben.

"On the snap count Ben would explode up into your face with the power of an IED and hit your head gear with a forearm shiver that was epic. On the first day, he hit me so hard he knocked me back into the quarterback, smashed my face guard into pieces, stunned me (I saw stars, etc.) and he tackled the QB and the runner causing a fumble—a perfect 10!

"Bill Dayton, our trainer, saw the event and replaced my facemask with another one with two plastic bars (the earlier one only had one) for practice the next day. At the next practice we had the same drill. On the count of two he exploded again and I tried unsuccessfully to parry the blow and get to his legs. He again destroyed my helmet and broke both bars on my face mask.

"When I arrived at practice the next day and saw my helmet, it was amazing. I had a full face steel bird cage bolted to my helmet. Bill stopped by my locker and said, 'He won't break this one.' As anticipated, the dive drill began about one hour into the normal practice. Now we had a regular gallery of observers. Some were there to pray for me. Eventually my turn came and I entered the pit. This time, I decided to try to explode into him and copy his move. When the ball was snapped there was a huge explosion. Turf, arms and legs flew everywhere. When the play stopped and I was able to observe the scene of battle, three things became apparent: first, I was still alive; second, my face mask was intact; and third, Ben did not make the tackle.

"As I left the practice field I noticed something was wrong. I couldn't get my helmet off. So I went to Dayton with the problem. Then he and trainer Dan Casman each grabbed the sides of the helmet near the ear holes and pulled out and up. This allowed the helmet to pop off. When they put it on the work bench the steel cage was so bent that it distorted the sides (ears) of the helmet into which it was bolted so they were out of alignment and twisted under my cheek bones preventing the helmet from coming off normally.

"We felt sorry for any center who had to block Ben, including some of our opponents!"

Peter Kiernan (guard) '60, '61, '62

ATTORNEY, U.S. SECURITIES AND EXCHANGE COMMISSION
BETHESDA, MARYLAND

"Jack Prendergast, the head line coach, had two little twin boys who would come to practice on occasion. One Friday we were practicing in the Bowl before a game, and Prendergast had his back to the goal line. Behind him, one of the twins shimmied up the goal post and was walking across the crossbar. It looked pretty dangerous. When Jack saw that we were distracted and turned around to see what was going on, he didn't seem alarmed at all—normal hi-jinks for him, I guess. He just said something like, 'You, get down' and turned back to the practice.

Dr. Hirata

"We had an exceptional staff of trainers in Bill Dayton, Dan Casman, and Al Battipaglia. Our doctor, Isao Hirata, was also very good. One day when we were scrimmaging I got hit, knocked unconscious, and lost my memory for a period. It was my third concussion. Dr. Hirata made sure I went to the infirmary, took me out of early practice for

Peter Kiernan
(YALE ATHLETICS)

a full week, got me a special protective helmet, and said if I ever got another concussion, I would never play again. He had that kind of sensitivity to the danger of concussions in an era when they were not looked at as seriously as they are today. On most teams if you were knocked out, they would put you right back in the game or practice. That's what happened to me the first two times it happened to me in high school. Luckily, my third concussion was my last, perhaps because of Dr. Hirata and that special helmet.

Rooting for Harvard

"I'm very proud to have been a member of that great '60 team, and my other three Yale teams, even though I never started a JV or varsity game. To be honest, I would be quite happy if, while I am still alive, no other Yale team duplicated our 1960 undefeated, untied season. If Yale goes into the Harvard game undefeated, I'm rooting for Harvard!"

Peter Kiernan had two brothers, Paul '66 and Kevin '73, who also were guards at Yale for four years.

THEY REMEMBER THE '60 TEAM

JACK DOLAN

"Perhaps the greatest season in Yale Bowl history was 1960. The unusual eight straight home games occurred because Columbia (which was supposed to play host to Yale in New York City) requested the site change to the Bowl since renovations to its Baker Field home site were not complete."

GEORGE MARTELON

"I can't forget the 1960 Colgate game. I usually sat with my dad around Portal 8 but that day we sat around Portal 9, because I recall it was Youth Day and the area around Portal 8 was filled with kids. Colgate was driving for a score in our direction and had the ball on about the 5-yard line. The Colgate QB called a misdirection play and the entire team did a student body left as he threw the ball to the wide receiver in the right corner of the goal line. Bob Blanchard picked off the pass in the end zone and ran for a TD. According to the record books, it was a 99-yard interception run.

"While the QB for Colgate got robbed, the one who really lost out was Blanchard on the interception record. To all of us, because it happened right in front of us, No. 35 (Blanchard) was clearly in the end zone when he intercepted the ball. While he was gone by the time he hit the 10-yard line because all of the Colgate players were at the other side of field, his interception run to us had to have been at least 100 yards maybe 101 yards. Only years later, while working in the press box as the PA spotter, did I realize how the official scorer could have seen it as a 99-yard interception runback. The angle of the view into that corner of the end zone from the press box clearly limits what you see."

ROBERT LEWIS

"In 1960 a watershed event in my life occurred the night before Labor Day when I got very sick. The doctors were confused, though they were suspicious of leukemia or rheumatic heart fever. They never did diagnose the problem, but I was assured there was no heart damage. I was in the hospital on September 24 when Yale beat UConn 11-8 on Wally Grant's field goal. The following day my father came into my room with a copy of the *New York Daily News* and I was able to read about the game.

"The next week I was home from the hospital but could not go to the Yale-Brown game in the Yale Bowl, and we could not pick up WELI in Great Neck, Long Island. But my father bought a radio antenna pole and installed it on the roof of our house and wired it into an intercom in my room so we could all listen to the game, which Yale won 9-0.

"I was unable to attend any games in '60 because of my illness. However, a few days after the Dartmouth game that Yale won 29-0, the postman came to the door with a package. To my surprise, it was a football autographed by the '60 Yale football team and inscribed, 'This ball was carried by Bob Blanchard over the Dartmouth goal line for the second touchdown of the game.'"

REMEMBERING SCOTTY MCDOWELL

Arthur Isbister McDowell, a.k.a. "Scotty," was the maitre d' at the Ray Tompkins House for many years in charge of the training table. He was a lovable, caring Pool shark and colorful personality to match. He stood about 5-feet-5, was bald with a little fringe of white hair. He spoke like a Scot and has been described as having "the biggest Coke-bottle glasses you ever saw."

MIKE PYLE

"We used to call 'Scotty' the 'one-eyed dishwasher.' Every Friday he would serve swordfish and none of us would show up."

KEN WOLFE

"We used to really tick off Scotty. On occasion, the first one in the dining room would get a basket of rolls and put them in a pitcher of water. We would then throw the water-soaked rolls at each other and make a mess, with pieces of dough splattered all over the room. Scotty had to clean up and used to bark, 'I'm not taking this shit from you guys.'"

PETER KIERNAN

"Scotty sold tickets in a football pool; he was, in effect, a bookie. We would each give him a

A group of players from the 1960 team gather at the 50th year reunion in 2010. L-R: Erik Jensen (hidden), Lee Marsh, Ken Wolfe, Tom Iezzi, Hank Hallas, John Stocking, and Jim Thompson.
(BILL O'BRIEN)

dollar and get a chance to circle eight winners on a betting slip from a slate of pre-selected games in the hope of getting a big payday. The slip often included Ivy League teams. That would probably be a big scandal today."

PAUL LOPATA

"During the early Fall practice in 1956, I happened upon a crate of oranges at the Ray Tompkins dining kitchen and made a rash decision to confiscate it. To my utter surprise, dear ol' Scotty somehow suspected me as the culprit and insisted he was right despite my denials. How I asked did he come to think I was the confiscator [thief]? His answer was that I was the only one with the guts [stupidity] to do such a thing.

"Know that I truly loved Scotty!"

HANK HALLAS

"The first time I saw Scotty was around the pool

table in the anteroom to the training table in Ray Tompkins House. My first reaction was 'what is that one eyed dish-washer doing at the pool table?' I soon learned why. The seniors had arrived before the Chippeo bus (of course) and were in the middle of a game of 'Eight Ball.' I seriously thought that the seniors were about to fleece the poor dish-washer. I remember thinking 'what kind of cruel guys are Singleton, Muller, and Wolfe?' It didn't take long before Scotty cleared the table and them along with it and didn't pick up a dime."

ROBERT LEWIS

A Ten-Year-Old Smuggled into Palmer Stadium

"In 1959 Scotty asked, 'How would you like to watch the game on the field from the sideline?' They gave me a sideline pass and I did small things like helping the Yale manager pour water etc. When we went to Princeton on November 14, there was a shortage of sideline passes. Princeton was being Princeton, and it looked like I would get bumped that game. But Scotty came to the rescue. He took me into the locker room at Palmer Stadium, and trainer Bill Dayton and his assistant Dan Casman were there. They worked out a plan where they literally smuggled me into the stadium. They had me wear a Yale helmet and a big blue hood. I was told to run onto the field with the team at the end of the line and nobody would notice that I was not part of the team.

"He was right!"

NEVER AGAIN HAS Yale had such a magic carpet ride as they did in 1960. Difficult times lay ahead. It would be several years before the Elis would regain its prestigious perch atop the Ivy League.

CHAPTER 16

A REVOLVING DOOR OF COACHES—1961-1965

The most memorable game I ever played in was the Princeton game in '64. The game was billed as 'The Battle of the Fullbacks,' Chuck Mercein vs. Cosmo Iacavazzi."

—Chuck Mercein

COACHING CHANGES AND the ballyhooed 1964 Yale-Princeton contest featuring running backs Chuck Mercein and Cosmo Iacavozzi highlighted this period in Yale football history. The assassination of President John F. Kennedy in 1963 cast a shadow over the era as well.

Before the 1961 Harvard game in the Bowl, there was a rumor that President Kennedy, a Harvard graduate who had played freshman football, was going to attend. The *Harvard Crimson* distributed a parody of the *Yale Daily News* with a headline touting Kennedy's appearance. In the Bowl, Harvard President Robert Ellis Smith donned a mask of President Kennedy. Nearby his friends were dressed as secret service agents and a military aide. Smith walked onto the field before the game while the Harvard band played *Hail to the Chief*. The stunt duped the 61,000 in attendance, but that was as close as the president came to the Bowl in 1961. According to later reports, President Kennedy listened to the game via radio in Hyannisport, Massachusetts. Not only did Harvard win the war of pranks, the Crimson blitzed the Elis 27-0.

Both Yale and Harvard elect only one team captain. Both captains have appeared together on the front cover of the game day programs every year since 1961, with the exception of the 2012 season when Yale captain Will McHale was stripped of his

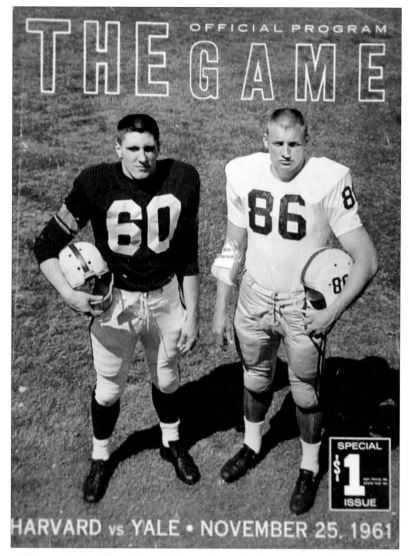

Yale captain Paul Bursiek and Harvard captain Pete Hart on the cover of the November 25, 1961, Yale-Harvard game day program. This began the annual tradition of the captains from both schools appearing on the cover of the game day program.
(YALE ATHLETICS)

captaincy because of an off-campus altercation. The photo is taken in the spring every year on the campus of the home team of that year's game.

The Players

Bill Leckonby (quarterback/ defensive back) '59, '60, '61

HIGH-TECH EXECUTIVE; OPERATED MULTIPLE SOFTWARE
COMPANIES FOR TWENTY-FIVE YEARS
PORTOLA VALLEY, CALIFORNIA

"During my entire football career, including high school and college, my father only saw me play one time and it happened to be the '61 Harvard game when I got ejected! Here's the story.

"My dad, Bill Leckonby Sr., was the head football coach at Lehigh from 1946 to 1965. Because of his coaching commitments, the only opportunity he had to see me play was the '61 Harvard game. Thanks to a scheduling quirk, we played the Harvard game after Thanksgiving that year.

Bill Leckonby
(YALE ATHLETICS)

"Harvard scored with about two minutes to go in the game in the end zone opposite the scoreboard to take a 27-0 lead. When they went for the extra point, I was lined up in the linebacker position and my assignment was to shoot the gap and try to block the extra point. I went in hard and laid out the holder with a forearm shiver. I hit him hard but it was a legal hit. He took exception and started swinging at me. Then I went after him and we were both ejected along with a couple of other guys. It was an old-fashioned ruckus. In case you're wondering what my father said about my ejection: He said absolutely nothing.

"Surprisingly, I only threw eight passes (and completed two!) that game even though Harvard had a commanding lead. 'Ollie' [coach Olivar] felt strongly that we could run against them. Also, Ruly Carpenter, a key potential receiver, got a concussion early in the game and was gone."

Hank Higdon (halfback) '60, '61, '62 (captain)

EXECUTIVE RECRUITER
GREENWICH, CONNECTICUT

"I was elected captain for the '62 team on the Monday night following the '61 Harvard game and got invited to speak at the Yale Club in Buffalo on December 30. I flew up in the morning and was expecting to fly back to LaGuardia Airport that night, but it started snowing during the luncheon and it turned into a blizzard. I could not get a flight out of Buffalo that night, so Charlie Yeager, the Yale student manager who scored an extra point in the '52 Harvard game, invited me to stay at his home. That day they fixed me up with an attractive but older airline stewardess. I spent the night in Buffalo, but not with the stewardess, although her company helped me to get through a Buffalo blizzard.

Hank Higdon
(YALE ATHLETICS)

Hinojosa Breaks Neck

"One of the most unusual things I ever saw on a football field happened in the Penn game at Franklin Field in '61. Lyn Hinojosa and I were both in twin safety preparing to return a punt. Lyn had snake hips and was an elusive runner. We were both about the same size, 5-9 and 160 pounds. The punt came to me and I ran to my left. 'Lynnie,' who was a good blocker, extended his body and made a cross-body block. Lynnie was injured on the play, but nobody knew to what extent. Bill Dayton, our team trainer, came out and they let Hinojosa walk off the field. They eventually placed him in a motorized stretcher and took him to the hospital where he was diagnosed with a broken neck. Dayton was severely criticized for allowing Lynnie to walk off the field. We went back to New Haven and Hinojosa remained in a Philadelphia hospital until after Christmas. He never played again.

"Running back Lee Marsh had a huge day for us that game which we won, 23-0. He was named the 'back of the week,' beating out Syracuse great [and eventual Heisman Trophy winner] Ernie Davis. We were graded on a scale of 1 to 5 on every play. Nobody ever got a 5. Marsh graded overall about a 1.5 that game despite rushing for 112 yards.

The Whiffenpoof Song

"One of my closest teammates was Connie Shimer. In the '60 Harvard game he caught two touchdown passes from Bill Leckonby. Connie roomed with Stan Snyder, an outstanding piano player. One of our favorite local pubs was Jocko Sullivan's on Chapel Street in New Haven. Jocko loved the Yale players and would buy us meals and give us drinks.

One night before an exam, Connie asked Stan if he wanted to go to Jocko's for a few beers. Stan nixed the idea, saying he didn't have any money. Connie, who was still on cloud nine over his big game at Harvard, said, 'Stosh,' you don't have to worry about money; I scored two touchdowns against Harvard.'

"Connie, who was an attorney and very active in civic affairs near Bethlehem, Pennsylvania, died in 1996. I went to the funeral with Snyder and Bill Madden, the captain of the great '62 Yale basketball team. We met on the west side of Manhattan, had a few beers then drove to Pennsylvania. Stan gave a beautiful eulogy and played *The Whiffenpoof Song.* There wasn't a dry eye in the place."

To the tables down at Mory's
To the place where Louis dwells,
To the dear old Temple Bar
We love so well.....

YALE FOOTBALL FORTUNES changed rapidly after the celebrated 1960 season. Heavy graduation losses and injuries led to losing seasons in '61 and '62 when the Bulldogs were a combined 6-10-2 with losses to Princeton and Harvard both years. Coach Jordan Olivar resigned under pressure from alumni after back-to-back poor seasons. Olivar, who lived in Inglewood, Calif., had one of Mutual of New York's largest life insurance agencies on the West Coast, numbering about 120 employees. He spent most of the year in the Los Angeles area. This did not please the old Blues who believed recruiting suffered because of his off-season absence. There was a bit of sniping in the *New Haven Journal-Courier,* but most likely the guns that fired Olivar were in Chicago, where Yale's recruiting czar, Bob Anderson, held court with a coterie of alumni.

By January 1963, Yale wanted Olivar to be a full-time coach, but Ollie chose his business. Overall he went 61-32-6 with two Ivy League titles. Only Walter Camp and Tad Jones had better winning percentages at Yale.

Jordan Olivar
(YALE ATHLETICS)

THE PLAYERS REMEMBER JORDAN OLIVAR

BOB BLANCHARD

"Jordan had a gifted mind. He and his wife were fabulous bridge players. Jordan was particularly creative when it came to devising a game plan to confront each opponent on Saturday. Because of his leadership skill, he had the confidence of his players as we prepared for each game. Each week in the fall of 1960 we presented the opposing team with new offenses and defenses to deal with.

"During my junior and senior years, arrangements were made to house the team off campus at a local motel the night before all home games. Coach Olivar decided that there were too many distractions on campus. Our curfew was 10 p.m. with bed checks."

TOM SINGLETON

"For the most part I called my own plays at Yale, but during my sophomore and junior years, Jordan would send plays in on a 3x5 card. He would do this with a young quarterback. If we

had a long drive I would sometimes end up with ten to fifteen 3x5 cards that I stored under my sweaty shirt. When I pulled them out they would be soggy and wet."

PETER KIERNAN

"In '59 we had an undefeated freshman team, and to me our prize prospect for the varsity for the next three years was our quarterback, Tim O'Connell. He was full of confidence, someone you knew would accomplish what he planned in the huddle, and a very good defensive player as well. He was a Billy Kilmer type. In our sophomore year, the great '60 season, I was on the third string when coach Olivar put us in the Brown game with a minute or two left and a 9-0 lead. I heard Ollie tell Tim as we went in to keep the ball on the ground and run out the clock. Tim ignored Olivar's instructions and called a pass play that he completed to Bob Jacunski for 23 yards that brought the ball to the Brown 36. It was Yale's longest completed pass of that game. I was amazed. To top that, Tim then called time out. I think this slanted Olivar's view of Tim, and he never had quite as much success on the varsity as I thought he deserved. Tim was a great player and, to me, could have started at just about any level school. Not that I am suggesting he should have played ahead of Tom Singleton, our wonderful 1960 quarterback— quite the contrary.

"Don't be fooled by the modest individual and team statistics from the '60 team. Because Jordan Olivar did not believe in running up scores, the first team often played less than half the game. I was on the third team and I played in every game except the UConn game. Yale was No. 3 in the nation in scoring, and most points scored against them came against our second team."

HANK HIGDON

"Jordan Olivar's insurance business probably affected recruiting whereas Bob Blackman, the Dartmouth coach, was recruiting year round. The same people who were cheering Olivar two years earlier were pressuring him to leave.

I had tremendous respect for him. He had a great football mind. When he played tackle at Villanova, he called the offensive plays. Where have you seen that before?"

CHUCK MERCEIN

"I played for Jordan Olivar my first varsity season and then for John Pont the next two years. Olivar was a very cerebral guy but I never really connected to him. He was kind of cold, detached, and not totally there regarding his commitment to Yale football. I found Olivar to be an uninspiring coach and in general a rather boring guy.

"I was ecstatic when Pont was hired. He had fire in his belly. He was demanding, passionate and emotional. I liked his enthusiasm, though a lot of guys didn't. Pont was right on board with me right away and built his offense around my running and pass-catching abilities as a fullback, the reverse of Olivar, who actually had me on defense as one of his starting linebackers my sophomore year."

THEY REMEMBER "OLLIE"

BUD SMITH

"During the '50s my late wife, Lee, and I were walking out of the Bowl following a Columbia game. We were walking toward the Lapham Field House to shake hands with the players when a tall gentleman walked by. Lee asked, 'Who is that?' I said, 'It's Jordan Olivar, the head coach.'

She went over and tapped Jordan on the shoulder and said, 'Mr. Olivar, I'm Lee Smith and I want to congratulate you on your victory.' From that little introduction we became life-long friends with Jordan and his wife, Stella. And three or four weeks later they came to our home for dinner.

"We went to many away games. When Yale played Harvard at Harvard Stadium, Lee would go down near the rail and would give Jordan a good luck kiss. There was a special bond between them."

ROBERT LEWIS

"My mother, Margie Lewis, was a very exuberant Yale fan and wasn't afraid to criticize coach Olivar's Belly-T offense. One game my mother excused herself to the ladies' room, and my father and I noticed that Jordan's wife, Estelle, was sitting to my mother's right. When my mother returned, my father said to her, 'Don't say anything critical of Olivar, because his wife is sitting next to you.' On the very next play, Yale runs and makes short yardage, if any, and "Stella" (that's what Jordan called his wife), yells out, 'What kind of play was that, Jordan? It's the most ridiculous call I ever saw in my life.' At that point, Stella and mom bonded and became very close friends. The Olivars had dinner at our Branford home several times."

GEORGE GRANDE

"I recall an experience I had in 1964 with Jordan. I was in Los Angeles, visiting the campus of USC, where I wanted to go to school. The Yale basketball team, led by Rick Kaminsky, happened to be there to play in the 'L.A. Classic.' Jordan invited the team to his home along with the coaches (Joe Vancisin, Vito DeVito and Bob McHenry), my brother Carlo, who was going to broadcast the game on WNHC radio, and me. The basketball players wanted to hear Jordan's

Yale football stories. He obliged and had them mesmerized, giving them a football-type pregame pep talk for the L.A. Classic.

STAN CELMER

"Following my retirement in the early '80s, I went to practice every day for about twenty-five years. Before that I would go on a semi-regular basis going back to when Howie Odell and Herman Hickman were the head coaches. Jordan Olivar gave me a pass to attend practice any time I wanted."

DON SCHARF

"Jordan was a great guy. The football banquet would be the Monday night after the Harvard game and he would go back to California on Tuesday. He would then return in April for one week to talk with candidates during the admission period.

"The alumni liked Jordan but wanted him to be at Yale the entire year. They even went so far as to tell him that they would get him an insurance business in the New Haven area. He thought about it but rejected the idea. He said, 'That's nice now because I'm winning. But my insurance business will go out the window when we start losing.' He didn't want the alumni to have any connections to his business.

"The alumni gave Olivar one year to think about it and he chose his business."

Chuck Mercein kicks a field goal vs. UConn in 1963 for the game's only score.
(YALE ATHLETICS)

OLIVAR WAS REPLACED by John Pont, who arrived from Miami of Ohio, known as the "Cradle of Coaches." *Register* sports editor Charley Kellogg called him "The little gladiator." He served two years and went 12-5-1 before moving on to Indiana University where he produced a Rose Bowl team in his third season. Pont's contribution to Yale football was significant in that he brought in such talented coaches as Carm Cozza, Seb LaSpina, Rich Pont and others. Cozza succeeded Pont in 1965. Thanks to Chuck Mercein's field goal, Pont's first game was a 3-0 win over UConn.

John Pont
(YALE ATHLETICS)

Chuck Mercein (fullback/ linebacker, kicker) '62, '63, '64

WALL STREET EQUITIES INSTITUTIONAL SALES TRADER/ NFL PLAYER
WHITE PLAINS, NEW YORK

Chuck Mercein was a first-team All-Ivy and All-East selection as a senior in 1964 and was a Chicago Tribune All-America selection. He ran with knees up high, averaged 92.1 yards per game and 5.7 per carry. The Elis, who finished 6-2-1, won their 600th game that season when they defeated Lehigh 54-0. Mercein played in the NFL from 1965 to 1970 with the New York Giants and Jets, Green Bay Packers, and Washington Redskins. He is best remembered for his performance in the 1967 NFL championship game, widely known as the "Ice Bowl," in which he accounted for half the yardage in the Packers' twelve-play, 68-yard drive that defeated Dallas 21-17. He then played in the Packers' 33-14 win over Oakland in Super Bowl II.

"My first game ever in the Yale Bowl was against UConn in '62. I honestly didn't know where UConn was. I was glad that it was a home game because I was afraid we might have to go to Alaska to play. The following year, coach John Pont's first game, I kicked the field goal to beat UConn, 3-0. People told me that I saved Yale's bacon because UConn had never beaten Yale."

ON NOVEMBER 22, *1963, the day before Yale-Harvard were scheduled to play the 80th edition of "The Game," President John F. Kennedy was assassinated in Dallas, Texas.*

At the time of the assassination, the Yale-Harvard Freshmen and JV games were in progress as well as the house and college games between the two universities. There was talk of playing the game the following Thursday, on Thanksgiving, but the idea was nixed. Yale president Kingman

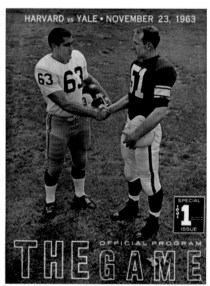

This program is dated November 23, 1963, but The Game was played on November 30, because of the assassination of President Kennedy. The captains are William Southmayd (left) and George Humphrey.
(YALE ATHLETICS)

Brewster and Harvard president Nathan Pusey agreed the game should be postponed for a week.

"The Game" that was televised regionally on CBS with announcers Lindsey Nelson, Jim Simpson and former Notre Dame coach Terry Brennan in the booth, was played a week later in a grim atmosphere under sullen skies on a cold day as the nation mourned the death of a president. Pregame tailgate parties were subdued and attendance was a modest 51,000. The Elis, led by quarterback Brian Rapp, won 20-6 behind Randy Egloff's two touchdowns and the running of Mercein.

When the day of gloom mixed with a morsel of celebration had ended, Charley Kellogg wrote, "A big yellow moon with a wraith of a windy cloud draped across its face peeped over the eastern rim of the Yale Bowl on the last day of November. Its light showed up the scars in the turf inside the big oval…"

MEMORIES OF A TRAGIC DAY

ROBERT KENNEY (END/KICKER) '64, '65, '66

Robert Kenney was an All-Ivy first team selection in 1964. In '66 he led the Ivy League with 32 receptions. On November 22, 1963, he played in the Yale-Harvard Freshman game during which time President John F. Kennedy was assassinated.

"That fateful day, our game started at 1:00 pm. Just before halftime, there was a murmur in the stands. I was on the sideline at the time. Naturally, I looked to the field because I assumed something on the field triggered the spectator noise. Nothing was happening on the field. The spectators had just heard about the shooting in Dallas.

"Eventually, the news filtered down to the field. The game continued because no one knew the details. I think [his] death was confirmed during the early afternoon.

Robert Kenney
(YALE ATHLETICS)

"The rest of the day was eerie. People walked around in a daze. Normally, Friday of H-Y weekend was the start of a major social occasion. All events were canceled. Most dates went home or never came. My date, and now wife, went back to Connecticut College. There were some informal gatherings that evening as people drifted from dorm to dorm. Yale came to a standstill and cleared out over the weekend as students went home for the Thanksgiving holiday. The varsity game was postponed for one week. Some colleges played on Saturday including Nebraska-Oklahoma. Many canceled their games.

"Sadly, the NFL went ahead with the Sunday schedule which Pete Rozelle later regretted. The AFL did not play their games."

CARM COZZA, ASSISTANT COACH, 1963

"I was watching the freshman and J.V. games when an alumnus came up to me and said, 'The president has been shot.' I looked at him and did not want to believe it. Later on, another alum came up to me and said, 'The president has been assassinated.'

"I went to John Pont, the head coach, and said, 'You know, there's a possibility they will cancel this game.' He said, 'I don't see how they can do that. I've been told it's sold out and people are coming in from all over the country and even from foreign countries for the ballgame.'

"Within a few hours we had heard that Yale postponed the game until the following Saturday. Every school in the country with a few exceptions waited to see what we were going to do. And as soon as we postponed the game, the rest with the exception of a half dozen postponed. In those days it was important to the whole country what Yale did."

CHUCK MERCEIN

"Previous to our going out to the Bowl for our light Friday workout to prepare for the '63 Harvard game, some of us had been across the street at the freshman game when word

The November 14, 1964, Yale-Princeton game day program.
(YALE ATHLETICS)

that the President had been shot reverberated through the crowd. While practicing in the Bowl we were called to circle up and informed that JFK had, indeed, died. I recall the pall which came upon the group on our learning of his death and also the uncertainty at the moment of whether or not we would be playing the next day which later, of course, we were informed we would not and that 'The Game' would be postponed till the next Saturday. That ended our practice and we all slowly and very quietly left the field for our locker room, all of us terribly shocked and saddened by the tragic news."

Chuck "The Truck" Mercein (30) was a punishing runner who led Yale to victory over Cornell in '64.
(YALE ATHLETICS)

IN A YEAR the Beatles led the British invasion of rock groups into this country, Mercein staged a memorable performance at Cornell in '64 when he ran for a TD and kicked three field goals (48, 30 and 46 yards) leading the Elis to a 23-21 victory. His publicized matchup with Princeton's Cosmo Iacavozzi drew 60,173 fans to the Bowl that was celebrating its 50th anniversary. Unfortunately for the Elis, Mercein's day ended early because of an injury while Iacavozzi ran roughshod out of the single wing. He rushed for 185 yards and scored two fourth quarter touchdowns on runs of 39 and 47 yards. After each touchdown he fired the football into the north end zone stands, a breach of football etiquette that Yale Nation would not let go.

CHUCK MERCEIN

"The most memorable game I ever played in was the Princeton game in '64. The game was billed as 'The Battle of the Fullbacks'—Chuck Mercein vs. Cosmo Iacavazzi. Princeton came into the Bowl undefeated in the Ivy. We were 6-0-1, having played a 9-9 tie game with Columbia. The score was tied 14-14 at the half and I had outplayed Iacavazzi. I scored the first touchdown of the game from the 1-yard line. I felt very strongly we were going to win the game. I also played linebacker that day. But just before the half I sustained an injury that ended my college career and perhaps ended any hope of Yale winning an Ivy League title and my dream of being undefeated. This is what happened.

"I used to run hard down field after I kicked off rather than just hanging back. I often broke

up the wedge and made the tackle, which was unusual for the kickoff man to do. Well, on this play, before I tackled the kickoff return man, a blocker stuck his helmet in my thigh, resulting in a hematoma to my right quadriceps. It was painless and at the time I wasn't aware when the injury occurred. But at halftime my leg swelled to twice its size because of internal bleeding. They had to cut off my football pants to remove them. I didn't play the second half and we suffered a letdown.

"Meanwhile Iacavazzi went wild while I sat devastated on the end of the bench, wearing a parka with hood up and my head down. I couldn't even watch and never saw Iacavazzi throw the ball up into the stands after scoring one of his touchdowns. We lost 35-14, and that game is still in my craw.

"I was hospitalized for a few days and the following week I couldn't play against Harvard, a game we lost 18-14. It was a tough way to end the season and my Yale career.

Cosmo Iacavozzi (32) humbled the Bulldogs in '64 leading the Tigers to a 35-14 win. Yale's Pete Cummings (35), Greg Weiss (64) and captain Ab Lawrence (79) chase Iacavozzi as he heads to the end zone.
(YALE ATHLETICS)

Front Row L-R: Steve Lawrence, (end) Ab Lawrence (tackle), Ralph Vandersloot (guard), Tim Merrill (center), Chuck Benoit (guard), Dave Strong (tackle), Dan O'Grady (end). Back Row L-R: Robert Kenney (split end), Jim Groninger (halfback), Chuck Mercein (fullback), Jim Howard (halfback), and Tone Grant (quarterback).
(YALE ATHLETICS)

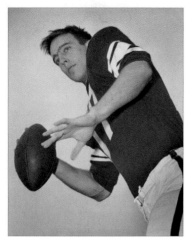

1964 Yale QB Ed McCarthy
(17) died in a car accidents two
months after he took his final
snap.
(YALE ATHLETICS)

"I met Cosmo for the first time in 2010 at the Waldorf Astoria in New York, where the Ivy League football dinner was held. I told him what a huge disappointment it was for me still (forty-six years later) that I was injured in that game and that I was unable to play in the second half and that I thought that if I had played the whole game, the outcome would have been quite different."

THE COZZA ERA BEGINS

Former Yale player and athletic director Ed Woodsum and former vice president and secretary of Yale University, Sam Chauncey, recall the hiring of Cozza.

ED WOODSUM

"I was on the Football Advisory Committee when coach John Pont left after the '64 season. Athletic Director Delaney Kiphuth interviewed a candidate for the position. The guy was a bright individual who was an assistant coach from a Southern school. Delaney explained to him that Yale was a non-athletic-scholarship program, but they did give financial assistance based on need. The candidate responded, 'You mean if you had a high school All-American quarterback who came from a wealthy family, you could not give him any aid? And if a third-string tackle qualified for financial assistance, you would give it to him? That's not only unfair; it is un-American!' He didn't get the job."

SAM CHAUNCEY

"I was on the committee that selected Pont and then Cozza. When we hired Pont, Joe Paterno, who was an assistant to Rip Engle at Penn State, was the runner-up. After Pont went to Indiana

the same committee was assigned to select a new coach. It was a short search. Half of us were enamored with Carm but felt we had an obligation to ask Paterno. We didn't necessarily want him but felt it was appropriate to contact him since he came in second when we hired Pont.

"Delaney Kiphuth and I were in the Carm camp. When Delaney offered Paterno the job, he did so without much enthusiasm. Based on the Yale offer, Engle got Penn State to make Paterno an associate head coach with the promise that he would get the head job when he retired. So Paterno stayed at Penn State and we hired Carm."

Carm Cozza (Head football coach, 1965-1996)

ORANGE, CONNECTICUT

Carmen Louis Cozza, an assistant under Pont, was hired in 1965 for the start of a thirty-two-year career that included ten Ivy League titles. Cozza was known for his modesty, dignity, and grace. He had an inner peace that was obvious to anyone who has ever met him. He was revered by his players. John Powers ('70) wrote, "Cozza had three daughters and nearly a thousand adopted sons," in reference to players who wore the Yale blue between 1965 and 1996.

"I never applied for the head coaching job at Yale and ended up here for thirty-two years. I was an assistant at Yale under John Pont in '63 and '64 and was offered the head job at the University of New Hampshire before the '65 season. I took my wife, Jean, and our two daughters up there, and it reminded us a lot of Oxford, Ohio, where my alma mater, Miami University, was located.

"But Delaney Kiphuth, the athletic director at Yale, called me and asked me to wait twenty-four hours before I accepted anything at New Hampshire.

"My first game [as Yale's coach] was a 13-6 loss to UConn. With two minutes left in the game, UConn's Gene Campbell picked off a Pete Doherty pass and went into the end zone. It was the first time UConn had ever defeated Yale. I was crushed and I second-guessed my ability. I got an awful lot of letters I'd like to forget. Most of them had nothing to do with the game. Instead they were about my religion, my nationality, and everything else. It was a very difficult time. Charley Loftus, the sports information director at the time, used to say that one alumnus wrote, 'There's a train leaving for New York at 4 o'clock; be under it.' But that wasn't true.

Lesson No. 1

"My first captain, Dave Laidley, taught me something. He was on the defensive side of the ball and I coached the offense. One day I got real upset with the defense. At the end of practice Dave asked if he could see me. He said, 'Aren't you our coach too?' Boy, did a light go on in my head! I said, 'Yes, I am.' From then on I went on both sides of the ball. Lesson No. 1 is you learn more from your kids than you do from any book or any clinic.

"I knew the defense was in solid shape with Bill Mallory, who was our coordinator. Bill went on to coach at Indiana and Colorado. He played for me when I was an assistant at Miami of Ohio.

The Jolly Green Giants

"In '65 we had two good defensive tackles known as the 'Jolly Green Giants,' Glenn Greenberg and Bob Greenlee. Greenlee was an exceptional player who could run like a deer. He was the first pick in the fourth round of the NFL draft, which is high for a defensive lineman. One day he came to practice with hip boots on. I said, 'What are you doing? This is a tough school. You just can't go out fishing and hunting.' He said, 'I like to do that, coach.' I said, 'So do I, but there's a time and a place.' Well, in those days we got the players' grades at the end of the semester, and Bob had five A's. So I never said another word to him.

"Bob had an opportunity to play in the NFL, but he was a great musician and ended up in the music business. I remember he played at Toad's Place. Unfortunately, Bob died of pancreatic cancer.

"Greenberg was the son of Hall of Fame baseball great Hank Greenberg. Ironically, Hank, who was the general manager of the Cleveland Indians in '52, signed me to a professional baseball contract when I graduated from college. I was signed as a pitcher, but because I had a strong arm and could run and hit, they made me an outfielder. I was traded to the White Sox organization the next year, and that's where my minor-league career ended. Hank came to New Haven to watch Glenn play a couple of times, but I never saw him.

"My first year, the quarterback with the strongest arm and the most athletic didn't move the ball like Watts Humphrey. Watts was the least athletic of the bunch, but he moved the chains."

Watts Humphrey
(Yale Athletics)

Watts Humphrey (quarterback) '63, '64, '65

PRESIDENT OF A PRIVATE COMPANY
PITTSBURGH, PENNSYLVANIA

Milty-to-Gilbert-to-Milty

"In '65, Carm Cozza's first year as head coach, I competed for the quarterback job along with Tone (pronounced Tony) Grant and Pete Doherty. I came into the Brown game, the third game of the season, with the game tied 0-0. We mounted a drive to set up the winning field goal. And that was the final score, which was Carm's first Ivy League victory. From that point on I was the regular quarterback. "Tone and I were very good friends. Jim Root, the quarterbacks coach, was a great guy who had a great sense of humor. Jim used to call me 'Gilbert,' and he would call Tone, 'Milty.' He designed a razzle-dazzle play called 'Milty-to-Gilbert-to-Milty' that involved the both of us. Tone would take the snap and I would line up at left halfback. I would sweep around the right side and Tone would lateral the ball to me. I would fake a run and pull up before the line of scrimmage and throw to ball to Tone, who ran up the opposite (left) sideline. It was a lot of fun, but it never worked.

A Family Tradition

"My father was a quarterback and a place-kicker at Yale. He kicked the tying point in the 9-9 game against Dartmouth in 1937. He was a Silver Anniversary All-American, an honor that combines business and football achievements. As for my brother George, who captained the '63 team,

he was one of the truly great Yale captains. He was an inspirational leader.

"My best all-around game was the '65 Cornell contest in the Bowl, when we won 24-14. I was voted the Ivy League Player of the Week. *Humphrey rushed 14 times for a team-high 93 yards and completed seven of 11 passes (one intercepted) for 91 yards.*

"The following week we lost to Dartmouth, 20-17, late in the game after giving up the lead. That was a tough one. My greatest disappointment was losing to Princeton and Harvard my senior year. In the Harvard game that we lost 13-0, there was no score at the half. I threw interceptions in the third and fourth quarters that were damaging. Both times Harvard took advantage of our turnovers and scored on short runs by Bobby Leo and Tom Choquette.

Thank You, Dr. Balme

"After graduation I enlisted in the military and was an infantry company commander in the United States Marines, serving in Vietnam. Little did I know that I would cross paths with a former great Yale player in a strange way. I was shot three times on separate occasions. In 1968 my unit was involved in operations south of Da Nang when I was hit by a rocket round of shrapnel. I was brought to a M.A.S.H. unit where Dr. Ben Balme, an All-America player at Yale in 1960, tended to me. I lost one-third of the muscle in my right forearm but if it wasn't for Dr. Balme, I might have lost the use of my arm. I was unconscious or delirious when I was brought in and I never did talk to Dr. Balme. Someday I would like to meet him and thank him for what he did for me."

Dr. Ben Balme at the 50th reunion of the 1960 team
(BILL O'BRIEN)

TOM SINGLETON (QUARTERBACK) '58, '59, '60

"After Ben Balme graduated from Yale Medical School he went into the Navy and volunteered to serve in a M*A*S*H unit in Da Nang, Vietnam. One day he was on duty when they wheeled in Watts. His arm had been shattered by grenade fragments. Ben said, 'I just watched this kid play football at Yale a year ago when I was at Yale Medical School, and here I am doing surgery on his arm.' Ben has been a renowned orthopedic surgeon in Portland, Oregon, for many years."

DON SCHARF

"When Watts Humphrey was rolled into the M.A.S.H. unit, Dr. Balme was told to let him go, he was too far gone. Ben wouldn't listen. Not only did he save his arm, he saved his life."

ROBERT LEWIS

"Tone Grant, a quarterback on Carm's first team in 1965 was a great guy. At Carm's retirement dinner, Tone asked all of his teammates from Carm's first team, including Bobby Lewis, 'our ball boy' to stand up. I was so honored!"

L-R kneeling: Tracy Whitaker (halfback) and Bill DuRoss (end); Standing: line coach Jay Fry, Tone Grant (quarterback) and Paul Kiernan (guard).
(YALE ATHLETICS)

SEVENTY FIVE CENTS
EST. PRICE .72   STATE TAX .03

OCTOBER 5
1 9 6 8

JAYCEE YOUTH DAY

COLGATE - YALE

OFFICIAL PROGRAM

CHAPTER 17
CHAPTER 17
THE DOWLING-HILL ERA

"What was so extraordinary about Dowling and his teammates was that somehow they managed to make football important (and even dear) at the very time American colleges were changing forever."

—Frank Deford, *Sports Illustrated*,
September 5, 2008

FOR MANY, THE period from the mid-1960s to the end of the decade marked the golden years of Yale football. The resurgence came at a time when Norman Rockwell's America was changing.

Only a few years earlier, a young American president had declared that "the torch has been passed to a new generation of Americans." One hundred days later, John F. Kennedy was assassinated.

A few years after he had led the March on Washington to promote civil rights, Martin Luther King Jr. was also murdered, and two months afterward Robert F. Kennedy met the same fate during his run for the presidency.

The Vietnam war triggered social and political upheaval throughout the country. In August 1968, as antiwar protesters chanted "the whole world is watching" at the Democratic National Convention, Chicago police used violence to break up the demonstration, with cameras rolling. The unrest was reflected on college campuses across the country, including Yale.

During this era of upheaval, Carmen Cozza and his staff assembled a team that would find a special place in Yale football history. The coaches recruited well early on, planting the seeds for a rich harvest in '67 with players like quarterback Brian Dowling and running back Calvin Hill. The two would become intrinsically linked in Yale football lore, as Kelley and Frank were in the 30s and McGill and Ward were in the 50s.

The 1967 and 1968 teams combined to go 16-1-1 with a conga line of talent. Yale won the Ivy championship in '67 and shared the title the next year with Harvard. During "The Game" in 1968, the Crimson had a near impossible mountain to climb, trailing the Bulldogs 29-13 with forty-two seconds remaining. The nightmarish 29-29 tie continues to haunt old Blues and has taken on a life of its own.

If Yale ever had an artist, it was Dowling, the magnificent quarterback. A skilled pianist, Dowling was the virtuoso of the Yale offense, and the Yale Bowl crowd noise was his chorus. He was the embodiment of Frank Merriwell, the fictional Yale athlete created by writer Burt L. Standish in his early 20th-century novels.

Dowling's record as a starting Yale quarterback was 15-0-1. But oh, that one tie!

Calvin Hill was a man among boys, arguably the greatest athlete in Yale history. He went on to an outstanding NFL career, spent mostly with the Dallas Cowboys. Former Dartmouth coach Bob Blackman said, "Calvin Hill is the only human being in the history of the human race to weigh more than 220 pounds and long-jump 25 feet. It's like trying to stop a locomotive."

THE PLAYERS

Brian Dowling (quarterback) '66, '67, '68 (Captain) '68

ENTREPRENEUR/BROADCASTER
NEW HAVEN, CONNECTICUT

A two-time first team All-Ivy selection in 1967 and 1968 and an honorable mention All-American in 1968, Brian Dowling finished ninth in Heisman voting in '68. He was the nation's Division I leader in passing efficiency in '68 with a 165.8 rating. He is currently Yale's career leader in passing efficiency with a 144.04 rating. During his Yale career, he completed 148 passes in 280 attempts, for 2,337 yards. He threw for 30 touchdowns, 19 of which came in '68. Dowling was drafted by the Minnesota Vikings in the 11th round of the 1969 NFL draft. He played with the Boston/New England Patriots (1970-1973) and Green Bay Packers (1977). In between he played for the New York Stars/Charlotte Hornets (1974-75) of the World Football League.

Brian Dowling. They said, "God Wears No. 10."
(Sabby Frinzi)

"I was heavily recruited out of St. Ignatius High School in Cleveland.

"Ohio State coach Woody Hayes put the full-court press on when he tried to recruit me. On his one allowed visit one evening, he spent four hours in our home. Woody had a lot of influence in the state of Ohio, which was manifested in a call from the governor's office. I was told that the governor wanted to pay me a visit. I had to ask my mother who the governor was. It was Jim Rhodes. Woody wasn't done yet. He got OSU alum Jack Nicklaus to invite me to play golf. Unfortunately, I was unable to accept playing with the legend, as a trip to USC was already scheduled.

"I vetoed Ohio State because they were predominantly a running team and I wanted to go to a school where a quarterback would do more than hand off. Paul Warfield, the Hall of Fame wide receiver, caught probably twenty passes in his career at Ohio State, where he played halfback. My father said to Woody, 'I can easily pay Brian's way to Ohio State should he decide to go there. Give the scholarship to a kid who needs it.' Woody answered, 'Mr. Dowling, you run your business your way and I'll run my business my way.'

"I loved Princeton's campus but wasn't wild about the single wing, primarily a running offense. In the summer of '64 my father and I visited the Yale campus. John Pont was the head coach but we found Carm, who was an assistant coach at the time, and he took us out to the Yale Bowl. He said, 'Wouldn't it be great to play in front of a full house at the Yale Bowl?' So I kept Yale as a favorite in the East.

"After the '64 season Pont went to Indiana University as their head football coach, and he invited me to attend a dinner in Cleveland with about 20 recruits. While I was there he pulled me aside and said, 'I still think you should go to Yale.' Finally my dad said, 'Why don't you go to Yale, and if you don't like it, I'll pay your way at one of the other schools.' I saw that guys like Mike Pyle and Bill Bradley had gone to Ivy League schools and were playing professional sports, which I found impressive. I also learned that Calvin Hill and Bruce Weinstein, two *Parade* All-Americans, were coming to Yale. My decision was made.

1965 Yale Freshman Team

"We had a very good freshman team and went undefeated. We had 125 players, including thirteen quarterbacks, six of which were all-staters. They moved one of the QBs, Calvin Hill, to running back and linebacker. Carm said that in his thirty-two years as Yale's head coach, Calvin is the only player who could have played all twenty-two positions.

1966: A Lost Season

"My sophomore year we opened the season with a 16-0 win over UConn. In the next game we played Rutgers in the Bowl and lost 17-14 on a very rainy day when I injured my knee and suffered ligament and cartilage damage. Calvin dislocated his elbow against Penn, so neither of us was there in losses to Princeton and Harvard, the season ending 4-5.

"The following year Lady Luck again was not on my side. While doing a tumbling drill I broke a metacarpal bone on my right hand 10 days before our first game against Holy Cross. I stood helplessly on the sidelines watching us lose 26-14, our only loss of the season. I dressed for the UConn game but didn't play. The next game, against Brown, I got in one play as a wide receiver, then started the following week against Columbia.

"When we beat Cornell 41-7 in our fifth game of the year, I think we realized that we had something special going. Then the next week we beat Dartmouth 56-15. Carm was at a loss of words when he met with us for our post-game meeting. After several seconds went by, middle guard Paul Tully shouted, 'See you Wednesday,' in reference to having a couple of days off from practice.

God Wears Number 10

"There was a lot of spirit on campus the week of the '67 Princeton game. They had beaten Yale six years in a row, and the Yale student body was wired. There were rallies that week and the mood was to smash the Tigers. I promised the students that if I scored, I would throw the ball up into the stands in retaliation of what Princeton running back Cosmo Iacavazzi did in the Bowl three years earlier when he fired the ball into the stands each time after he scored two touchdowns in the second half. In the first quarter we ran a play where Calvin rolled out and threw a pass to me for a touchdown. I kept my promise and tossed the ball up in the stands. We finally broke Princeton's hex with a 29-7 win.

"I wore No. 10, and it was after that game that the cry around the Yale campus was that 'God Wears No. 10.' It was raining for a time, and someone said I raised my hands with palms up and the rain stopped. Of course the story is apocryphal.

"Entering the Harvard game, we had already clinched the Ivy League title because every team had two losses in the league and we had none. The Bowl was packed with over 68,000 fans. They were even sitting in the aisles and it was a beautiful day. This is what I had imagined it would be like when I visited the Bowl with my dad in '64.

"We jumped to a 17-0 lead in the first half, with one of the touchdowns being a long pass to Calvin on a scramble play. He had an uncanny ability to get open on scrambles and was easily the best I played with in twenty years of amateur and professional football.

"In the second half Harvard dominated play. Vic Gatto scored on a 3-yard run and Harvard went ahead when Ric Zimmerman hit Carter Lord on a 31-yard touchdown pass to take the lead 20-17.

"We got the ball with 2:06 remaining in the game on our own 22. I handed off to Bob Levin for a 5-yard gain. Then I called a quick-out to Del Marting, who got a first down on our 35. On the next play I rolled out and threw back deep to Del. He caught it and ran 30 yards for the TD.

"Harvard roared back but fumbled on our 10 and we hung on to win 24-20 and remain undefeated in Ivy play.

"Following the season I was elected captain of the '68 team. To this day that remains the greatest thrill I had at Yale. I didn't expect to be chosen captain because quarterbacks are normally not picked.

"We entered the '68 season with a lot of optimism, as nine starters were returning on offense. We opened with wins against UConn and Colgate before meeting Brown in the third game of the season, when something weird happened that I'll never forget.

"I always wanted to make a long run. Once in high school I ran for a 70-yard touchdown but never had a long gain at Yale. In the Brown game I pulled off a 54-yard touchdown run off an option play to make the score 28-0 before the half. When I crossed into the end zone someone shot off a cannon; that was custom when we scored. The cannon was loaded with wads of paper, and I was hit on the side of the calf. I was not hurt but asked the cannon caretaker to please aim it in a different direction. Six times we scored thirty or more points in a game in '68. We had a very potent offense, outscoring our opponents 317-147.

"I had another first when I ran back two punts in the Princeton game that we won 42-17. Bob Sokolowski, who normally ran back punts, got hurt and Carm put me in. Carm had said that if I stayed healthy for the whole season, he would give me a chance to run back kicks. I ran one back for 42 yards and made no gain on the other. In that game Calvin bit his tongue, and he was in the infirmary the week before the Harvard game.

Doonesbury

"My notoriety has lived on as 'B.D.' in the 'Doonesbury' cartoon strip that was created by Garry Trudeau, who was at Yale at the same time. Everybody on the team loved it. It began in the *Yale Daily News* under the title 'Bull Tales.' I met Trudeau only once at Yale, at the end of the '68 season when he was putting his strips together for a book and asked if I would write a foreword for it.

Howard Cosell and the NFL

"Famed announcer Howard Cosell was on campus for a master's tea that fall and stopped by my room. Five years later, during a *Monday Night Football* game (Patriots vs. Colts), he remarked as I tried to make something out of a bad snap on a field goal attempt, that that kind of play may have worked in the Ivy League but would not work in the NFL.

"I played ten years of professional football and did fairly well in the limited opportunities I got, but the experience paled in comparison with my time at Yale. Because I got drafted in the late rounds, I don't think the decision makers ever had me in their long-term plans.

"If I have one regret from my Yale career, it is that I played in seventeen games out of a possible twenty-seven because of the injuries I had. I was so fortunate to have played with so many good players, never having finished a losing game going all the way back to eighth grade.

"Looking back, I know I was a part of a very special time in the history of Yale football, but 'Father Time' waits for nobody. About twenty-five years ago Calvin and I were reminiscing about the old days. Calvin said, 'Do you remember when those old alumni would come into the locker room? We used to call them old farts. Well, we're the old farts now.'"

Calvin Hill (tailback) '66, '67, '68

NFL PLAYER/SPORTS ADMINISTRATION CONSULTANT
GREAT FALLS, VIRGINIA

Calvin Hill was an All-Ivy first team selection in 1967 and 1968 and an honorable mention All-American in '68. During his Yale career he collected 1,512 yards rushing, 858 yards receiving, and 24 touchdowns; he also passed for 298 yards and six touchdowns. He holds Yale receiving records for a season (22.2 yards per catch) and career (18.8 yards per reception). In track and field, he still holds the Yale record for the triple jump (51' and 5 ¼').

Hill spent twelve years in the NFL, six of those years with the Dallas Cowboys. Twice he returned to the Bowl as a member of the Cowboys to play the Giants. The 1969 NFL Rookie of the Year and a four-time Pro Bowler, Hill also played for the Washington Redskins and Cleveland Browns. In 1972 he became the first Dallas running back ever to rush for 1,000 yards (1,036). He played in two Super Bowls with the Cowboys, including Super Bowl VI, where they defeated the Miami Dolphins for their first Super Bowl victory. In 1975 he played for the Hawaiians in the World Football League, returning to the NFL the following year. In his NFL career he rushed for 42 touchdowns and had 23 TD receptions. In 1975 Hill and former Yale running back Dick Jauron were Pro Bowl teammates. The Calvin Hill Day Care Center in New Haven is named in his honor.

"Although I am from Baltimore, I attended and boarded at Riverdale Country School in New York City. While there I was introduced to organized football and went on to become the quarterback of a team that was undefeated for fifty-one straight games. In addition, I played varsity baseball and basketball and participated in track.

"Because of my high school success, I was heavily recruited to play college football. I made my first Yale recruiting trip in the fall of 1964 during the Dartmouth weekend. I was hosted by Tone Grant ('66), one of the Yale quarterbacks. I had a wonderful time. It was a joyous weekend: Yale won, the Yale Bowl was filled to the brim and the atmosphere was electric. I always wanted to go to a college where I would play in a big stadium in front of large crowds. On that trip I also learned about Yale's storied football tradition including Walter Camp, Levi Jackson,

Clint Frank, Larry Kelley, and others. That weekend I was also introduced to former VP of Pan Am Alvin Adams ('24), who became my great personal friend and mentor until he died.

A Humble Beginning

"When I arrived as a freshman in the fall of 1965, I fully expected to be the quarterback of the freshman team. That assumption lasted four snaps into the first practice, at which time I was moved to linebacker and third-string fullback. My expectations were dashed. My disappointment was exacerbated

Calvin Hill was a talented runner and the 1969 No.1 draft choice of the Dallas Cowboys.
(SABBY FRINZI)

A quarterback in high school, Calvin Hill was often used as a passer at Yale.
(YALE ATHLETICS)

by my realization there were lots of smarter people in every class with me. During the first six weeks, I studied harder than I ever did in my life, earned C-pluses in my classes and played football behind Bob Sokolowski and Bob Levin, both of whom were running wild down the field. I didn't see a silver lining in the classroom or in practice. But fortunately for me, there were people such as Alvin Adams, Tone Grant, Ernest Thompson (dean of Stiles College), and John Hersey (master at Pierson College) who encouraged me to keep working, keep 'sawing wood' and not to lose faith.

"Fortunately things turned around and by the fifth freshman game, against Princeton, I started at fullback. I had possibly the best game of my football career, scoring five touchdowns, blocking a punt, intercepting a pass and causing a fumble on a tackle. At the same time, I improved academically.

"By sophomore year, my classmates and I were excited to follow up our undefeated freshman year with positions on the varsity team and the chance to

play on the hallowed grounds of the Yale Bowl. Despite the excitement over playing in the Bowl and on the varsity squad, the season was not what we expected. Our quarterback, Brian Dowling, was injured in an early game and I dislocated my elbow against Penn. We lost to Princeton and Harvard and, as any Yalie knows, those were unforgivable outcomes. The Yale Bowl ghosts were crying.

"We redeemed ourselves the next two years with sixteen straight wins, an Ivy League championship in 1967, and a co-championship in 1968 with You Know Who.

Two Jazz Musicians

"I've been asked if it ever bothered me that Brian (Dowling) seemed to get the most publicity even though I had a great career myself. The answer is no. Brian was the most self-effacing guy you'll ever meet. We were pretty close and were in the same fraternity (DKE). The longer we played together, a telepathic sense developed between us. We were able to improvise in the middle of a play and did it often. We were like two jazz musicians. If one started to improvise, the other knew exactly what to do. In '77 when I was with the Redskins, Brian was on the team for six weeks until mid-October, waiting for the deadline to be re-signed. He never did appear in a game. Then coach George Allen decided to go with just two quarterbacks—Billy Kilmer and Joe Theisman. In my opinion, Brian was better than both of them.

NFL Draft Was No Joke

"On the morning of the draft I had breakfast and returned to my room in Pierson and decided to call Bruce Weinstein, who was also expecting to get drafted. I thought I would have a little fun with Bruce by pretending I was Wellington Mara, the New York Giants owner. So I called Weinstein and, masquerading my voice, said, 'Congratulations, Bruce, I'm Wellington Mara. We have just drafted you for the New York Football Giants!'

"Bruce, who was from the New York metropolitan area, was very excited and began to thank me. He was talking about his dream coming true. I soon decided to let him know that it was only a joke. Bruce was furious that I would play such a joke. I'm glad we weren't in the same room. Bruce, who was later drafted by the Miami Dolphins, was a lot bigger than I but usually very gentle unless he was riled. On this day I had riled him.

"A half hour or so later my phone rang. I answered. The voice said, 'Hi, Calvin, this is Gil Brandt of the Dallas Cowboys. Congratulations, we've just drafted you in the first round.' I thought this was a joke, maybe Bruce's way of retaliating. But I played along. I talked to purported members of the Dallas press and to a guy named Tom Landry. I continued to play along

with the joke. I thought that Bruce, Brian Dowling, or Ed Franklin would call and say the joke was on me. The next call I received was from Bill Ahern of the *New Haven Register,* congratulating me on my being selected by the Cowboys. I soon received congratulations from all corners. It dawned on me that I may have been too cavalier, too smug in my phone conversations with the Dallas people. I might have said the wrong thing and perhaps offended Landry!

"Because I was too smart, I unwittingly played the biggest joke on myself.

"What a way to start a professional career!"

A Yale Degree

"Reminiscing about Yale, my greatest thrill was the day I received my Yale degree. At that moment I knew I was a Yale man. Following the ceremony on the Old Campus, we went back to our resident colleges to actually get the degree. I got it framed and gave it to my father. He was so proud of that. He put it in his bedroom so that would be the first and last thing he would see every day. My father, who had no formal education, was a construction worker from South Carolina, and my mother had a high school degree. Yet, they both understood the value of a strong education."

Del Marting (left end) '66, '67, '68
INVESTMENT BANKER
RENO, NEVADA

Del Marting was an All-Ivy first team selection in 1968. His father, Walter, scored a touchdown for Yale in the 1932 Harvard game giving Del and his father the distinction of being the only father-son Yale combo to score a touchdown against Harvard.

"I used to work out in the summer with Brian Dowling at the University School in Shaker Heights, Ohio, and would run different pass patterns. We worked

Del Marting (91) in end zone with ball scored the winning touchdown in Yale's 24-20 win over Harvard in '67. Calvin Hill (30) and Harvard's Tom Wynne (45) are in photo.
(New Haven Register)

well together. My senior year Brian threw twenty-three passes to me and there were no incompletions, none were dropped and none over- or under-thrown.

"The touchdown I scored at the end of the '67 Harvard game is remembered by a lot of people, probably by more than could possibly have been at the game. We were down 20-17 late in the last quarter when Brian called a roll out play to his right. I lined up at the left end spot and Bruce Weinstein lined up at right end. Bruce would run a short route and curl back and Calvin Hill would run a deeper route on the same side. I was the third target on the left side. I was supposed to go down and come across the middle of the field.

"Harvard was focusing on Bruce and Calvin. We were all supposed to release on the snap. I figured if I hesitated a second or two, Harvard might forget about me which is what happened. Harvard's defensive back Mike Ananis took off toward Hill and Weinstein. Brian rolled out and saw that I was wide open. I caught the pass and ran 30 yards for the touchdown. Ananis recovered but it was too late. He hit me but didn't really stop me and I made it into end zone. Ironically, we were good friends who both went to Exeter.

"Two things people forget about that game. (1)

With two minutes remaining Harvard rallied behind quarterback Ric Zimmerman and got down to our 10-yard line when Ken O'Connell fumbled and Pat Madden recovered, really saving the game; and (2) I scored the first as well as the last Yale touchdowns that game. The first one came in the second quarter when I recovered a fumble by teammate Jim Fisher for the touchdown. Cozza actually used to make the ends practice a 'fumble recovery' route on the goal line. None of us ever expected it would come into play and Jimmy didn't so much as fum-

Del Marting's father, Walter, scored a Yale touchdown in the 1932 Harvard game.
(Yale Athletics)

ble as cough it up when he was hit at the goal line and the ball kind of just floated into my hands in mid-air and I fell into the end zone. On our other touchdown, a run by Calvin, I actually threw the down field block on the Harvard d-back that sprung him loose. Somehow the stars must have been aligned that afternoon!

"It was a thrilling day but the most important thing was being together with my teammates and how we all celebrated a great victory!"

Bruce Weinstein (tight end) '66, '67, '68

Nursing homes owner
Palm Beach Gardens, Florida

Bruce Weinstein was an All-Ivy first team selection in 1968. He ranks tied for eighth place in touchdown receptions for Yale with 11.

Bruce Weinstein
(SABBY FRINZI)

"The night before the Brown game my senior year, tackle Gyle Gee and I tooled around New Haven on his new Triumph Bonneville motorcycle. The two of us, with a combined weight around 500 pounds, dwarfed the bike. We looked like a couple of trained bears in the circus. We stopped at a red light on the corner of Tower Parkway and Dixwell Avenue in New Haven. When the light turned green, Kyle gave it the gas. The front wheel of the cycle came up pointed at the sky and we almost wiped out. We were absolutely sober with kickoff less than twenty-four hours away. If we ever got injured, I don't think our coaches would have been very happy."

Ted Livingston (tackle)
'65, '67, '68

SENIOR MARKETING EXECUTIVE FOR A CABLE TV COMPANY
BROOKLINE, MASSACHUSETTS

George W. Bush's Roommate

"I guess my claim to fame is that I was the roommate of George W. Bush, the 43rd U.S. president. George,

who was born in New Haven, was the president of DKE (Delta Kappa Epsilon), a jock fraternity that had the reputation as the most boisterous frat on campus. George liked to party, but he wasn't much different from any other student in that respect. There are some accounts of George being arrested at the 1967 Yale-Princeton game in New Jersey, but I don't think it's true. He allegedly was arrested for sitting on a goal post and refusing to come down after Yale had defeated Princeton to end Princeton's six-year jinx over Yale. There was no doubt that he was sitting on the goal post. I've seen a picture of him hanging from the goal post, but as to anything else, I don't believe it. It has also been falsely written that he was a cheerleader at Yale. George was a cheerleader at Andover, where he prepped before coming to Yale.

Ted Livingston (75), Jack Perkowski (59), Fred Morris (50) and Kyle Gee (70) block for Brian Dowling (10) in the '68 Yale-Harvard game. The Harvard players are Lonny Kaplan (77) and Steve Zebal (52).
(SABBY FRINZI)

A Tumultuous Time

"Ninteen-sixty-eight was the beginning of a tumultuous time on campus as the Vietnam war raged on. I couldn't believe the impact that the football team had on the student body during this difficult time. They came out to the Bowl every week in droves and supported a great team. And there was no division among the players concerning those who were in favor or against the war. I was in the Marine Corps Reserves in 1966, and I never encountered any protest regarding my involvement in the military.

Deep Roots

"My dad, who was a swimmer and was on the crew at Yale, began taking me to Yale games in 1956. My Yale roots are deep and I lived Yale football in one of its greatest eras. I've been fortunate!

"I enjoy collecting and have 575 Yale game day programs. They are jewels of Yale football history. I have every one from 1940-1985 and many before that. I have some rare ones like the 1909 Yale-Princeton and the 1913 Yale-Harvard programs. My father handed down many he had collected and I continued the collection when I played."

Bob Sokolowski (running back; punt and kickoff returner) '66, '67, '68

ATTORNEY; BIG EAST FOOTBALL OFFICIAL
MERIDEN, CONNECTICUT

"Brian Dowling was the best overall athlete that I've ever played with. He had an aura and mystique about him that willed himself to win. When they said, 'God wears No.10,' that was true.

"In the spring of '69, I captained the baseball team and played left field while Brian, a .300 hitter, played

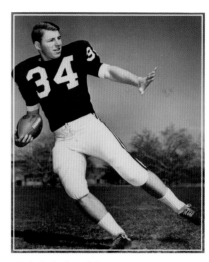

Bob Sokolowski
(SABBY FRINZI)

alongside me in center field. The team was returning to Connecticut from our southern trip to Florida and stayed in a small motel in North Carolina. Brian and I were roommates and when we saw that there was just a double bed in the room, he said, ' 'Sok,' let's flip for it.' I said, 'No way, B.D. When you're the C-A-P-T you don't sleep on the floor.' Guess who slept on the floor?

"The next morning B.D. told coach Ken MacKenzie how he spent the night on the floor. MacKenzie thought it was hilarious and mentions the story to me to this day whenever I run into him on the Yale golf course.

"I played football at Choate with Michael Douglas, the popular actor. His father, Kirk, another great actor, would sometimes visit the campus. I was amazed that he was a small guy. He comes across much taller in the movies. He was only about 5-feet-5.

"In '67 Calvin got dinged running back a punt. Carm decided that he was too valuable to be running back kicks and punts, so I replaced him our final two years, and that's where I got my little niche on the team.

"One of my highlights was running back the opening kickoff of the '67 Princeton game to the Princeton 40. It was a bad weather day at Palmer Stadium, but I helped to put us in a good position to score early, which we did. In the '67 Cornell game we made them punt six times in our 41-7 win and I was able to return all punts for 77 yards. I never called for a fair catch in my collegiate career. I didn't get to play that much, so when I got in there I put my hands on the ball and tried to do something with it.

Paper Bulldog

"I'll never forget the time Jon Stein, the sports writer from the *New Haven Register,* did a George Plimpton-type story. He put on the pads and scrimmaged with us. He was positioned at linebacker and the guys ran a couple of plays right at him. Needless to say, he didn't last very long.

"Hello George"

"In 1991 Carm Cozza was honored for his 25th anniversary as the Yale head football coach. It was a black-tie affair in New York and I went with Vincent Morrissey, who is the clock operator at the Bowl. We had hors d'oeuvres and mingled socially. George W. Bush was there and had a Secret Service guy with him because his father was president of the United States. George and I were both in Delta Kappa Epsilon and he recognized me. I said, 'Hi George, how are you doing?' He said, 'Hi, Sok, how are you?' I then asked, 'What are you doing these days?' He answered, 'I'm the president of the Texas Rangers.'

"Morrissey could not believe that I didn't know that. Well, I didn't."

REMEMBERING THE DOWLING–HILL ERA

CARMEN COZZA, HEAD COACH (1965-1996)

"Brian Dowling called his own plays. We met with him every Wednesday and went over downs and distance and our place on the field with Jim Root, the offensive coordinator. We discussed what we wanted on various plays. He was like a road map but he would improvise. I always felt when you rushed him, you were in trouble because he would use everybody to screen for him. He almost got me killed a couple of times in practice doing that. During games he would even use a referee to screen for him. Then he would find Hill, Weinstein or somebody else.

"Brian didn't have the greatest arm because he had broken his collarbone when he was in the sixth grade and he couldn't get his arm all the way up. But he had great wrists and he saw more of the field than any kid I've ever seen. He used everybody too. He had that Fran Tarkenton knack. I don't know if he ever got sacked.

"The student body was at fever pitch the week of the Princeton game in '67. The day we left for Princeton with a chance to clinch the Ivy League championship, the passion of the student body ran high. There had to be 100 or more people outside the bus. They rocked the team bus back and forth and were throwing oranges. I thought the students were going to tip over the bus. So I said to the driver, 'Let's get out of here before we get dumped.'

"During the week of the game, I kiddingly said to Brian Dowling, 'If we are safely ahead, I want you to throw the ball into the stands to their president.' The very first score we caught them in man coverage in the red zone. Calvin rolled to his right and threw the ball back to Brian. Dowling caught the ball on a dead run and went to the far corner of the end zone and threw the ball up in the stands. But being on the sidelines, we have the worst seat in the house and I never saw him throw the ball into the stands until I saw the film. I couldn't believe it. He threw the damn ball up in the stands on the first touchdown of the game.

"Calvin was the one guy that could have started at every position. Because of his size, speed, and jumping ability, I don't know of a position in college at that time that he couldn't have played. The week of the '68 Harvard game Calvin was in the infirmary until Thursday. He had bit his tongue in the Princeton game the week before and had an infection. But I wasn't worried about it because he was so good I knew he was going to play. He was a quarterback in high school. His senior year at Yale he accounted for 12 scores either throwing, two point conversions or touchdowns.

"Defensively we were solid but not as good as we were in the early '80s."

NORMAN BENDER ('68)

"By the fall of 1967 the Bulldogs had lost six straight games to Princeton. Additionally frustrating was the fact that their young Lochinvar of a quarterback, Brian Dowling, had been hurt and unable to play in the '66 Princeton game.

"At a rally the week of the game, the students were at fever pitch. Brian came out on the balcony of his upper floor dorm room and his classmates got rowdier still. We could see campus police gathering, obviously becoming concerned but Brian did then as he was to do two days later on the football field, he took over. He held his arms up in a papal gesture as the crowd drew silent. He spoke briefly but to the point and said, 'I have never met anyone from Princeton but know I wouldn't like them very much.'

"We all hollered louder still. He then held up an orange, hesitated and crushed it against the wall: the crowd burst loose. Almost immediately and quite happily everyone dispersed and Brian's gesture was quite prophetic as Dowling, Hill, and company were to convincingly whip Princeton two days later. But anyone who had witnessed that scene Thursday night was already convinced."

BUD SMITH

"I have a piece of the goal post from the 1967 Yale-Princeton game at Palmer Stadium. My late son, Paul, was there with us and he got a piece of the goal post after the game."

AL BATTIPAGLIA, YALE TRAINER

"One time Brian Dowling broke his nose in a game. As the team doctor and I took him off the field, Brian pointed to his nose and kept saying, 'U.S,' 'U.S.' The doctor had no idea what Brian was trying to say but I knew. He was simply saying 'Ugly Squad,' 'Ugly Squad.' He wanted to be put on the 'All-Ugly Squad.' Heck, Brian was a handsome guy. I wasn't going to put him on that team."

REMEMBERING THE 29-29 TIE GAME

THE '68 YALE-HARVARD game was played in Boston on an unseasonably warm day under a blue windless sky. Both teams entered "The Game" undefeated and untied. Yale, the favorite, cruised to a 22-0 halftime lead aided by Brian Dowling, Calvin Hill and Del Marting touchdowns. In the second half Harvard coach John Yovicsin

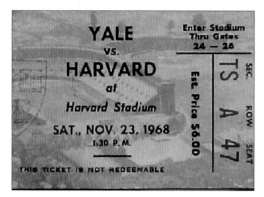

Ticket for the November 23, 1968, Yale-
Harvard game
(YALE ATHLETICS)

replaced quarterback George Lalich with Frank Champi who brought the Crimson to within 22-13 on TDs by Bruce Freeman and Gus Crim. Dowling then scored in the fourth quarter on a five-yard run to make it 29-13 after Bob Bayless converted the extra point.

With forty-two seconds remaining in the game, Freeman scored again on a 15-yard pass from Champi before Crim ran it over for two points making the score 29-21. Harvard's Bill Kelly then recovered an onside kick at the Yale 49. With three seconds remaining in the game, Harvard subsequently scored on a pass from Champi to Vic Gatto (29-27). Champi then found future major league catcher Pete Varney in the end zone for the tying two-point conversion.

The *Harvard Crimson* bannered, "Harvard Beats Yale, 29-29."

CARMEN COZZA

"In '68 we were undefeated and ranked 18th by UPI going into the Harvard game. We were heavy favorites to beat Harvard. But everything that could go wrong in a game did in two minutes and forty seconds which ended in the 29-29 tie. There was an inadvertent whistle, a couple of questionable calls, and a fumble that a Harvard player picked up. Our kids stopped because they heard whistles and so did I. The clock never started on the kickoff when there were forty-two seconds left. Many say that was the greatest game of all time. But it was not to me.

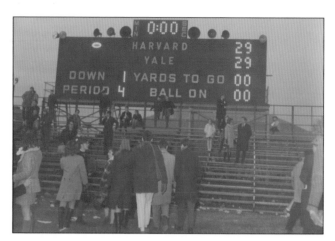

The scoreboard tells the story in the dusk of Harvard Stadium.
(SABBY FRINZI)

"When Harvard got to within eight points [29-21], they recovered an on-side kick on our 49. Dowling and Hill pleaded with me to put them in the game on defense. We were in a three-deep setup and I could have sent them on the field. They were very good athletes. But it would have meant taking two players out of the game. I don't know which two we would have taken out, but it would have destroyed two young men if we had taken them out.

Tackle Kyle Gee (70), a two-time All-Ivy first team selection, blocks for Nick Davidson (44) in the '68 Yale-Harvard game.
(YALE ATHLETICS)

"I've been asked if Brian threw the ball too much that game and perhaps could have used the clock more when we had a good lead. There's two schools of thought. One is we turned the ball over seven times. We made some costly mistakes. But this team was a free-wheeling type of team, which is why I didn't want to correct Brian [on his play calling]. I told him to run our offense like he always did. Statistically we killed them. It was the turnovers and the calls [that decided the game]. Somebody upstairs wanted this game to end in a tie, because there's no way it could ever happen again.

"I have also been questioned about the players we had on the field to defend the onside kick when we fumbled. I have been criticized for not having enough players on the front line with good hands. Keep in mind that the player who fumbled [Brad Lee] was a pitcher on the baseball team who had good hands. I think this

Dowling connects with Calvin Hill on three yard TD pass in second quarter of '68 Harvard game. Bob Levin (41) and Harvard's Steve Renere (89) are also in photo.
(YALE ATHLETICS)

idea of putting players with the best hands on the front line for onside kicks is overdone. You want some big bodies there also to absorb the hits. Looking back, I'm satisfied with the group we had on the field at the time.

"During my tenure at Yale we lost three games at Harvard with less than two minutes to play. I think my greatest disappointment might have been the '68 tie game or losing the last game I ever coached, when Harvard beat us up there on November 23, 1996. I ripped the team at halftime as we were getting blown out. We came back but lost 26-21."

BRIAN DOWLING

"Some critics said that I passed too much and didn't use the clock in the 29-29 tie game against Harvard. I did not feel a two-touchdown lead was excessive, even with three minutes left, and was not in the habit of sitting on a lead.

"During the final drives by Harvard, Calvin and I asked Carm if we could go in on defense. I had played safety in high school and some as a freshman, and Calvin was such a great athlete, he could have played anywhere. Carm rejected the idea because it would have demonstrated a lack of confidence in his defense and be psychologically damaging.

"A lot had to happen for Harvard to score two touchdowns in the last two minutes, and they all did."

CALVIN HILL

"As for that game, which Harvard declared a victory, I have my own take. In sports lore, a tie is said to be like 'kissing your sister.'

The fact that the Harvards celebrated that tie substantiates what I've always thought of the Harvard character or lack thereof.

"That weekend was not a total loss because after the game I met my wife, Janet, at a party. She was with a Harvard guy, so there was no heavy lifting associated with impressing her. We have been married forty-three years.

"The bizarre thing about that Harvard game is I thought we had lost until I read of the tie in the *Yale Daily News* the following Monday in New Haven. I was initially shocked, but then relieved that we had at least won a share of the Ivy League title."

Ted Skowronski, Harvard center ('66-'68)

ATTORNEY
SOUTHBURY, CONNECTICUT

"Emotions were high on the campus the week before the '68 game as both Yale and Harvard were undefeated. The Harvard players were each given four tickets. My roommate sold his for $50 apiece. Because of all the hoopla and commotion, the night before the game coach [John] Yovicsin decided to take the team to Framingham, Massachusetts, which is twenty miles west of Boston. We watched the movie *Von Ryan's Express,* starring Frank Sinatra. It was inspirational in regard to the overly matched Americans trying to get through the German lines on a train. Don't forget that Yale was heavily favored to beat us.

"George Lalich was the starting quarterback that game for us, but Frank Champi replaced him for the start of the second half. Lalich was very upset about this and has not returned to Harvard for many functions. And oddly enough, Champi did not play his senior year. I understand he had a falling out with Yovicsin.

"Following the game a wire photo was taken of my girl friend, Ellen Loggee, and me on the field. It went all over the country. I was interviewed by the *New Haven Register,* and it was special because as a kid I delivered that paper. My brother Bob was captain of the Green Bay Packers and his games were always the most important in our family, but after that game he called me and for the first time I felt that my game was more important than his.

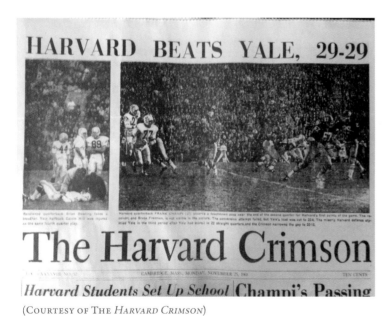

HARVARD BEATS YALE, 29-29

Harvard Students Set Up School | **Champi's Passing**

(COURTESY OF THE *HARVARD CRIMSON*)

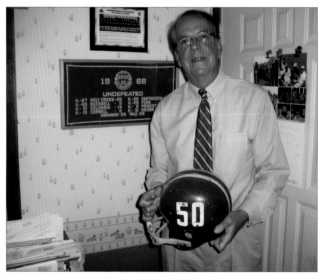

Harvard center Ted Skowronski holds the helmet he wore in the '68 Yale-Harvard game.
(DON KOSAKOWSKI)

Harvard's Vic Gatto scores the TD to make the score 29-27. The Yale player on Gatto is Don Martin. Other Yale players include Ed Franklin (15), Tom Neville (79) and Dick Williams (63). Harvard players include Ted Skowronski (50) and Fritz Reed (75).
(YALE ATHLETICS)

famous in the arts. Such prominent names as Henry Thoreau and Jack Lemon have been honored by having their names on the wall.

"The movie about the '68 game [*Harvard Defeats Yale, 29-29*] was made in 2008 and premiered the night before the '08 Yale-Harvard game at the Brattle Theater in Harvard Square. It was forty years later, and almost every player from both teams was present. Following the movie there was a panel discussion, which continued in a hotel bar after the theater had closed. For the most part, the players from that '68 game had never met, yet a strong bond was produced."

Gene Skowronski, Harvard Guard ('62, '64)

ATTORNEY
DERBY, CONNECTICUT

Gene Skowronski received honorable mention for the AP All-East team in 1964.

"I still love the Yale-Harvard game and all that goes with it. Who can forget the '68 game? It was a thrill to watch my brother Ted, who was the center on that team.

"Every play of a Yale-Harvard game is like Armageddon. It is so intense. During the week leading up to the game, there are no rallies and bonfires. However, the Harvard fight songs sound throughout the locker room, and a photo of the Yale player that you would be playing against is taped to your locker."

"Our locker room was pandemonium and we didn't want to leave. It was a tie game, but we felt like we won. We partied at Winthrop House until 5 or 6 in the morning, and many didn't attend classes for a week.

"The weekend following the game, the Harvard Club of New York flew down members of the football team for a special dinner and the showing of the game.

" Actor Tommy Lee Jones was a starting guard on our team. At times he would show up to practice in his acting outfits. He flies up for every Yale-Harvard game in Boston and hosts a dinner at a club, the Signet Society, which honors Harvard alumni who are

---

THEY REMEMBER

JON STEIN

"My first Harvard game was 1968, which spoiled me for all the rest: 29-29, an outcome that lives

in infamy at Yale and is a cherished Harvard memory. Never did I see a team as devastated as Yale.

"First, a little name-dropping. I lived in a co-operative apartment on Elm Street in New Haven, where I got to know Yale senior Jonathan Weiner. He suggested I interview Harvard All-Ivy guard Tom Jones, an old friend of his from St. Mark's School in Dallas. 'He's a wild man, he rides his motorcycle in Mexico during the summer and he's an actor,' Weiner said. When I called, the man who answered may have been Al Gore, Jones' roommate. He handed the phone to Jones, who predicted 'an hellacious game.' He wasn't wrong. The next I heard of Harvard's guard, he was calling himself 'Tommy Lee Jones' and drawing his paycheck in Hollywood. And of course, Gore became vice president of the United States in the Clinton administration.

"My assigned seat for the Yale-Harvard game was next to Red Smith, the great sportswriter who was between newspapers and was writing a syndicated column. Smith left early and never saw one of the wildest finishes in college football history. I was curious to read his column and bought the *Boston Herald*, which carried it. Smith wrote about only what he saw, which was equivalent to writing about the final game of the 1951 National League playoffs and not mentioning Bobby Thomson's home run.

"At the post game press conference, Carm Cozza had a tough time keeping his composure. He kept looking up to the ceiling in an effort to restrain his comments about the officiating.

"For me, Yale has never had a better combo than Brian Dowling and Calvin Hill. The '68 Harvard game tarnished their legacy, but only a little bit."

DON HARRISON

As sports editor and later executive sports editor of the *Waterbury Republican-American*,

I covered more than 100 Yale games during a 14-season span (1968-81).

The most memorable? Easy answer. The unfathomable 'Harvard Beats Yale, 29-29' tie at Boston in 1968. Brian Dowling, the living, breathing 'B.D.,' passed for two touchdowns and ran for two more scores on that long-ago Saturday afternoon. Yale's lead, 29-13, seemed secure. Alas, the fates—and perhaps the timekeeper—conspired against the Elis in the final 42 seconds. Remember, no time elapsed between the Harvard touchdown and 2-point conversion at the 42- second mark and the Crimson's recovery of an onside kick."

JOEL SMILOW '54

"After the disaster we went to a party where ninety-nine percent of the crowd was Harvard people. It was as bad a night as I ever spent in my life. I refused to watch the 2008 documentary, *Harvard Beats Yale 29-29*, the first year it came out. The game was like a bad dream. When I finally watched it, I still thought Yale would win when we're ahead by 16 points with less than two minutes to play."

CHARLIE YEAGER '52, MANAGER/END

"Sixteen years after I made my appearance against Harvard, I was in Harvard Stadium in '68 for the 29-29 game. I took former New England Patriots owner Billy Sullivan, his wife, Mary, and their son, Patrick, to the game. I tailgated with Bob Anderson, the great Yale recruiter out of Chicago, before and after the game. Following the heartbreaking ending he lamented, 'Our ice cream turned to shit.'"

BUD SMITH

"The height of my passion for Yale football was the Dowling-Hill era. I was at the 29-29 tie game. That was a terrible day. It was the biggest hurt I ever had as a Yale fan. It was a loss."

The Harvard Toilet Seat

"My late wife Lee, who became a rabid Yale football fan, decorated the walls of a bathroom in our house by pasting covers of Yale game day programs we had accumulated over the years. We used to exchange gifts with Eddie Silver, a friend from West Haven. One year Eddie gave us a Harvard toilet seat that I've been sitting on for over 30 years. There is a Yale helmet on the overhead lamp above the toilet that symbolizes Yale over Harvard. I think my wife built our house around the Harvard toilet seat."

BILL KAMINSKY, YALE TRAINER 1969-2010

"I remember standing on the sidelines next to Brian Dowling at the 1999 Yale-Harvard game in the Bowl. He was still as competitive as when he played. When Eric Johnson caught the winning touchdown pass from Joe Walland there was twenty-nine seconds left in the game. The number twenty-nine brought back haunting memories of the 1968 29-29 tie game. Brian didn't say a word and neither did I. "

MICHAEL AMATO

"I graduated from the University of New Haven and served in the Vietnam War from March 17, 1968, to March 15, 1969. I heard about the 29-29 tie game on Armed Forces Radio and from letters sent to me by my brothers and friends, who attended the game. They stated that I missed the greatest game ever played. That stung. A few weeks later my neighbor sent me a copy of the November 24, 1968, edition of the *New Haven Register* that covered the game. When I received the *Register,* everyone in my platoon wanted to read the articles. Put simply, it was the greatest game I never saw."

ROBERT LEWIS

"In '68 I was a cheerleader at Lafayette but went to the famed tie game at Harvard on Nov. 23 rather than cheer against Lehigh, our rival. My gut told me I had to attend that game after Charley Loftus had referred to me as "Yale's good luck charm" when he saw me on the sidelines the week before as Yale beat Princeton, 42-17. I guess I wasn't."

SABBY FRINZI

"I got a great shot of Brian Dowling with his hand in a Harvard's player's face. I cried after that game."

THE YALE CLASS of '68 never did achieve their expected perfection. Again, like the '21 and '37 teams, the Bulldogs met their Waterloo on Harvard turf. But the Dowling-Hill teams of '67 and '68 will have an everlasting legacy that unified a campus and a fandom that perhaps will never be seen again.

Bob Milligan hauls in a touchdown pass in Yale's 21-3 win over Penn in 1969.
(YALE ATHLETICS)

CHAPTER 18

THE IMPROBABLE '69ERS

"We've helped [the program] because we haven't broken the tradition of winning."

—Andy Coe (1969 Yale Captain)

IN JULY 1969, Neil Armstrong became the first man to walk on the moon. Later that year it appeared that Carmen Cozza could walk on water when he took a cadre of no-name players and won a share of the Ivy League title. The accomplishment was a rebuke to critics who'd claimed that Cozza had won previously solely because of outstanding players like Brian Dowling and Calvin Hill.

Dowling had been drafted by the Minnesota Vikings in '69 but was cut by the team in training camp. Hill was on his way to earning NFL rookie of the year honors and making the first of four Pro Bowls with the Dallas Cowboys.

Back in New Haven, the '69 Bulldogs started eleven sophomores and several players had changed positions. On paper this was earmarked as a rebuilding year but nobody got the memo. The heartbeat of this team was special. Led by captain Andy Coe, the Elis won a share of the Ivy title giving Cozza three straight championships. Quarterback Joe Massey, who quit the freshman team to join the glee club, returned in '68 as a third string quarterback but did a yeoman's job in '69.

The war raged on in southeast Asia, and in a show of solidarity with antiwar demonstrators several Yale football players sent a letter of protest to the *New York Times*. The Sixties were coming to an end, but social unrest in the United States continued. So did Yale's winning ways on the football field.

THE PLAYERS

Andy Coe (linebacker) '67, '68, '69 (captain)

CHIEF GOVERNMENT AND COMMUNITY RELATIONS OFFICER FOR
STANFORD HOSPITAL AND CLINICS
PALO ALTO, CALIFORNIA

Andy Coe was an All-Ivy first team selection in 1969.

Woody Knapp, who lettered in '62, '63 and '64, is the only Yale football player to lose his life in Vietnam. An award in his honor is given to a Yale football player each year. (YALE ATHLETICS)

"I grew up in Hamden, Connecticut, listening to the great Yale teams of the '50s and early '60s over WELI. I was a neighbor of Bob Blanchard and used to play football on his parents' lawn. I sold programs at the Bowl for a couple of years when I was a kid, getting into the game for free after the first quarter as payment for selling the programs. My prime spot was outside Portal 16, the 50-yard line on the Yale side. I used to get the players' autographs as they emerged from the tunnel after the games. Who would think that a few years down the road the role would be reversed?

"My family moved to Wilmette, Illinois, for my high school years, where I was fortunate to go to New Trier High School, home of what seemed to be half the starting lineup of the '60 team as well as other Yale greats.

A Hard Hit

"The hardest I ever got hit by a running back was by Calvin Hill in a preseason scrimmage when I was a sophomore. But the hit I put on him impressed the coaches, which led me to starting as a sophomore. Watching Hill and Brian Dowling those years was something. Brian could weave magic.

Andy Coe, 1969 captain
(YALE ATHLETICS)

"Bill Narduzzi, our defensive coordinator, was the coach that I had most contact with. He was known as 'The Doozer.' He would say things like, 'That's not rain, it's liquid sunshine.' Or, if we were doing terribly on defense, he would say, 'Gentlemen, this defense is horseshit.' Guys on the team like J.P. Goldsmith would do a great job of imitating him. I loved The Doozer.

The Surprising '69 Team

"Not many expected us to do much my senior year in '69 after Dowling, Hill, and company departed, but we surprised a lot of people. Our quarterback, Joe Massey, did a super job for us. Defensive end Jim Gallagher had a season for a lifetime. Ron Kell had a great year as my running mate at linebacker. Tom Neville was an outstanding defensive tackle and an eventual Rhodes Scholar. He had an amazing mind for numbers. Frannie Boyer, a backup linebacker, dubbed Neville 'The Computer' at a time when computers were not well known to the general public.

"Going into the Harvard game, our only chance for a share of the Ivy title was if we beat Harvard and Princeton beat Dartmouth. We beat Harvard in the Bowl 7-0 as Bill Primps scored the only touchdown of the game. Late in the third quarter we got word that Princeton was crushing Dartmouth in Hanover. Dartmouth had beaten us earlier. But Princeton ended up beating Dartmouth, and we finished in a three-way tie with Princeton and Dartmouth for the Ivy league title. It was a great way to end my football career.

A War Protest

"In '69 the Vietnam war did create a lot of division among the student body as students did take both sides. Most were against the war, as were most players on the team, as I recall. In the spring of my senior year I drew the number 137 in the draft lottery. I eventually obtained "CO"—conscientious objector status—from the Selective Service System. My father was a minister, as were several other family members, and we had strong religious and moral feelings about war. University President Kingman Brewster and Yale Chaplain Bill Coffin demonstrated terrific leadership during this very difficult time. I'll always remember Kingman in the Bowl wearing his fur coat and sitting just above the tunnel where we entered and exited. He was always cheering us on.

"On the same day as the Princeton game in '69 there was going to be a large anti-Vietnam war march in Washington. On the Sunday before the game I talked to Carm and Athletic Director Delaney Kiphuth about the possibility of providing a vehicle to express support for the march for those that wanted to. Our first commitment, of course, was to play in the game that same day. One idea was to wear black armbands. Delaney said that rather than wearing armbands, why don't you put together a letter and get signatures. Then we'll get it published in the *New York Times,* which is what happened. About two-thirds of the team signed the letter.

"I didn't know how the team would react against Princeton. Would the letter be a distraction? Would it affect the morale of the team? The answer to both questions was no. The Princeton game was a gem. We played the best team game I was ever involved in, and we won 17-14. It was in Princeton at Palmer Stadium, which made it doubly sweet."

Bill Primps (fullback) '68, '69, '70

ATTORNEY
OSSINING, NEW YORK

"Joe DiMaggio and Marilyn Monroe married in 1954 and honeymooned in Japan. While in the Far East, Marilyn made a side trip to Korea to entertain the troops. When she returned she said, 'Joe, you never heard such cheering.' The Yankee Clipper replied, 'Yes, I have.'

"I can say that I have experienced on numerous occasions the 'Joe DiMaggio moment' of cheering and roaring crowds during my football career at Yale. One of the funny things about the Bowl is that a huge crowd there makes a lot of noise but the size of the Bowl diffuses the crowd noise. At Harvard Stadium or the former Palmer Stadium, the crowd echoes more, maybe because the stands are more vertical.

"For me, the crowd noise magical moment in the Bowl was the '69 Harvard game, when I scored the only touchdown of the game and we beat Harvard 7-0 before over 62,000 roaring fans. Don't forget that this game was played the year after the horrendous 29-29 tie game. It had a little extra edge to it. At halftime the game was scoreless when our captain, Andy Coe, came over to the offensive room and said, 'Just get us one touchdown.'

"Harvard took the opening kickoff of the second half and moved the ball to about the 50-yard line. They punted and we began an 80-yard drive, covering 10 plays, the biggest of which was a Don Martin 36-yard run that got us over midfield to the Harvard 43. Quarterback Joe Massey then ran for 10 before throwing to Lew Roney over the middle for a significant gain. Lew was flagrantly fouled by a Harvard late hit, which brought the ball half the distance to the goal line, down to the 6. It was first and goal on the 6 in a scoreless game.

"The first two plays I ran were off tackle smashes to the left behind strong double team blocks by Roney and Earl Matory. It was third and goal on the two. I was set in my fullback stance in the I-formation. I

Bill Primps scores the game's only TD in Yale's 7-0 win over Harvard in '69. Brad Lee (60) blocks for Primps. Joe Massey (14) is the Yale quarterback. Harvard's No. 14 is Rick Frisbie.
(YALE ATHLETICS)

looked left and right, not to give away the direction I would be going. I was very aware of where everybody was and what was going to happen. The main noise I heard was the motor drives of the cameras that surrounded the end zone opposite the scoreboard. The tension was growing with every passing second. I then ran for 2 yards and scored behind a good double-team by tackle Terry Kessler and tight end Rich Maher. Woody Hayes taught Carm the play when Carm played for him at Miami of Ohio. They were the hardest 6 yards I ever picked up.

"A little sidebar here: Harry Klebanoff, my high school teammate at Ossining High School in New York, kicked the extra point. My high school coach, Don Hess, quipped, 'Ossining beat Harvard 7-0.'

"Needless to say, it was a happy campus that night as the euphoria of beating Harvard and gaining a share of the Ivy League title carried over to a Sha-na-na concert in the Freshman Commons. A lot of the social life and extracurricular activities at Yale at the time were influenced by Garry Trudeau, who was a senior in '69. And not having B.D. to cartoon anymore, he took his talents into other areas, like arranging for Sha-na-na to come to Yale.

"Most significant for me was that my date that night was a 19-year-old from Mount Holyoke College, Sophia Beutel, who 45 years later is my wife and mother of my three kids.

"Looking back, I guess I had several Joe DiMaggio moments."

Jack Ford (defensive back) '69, '70, '71

TELEVISION JOURNALIST/ATTORNEY
SPRING LAKE, NEW JERSEY

"My biggest thrill at Yale was winning a share of the Ivy League title in '69, my sophomore year, and the interception I had against Penn that season. Carm and his staff did a great job putting players in different positions, and we had only one loss in the Ivy going into the Penn game on Nov. 8.

Jack Ford is about to score after intercepting a pass in the '69 Penn game. Penn's Greg Leavitt (27) chases Ford into the end zone. Ford went on to become an Emmy-Award winning television news personality.
(YALE ATHLETICS)

"Penn battled injuries that year, but they were a dangerous team. The Bowl was a muddy field because it had rained all week, and I think the field conditions kept our offense from getting untracked. In the third quarter the Penn quarterback threw a long pass over the middle. I dropped back into a zone and stepped in front of the receiver. I lunged to get the ball and banged into Andy Coe, falling to the ground with the ball. To this day Andy says he picked me up and headed me in the right direction. I proceeded to run for a 77-yard touchdown.

"In that era there wasn't much celebrating after a touchdown. But as I turned in the end zone after I scored, in celebration I instinctively held the ball up in the air. The photo of that is hanging in the Payne Whitney Gym today. As I was jogging off the field I saw Carm coming toward me. I was scared. To me he was on Mount Olympus and was a strict disciplinarian. I thought he was going to give me a tongue-lashing about my celebratory actions, but all he did was give me a big smile and a hug.

"Carm, who helped get me into the Fordham Law School, was like a father figure to me, as were my Pop Warner and high school coaches, because my father abandoned the family when I was 5 years old. My mother, who was a schoolteacher, raised four children on her own. She has been the hero of my life."

Bob Milligan (wide receiver) '69, '70, '71

ENTREPRENEUR
NEWPORT, RHODE ISLAND

"I had a chance to start my sophomore year in '69 because of injuries to Earl Downing and Bernie Sowley. Running out of the tunnel to play UConn in front of a large crowd in the Yale Bowl was an awesome, overwhelming experience for a sophomore.

Little did I know the amazing experience that was about to come my way.

"The game was a low point and high point for me. I was the punter that year, and early in the game I had to punt from our own 20. I kicked the ball and it went almost straight up in the air. The ball took a backward bounce and hit me in the chest. I learned fast that fans would be unforgiving as the crowd booed when I ran off the field. But Carm, knowing how bad I felt, restored my confidence when he said, 'Don't worry about it, Bobby, you'll get the next one.'

"Later in the game I caught a then-record 93-yard touchdown pass from Joe Massey, topping Brian Dowling's 75-yard TD toss to Calvin Hill against Brown the year before. Then the crowd cheered me. I learned if you play well the fans will support you; if not, you better not be too thin-skinned.

"Things appeared to be moving in fast forward. The following week we beat Colgate 40-21 in the Bowl and I caught three touchdown passes, tying a Yale record held by many. I was on top of the world and I loved being a wide receiver. I no longer had the pressure of calling the plays and found that I had pretty good hands. Rich Pont, one of our assistant coaches, used to call me 'SH' for 'soft hands.'

"Some of my greatest memories were garnered during my years at Yale. But it was

Joe Massey quarterbacked Yale's improbable 69ers.
(YALE ATHLETICS)

also a sad time for me because of the tumultuous political and social unrest of the time. I was a traditional, hard-line conservative kid surrounded by the clouds of the Vietnam war, the Bobby Seale Black Panther trial in New Haven (1970), and Yale employees going on strike. Attendance at the games dropped, and I think football had lost some of its magic. I straddled the good times (1968-69) and the bad (1970-71).

Caught in a Birthday Suit

"Yale became a co-ed institution in 1969, and that made for some interesting tales. Before Yale became coed, males swam naked in the Payne Whitney Gym pool, like they did in YMCAs throughout the country. One day I was in the pool and there were several female students on the other end. One of the football players, I don't recall his name, entered the pool area in his birthday suit. He got about halfway when he noticed that there were several girls in the water.

Bob Milligan is one of eight Yale players to score three touchdowns in a game on pass receptions.
(YALE ATHLETICS)

Two-time All-Ivy first team defensive tackle and Rhodes Scholar Tom Neville sacks Columbia quarterback James Romanosky in a 1969 game at Baker Field.
(YALE ATHLETICS)

Tailback Don Martin played three years in the NFL as a defensive back with the Tampa Bay Buccaneers, Kansas City Chiefs, and New England Patriots. He returned to Yale as an assistant coach.
(YALE ATHLETICS)

I saw panic in his face. He did the quickest 180-degree turn you ever saw and ran back into the locker room. It was hilarious!"

YALE FOOTBALL PROSPERED during the tumultuous 1960s and the best was yet to come. The 1970s produced four Yale Ivy League championships and a bundle of players who went on to play in the National Football League.

Yale Athletic Director Frank Ryan and Coach Carmen Cozza, 1977
(YALE ATHLETICS)

CHAPTER 19

THE 1970S—A FLOURISHING DECADE

Two of the greatest running backs in Yale history—indeed, in Ivy League history— were the face of Eli football in the 1970s: Dick Jauron and John Pagliaro. And then Rich Diana came on the scene in 1979."

—Don Harrison, Executive Sports Editor, *Waterbury Republican-American*

CARMEN COZZA FIELDED championship football teams in '67, '68, and '69. But his winningest decade was the seventies, when the Bulldogs compiled a record of 67-21-2 and won four Ivy League championships. The Yale Bowl was an inhospitable environment for opposing teams; the Bulldogs' home record was 46-10-1 during the decade. If it's true that a coach needs chicken to make chicken salad, Cozza had a smorgasbord of talent to feed his program. Eight players who wore Yale uniforms during this decade went on to play in the NFL: Dick Jauron (fullback/halfback); Don Martin (defensive back/running back), Gary Fencik (split end), John Spagnola (tight end), Greg Dubinetz (offensive guard), Ken Hill and Rich Diana (running backs), and Jeff Rohrer (linebacker).

Running back John Pagliaro and offensive guard Steve Carfora were both two-time All-Ivy first-team picks as were defensive players Jim Gallagher (defensive end), Tom Neville (tackle), Elvin Charity (halfback), John Cahill (middle linebacker), and Bill Crowley (linebacker). Pagliaro was twice named the Ivy League MVP.

Cozza resurrected the full-house T-formation in '72 to take advantage of his three explosive running backs—Rudy Green, Tyrell Hennings, and Jauron.

Brown spoiled a perfect season for Yale in '76 when the Bears beat the Bulldogs 14-6 in the first game of the campaign. (The Bears would do likewise in 1999.)

For the 1977 front cover of the Yale-Harvard game day program, longtime Yale photographer Sabby Frinzi cleverly shot the captains—Yale's Bob Rizzo (No. 19) and Harvard's Steve Kaseta (No. 77)—standing side-by-side. Yale punter Mike Sullivan's 66-yard TD run during that game is one of the more memorable moments in the history of the storied series.

Several Yale players made national news that year when they socialized with former President Gerald R. Ford on campus. Ford met with the team and former coach Ducky Pond, who'd hired him as an assistant coach in 1935 for $2,400 a year.

Ken Hill's school record 100-yard kickoff return against Cornell in '78 remains etched in Eli glory.

In 1979 captain Tim Tumpane (LB) became the first defensive player to win the Asa S. Bushnell Cup as the Ivy League MVP. During the year he made 148 tackles and held together a defense that led the nation in total defense: 175.4 yards per game.

THE PLAYERS

Dick Jauron (running back) '70, '71, '72

NFL PLAYER AND NFL COACH
WESTLAKE, OHIO

Dick Jauron was the first Yale football player selected to the All-Ivy first team three times. A Kodak All-American and AP second-team All-American his senior year, he was also the first Yale player to win the Asa A. Bushnell Cup as the Ivy League's most valuable player in '72. In Yale's 28-7 win over UConn that year, Jauron ran for a then record 194 yards, breaking Clint Frank's single-game rushing record. Jauron's epic 87-yard run against Columbia provided the deciding touchdown in a 28-14 comeback win. He helped defeat Harvard in Boston in '72 by rushing for 183 yards, including a 74-yard touchdown gallop, as Yale rallied from a 17-0 deficit to win 28-17. At the end of the season he played in the annual East-West Shrine Game and scored the only touchdown on a 5-yard run in the East's 9-3 victory.

A Parade All-American out of Swampscott (Massachusetts) High School, he became the first Yale runner to gain 1,000 yards in a season when he collected 1,055 in 1972. In his career he rushed for 2,947 yards and scored twenty-seven touchdowns. Consistency was his game. For thirty-four years he owned the school record of sixteen consecutive 100-yard rushing games.

The quiet and humble Jauron was selected in the fourth round of the 1973 NFL draft by the Detroit Lions and also was drafted as a shortstop by the St. Louis Cardinals in the 25th round of the 1973 baseball draft. He chose the NFL and became a defensive back with the Detroit Lions for five years and the Cincinnati Bengals for four. He later was head coach of the Chicago Bears (1999-03) and Buffalo Bills (2006-09) and has been an assistant coach with several teams.

Dick Jauron was the first running back in Yale history to gain 1,000 yards in a season. (Sabby Frinzi)

"Why did I choose Yale? My mom and dad were very directed people. My mom believed in family, education, healthful living, and doing right by everyone. My dad was extremely competitive and tough-minded. He loved sports, his family, reading history, and competing.

"I was a history major and aware of the great reputation of Yale's history department. I was very impressed with coach Cozza, coach Pont, and the entire Yale coaching staff.

"I attended the famous Yale-Harvard 29-29 game in '68. At the time, I was a high school Yale recruit, and I'll never forget how somber the locker room was after the game. I was very impressed by the way Calvin Hill handled himself at that time and remain impressed by Calvin to this day. He was and is a great athlete and role model.

"My dad (Bob Jauron) undoubtedly had a great impact on my sporting life. He was a great high school athlete in Nashua, New Hampshire, who went on to play for Frank Leahy at Boston College. He was a member of BC's squads for the 1940 Cotton Bowl and the 1941 Sugar Bowl. He was a great coach who coached at all levels, including professional football in Canada. He was the best coach I ever saw.

The Cutback

"In '72 we were losing to a good Columbia team 14-12 in the Bowl in the fourth quarter when the coaches made the right call at the right time. We executed the play well, it was blocked perfectly and I carried the ball (87 yards) for a touchdown. I love

the fact that the play was critical to the outcome of the game, and that everyone had a hand in its execution and success. When you can get that moment where you can cut back and see it and feel

L-R: Former U.S. Attorney General John Mitchell, President Gerald Ford, and Dick Jauron (Yale Athletics)

it, then you're just worried about getting caught. Once I was able to cut back against the grain, I didn't think much about anything but getting to the goal line. I know coach Cozza was running step for step with us down the sideline, and I also know he beat me to the end zone!

"I enjoyed cutting back. My pure speed was good, not great, and generally not fast enough to just outrun defenders to the edges and turn the corner. The touchdown against Harvard in the 1972 game (74 yards) was also on a cutback. I was proud of that moment because it impacted the outcome. We were losing 17-6 in the third quarter when we scored on that play. That was the only time we beat Harvard in my Yale career, and if I had to choose one win, it would be that. I would be remiss, however, if I didn't mention that we beat Princeton all three of our varsity years.

The East-West Shrine Game

"We had a great time in San Francisco following my senior season. I got to spend more time with coach Cozza and his family than I had as an undergraduate player for Coach at Yale. Coach Cozza was the head coach of the East team, with a staff that included University of Michigan coach Bo Schembechler. Carm and Bo were fast friends and teammates at

Miami of Ohio in both football and baseball. It was great to watch them coaching together.

Highs and Lows

"My biggest disappointments at Yale? My junior year we went 4-5 and I didn't play at a high enough level to help us win more games. And we never won an Ivy title during my varsity years. I had many thrills, but my greatest thrills will remain my association with my teammates and the many friends that I have been blessed with through the years."

Brian Clarke (kicker) '71, '72, '73

ActorOrlando,
Florida

Brian Clarke set school records for field goals in a game (three, tying Chuck Mercein), season (nine) and a career (twenty-one) before becoming Grant Putnam on TVs *General Hospital* and New York Mets pitcher Merle "the Pearl" Stockwell on ABC's *Eight Is Enough*.

Brian Clarke (31) lays a hit on Harvard's Burrelle Duvauchelle (45) in Yale's 35-0 win over Harvard in '73.
(Sabby Frinzi)

"Though the ultimate outcome would suggest that three points meant little in our Dartmouth matchup at the Bowl in '72, the 42-yard field goal I had early in the game remains with me for a variety of reasons: into a tough wind, at a time when every point mattered and going against a Big Green undefeated-and-on-a-roll team. A week earlier, we'd lost—after a 4-0 start to the season—to Cornell, in Ithaca, 24-13. We needed that game and needed that kick, and so the memory endures with me. Our completely destroying them, 45-14, endures even more!

Cambridge Voodoo?

"Now, Harvard 1973 in the Bowl! We were not enthralled by the way the Harvard players had evil-eyed us (Cambridge voodoo?) outside Lapham Field House after our pregame workout the day before. As I recall, our collective reaction was on the order of 'Fuck that,' but perhaps not as eloquent. Compounding it a day later, the Johns came out of the tunnel (where they'd been standing and waiting) late for the start of the game, while our kickoff unit was already on the field and waiting.

"I was—we all were—incensed! My kick was high, three yards deep in the end zone, and as I headed downfield (I never played safety on kick-offs), I remember watching this big mofo running at me, growling. Yep, growling! What the hell was that? Apparently, the return man, No. 45 (Burrelle Duvauchelle) took that growl as his 'enter stage left' cue, and we introduced ourselves, nose to nose, inside the Harvard 20-yard line. Evidently, the 'big fella,' No. 88 (Walt Herbert, 6-5, 240) was supposed to block me when he 'rabidly' ran into me. And then we met. And then there was none.

Our 'D' ate up the vaunted Crimson 'O,' turned Pat McInally into a non-factor, and Kevin Rogan, whose nearly unfathomably patient wait (four full seasons after injuring himself as our starting QB on the first offensive down for our 1970 frosh team) availed himself to the max! In the only start he ever had in his Yale varsity football career, Kevin kept our offense firing on all eight and etched his 'Finis' on the annals of 'The Game' with our 35-0 'romp in a swamp.' Beautiful, beautiful day—despite the horrible New England weather."

Don Gesicki (running back) '73, '74, '75

ATTORNEY
CHESTER, NEW JERSEY

Halfback Don Gesicki was an All-Ivy first team selection in 1975.

A Record Touchdown Pass

"I was a quarterback in high school but played the position for only a short time on the Yale freshman

Don Gesicki leaps over UConn tacklers behind the blocking of Steve Carfora (66) and Vic Staffieri (65) in '75 game.
(SABBY FRINZI)

Stone Phillips (16) confers with Carm Cozza and coach Seb LaSpina. Phillips was anchor of NBC TV's *Dateline* for fifteen years.
(SABBY FRINZI)

team. Ironically I threw, what was at the time, the longest touchdown pass in Yale history to Gary Fencik, our outstanding wide receiver.

"We were playing at Princeton in '75 and on our own 3-yard line when our quarterback, Stone Phillips, who would gain national fame as host on NBC's *Dateline*, called the play in the huddle. I thought there must have been miscommunication somewhere along the play-calling process. We were primarily a running team with a dominating offensive line and very skilled blocking fullbacks. As Coach Cozza was known to say, 'Three things can happen when we pass, and two are bad.' The play was designed for me to take the pitch from Stone and roll to my left. Since I am right-handed, it added to the difficulty of the play. I was to fake the sweep play and throw a pass to Fencik, who had lined up as a receiver on the left side of the formation.

"Fencik was an extraordinary player, so I suppose that Coach Cozza and Coach LaSpina knew that if I could just throw the ball anywhere near Gary, he would turn it into something special, and he did in a big way. Gary caught the ball on our 35-yard line and used his speed to outrun the Princeton defense, resulting in a 97-yard touchdown." [The record was broken in 2012 by freshman quarterback Eric Williams who threw a 98-yard TD pass.]

Stunning Field Goal

"In '75 we led Dartmouth 13-7 with 44 seconds remaining. The Big Green had third and goal from the 6 when their quarterback Kevin Case fumbled the ball into the end zone. Dartmouth split end Harry Wilson recovered for the touchdown. In exhilaration, Wilson ran in front of our bench, taunting the Yale team with the ball. Dartmouth was flagged 15 yards for unsportsmanlike conduct.

"After Nick Lowery converted for a 14-13 lead, the penalty made him kick off from his own 25. John

Gary Fencik, a 1975 All-Ivy first team selection, played defensive back for the Chicago Bears from 1976-87.
(Sabby Frinzi)

Pagliaro returned it to the Yale 44. Stone Phillips threw three straight incomplete passes to Fencik, but on the third pass Dartmouth linebacker Reggie Williams was called for interference, which put the ball on the Dartmouth 46. After another incomplete pass to Fencik, Phillips found Al Barker, who brought the ball to the Dartmouth 30. Yale called a timeout with 2 seconds remaining. Randy Carter then jogged onto the field and kicked a 47-yard field goal to win one of the most exciting games ever played in the Bowl.

[Carter died of cancer in 2009, a few days before the opening of the Kenney Center at the Bowl. The featured photo of the Cozza era in the Kenney photo gallery is a shot of Carter and Cozza in embrace after the historic kick. Locker No. 5, the number Carter wore, has been endowed by the team.]

"When I was in high school, I never imagined that I would attend Yale and have the honor of playing in the Bowl. In '75 we played Harvard at the Bowl for a shot at the Ivy League title before a crowd that approached 67,000 fans. Unfortunately, Harvard won 10-7 when Mike Lynch kicked a field goal late in the game.

"I carried the football a number of times in the Yale Bowl, but I've carried away many more fond memories. I have been blessed to be part of the Yale football tradition."

Greg Hall (tight end) '74, '75, '76

Managing Director at Barclays Capital
Larchmont, New York

"My only TD came against Lehigh in 1976 after which Ronald Reagan approached me at Mory's to congratulate me. He was there for parent's weekend. His son, Ron, was a freshman at the time. It was the highlight of my very modest career.

Greg Hall's TD vs. Lehigh
(SABBY FRINZI)

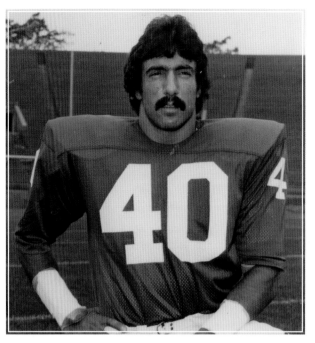

John Pagliaro is the only Yale player to twice win the Asa
A. Bushnell Award as the Ivy League MVP.
(SABBY FRINZI)

"We talked about his days as a radio broadcaster on WHO in Des Moines, Iowa, when he did re-creation of Chicago Cubs games in the studio off a ticker tape and made it sound like he was at Wrigley Field. I got a kick out of that since I'm originally from Sioux City, Iowa."

John Pagliaro (running back) '75, '76, '77

MAGAZINE PUBLISHER
LUTHERVILLE, MARYLAND

John Pagliaro an All-Ivy first team selection in 1976 and 1977, received All-America mention in '76 and made the AP third team in '77. He was selected the Ivy league's MVP in 1976 and 1977. "Pags" and Harvard's Carl Morris are the only players to twice receive the Asa A. Bushnell Cup as the Ivy League's MVP. In '77 he ran for 1,159 yards, breaking Dick Jauron's single-season mark of 1,055. Pagliaro, who played the game at full throttle, rushed for 2,476 yards in his career, averaging 5.2 yards per carry, and was the first Yale running back to have back-to-back 1,000-yard seasons. The first team Walter Camp All-American currently ranks sixth among Yale's career rushing leaders.

"I've been asked why I ran with very high knee action. Directly after high school I played in the Nutmeg

Bowl, a Connecticut high school summer all-star game, and tore cartilage in my knee on the first play of the game. I tried to play freshman ball but didn't have any mobility because of the injury. After surgery, Bill Dayton, our trainer, had me do workouts to strengthen my knee. I ran track at Yale and while on our winter trip to Tallahassee, Florida, in the spring of my freshman year, my coach, Lee Calhoun, an

"Pags" makes big gain in the '76 Princeton game won by the Elis, 39-7.
(SABBY FRINZI)

Olympian, had me pull a heavy sled every day for forty or fifty yards at a time. The only way I could pull the sled was to pump my legs high and drive it forward. After a few times, it felt great and I found myself getting stronger day by day. I can only believe that these workouts had something to do with my high knee action on the field, as it became a natural thing for me to do when I felt someone around my legs.

"A lot of my success as a running back has to go to Rich Pont, my backfield coach. He was a true technician when it came to the art of running. He turned running into a science by dissecting every body and eye movement. He took me to the next level of running through constant repetition of small movements and total commitment to the game.

Perfect Attendance

"In my three varsity years at Yale I never missed a practice or a game. I always felt so much a part of the team, whether in high school or college, and never wanted to let my teammates down. Plus, I feel I had a certain paranoia about losing my position that was always hidden in the back of my mind. I'm not sure why; it was just there. But the good thing about that feeling is it inspired me to be in the best shape and always drove me to practice as if I were playing in a game. When I got the ball in practice, I would always run 20 or 25 yards after the line of scrimmage. It kept me in top game condition and gave me that all-important game feeling.

"I think the best overall game I had was my junior year in '76 against Penn on the new, hard Astroturf of Franklin Field. Carm's game plan was to keep Penn off the field due to their explosive offense. So we proceeded to grind it out and still have the school's single game record for most total first downs (thirty-two), most rushing first downs (thirty) and most rushing plays (eighty-four). Talk about ball control—we

possessed the ball for forty-five minutes. I had 187 yards on thirty-three carries and three TDs. I also made thirteen first downs. Our linemen had a great game, opening nice holes, blowing Penn off the ball, and we had fun staying on the field, just like Carm planned it. Due to the five-yards-and-a-burn-of-Astroturf style of play, the game was still fairly close (21-7), but a convincing win nonetheless. That was our first experience playing on Astroturf and it was fun. You could cut on a dime, but since it was such a hard surface, I was extremely sore the next day.

"Although the '76 Penn game might have been my best game, my greatest thrill was beating Harvard my senior year ('77) in the Bowl, 24-7 and winning the Ivy title outright. It was a magical feeling. I ran for 172 yards and scored the final touchdown. Lou DeFilippo, my coach at Derby High School, was on the sidelines watching the game with a few of his coaches. He picked me up after my last touchdown and told me how proud he was. He also picked up and hugged another former player of his, Mike Sullivan, who ran for a 66-yard touchdown in the last quarter. Can you imagine the day coach DeFilippo had, seeing two of his former players score touchdowns against Harvard?

A Proud Dad

"It was also a special experience watching my son John play at Yale from 2008 to 2010. I remember him leading his J.V. team to victory over Harvard his freshman year in '07 and running for 150 yards and two TDs. It was a very proud time for me. Every time he played as a member of the Yale team, he performed and made big plays.

"In retrospect, it's a unique experience to have shared two championships with so many great guys. I feel winning a championship kept us closer, and it's something we will always have with us."

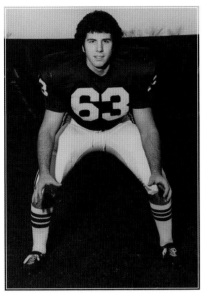

Joe Zuraw
(Sabby Frinzi)

Joe Zuraw (linebacker) '76, '77, '78

Patient advocate
Seymour, Connecticut

"Coming from a working-class family in Ansonia, Connecticut, I grew up a UConn fan and thought Yale was for the elite. I was all set to go to West Point before Yale assistant coach Buddy Amendola recruited me. After meeting with Buddy and Carm, I realized the opportunities that Yale would afford and decided to go to Yale. It was the right decision.

"I started at linebacker and fullback my freshman year in '75. I was slated to be a starting linebacker my sophomore year when I hurt my back. I finally got healthy my senior year, but by that time I had to earn my way back. Bill Crowley, an All-Ivy player and a Rhodes Scholar, took my place. So I guess you can say I lost my job to one of the best.

"But I did get to play and my father, who came to all my home games with my girl friend, Cindy, got a chance to see me play. Dad and Cindy would go to a Kentucky Fried Chicken the morning of the game, get a bucket and tailgate together."

"Spags"

"I roomed with John Spagnola for a time. 'Spags' was not the fastest or the strongest player, but he had the greatest hands of anyone I ever saw. When we were freshmen we were playing Princeton. Coach Harry Jacunski benched Spags for being late to a meeting. Well, the game was close, and there was about three minutes remaining when Harry sent Spags into the

game. He casually caught a few passes, then scored the winning touchdown on one of the most incredible catches I ever saw, leaping in the air with three or four defenders on him. When he came off the field he said to Harry, 'Is there anything else you want me to do?'

"My defining moment as a Yale football player occurred in the Ray Tompkins dorm where we stayed during our two-a-days in August. We lived in an Army barracks style, lights out early and bunk beds. One night one of the underclassmen was complaining to the guy under his bunk. He said, 'I'm captain of the players sitting on the bench.' One of the seniors yelled, 'Who made you captain?'"

An Invitation to President Ford

"I was the master's assistant at Timothy Dwight College (TD), my residential college. Every year we had the opportunity to invite dignitaries because of a Chubb Fellowship program run by the master of Timothy Dwight. The master invites public personalities to reside in TD and hang out with the students, in order to foster an interest in public affairs. In 1977 we invited former President Gerald R. Ford, who had played football at the University of Michigan and was an assistant coach here at Yale when he went to Yale Law School.

"The president arrived on Sunday, February 7, but on Friday morning I met Robert Barrett, his chief of staff, in the cafeteria. We had coffee and talked for about 15 minutes. I asked if there was a possibility of arranging a meeting with Ford, my roommates and me. Barrett could not assure me of that, so I wrote a letter to the president inviting him to our room and gave it to Barrett to give to Ford.

"I didn't think much would happen. On Friday afternoon I met Cindy, at a bus stop in New Haven and we rode back to Ansonia, where we lived. Cindy, who has been my wife for more than 30 years, was in nursing school in Hartford at the time, and this was a regular Friday afternoon ritual. I did not return to the campus until late Monday evening or early Tuesday morning.

"To my amazement, on Monday night President Ford agreed to my long shot request of meeting him along with my roommates. Unfortunately, I was unaware of this because I had gone home. So my roommates met with the president, had a few beers, and talked football and sports in general. This was almost surreal. I could not believe that I was the catalyst for the meeting and I missed it. However, I was part of a group that had breakfast with him on Tuesday morning and I gave him a No. 48 Yale jersey. That was my number at Yale and his number at Michigan.

"When Cindy and I got married, I invited the president to our wedding. He wasn't able to come, but he did send me a nice letter and a gift—a presidential ashtray from the White House. There was no stamp on the envelope. Apparently when mail is sent out from the White House, a presidential seal is used in place of a stamp.

"My four years at Yale was a wonderful experience. I only have one regret. I wish I had stayed on campus the weekend that President Ford was there."

Drew Pace (defensive back) '78

FINANCIAL SERVICES
BOSTON, MASSACHUSETTS

Partying with a President

"There is no doubt that the highlight of my Yale career was the time I had a few beers with President Gerry Ford.

"We knew for a while that President Ford was coming to TD, and being Gerry Ford fans, my

Drew Pace and President Gerald Ford
(DREW PACE)

friends and I knew we wanted to meet him personally. He arrived on Sunday, and for the first two days he was on campus, we weren't having much luck meeting him. The president addressed the entire football team at a gathering at Ray Tompkins House on Monday afternoon, so we got a chance to see him, but not meet him personally. Monday night was Ford's last night in TD, so we knew we were running out of time. At dinner that night, we decided to write Ford a letter expressing our interest in meeting him in a private setting. Five football players signed the letter—Rich Faschan, Lou Orlando, Bob Skoronski, Tom Ventresca, and I. After dinner, we walked over to the suite in TD where Ford was staying and gave the letter to a Secret Service guy. He asked what was in the letter and we said we were inviting the president to come up to our room. He laughed and said, 'I don't think it will happen, but I'll give him the letter.'

"We went back to our room and waited. It seemed like hours, but it wasn't actually that long before the phone rang. On the other end was Robert Barrett, the president's chief of staff. Barrett said, 'The president can't come up to your room, but he would like the five of you to come down to his room.' We found out later that after Ford read our note, he told Barrett, 'Call 'em up. Tell 'em to come over.'

"It was difficult to control our excitement. Barrett stressed that we were not to tell anyone, and only the five of us who signed the letter could come. We grabbed two six-packs of beer and headed across the courtyard to Ford's suite. When we got to the president's room, we were greeted by the Secret Service, who confiscated our beer — probably for security reasons — but said, 'Don't worry, he's got plenty in there.'

Inside the room, there was just the president and one other guy. After introductions and handshakes, Skoronski, whose father was the captain of Vince Lombardi's great Green Bay Packers teams in the '60s, walked over to the refrigerator and boldly asked, 'Can I crack one open for you, Mr. President?' I couldn't believe it. Skoronski took out beers for all of us, and we sat around and had a couple of cold ones, talking to the president of the United States. We had actually pulled it off.

"Ford took off his shoes and tie and put his feet up on the table while he drank a cup of coffee. We talked about football in general. He talked about his days when he played football at Michigan and when he coached at Yale. At the time, he coached under 'Ducky' Pond, who, like myself, was from Torrington, Connecticut. We also talked about golf, skiing and professional wrestling. Politics never entered the discussion; it was just a bunch of guys talking sports. After about an hour, Ford put his tie back on, posed for photos with us, signed some autographs, and we said our goodbyes.

"We walked back to our room, hardly believing what had just happened. We all called our parents to tell them the news, but we decided not to tell anyone else just yet. Nevertheless, about an hour later, our phone began to ring. Apparently, Ford's press people got the word out and we got calls from the *New York*

Times, New Haven Journal-Courier, and the *Hartford Courant*. We attracted national attention when *Newsweek* ran a story about Ford's visit to Yale, mentioning that 'five Eli football players, armed with two six-packs of Michelob, dropped into his suite one night to shoot the breeze.' The *Journal-Courier* article talked about our 'good old-fashioned bull session with the president.' In that article, Ventresca said, 'If everyone had a chance to meet him (Ford) like this, he would have won the election in a landslide.' To which Orlando added, 'Yeah, instead of playing golf in the Bob Hope Desert Classic.' [Gerald Ford was defeated by Jimmy Carter in the presidential election of 1976.]

"The morning after our party with the president, we were part of a group of fifteen TD football players who met with Ford for breakfast in the TD dining hall before his departure. When Ford came into the room, he walked around the table to shake hands with everyone. When he came to us, he said, 'Hi, Lou. Good morning, Drew.' The rest of the group was dumbfounded—what's going on here? We said, 'Oh, we just had a few beers with him last night.'

"Joe Zuraw came back in time to attend the breakfast with Ford, but we had to break the news to him about what happened the night before. He couldn't believe he had missed it. We knew how much he wanted to meet Ford, probably more that the rest of us, but we couldn't call him to join us because the Secret Service guys were adamant about limiting the party to only the five of us.

"My connection to Ford lasted a little longer than the party in TD. After his visit, the college established the Gerald R. Ford Scholar-Athlete Award. The inaugural award went to John Pagliaro in 1978. Then when I graduated in 1979, I received the award. It was obviously great to get the recognition, but it meant a little more to me since I had the chance to meet Ford.

"But the connection didn't stop there. After Yale, I went to business school at Dartmouth. In the fall of 1980, Ford came to the campus to speak. I was able to touch base with him again.

"Meeting him was unquestionably the highlight of my college years, and it is a story the five of us retell often."

John Spagnola (tight end) '76, '77, '78

NFL PLAYER, ABC-TV COLLEGE FOOTBALL COMMENTATOR, AND INVESTMENT CONSULTANT
BRYN MAWR, PENNSYLVAINA

Tight End John Spagnola, an All-Ivy first team selection in 1978, finished his Yale career in 1978 with 88 pass receptions, at the time a school record. He averaged 17.6 yards per reception, totaling 1,554 yards. Ralph Plumb (2001-04) is the current career leader in receptions with 195. Spagnola spent eleven years as a tight end in the NFL with the Philadelphia Eagles (1979-87), Seattle Seahawks (1988), and Green Bay Packers (1989).

Controversy at Penn

"Although we finished the '78 season beating Cornell, Princeton and Harvard, it was a disappointing year since we didn't win the Ivy League after winning it the two previous seasons. We had a bad October, losing to Rutgers and Dartmouth and playing back-to-back tie games with Columbia (3-3) and Penn (17-17). I found myself in the middle of some controversy for the Penn game.

"I roomed with tight end Bob Krystyniak on the road for three years. We never made it together for the 7:30 a.m. team breakfast, when we were served steak and eggs. I didn't think it made much sense to get up that early, so Bob and I would take turns and bring food back to the room. On the morning of the Penn game, Krystyniak brought back breakfast, and for some reason this time Carm was angry that

I wasn't there. He informed me before the game that I would not be starting because I didn't make breakfast. I said to him, 'I hate to tell you, but I never made breakfast.' This was upsetting, because I was from Philadelphia and the game that day was at Franklin Field. I sat the first two series before Carm put me in.

"We fell behind 17-3 early in the last quarter. But we rallied and the game ended 17-17. Overall I had ten receptions for 154 yards, most coming in the second half. I think it was that half that jump-started our offense the rest of the season.

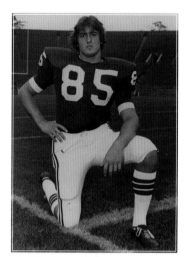

John Spagnola enjoyed an eleven-year career in the NFL after graduating from Yale and served as a player representative and executive vice president of the NFL Players Association.
(SABBY FRINZI)

Pilfered Six-Packs

"Krystyniak and I enjoyed having a few beers together. I'll never forget our '76 trip to Harvard. The coaches would take a few six-packs for themselves and load them in the back of the bus. When we arrived at the hotel they would take the beer to their rooms.

"When the bus emptied the day before the game, we pilfered a couple of six-packs for our room in the Marriott at Newton. That night we uncorked a few and were relaxing when backup quarterback Bob Rizzo stopped by our room and had a few pops with us. I was getting concerned and said to him, 'Hey, you better slow down in case you play tomorrow.' Rizzo shrugged, 'Don't worry; I'm not getting in.'

"In the second quarter Stone Phillips, our regular quarterback, got his bell rung and Rizzo unexpectedly entered the game with Harvard winning 7-0. Rizzo ended up rushing for 53 yards and throwing for 30, including a couple of big passes to me and we won 21-7. Despite his lack of varsity experience, Rizzo was so well respected he was elected captain of the '77 team."

A Fun Time

"I had my share of fun at Yale, and so did others. After the team banquet our senior year, one of the players got into a little trouble and got arrested. But they didn't hold him too long. That night I went into a few bars holding my team MVP trophy over my head.

"I think my biggest thrill at Yale was that my class never lost to Princeton or Harvard during the four years I was there. I never enjoyed playing football on any level as much as I did at Yale. We played because we loved the game and the players were there for the right reasons.

"Downtown Left"

"I threw one pass my entire football career, including high school, college and the NFL, and that pass in the '78 Harvard game established a record as the longest scoring pass by a Yale player in the history of the Yale-Harvard series. A little background:

"At Friday practices we used to throw the ball around in the Bowl and have a little fun. The interior linemen, called the 'Toads,' would be having their fun while quarterback Pat O'Brien, Krystyniak, running back John Hatem, and I would create some crazy razzle-dazzle, flea-flicker type plays. One play that we devised was called 'Downtown Left.' As soon as the ball was snapped, I drifted back a few feet from my left end spot and caught a lateral from O'Brien. Krystyniak jogged slowly down the right side then took off deep, and I fired the ball to him.

"Cozza saw it and liked it. We ran the play twice in practice, and it failed miserably both times. I never thought we would use it, but was I in for a surprise. In the '78 Harvard game we got off to a 14-0 lead and Harvard came back to tie it in the second quarter. On our first play after the kickoff we were on our own 23, facing the open end of Harvard Stadium, and the ball was on the right hash mark. The play came in from the sideline calling for "Downtown Left." I couldn't believe it. I said, 'Oh ##%&#.'

"We ran the play, and I had a little trouble locating Bob. But I found him and let it go about 53 yards. Bob put it in another gear and caught the pass for a 77-yard touchdown. We ended up winning the game 35-28. Maybe this was our version of Harvard end Pat McInally's flea-flicker of four years earlier when McInally took a lateral from Harvard's Hawaiian quarterback Milt 'Pineapple' Holt and connected with Jim Curry.

"Every time I watch a Yale-Harvard game, I know that record won't be broken once Yale gets the ball to their own 24. Ed Marinaro, the great running back from Cornell, once said, 'People who say records are made to be broken never held a record.'"

Bob Krystyniak (right end) '76, '77, '78

BUSINESS DEVELOPMENT AND STRATEGIC ALLIANCE WITH THE PPG INDUSTRIES
PITTSBURGH, PENNSYLVANIA

"'Downtown Left'—When the play came in, Spags and I looked at each other. I was truly shocked. I think Seb LaSpina, our offensive coordinator, further developed the play by pulling a guard to block for John when he got the ball from Pat O'Brien. When the ball was snapped I sauntered the first 15 or 20 yards down the field. The D-back on my side sprinted to the other side, anticipating a screen. The

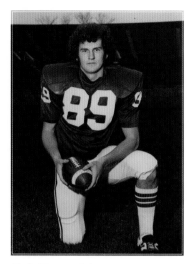

Bob Krystyniak
(Sabby Frinzi)

safety came up to cover the apparent screen, and there was not one Harvard player within 20 yards of me when Spags let it fly. He threw the ball across the field, and I think he threw it as far as he could throw it. It was perfect timing, even though I had to run another 30 yards to catch it. I caught it around the Harvard 24 and ran for the touchdown to give us a 20-14 lead before Dave Schwartz kicked the extra point to make it 21-14. The 35 points scored in the second quarter of that game remains the highest scoring quarter in the history of the Yale-Harvard series.

"Spags gave me a picture of the Harvard defender chasing me toward that end of the field so I could remember my last touchdown. I also recall a photo of Yale President Bart Giamatti, Athletic Director Frank Ryan, Spags, and me in the locker room after The Game with champagne being sprayed. That is a classic. Giamatti and Ryan being there showed the support and pride in the football program at that time, as well as the importance of the rivalry.

"Spags and I were like bookends. When we graduated, we gave Seb slate bookends with our numbers engraved on them.

Toe-to-Toe with the Scarlet Knights

"This might surprise you, but my biggest thrill at Yale was the '78 game we lost to Rutgers, 28-27. We threw the ball extensively, which was rare during the Pagliaro-Cozza years. When we went for the two points in the last quarter, I thought we should have called a play to the outside. Instead, we called a crossing pattern where Spagnola and I picked for each other.

"But playing against that level of competition and being able to go toe-to-toe with the Scarlet Knights was impressive.

"We had some good parties. Keep in mind that the drinking age then was 18. I remember getting inebriated after the 1977 postseason banquet when we were awarded the Ivy League trophy. We took it around the campus and carried it into Toad's and Rudy's [two local taverns]. The guy at the door at Toad's didn't want to let us in, but we just blew through the door.

An Intoxicated Teammate

"We beat Princeton 39-7 my sophomore year in the Bowl. Before the game Andy Horvath, a third-string safety, went out and tailgated with friends before he put on his uniform. Horvath, who was a playboy, had several Bloody Marys and returned intoxicated. You could smell the booze, and he was hollering and raising hell. During our pregame warm-ups on the field, we had one drunk teammate. But I'm sure he was sober by the time he got into the game late in the fourth quarter. And would you believe he intercepted a pass to end the game. If Carm ever knew what Andy had done that day, I think he would have thrown him off the team.

"In retrospect, it was a great time playing football and getting an education at the same time. It is the way college football should be—competitive, but not a profession. And boy, did we have fun!

A Tragedy at Harvard

"My two trips to Harvard were both interesting. In '76, my sophomore year, we came back to win after trailing early in the game. But it was something that happened to a Harvard player off the field a few days later that will stay with me forever.

"The Game was played on November 13. On November 16 the Harvard football team had their annual breakup party at the Harvard Club. Following the party, a group of Harvard players, including Andy Puopolo, a senior cornerback, went to a section of Boston known as the Combat Zone, notorious for prostitutes, strip bars, back alleys, and lawlessness. Puopolo, an aspiring physician, was stabbed there during a street altercation. He suffered extensive brain damage from a lack of oxygen and was in a coma for thirty-one days before he died on December 17 at the Tufts-New England Medical Center. It's hard for me to believe that I played football against Andy just a month before.

"The entire Harvard football team served as pallbearers at the funeral service, held December 20 at St. Leonard's Church in the North End of Boston. It's estimated that 2,000 people attended the service."

The Puopolo stabbing occurred as the Harvard players left a bar after a night of revelry. They were in their van when a prostitute reportedly reached into the van, rubbed her hands on one of the players, and in the process took his wallet. Puopolo chased the woman but encountered three men who came to her aid. One of them, Leon Easterling, was charged with stabbing Puopolo.

Bill Crowley (linebacker) '76, '77, '78 (captain)

FORMER PRESIDENT OF ESL INVESTMENTS
BRANFORD, CONNECTICUT

Bill Crowley was an All-Ivy first team selection in 1977 and 1978. In '78 he received honorable mention AP All-America. He led Yale in tackles the three years he lettered. Crowley is one of six Yale football players selected as Rhodes scholars. The others are Larry McQuade '50, Tom Neville '71, Kurt Schmoke '71, Roosevelt Thompson '84 and Chris Brown '90.

"Yale assistant coach Seb LaSpina recruited me to go to Yale. I had signed a letter of intent at Northwestern but changed my mind. My father, who is a Yale

1978 captain Bill Crowley was a Rhodes Scholar.

graduate ('48), gave Sebby a hard time. My father questioned if it was really worth $7,000 to go to Yale. Sebby came to me after we won the Harvard game in '77 and said, 'Aren't you glad you came here? Northwestern is 0-10.'

"Yale was pretty good in the late '70s and the Bowl was a hallowed and formidable place to play football. In 1977, we scrimmaged C.W. Post, a smaller school. After one particularly explosive tackle, defensive end Mike Tomana stood over a crumpled C.W. Post ball carrier and intoned, 'Welcome to the Yale Bowl.' It was sort of a jerky thing to do, but it seemed pretty cool at the time."

Mike Sullivan (running back, punter) '77, '78, '79

ATTORNEY
ORLANDO, FLORIDA

"How can I ever forget November 12, 1977? We beat Harvard 24-7 in the Bowl, I scored a touchdown on a 66-yard run and later that evening went on the first date with the girl I would marry.

"We were ahead 10-7 early in the fourth quarter. It was fourth and 20 on our own 34, which placed me on about our 20. There was no instruction from Carm to consider a fake, and that would have been unthinkable given our field position. However, every punter considers what will happen with an errant snap from center, including Carm's pregame standard: 'Know when to take a safety.'

"As a punter, you're always looking, always studying the defense. I had already had two punts during the game and noticed their ends were crashing. They were taking a hard inside rush that caused me to line up a little deeper this time. I also noticed that Harvard rushed nine men from the line of scrimmage, with a short safety about 20 yards downfield and the punt returner about 40 yards downfield. The Harvard defense wasn't leaving anyone in the short to intermediate area.

"The snap from center Jim Browning was eye-level high and sailed to my right. I could see Russ Savage, Harvard's big, fast, rangy left defensive end,

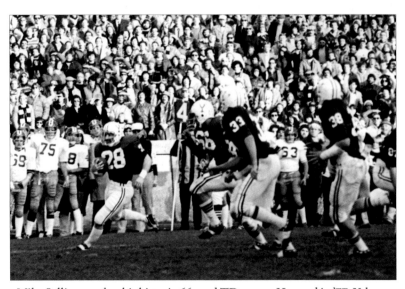

Mike Sullivan makes his historic 66-yard TD run vs. Harvard in '77. Yale blockers are Steve Carfora (66), Mike McIntyre (33) and Rick Angelone (38). (SABBY FRINZI)

had his eyes on the ground and was taking a hard slant in. I was a left-footed punter. I thought about punting with my right foot but was afraid I would whiff the ball.

"Because I caught the ball a few yards to my right, I had a certain momentum moving in that direction. As I looked up field I saw 20 yards of green grass from the right hash mark to the sideline. It was a pleasant, unexpected sight. I took off and it was just wide open. I didn't see anyone until one of our linemen, Steve Carfora, at midfield, blocked the short safety on his left ear hole. It was a vicious hit, a little to the left of the hash.

"I ended up hopping over the two of them. At that point it was just me and the deep safety. Mike McIntyre, the up back in the punt formation whom I shared the punting duties with that year, released probably before I crossed the line of scrimmage and cut the deep safety at his knees. At that point the field opened up like the Red Sea and my teammates Keith Bassi and Kevin Kelly accompanied me into the end zone. They were yelling and both patted me on the helmet before we all trotted off the field .

"I turned to my left and looked back: no flags. I thought that couldn't possibly be. No doubt it was the highlight of my Yale career. Ironically, if the snap had been good it never would have happened. And if it weren't for Carfora's block, the play might have resembled the 2009 fake punt or worse.

"When I got to the sideline, I was greeted by my high school coach, Lou DeFilippo, who was on the sideline the entire game. I jumped into his arms as I had done so many times at Derby High School. I then reached Carm. He said with a smile, 'If you hadn't scored, you could have kept running out of the Bowl.'

"Following the game I tailgated with family and friends in a parking lot outside the Bowl, then went to a party in the courtyard at Timothy Dwight College. Frank Maturo, an outstanding basketball player, had previously introduced me to Lynn Cocorullo, who is now my bride of over 30 years.

"I guess you can say I had some day!

Relaxed Huddles

"A constant theme at Yale was how relaxed the huddles were. During my senior year ('79) we were playing Brown. The game was being televised on ABC, with Keith Jackson and Frank Broyles in the broadcast booth. During a timeout, our band played a Led Zeppelin song. Rich Diana, a sophomore at the time, called out the song and one of our linemen disagreed. Imagine arguing about the title of a rock song during a timeout! Some of the funniest guys were the offensive linemen. I'm sure it would surprise the fans that it was common for guys to tell jokes in the huddle."

Ken Hill (running back) '77, '78, '79

NFL Player; real estate developer
Morris County, New Jersey

Ken Hill was an All-Ivy first team selection in 1979. In 1978 he averaged 29.3 yards per kickoff return, a Yale record (11 returns, 322 yards). In the '78 Cornell game, he made a jaw-dropping 100-yard kickoff return leaving 11 Big Red jerseys in his wake.

Hill played 10 seasons in the NFL (1980-89) as a member of the Oakland/ Los Angeles Raiders, New York Giants and Kansas City Chiefs. He played in Super Bowl XVIII for the Raiders and Super Bowl XXI with the Giants.

"I grew up in Oak Grove, Louisiana, a town a little bigger than *Mayberry RFD*. My parents, who raised nine children (five boys and four girls), were both educators. We didn't have a lot of money, but my father wanted us all to go to an Ivy League school, which three of us did. Fortunately, all of my siblings have been successful in their chosen fields.

A Record Kickoff Return

"In the '78 Cornell game I ran back a kickoff 100 yards in our 42-14 victory in the Bowl. I hadn't been playing well that game. Before the start of the second half I sat on my helmet on the sidelines pouting instead of getting loose and preparing myself to play. Coach Seb LaSpina said to me, 'Don't you think you should be getting ready?' I looked at him, and ran out on the field, caught the kickoff and ran it back 100 yards.

"When I caught the ball I took a step back, which is a cardinal sin because my weight was on my heels. I brought it out and went up the sideline. There were some great blocks in the wedge and I wasn't touched. I found myself one-on-one against the kicker. I shimmied my shoulder a little, causing him to stumble. In the midst of this I kind of chuckled to myself. I looked over my shoulder 20 or 30 yards from the end zone and just took it in. After I scored I ran back to the sidelines, where I was greeted by Seb. 'I guess you were ready,' he said.

The '78 Harvard game

"The '78 Harvard game was my greatest thrill at Yale. We won the game 35-28 in Boston. It was one of the most exhilarating experiences of my life, including the two Super Bowls I played in. In the second quarter I scored on an 18-yard run and for the day gained 154 yards on 25 carries. Rich Angelone (93 yards rushing and one touchdown) and Mike Sullivan (51 yards rushing) also had big games.

Ken Hill (left) chats with John Spagnola. Both enjoyed productive careers in the NFL.
(SABBY FRINZI)

Greatest Disappointment

"My greatest disappointment during my Yale career was losing the '79 Harvard game, 22-7. We had gone into that game undefeated. I dropped the ball five times. We fumbled six times and lost three of them. As far as I'm concerned the '79 season was a truncated season. We only played eight games. I don't count the Harvard game. It never happened.

"I knew Calvin Hill had fumbled a couple of times in the '68 Harvard game and we commiserated about it. For a long time, people asked me if I was Calvin's brother. At some point when I was playing in the NFL they began asking if he was my father. I love to point that out to Calvin every time I get the opportunity.

An Ivy Leaguer in the NFL

"Following the '79 Harvard debacle, I developed a deeply rooted distaste for football. I didn't work out and got kind of heavy. Seb notified me that there were NFL scouts looking at me and they wanted me to work out for them. I did and it went pretty well, even though I was fifteen pounds overweight.

"I had my share of success in the NFL. Of course, being from an Ivy League school, I caught my share of snide remarks. They knew about my fancy major (molecular biophysics and biochemistry) and would let me have it on occasion.

"I had a great relationship with coach Bill Parcells when I played for the Giants. We were friends, but he would come at me on occasion. After one game he said, 'I hope you understand what you did.' Then with a wry smile he added, 'I'll never bring another Yalie in here again.'

Racial Issues

"Race wasn't an overriding issue at Yale, but I felt it. I played fullback initially, and some folk in the stands thought that other players should be playing fullback. It is my understanding that there was lots of racial stuff being said in the stands.

"I grew up in Louisiana running from the Ku Klux Klan. I had a cousin that was murdered by the Klan, so I was acutely aware and sensitive to racial bigotry long before I entered Yale.

"I was stopped many times by the campus police. I had a history with one female officer involving two different situations. Here's one of them.

"One year we ate our pregame meal at the Hall of Graduate Studies, near Toad's. All of the locks for the residential colleges were keyed. You had to use your key when you entered and exited. One day, which happened to be a game day, I was leaving the Pierson College gate with a teammate, Fred Hayward, when this officer was sitting in a parked car that looked like it had been in demolition derby and didn't fare very well. I chuckled when I saw her, but it was actually a nervous chuckle because of the game a few hours away. She jumped out of her car with her hand on her gun and yelled, 'Stop.' I answered, 'I am not going to allow you to denigrate or disrespect me by forcing me to put my hand in my pocket and take out my Yale ID when you saw me put the key in the gate.' I then asked, 'What's the issue?' and she replied, 'You fit a description.'

"An anthropology professor I had happened to be coming from Greek Village and observed the encounter. He just shook his head. I eventually showed her the ID card and she let me go.

"During that time there was an organization on campus called 'Black Athletes at Yale.' I went to a couple of meetings. Some of the stories I heard were ridiculous. Although there were some rumblings and grumblings about the football staff, most of the acrimony was directed at the basketball program. Remember, most football players came to Yale because of Carm, so there weren't too many problems voiced by the players.

Tradition

"Going to the Ray Tompkins House and being around Carm in that facility, there was the expectation that we would win, just like Lombardi's Packer teams did in the '60s. No matter how well we played, it was never good enough. That's the making of championship-caliber teams. During my career (1977-79) we were 20-5-2, including Ivy championships in '77 and '79. Plus I have my Super Bowl rings. Football has been very good to me."

THE PLAYERS REMEMBER DICK JAURON

RON DARLING—MAJOR LEAGUE BASEBALL PITCHER/NEW YORK METS TV BROADCASTER

Ron Darling was a QB and CB on the freshman team in 1978.

"I developed a friendship with Dick that still lasts to this day. Dick was the sweetest guy. He was a good guitarist who taught me the intro to *Roundabout* by Yes. That was worth the price of a Yale education. I can still play it."

PAUL SORTAL (RUNNING BACK/WIDE RECEIVER/KICK-OFF RETURNER) '71, '72—FINANCIAL ADVISOR, WILMETTE, ILLINOIS

"The highlight of my experience at the Bowl and as a Yale football player was to be a teammate of Dick Jauron's. The spirited Yale alum who recruited the Chicago area, the renowned Bob Anderson, told me about Dick with his first allowed phone call after acceptances went out. Dick was the most highly sought-after Massachusetts schoolboy football player, a high school All-American whom Boston College and Notre Dame wanted. Anderson also said that Boston Celtic legend John Havlicek said that Dick was the best high school defensive basketball player he ever saw and that some considered Dick the best shortstop in New England that year, in high school or college. Yet more rare than his astounding athletic ability were his impeccable character and his absolute modesty about his achievements."

The Paul Sortal Award is given annually to the Yale varsity baseball player who uses his ability to the fullest.

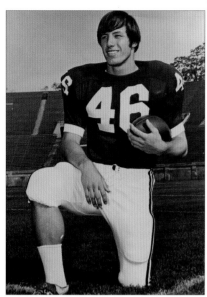

Paul Sortal
(SABBY FRINZI)

BOB MILLIGAN

"Every Friday afternoon before a game we had light workouts in the Bowl and Dick used to fantasize that he was Lem Barney, the great Pro Bowl defensive back of the Detroit Lions. I got the biggest kick out of that. When have you ever seen an offensive player practice defense? And who would believe that in a couple of years Dick would be playing alongside Lem in the same defensive backfield with the Lions as a free safety?"

THE WRITERS REMEMBER DICK JAURON

JON STEIN

"Carm Cozza was an emotional man underneath, and sometimes his emotions spilled out, such as after Dick Jauron's climactic 87-yard run to beat Columbia in 1972 at the Bowl. Cozza ran into the end zone, hugged Jauron and lifted him up. Another memorable image of that play was caught by *Register* photographer Kirby Kennedy, who captured the look of disbelief on the faces of the Columbia players as Jauron ran past their bench. This was a play that destroyed Columbia's season."

DON HARRISON

"I was blessed to know and cover four of the greatest backs in Yale history—

Calvin Hill, Dick Jauron, John Pagliaro, and Rich Diana. Without casting aspersions on the others, I would declare Jauron as the most electrifying, the most elusive and the most reticent. 'Yale's Jauron Runs Long Except in Interviews,' crowed a *New York Times* headline that fall. "

OPPONENTS REMEMBER THE SEVENTIES

GLENN GAETANO (LINEBACKER) PENN, '71-'73—ASSISTANT DIRECTOR WITH THE U.S. DEPT. OF LABOR, WAGE AND HOUR DIVISION IN NEW HAVEN; SHELTON, CONNECTICUT

"It was incredible playing in the Yale Bowl. As a kid my father would take me there, and to have him and my family and friends see me play in the Bowl was a great experience. Two of my teammates were Vinny and Pete Sgro from West Haven. And on the other side of the field was my longtime friend and high school teammate from Derby, Rick Volo, who played for Yale.

"The whole weekend was special when we played Yale. We stayed at the motel by the West

Rock tunnel on the Wilbur Cross Parkway and had tremendous dinners at Les Shaw's restaurant, which was located adjacent to the motel."

DENNIS O'CONNELL (LINEBACKER) UCONN '76, '77, '78—STATE OF CONNECTICUT PROBATION OFFICER/ RECREATION AND PARKS DIRECTOR; DERBY, CONNECTICUT

"I was really pumped for the '77 game against Yale. John Pagliaro was a high school teammate

of mine, and I was looking forward to going against him and guard Steve Carfora, Yale's captain. When John set up in the backfield in the first quarter, I gave him a wink. That game I made 22 tackles; 19 were solos. I think I got John about 15 times. In the second half Yale made some adjustments and neutralized me. Yale won that game 23-12."

THE COACHES REMEMBER THE SEVENTIES

CARM COZZA—HEAD COACH

"I have met many great people during my time at Yale, and one was President Gerald Ford. When I found out that my players had a beer in his room, I wisecracked, 'Mr. President, I don't like our kids drinking.' And he replied, 'Well, you weren't supposed to know about that.'"

Running back Tyrell Hennings has fun with coach Cozza and 1974 All-Ivy first team (offensive tackle) Al Moras.
(SABBY FRINZI)

DAVE KELLEY— DEFENSIVE LINE COACH

"Globe Master"

"I've witnessed my share of strange things over the years but one of the most unusual involved Al Moras, a 6-foot-2 offensive tackle ('72-'74). The kids called him 'Globe

Master' because his hat size was 9 ¼. His head looked like a basketball bowl. We were playing at Penn. Midway through the first quarter the suspension in his Rydell helmet broke causing the helmet to slip below his forehead. The face mask bar was rubbing against the bridge of his nose which was bleeding. He came off the field cussing in search of our trainer, Bill Kaminsky, who unsuccessfully attempted to lift Al's helmet off his head. Al said to him, 'Just put something on my nose so I'm not drinking my own blood. '

"At halftime we still couldn't remove the helmet and his head started to swell and his nose was still bleeding. They did whatever they could to get his helmet off his head but failed. He played the whole second half with a damaged helmet.

"When the game ended he had two black eyes and looked like a raccoon. His teammates were calling him 'Darth Vader.' But our challenge was to get the helmet off his head. A short time later they got a big metal cutter and cut the cage off but the helmet was another story. It was finally extricated by using a saw blade. When the ordeal ended, they had to tape four ice bags to his head. Today Al is a brain surgeon."

An Embarrassing Moment

"After we beat Harvard in '78, Spagnola and Krystyniak stayed at the Marriott Hotel in Newton, Massachusetts. They decided to have a little party and went out shopping for some libations. When they returned to the hotel, they were waiting for the elevator with their supplies in hand. When the elevator door opened they were greeted by Seb and me who were headed out. We met the party boys face-to-face and you could have colored them Harvard Crimson. Spagnola, thinking quickly, offered us his bag of goodies and said, 'Guys, this is for all your hard work this season.'

"In the '79 Harvard game captain Tim Tumpane

1979 captain and All-Ivy first team linebacker Tim Tumpane lays a vicious hit on a Penn opponent.
(SABBY FRINZI)

out of Mount Carmel High School in Chicago dislocated his finger and broke his hand while making a tackle. Dr. Goldberg took him under the tunnel and put the finger together and placed a cast on his hand. He played the entire second half with a broken hand."

<hr/>

THE TRAINERS REMEMBER THE SEVENTIES

<hr/>

BILL KAMINSKY

"Kevin Rogan started one game at quarterback during his college career and it happened to be the '73 Harvard game. Subbing for Tom Doyle, who separated his shoulder against Princeton the week before, Kevin stepped to the plate and led Yale to a 35-0 win. Kevin was the most unselfish athlete we ever worked with. We used to call him 'Iron Man.' He assumed his role as a backup and was a hard working player. His brother, John, had a more prominent career (1979-81) as a Yale quarterback. I used to call him 'Three Ring Rogan' because he was on three Ivy League championship teams.

"Gary Fencik was a tough nut. One time he broke

his nose and all he said was, 'Stop the bleeding.' Our head trainer Bill Dayton ran a piece of wire under his helmet and took care of the problem.

"The trainer's room is often a necessary stop for football players. John Cahill, who captained the '75 team and was All-Ivy as a linebacker in '74 and '75, prided himself in not coming into the training room. He would come by and peek at the clock but would not enter the room. One day I moved the clock on him. But John, who is a cardiologist in Chicago, did come in the room once but he doesn't remember it because he had a concussion.

"We always were careful in dealing with concussions. Any player who suffered a concussion would not play for ten days. Now there is a pre-test that every player takes. If a player is concussed, he is tested and you can run that test against the pre-test and study any changes. There are times when a player is stunned but not concussed. The team doctor makes that determination."

AL BATTIPAGLIA

"I was driving my car one day when I heard a radio interview with John Spagnola. He was asked about his Yale background. He said, 'I'm part of the trio.' The interviewer asked, 'What trio?' John said, ' 'Pags,' 'Spags,' and 'Battipags,' in reference to John Pagliaro, himself and me.

The interviewer asked, 'Who is 'Battipags?' Spagnola answered, 'The trainer.' I couldn't get over that."

The First Female Acting Head trainer

"In September 1978 Frank Ryan, the athletic director, named Daphne Benas as the first female acting head trainer. I had been in that position for a year or so. We got along well together. Yale had become a co-ed school in '69 and Ryan saw the need for a female in the training department and five women were added in the athletic dept."

THEY REMEMBER THE SEVENTIES

RICH SCHYNER

"I'm probably the only field superintendent that ever got credit for a tackle. Every Friday defensive line coach Dave Kelley used to post a list of players and the number of tackles they made. My name was on the bottom of the list. If an opposing player slipped or fell on the Yale Bowl turf, he gave me credit for a tackle."

FRED CANTOR '75

"I was a member of the Yale varsity soccer team from 1972-74.

"In 1973, the Yale soccer team earned its first-ever NCAA tournament berth. On Saturday morning of Thanksgiving weekend, we hosted Bridgeport, the No. 1 seed in New England, at Coxe Cage field, adjacent to the Yale Bowl.

"We upset Bridgeport 3-1, and shortly after the game I had the great pleasure of walking inside the Bowl and watching the Yale football team rout Harvard 35-0, thereby depriving the Crimson of a share of the Ivy title.

"Considering what was at stake in both games, and the experience of being a participant and then a spectator in rapid succession, it probably ranks as the greatest sports day in my life."

STEVE CONN—YALE ASSOCIATE ATHLETICS DIRECTOR, DIRECTOR OF SPORTS PUBLICITY; WOODBRIDGE, CONNECTICUT

Fridays in the Bowl

"My friends, Bill McNeil, Ken Moscovic, and I got dropped off on Central Avenue on fall Friday afternoons to encounter a football bonanza.

"Head coach Carm Cozza held light Friday afternoon workouts in the venerable stadium with very little fanfare. I don't believe the Bowl was actually supposed to be open, and my friends and I certainly felt we were not supposed to be there, but we jumped at the opportunity.

Toad Ball

"Fridays in the Bowl meant Yale offensive linemen playing 'Toad ball.' In Cozza's era offensive linemen were known as Toads; a toad jumps forward out of a squatting stance. Mark Noetzel, who played from 1976 to 1978, was a 6-foot-1, 215-pound guard and three-year letterman from Ohio. He said, 'Toads would be transformed into princes on Fridays. We had the chance to be skill players for a moment.'

"Other players had field goal kicking contests or just fooled around before the coaching staff arrived to blow its first whistle. The players allowed us to compete in their kicking contests, but we were too small or probably too fast to play with the Toads.

"Cozza was not enamored of the idea of his big linemen, in full uniform with pads, pretending to be skill players. In fact he was very worried about the consequences of a wrong turn or tumble. We were glad he didn't like to watch them play, because it gave us more time with the Bulldogs.

Veteran broadcaster George Grande (left) playfully grabs the mike of Steve Conn, the Yale Associate Athletics Director, Director of Sports Publicity.
(RICH MARAZZI)

'I watched them one time and that was enough,' Cozza said. 'It was like watching a circus.' He left Toad ball in the hands of his offensive line coach and once told him, 'You better not get any of these guys hurt. They're not very good attempting to be skill players, and they even look dangerous to each other.'

"Just being on the field with guys like receiver John Spagnola, quarterback Pat O'Brien, tight end Bob Krystyniak, and linebacking star Bill Crowley as they goofed around was worth whatever time we were allowed to stay. In fact, I would bring a camera and those players would organize themselves into crazy posed-action scenarios. Later in the season I brought black-and-white prints that I made in our darkroom. I gave some out and had some signed by Spagnola, O'Brien, Krystyniak, and Crowley.

"When it was time to go, we reluctantly scooted out the players' tunnel, peeked inside the halftime room while wondering what Cozza's speech the next day might sound like, and then raced across Central Avenue to watch the inter-college games."

Inter-College Games

"The number of residential colleges grew from ten in 1933 to 12 in 1962 and for many years each one of the colleges fielded a team. The team captain, usually with the help of a coach obtained from one of the graduate schools, took charge of the college team organizing its players into a working unit. Each team played a nine-game schedule. The day before the Yale-Harvard game, the Harvard football House teams played Yale's college teams.

"For many years and up until 1992, tackle (not flag) intramural games known as inter-college football were played among Yale's 12 residential colleges. There were six teams, each a combination of two colleges, which squared off on Friday afternoons. The officiating crews were more than happy to have volunteers work the down markers as part of the chain gang. These spirited contests were amazing displays of emotion and desire but lacked enough medical trained help to cover all the injuries suffered by poorly prepared bodies.

"I recall seeing a much older man banging heads with young college kids and wondering why he would be out there putting his body at great risk. I later discovered that man was my first athletics director at Yale, Don Kagan, the Sterling Professor of Classics and History, who served as interim Yale A.D. in 1987-88.

'It was a fulfillment of a life's love of playing football. I was in reasonable shape and could play without getting killed,' said Kagan, who played defensive tackle and linebacker up until the age of 45 for the Timothy Dwight-Silliman squad. 'I also got to play against my son (fullback for Pierson-Davenport), but I don't remember tackling him.'

"Medical and financial issues forced the end of residential college tackle games, which have been replaced by flag football."

Bobby Kennedy Hoax

"The day before the Yale-Harvard game, the Harvard football House teams used to play Yale's college teams. This was a tradition that vanished many years ago. Injuries and insurance issues led to its demise.

"Bobby Kennedy and brother, Ted, pulled off the greatest hoax in the history of these games when Bobby played in the November 20, 1953, contest in New Haven six years after he appeared in the Bowl as a Harvard varsity player. These games were reserved for undergraduates. At the time, RFK was a lawyer on the staff of the Hoover Commission in New York City and was celebrating his 28th birthday.

"It all came about when Ted, who played for the Winthrop House team in '53 before playing varsity the next two years, asked Bobby to come to New Haven for the game. Bobby declined the offer saying he would rather play. Teddy granted Bobby his wish and Bobby played as Teddy's sub.

"The sham remained unreported for 43 years until George Sullivan exposed the masquerade in an article he wrote in the 1996 Yale-Harvard program.

"Sullivan wrote, 'So Bobby drove to New Haven. He borrowed a red and white Winthrop uniform and dressed in the back seat of his car. He arrived unnoticed on the field just before kickoff and made several tackles and pass receptions helping lead Winthrop to a 6-0 victory. With victory in sight he decided he was not needed any longer. He changed again in his car and drove back to New York.'"

REMEMBERING JOE LOPRESTI

Joe LoPresti was the co-owner of "Phil's Barber Shop" from 1964 to the time of his death in 1993. He was a friend, father figure and counselor to many Yale players in this era. To many, he was Yale's No. 1 sports enthusiast.

SABBY FRINZI

"One tradition that I'm proud to be associated with as the Yale football photographer was providing photos for 'Phil's Barber Shop' that was run by Joe LoPresti. I would give Joe about 20-25 photos on a Sunday following Saturday's game and he would put them in the window. Players would come by and order the prints for their family."

MARIA GARGANO (DAUGHTER OF JOE LOPRESTI)

"Greg Dubinetz, '75, inscribed one of Sabby's photos to my dad. It reads, 'To my Yale Dad, … much love and respect.' When my father learned that Greg was tragically killed in a car accident, he was very upset. It was like losing a son.

"Jeff Schulte, '84, was in the hospital and my dad was in constant contact with Jeff's mom, Marjorie. My father secretly surprised Jeff and flew his mother here to be with him.

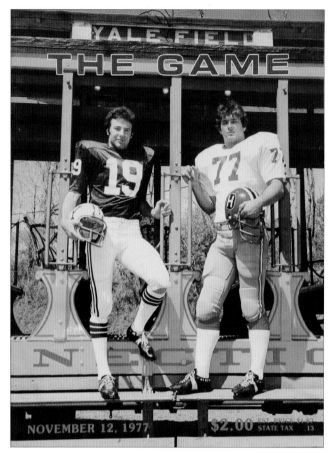

November 12, 1977, Yale-Harvard game day program. This is the only year when the uniform number of the captains corresponded to the year. Yale's Bob Rizzo (19) and Harvard's Steve Caseta (77).
(SABBY FRINZI)

"That's the kind of man he was!"

Y ALE'S PRESTIGE AS an Ivy League power in the 1970s changed drastically when the NCAA moved Yale and the other Ivy programs from Division I-A to Division I-AA in 1982. Yale University president A. Bartlett Giamatti was vilified for an apparent call to de-emphasize college athletics. Before that, however, Yale enjoyed one its greatest victories when the Bulldogs beat Navy in 1981.

CHAPTER 20

THE **1980S**—A CHANGE OF FORTUNES

*"Beating Air Force in '80, which was my
100th win, and Navy in '81 were the
biggest non-Ivy wins of my coaching career."*

—Carmen Cozza

COMING OFF ITS winningest decade under coach Carmen Cozza, the Yale Bulldogs began the 1980s on a high note, winning Ivy titles in 1980 and '81. Unfortunately, the program quickly descended from this peak into a valley, putting together only two winning seasons over the next six years. The Elis would have to wait until 1989 before winning another championship.

The decade included some milestones. Cozza's 100th victory came against the Air Force Academy in 1980. And the following year he enjoyed his biggest non-league win when Yale sank the Navy 23-19. Princeton spoiled a perfect Yale season in '81 after the Elis had dominated the Tigers for fourteen consecutive years. On November 4th, it looked like the trend would continue against the 3-4-1 Tigers. But Princeton quarterback Bob Holly scored with four seconds left to seal a 35-31 victory.

Despite having that blemish on its record, the '81 team was named the ECAC Team of the Year and finished third in the Lambert Trophy balloting behind Penn State and the University of Pittsburgh. The seniors on the '81 team finished 25-4 during their careers, winning three Ivy League titles, two outright.

In 1982 Yale's football status and fortunes changed when the NCAA moved the Ivies to the new and less celebrated Division I-AA, now known as the Football Championship Subdivision, or FCS. This affected recruiting as did a speech delivered by Yale president A. Bartlett Giamatti on April 10, 1980, in which he asked whether "organized games and physical training have any role in our modern University, and if they do, what are their purposes?" The speech—in which Giamatti referenced Sophocles, Aeschylus, and Euripedes—was widely interpreted as a call for the de-emphasis of college athletics. The trend, nationwide, was toward an emphasis on

Former Yale president and major league baseball commissioner Bart Giamatti (on left) at the 1982 Yale-Harvard game. (YALE ATHLETICS)

implementing Title IX, which required adjusting athletic budgets to accommodate women's sports.

Yale's athletic director Frank Ryan and Giamatti came under fire.

In the November 28, 1983, edition of *Sports Illustrated*, Phil Tarasovic, the 1955 Yale captain, was quoted as saying that "Ryan and Giamatti are destroying the program."

The Lund brothers (Ken-'86 and Don-'88) are the only brothers to serve as Yale captains. Don (No. 40) is pictured above. Ken (No. 67) is photographed on next page. (YALE ATHLETICS)

Ken Lund
(YALE ATHLETICS)

Figurative storm clouds were replaced by real ones when the 1985 Yale-UConn game, scheduled for September 28th, was canceled because of Hurricane Gloria, which brought power lines down throughout New Haven. UConn had won the previous three contests between the two teams, and both the Elis and Huskies had undefeated records at the time they were to play. "Our seniors were disappointed, because this was their last chance to beat UConn," according to Yale's SID at the time, Mark S. Curran. At least 40,000 fans were expected at the game. Not only did Gloria disappoint fans, but someone missed out on a chance to win a car as well. A UConn booster club had organized a halftime raffle of a 1986 Chevrolet, but wound up sending the car back to the dealer.

"Yale's athletic director Frank Ryan wanted to play the game," said Rich Schyner, former superintendent of Yale athletic fields. "I was against it because access to the Bowl was nearly impossible. There were trees down and many people were without power. Traffic lights weren't working and the ticket sellers couldn't get there. In the end, New Haven Mayor Biagio DiLieto ordered the game canceled."

In 1987, the Bulldogs encountered a tsunami in Hawaii where the Rainbow Warriors pummeled the Elis 62-10, the widest margin of defeat (52 points) in the history of Yale football. The season, however, saw three thrilling last-minute comeback victories engineered by quarterback Kelly Ryan, against UConn, William & Mary, and Penn.

In 1989, quarterback Darin Kehler, drafted off the baseball team, and linebacker Jon Reese, led the Elis to an 8-2 record and Cozza's tenth and final Ivy League title.

THE PLAYERS

Kevin Czinger (middle guard) '78, '79, '80

SERIAL ENTREPRENEUR
GREENWICH, CONNECTICUT

"Kevin Czinger is the toughest player I ever coached."-Carmen Cozza

The 5-foot-9, 185-pound defensive dynamo played with a heart as big as the Yale Bowl. Many consider him the greatest Yale defensive player in the modern era. In 1980, Czinger was an All-Ivy first team selection and an honorable mention All-American. He also won the Bushnell Cup as the Ivy League's MVP giving him the distinction as the first lineman to win the award that was begun in 1970.

Czinger, who played with a chip, holds the Yale career record of 27 sacks. Still weak from a bout of mononucleosis, the fearless Bulldog knifed through the line and blocked two punts that led to Yale's two touchdowns in a 13-12 win against Brown in the 1979 opener. Against Boston College in 1980, he made 13 tackles including four in the Eagles' backfield. With Czinger plugging up the middle, Yale led the nation in defense against the rush (75.0 yards per game)in 1979 and was second (83.3 per game) in 1980.

"Harry Jacunski was exactly what I needed as a freshman football player. I was recruited for Yale football, but I didn't show up for the first week of freshman practice. I was scared and intimidated by Yale and, frankly, I didn't believe I could compete academically with the kind of sophisticated and intelligent students I was facing at Yale for the first time. I had never been outside of Ohio for more than one to two days. I also had my doubts about competing athletically.

"Having recruited me, however, Yale didn't accept my not showing up for football practice. And so I was tracked down and asked to come speak with the coaches. I went to the Ray Tompkins House and met with Carm and Harry. Looking back, if Harry had been a strict disciplinarian, that meeting might have

Kevin Czinger, a great defensive player, was a cult figure among his peers. (YALE ATHLETICS)

been the end of my football career and perhaps (or likely) my Yale career. Instead, there was a man who looked at me and spoke to me with empathy and without pressuring me, a man who had been an NFL champion and college legend. Instead of being convinced that I couldn't handle the pressure of both Yale academics and football, I realized that this man would give me a chance to make it all work. He was a good man.

"When I would see Harry and his wife Grace in the stands at the Bowl over the years, I would stop where he was seated. We would hug and I would be filled with tremendous affection for the man.

"Because of the success I had against Brown it has been written that the Brown coach awarded me a letter because I was in their backfield so much. I wouldn't have minded a letter from Brown, but it must have gotten lost in the mail."

Phil Manley (quarterback) '80

DIRECTOR OF CORPORATE ACCOUNTS FOR A LARGE
PHARMACEUTICAL COMPANY
ELKRIDGE, MARYLAND

Yale's First Black Quarterback

"I have the distinction of being the first black quarterback to start a varsity football game at Yale. It sounds like a nice achievement, but the truth is, my Yale football experience was bittersweet. I loved my teammates, but I was frustrated because I wanted to play more.

"I deeply admire and respect former Yale head coach Carm Cozza. He is as honorable as they come and is unquestionably the greatest coach in the history of Yale football. Still, that did not stop me from giving him more grief than probably any player he

ever coached. We had some intense discussions back then concerning my lack of playing time. And to this day, when we are together, after exchanging greetings. I remind him: 'You should have played me more.'

"As a nineteen- or twenty-year-old there is no doubt I felt that being black was part of the reason I did not curry more favor with Carm. Don't get me wrong. I don't believe that Carm looked at me and said to himself, 'No way I'm starting a black guy at quarterback.' And he never treated me any different from any other player. Quite the opposite, in fact. As a quarterback I had opportunities to interact with him much more than most of the players on the team. Other than our disagreements about playing time, never were our interactions unpleasant.

"Regarding his preference of [John] Rogan, I think Carm looked at him and saw a guy who was 6-feet-2, had a great arm, and was cool under pressure. With me I presume he saw a guy who was also confident under pressure, was only 5-8, and possessed only average passing skills. My asset was my quickness—I could make plays with my feet. I honestly think I was the quickest player, not just on our team, but in the entire league. But at the time my feeling was that Carm either didn't recognize my abilities or didn't value them. I'm sure I felt that I had to do more than play well, that I would have to be significantly better than Rogan to beat him out for the position.

"As it turned out, Rogan was not just good, he played so well over the course of his career he is considered among the all-time great Yale quarterbacks (God, it was hard to say that). He deserves every accolade. He was good. And with his play he justified the confidence Carm placed in him. He earned the right to be on the field. My argument has never been I was better than he was (nor did I accept that he was better than I was). My argument was that I could play football. If given the opportunity, I could lead this team.

"I take a lot of pride in the fact that during the 1980 season, my senior year, I played well enough that Carm decided to split time with Rogan and me. I outplayed Rogan in the preseason (no one else remembers this stuff), but prior to the first game I read a quote from Carm in one of the local papers that stated something to the effect, 'Both Manley and Rogan will play, but Rogan deserves the start because of what he accomplished last year.' I remember thinking to myself: it is pretty hard to accomplish anything when I'm standing on the sideline with a clipboard in my hand. But by that time I was so thrilled to just get in a game, I accepted my status without complaint.

"With the exception of Harvard, I had meaningful minutes in every game. I typically played anywhere between one and two quarters, and I got to return punts on occasion, something I loved doing. Despite my frustrations as a junior, there was never any tension between John and me

"On October 11, 1980, we played Boston College and lost 27-9 in Boston. It was the first night game Yale ever played. This was the biggest and strongest team we faced that year. It was a very rainy night. Carm put me in late in the first half and I moved the team, eventually driving our offense to our lone touchdown. I distinctly remember how much my quickness came into play that night. Their linemen were big and slow. It was so easy to run around them.

"Because of my performance against BC, Carm named me the starter for the Columbia game. I was aware that I was the first black quarterback to ever start a game at Yale, but to be honest, there wasn't much fanfare about it. My girlfriend didn't even attend the game. (Her mother was in for a visit. Still, you would think she could make the time—not that I'm still bothered by it.)

Despite losing, quarterback Phil Manley (5) moved the chains in Yale's first night game ever against Boston College. (YALE ATHLETICS)

Locker Room Hi-Jinx

"My teammates, whom I loved, had some fun with me in practice the week of the game. One day I entered the locker room and found my uniform stuffed and hanging from my locker with a noose around the neck and a sign pinned to the chest saying, '*No way a black guy is going to start at quarterback for Yale.*' Before the 'PC police' suggest how offended I should be by this act—save it. This was a college football locker room. Race, sex, politics, religion—even sisters and mothers—nothing was off limits. Everyone who walked in that locker room caught hell. And we loved it. These guys were my brothers. Strange as it may seem, hanging me in effigy was their way of saying, 'Congratulations, Phil ... we are proud of you.'

"So I get the start against Columbia. The Lions came out strong and took an early lead. I remember one pass I threw that hit my receiver right between the numbers. Instead of pulling in the catch, he bobbled the ball, was hit, and I watched helplessly as the ball bounced high into the air, floating down into the waiting arms of a Columbia defender. Just my luck. We were trailing at the half, but we rallied in the third quarter. I led a drive late in the quarter that gave us the lead. We were driving again early in the fourth when I took a shot to the head and was forced out of the game. I should have just run out of bounds, but my mindset was that I had to make plays or I'd be yanked (a learned response). So once I reached the sideline I attempted to cut back up field, only to have my chin introduced to the crown of a Columbia player's helmet. Like a self-fulfilling prophecy, Rogan came in the game and completed the drive, and he must have led us to another score as well. We ended up winning the game 30-10. The next day Jon Stein of the *New Haven Register* wrote an article with the headline, 'Rogan Saves Yale.' All I could do was laugh. Needless to say, my career as a starter was over."

It would be 32 years before another African American started at QB for Yale when Derek Russell started against Harvard on November 17, 2012.

Rich Diana (halfback) '79, '80, '81

ORTHOPEDIC SURGEON
HAMDEN, CONNECTICUT

A first team All-America selection of the Football Writers Association of America in 1981, when he rushed for 1,442 yards, Rich Diana was also UPI's 1981 New England Player of the Year and was 10th in voting for the Heisman Trophy. He was All-Ivy first team in both '80 and '81. In the '81 Princeton game he ran like a runaway mustang garnering a team record 222 yards, sadly in defeat. For his career he rushed for 2,576 yards, at the time Yale's second highest total, and 19 touchdowns, averaging 4.8 yards per carry. He also caught 34 passes for 426 yards and four touchdowns. He played for the Miami Dolphins on special teams in 1982 and appeared in Super Bowl XVII against the Washington Redskins.

"When I was being recruited at Yale, I saw John Pagliaro at the dining hall at Timothy Dwight College, and I was in absolute awe. But to be truthful, I grew up a UConn fan. My brother, Vinnie, played his freshman year there, and my family followed the

Huskies. I saw three Yale games in the Bowl when I was a kid. One of them was when Mike Zito of UConn knocked Calvin Hill out of the game.

Geometric Function Theory

"Yale was a unique place to go to school. One year I had a tough math course and was unable to contact my professor for some extra help. So I met with Yale Athletic Director Frank Ryan, the former Cleveland Browns quarterback. Frank had a Ph.D. from Rice and was a math whiz who had brilliant thoughts on geometric function theory. His doctoral thesis was titled 'Characterization of the Set of Asymptotic Values of a Function Holomorphic in the Unit Disk.' When Frank played with the Browns, Red Smith wrote that the Browns' offense consisted of a quarterback who understood Einstein's theory of relativity and ten teammates who did not know there was one. The two of us sat and did math problems together. Where else but Yale could a student do advanced math problems with the athletic director?

"The coaching I got was excellent. My senior year I would sit with the running backs coach, Rich Pont, and watch film. He put together cut-ups of the great running backs like Calvin Hill, Dick Jauron, and John Pagliaro, focusing on their footwork. He had steps named after each of those individuals. We were expected to execute these steps to perfection in our base plays.

The Historic '81 Season

"The '81 season was historic in many ways. We opened with a 28-7 win over Brown in the Bowl. Before the game I was interviewed by John Papanek, a writer from *Sports Illustrated*. I was told that if I had a big game against Brown, *SI* was going to do a feature story on me. In the first half Brown shut me

Rich Diana, in his most memorable day at the Yale Bowl, scores one of his two touchdowns in Yale's 28-0 win over Harvard in 1981.

down pretty good, but in the second half we started to click. In the third quarter I had an 80-yard run that solidified the game. Carm took me out late in the game and the *SI* photographer told me to stand on a four-foot-high bench. He lay on the ground on his back and took a very creative shot of me. Because of the position of the photographer, it appeared that my head was almost touching the blue sky.

"I thought my day was over when Carm notified me that I was a couple of yards short of Dick Jauron's single-game rushing record. He asked if I wanted to go back in the game. I said, 'Of course.' I was stopped on a couple of plays and even lost yardage, but when the day ended I had a record 196 yards, including three touchdowns—good enough for a feature in *Sports Illustrated*.

Beat Navy

"One of my biggest thrills at Yale was beating Navy in '81. The tradition at Yale was extraordinary when I played, but at the same time we were an Ivy League institution. The year before, we played Boston College and had been beaten. We needed to establish the fact that we could play with the big schools. In '81 I was in competition with Navy's Eddie Myers

in the national rushing category. There was Marcus Allen, Herschel Walker, Barry Redden and myself, followed by Myers in that order at the time of the Navy game. When Navy came to town, we didn't know that Myers was injured and wasn't going to play. Everyone thought they we would go *tete-a-tete*.

"Navy had a strong defensive line and out manned our offensive line by 30-35 pounds per man. Apparently to keep our spirits up, the coaching staff never told us about the size of the Navy defensive line. The game was nationally televised and Ara Parseghian was doing the color. Before the game he proved to be prophetic when he said, 'Rich Diana will not be able to run against Navy.' In my 23 carries that game, 21 of them totaled 20 yards. Overall I had about 80 yards because I had two carries that gained good yardage. They should have beaten us easily, but our defense came on like gangbusters and what looked like a Navy rout early in the game turned into a 23-19 Yale win. Quarterback John Rogan and receiver Curt Grieve were sensational that game and Tom Kokoska scored a touchdown. Would you believe that I never saw a replay of the game until our 30th reunion in 2011!

A Heartbreaking Loss

"Then there was the Princeton game, our only loss. We were two minutes away from Yale football immortality. We were leading 31-28 with a little over two minutes remaining in the game when we ran a pass play on third and 4 that failed. We punted and were subsequently charged with pass interference in the end zone, which put the ball on the 1-yard line. By today's rule the penalty would have been 15 yards from the line of scrimmage, which was the 20.

"That game I carried the ball a school-record 46 times for a then-record 222 yards. Most people weren't aware that I played that game in excruciating pain. Three weeks earlier, in the Penn game I cracked two ribs. I had to wear a flak jacket the rest of the season. And at Ithaca the week before the Princeton game, I cracked two fingers in my left hand against Cornell. If that wasn't enough, in the Princeton game I had a neck stinger in the first half. But when you get the chance to carry the ball, you do it. We just came up a little short.

"After the game I was walking to the locker room with my brother and Seb LaSpina, our offensive coordinator. Sebby said to my brother, 'We should have given the ball to Richie one more time.'

The "Diana Clause"

"I was involved in some controversy my senior year when I was ruled ineligible to play baseball. I had enjoyed a very good baseball career at Yale, and we had some great teams. Had I not chosen to go to Yale, I would have been a first-round draft choice of the Baltimore Orioles in the 1978 draft. But here's what happened.

"At the time there was an Ivy League rule that said if you participated in more than one post-season bowl game, you were academically ineligible. I played in the Blue-Gray game and the Japan Bowl during my Christmas vacation. What right did anyone have to tell me what to do during my Christmas vacation? The following year the 'Diana Clause' was added to the rule book, which basically changed that rule so someone no longer would be academically ineligible because they played in more than one bowl game."

John Rogan (quarterback) '79, '80, '81

EXECUTIVE RECRUITER
GREENWICH, CONNECTICUT

John Rogan was the first player to lead Yale in passing for three seasons (1979-81) since Dean Loucks (1954-56).

The numbers tell the story. John Rogan (19) and Curt Grieve (81) were key offensive players for Yale in 1981.
(SABBY FRINZI)

"Rich Diana was an outstanding talent. We beat the Air Force Academy 17-16 in 1980. Air Force had tied Illinois 20-20 the week before and were heavy favorites to beat us. Rich made an amazing catch of a pass I threw that went for a touchdown. He one-handed it and rode into the end zone with an Air Force player on his back. After the game our captain, John Nitti, presented Carm with a plaque from the players.

John Nitti (41) carries the ball in the 1980 Air Force game.
(EWING/ YALE ATHLETICS)

"Beating Navy in '81 was the pinnacle of my career at Yale. The Tuesday night before the game we watched game films like we always did to prepare for the next game. So we watched the Navy-Michigan game played in front of 105,000 fans at Michigan Stadium. We were trying to concentrate on the game, but looking at the background of fans at 'The Big House' was intimidating. The week before, we watched film of the UConn game, and they certainly didn't play in front of 105,000.

"October 3, 1981, was such a memorable day. Ara Parseghian, Carm's coach at Miami of Ohio, and Al Michaels were there to broadcast the national regional game that was televised on ABC-TV. It was Ara's first time on the Yale campus.

"Navy got off to a 12-0 lead. The first three times they touched the ball they went through us like Swiss cheese. But then we had a stop, and making Navy punt for the first time was important. Late in the first quarter we started throwing the ball and got two or three consecutive first downs. This is when momentum, I think, swung to our side. The linemen in the huddle were saying things like, 'C'mon, guys; we can do it.' At that point I thought that we could take them. For years Yale was a tailback offense but I threw thirty passes that game, which was about ten more than I usually threw. Curt Grieve caught the game winning touchdown pass with about 3:19 left in the game.

"Throwing to Curt during my days at Yale was a pleasure. Curt and I had a sense of invincibility. I think we felt that nine out of 10 passes would be completed. We knew that not many teams would stop us. Curt was 6-feet-4 and had an amazing vertical leap. He was a real technician on how he ran his routes. If he had to make a cut after running 8.1 yards, that's what he would do—8.1 yards on the button.

A Painful Loss

"In '81 we went into Princeton undefeated and blew a 21-0 lead and lost 35-31 on the last play of the game. That was painful because it prevented us from being mentioned among the all-time great Yale teams. Since we beat Harvard the following week, a win against Princeton would have enshrined us. However, I do believe that among the players, the '81 team is recognized as being as good as any other Yale team in school history.

The Rogans vs. Harvard

"My brother Kevin is a great story. He was the starting quarterback his freshman year in '70 when he separated his shoulder. He didn't play again that year, which set him back on the quarterback depth chart for the next three years. He was, however, backing up a quality quarterback in Tom Doyle. As fate would have it, Tom got injured before the '73 Harvard game and Kevin made the first start of his career. How many Yale quarterbacks have made their first start against Harvard?

"Kevin not only answered the bell, he led the team to a 35-0 win. He was 8-for-17 in the passing department with one pick. By the way, the two years I started against Harvard (1980-81), we beat them 14-0 and 28-0. If you're keeping score, it's the Rogans 77, Harvard 0."

Curt Grieve (wide receiver) '78, '80, '81

PROJECT MANAGER FOR A TECHNOLOGY COMPANY
VALDOSTA, GEORGIA

Curt Grieve caught a Yale-record fifty-one passes for 791 yards and thirteen touchdowns in 1981. He had twenty career touchdown receptions and is second only to Eric Johnson (23) in that category. An All-Ivy first team selection in 1981, he played in the Blue-Gray game and was a sixth-round draft choice of the Philadelphia Eagles.

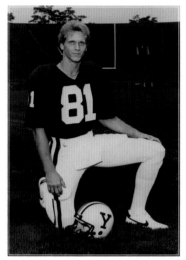

Curt Grieve

"Fans often are curious regarding a player's game-day routine. This is what I did for our six home games my senior year in 1981:

"Team breakfast: This was a low-key affair at a dining hall on campus. Everyone showed up. Although I had a huge appetite in those days, I never ate much at these breakfasts.

"Team meetings: Mid-morning, the team would assemble at Ray Tompkins House, the athletic building adjacent to the Payne Whitney Gymnasium, built in the same neo-Gothic style. The second floor of this building had a long hallway with coaches' offices and meeting rooms. A large meeting room at the end of the hall had wood-paneled walls, and a large sculpted stone fireplace with a leather sofa and chairs in front. It felt like being in the great room of some country estate in England.

"The ride to the Bowl complex: Buses took us from the Ray Tompkins House out to the Yale Bowl. The buses would pass the columns of the Walter Camp Gate and deposit us at the Lapham Field House. The Walter Camp Memorial Gateway, an imposing entry to the Yale Bowl had six columns that are at least two stories high. I loved those columns. The columns, together with the arena of Yale Bowl, made me feel we had our own piece of the grandeur of ancient Rome.

"Lapham Field House: Now called the Smilow Field Center, it was finished in 1923. I don't think it had changed much between then and the early 1980s when it was home to my football locker. I loved its aura. It made me feel a direct connection with the leather-helmet guys on the fabled Yale teams of old.

"Dressing for the game: This involved a fixed routine for me, particularly in 1981. I wasn't overly superstitious, but we were undefeated at home, so same socks, same wrist bands, same everything. Why mess with a good thing?

"The walk to the Bowl: Once ready, players would take the short walk from the Lapham Field House over to the Bowl.

"The Yale Bowl: I recall the Bowl in the early 1980s as crumbling in some parts but still retaining its classic dignity. Like other elements of the Yale athletic fields complex, the Bowl made me feel I'd been transported back in time.

"Pregame warm-ups: This was a fixed routine for the whole team. Being a receiver, I most valued the portion of the agenda where we took turns running pass routes and catching balls the quarterbacks would throw as they loosened up their arms.

"Between warm-ups and the game: Several yards back from the sideline, in the middle of our team area, was a table. The table held the telephones that connected the sideline to the coaches' booth in the press box and a spaghetti-like cluster of wires. After warm-ups at our first home game in 1981 against Brown, I was running toward the table without looking where I was going. At the last second before crashing into it, I looked ahead and saw the obstacle. So I did what was natural to me at the time. I jumped up and sailed over it. After that, I had to do this at every game. Again, in '81, we were undefeated at home. Why mess with a good thing?

"Coming out for the game: When we returned to the field for the start of the game, the day's crowd would now be fully present. For the Harvard game that year, over 72,000 came out. I'll never forget that noise.

"The post-game routine: I was fortunate enough to have my parents at my games, and at times my sisters as well. After one game in the 1980 season, my father and I decided to hoof it and walk back to the campus from the Bowl while the rest of the family rode back in a cab. This started another routine that was then repeated after each game I had played in the Bowl. On a warm fall day following a win, walking back to campus and talking to my father about some catch I had made was really the icing on the cake, and something that I'll always cherish."

Tom Giella (defensive tackle) '81, '82, '83 (captain)

MANAGING DIRECTOR FOR A HEALTHCARE SERVICES COMPANY
EVANSTON, ILLINOIS

Defensive tackle Tom Giella was an All-Ivy first team selection in 1983.

"We went from 9-1 my sophomore year in '81 to 1-9 my senior year in '83. The ball bounced the wrong way in '83, and we had a lot of injuries including players like Paul Andrie, Steve Skwara, Mike Curtin, Peter Gates, and others.

The 100th Playing of the Game

"The '83 Yale-Harvard game was the 100th playing of The Game. Playing the last game of my life in the Bowl in front of over 70,000 people was a real thrill. That day a total of 32 living captains from Yale and a like number from Harvard walked out to midfield for the coin toss with Harvard captain Joe Azelby and me. It was a great way to end my career. Henry Ketcham, who captained the 1913 Yale team, was there. He came out to practice the day before the game and was quite inspiring. Such Yale greats as Larry Kelley and Clint Frank were also in attendance, as was Brian Dowling. Hamilton Fish, who captained the 1909 Harvard team, was the patriarch of all the captains who showed up that day.

1983 captain Tom Giella
(SABBY FRINZI)

"Harvard had a very good team that year and ended up winning the Ivy championship. We played them tough, with the score 13-7 going into the fourth quarter, but lost 16-7. As with every other game that season, we played our hearts out, didn't quit, and left the field with no regrets. To honor the 100th anniversary of The Game, the cover of the program featured a painting by artist Andy Yelenak of both Joe Azelby and me along with the 1875 captains William Arnold (Yale) and William A. Whiting (Harvard). That was the first year the teams played each other to start this heralded tradition.

"Overall, it was a privilege to play football at Yale and an honor to captain a team. The lessons I learned playing football at Yale and in the Yale Bowl are life lessons that will be with me forever."

After the 1983 Harvard game, Harvard students climbed the aluminum goal post at the scoreboard end of the Bowl. The post toppled and fell on Meg Cimino, an 18-year-old Harvard freshman. She suffered a fractured skull and damage to her brain stem and cerebellum. She reportedly received a $925,000 settlement from Yale and the city of New Haven. At length she recovered, returned to Harvard and graduated. She then earned a law degree from the University of Pennsylvania and became a writer and lawyer in New York City.

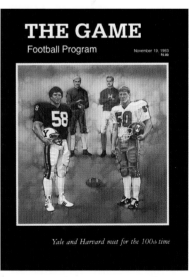

The November 19, 1983, 100th Anniversary Yale-Harvard game day program
(ARTIST, ANDY YELNEK/YALE ATHLETICS)

Mike Curtin (quarterback) '83, '84, '85

ORTHOPEDIC SURGEON
BOISE, IDAHO

When Mike Curtin graduated he held the Yale record for most completions in a career (207). The mark was broken two years later by Kelly Ryan. Curtin currently ranks seventh in career completions among Yale quarterbacks.

"The highlight of my career was the '84 Princeton game. With 91 seconds to play and no timeouts remaining, we launched a drive that covered 98 yards in 12 plays and scored. Princeton, with a 24-21 lead, had reached our 2-yard line. Instead of going for the field goal on fourth down, they went for the touchdown and our defense shut them down. Sophomore Ted Macauley, an undersized tailback who was tough as nails, caught a couple of screen passes to get us out of the hole. Senior tight end Andy Marwede made a big catch on a third-and-10 with fourteen seconds left and brought the ball to the Princeton 14. When we were on our side of the 50, we had our backs to the wall. Once we got on their side of the 50, you could feel the momentum shifting. With five seconds remaining, I threw a 14-yard touchdown pass to Kevin Moriarty, who made two big catches during the drive. He caught the ball in the northwest corner of the end zone. We had beaten Princeton 27-24, and the place went crazy.

"My biggest disappointment was the '85 season when we finished a mediocre 4-4-1. Our expectations were much higher. Since this was my senior year, I still feel responsibility for that. We opened with a win against Brown. Our next game, against UConn, was canceled because of Hurricane Gloria. We were 3-2 overall and 2-1 in the Ivy when we went up to Hanover on Nov. 2 and played Dartmouth to a 17-17 tie. I believe that game changed the momentum of our season, and I always looked at that game

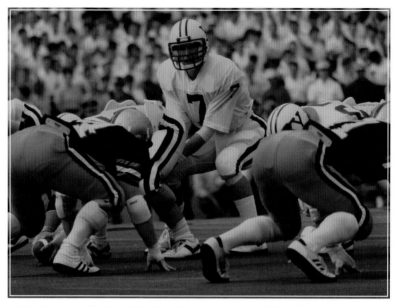

Mike Curtin calls signals in the '85 Army game at West Point. (YALE ATHLETICS)

as the dividing point of a season in which we underachieved. We lost our next two games to Cornell and Princeton but finished with a win over Harvard.

"Perhaps my senior season wasn't what I had hoped it would be, but the memories I garnered at Yale will always be close to my heart. I have a picture in my home of an aerial shot of the Yale Bowl from the 100th Yale-Harvard game played in 1983."

Jim Pucci (kicker) '83, '84,'85

PERIODONTIST
NORTH HAVEN, CONNECTICUT.

"My story is like a bad dream with a happy ending. But first a little background. My freshman year I shared the quarterback duties with Mike Curtin. Then I played fullback on the junior varsity team the next two years. I felt that I wanted to make a contribution to the varsity, so I asked if I could try out as a kicker. So my senior year in '85 I was used as a kicker on the JV team and was a backup to John Duryea, the varsity kicker.

"Normally our traveling squad included one kicker and a punter. But when we played Army at Michie Stadium on October 5, the athletic department felt it would be a good idea to take the entire

266   A BOWL FULL OF MEMORIES

team to experience the history of West Point and the overall atmosphere of the United States Military Academy.

"Army was trouncing us 59-6 with about 2 minutes to play. With Army in possession of the ball at their 35 yard line and feeling as though they would run out the clock, I removed my squared-toe shoe for kicking that I had been wearing the entire game and put on my regular shoe. On fourth down and Army in punt formation, the snap sailed over the punter's head and we took over with just over a minute to go in the game. On the very next play we scored a touchdown. Carm turned to me and said, 'Pucci, go in and kick the extra point.' He caught me by surprise. I didn't have my square-toe shoe on for kicking. So I grabbed my kicking shoe and threw the regular shoe I was wearing on my right foot to the sideline and ran onto the field. Once I got into position to kick the extra point I tried frantically to tie my shoe so we wouldn't get penalized for delay of the game. The clock was ticking and my holder, John Andrews, kept asking, 'Are you ready?' I answered, 'yes' but I wasn't laced up. Anyway, I made a perfect kick for the extra point.

"My next job was to kick off to Army. My shoe was still unlaced and as I tried tying the shoe, my lace broke. So I kicked off with my shoe untied and unlaced and drove it down to the goal line. I made two perfect kicks with an imperfect shoe."

Carmen Ilacqua (linebacker) '82, '84, '85 (captain)

Investment advisorMayfield Village, Ohio

"My freshman year the late Jim MacLaren and I were appointed captains for our first game against Army's JV team. We played the game in front of 40,000 or so

Jim Pucci
(Sabby Frinzi)

empty seats at West Point's Michie Stadium. Jimmie suffered a concussion and I a compressed vertebra in my upper back. We both had to spend the evening back in New Haven in the hospital.

"We shared a room with do-not-move-or-get-out-of-bed restrictions. I could barely take a breath and Jimmie was still loopy, but we both decided we were very hungry. So, we called Domino's Pizza and had them deliver a pizza and some soda to our hospital room around 11 p.m. I managed to get out of bed, and Jimmy Mac and I enjoyed Pepsi and pizza, until the nurse walked in and nearly fainted at the sight she saw—me, barely able to take a breath, and Jim not knowing what town he was in. Our impromptu pizza party in the hospital was short-lived.

The Resolve of Jim MacLaren

"While undergoing his master's studies, Jim was hit by a bus in New York City and had to have a leg amputated at the knee. Undaunted by his disability, he competed and set many records in some of the toughest races, including the New York City Marathon and the Ironman Triathlon in Hawaii. Not

1985 captain Carmen Ilacqua
(SABBY FRINZI)

only did Jimmy compete, he often finished ahead of most of the so-called able-bodied athletes. He was subsequently struck by a van in Mission Viejo, California competing in a triathlon. He broke his neck at the C5 vertebra, paralyzing him from the neck down.

"He received numerous awards, including the Arthur Ashe Courage Award at the 2005 ESPY Awards, the 2008 NCAA Inspiration Award and the distinguished Kiphuth Medal, the highest honor bestowed by the Yale athletic department.

"Unfortunately, Jim died on August 30, 2010, of pneumonia. How much of a cross should one man have to bear in his life!

A Screaming Lunatic

"In my sophomore year I broke my collarbone the first day of practice and missed the entire season. My junior year in '84 we are playing at Harvard, a game we won after being down 14-0 real early, thanks to a career day by Paulie Spivack at tailback. In the second quarter I got tangled up with a receiver who had just caught a pass, and when I slung him to the ground my right thumb got caught up in his belt, tearing the muscle between my thumb and forefinger. Harvard punts, I come off the field holding my right hand. The trainers immediately looked after me and started manipulating my thumb.

"At Harvard Stadium, the fans are right on top of you. All of a sudden, I hear someone yelling, 'You have nine more, just tape it up!' I'm thinking, who is this lunatic screaming at me? I turn around and it is my older brother, Frank, flanked by two members

of the stadium security crew, as his seats were up high. Frank, showing me no mercy, was calling me out to toughen up. No ice or treatment; I just had them tape it up a bit more and resumed playing. My thumb ached for about two months but the pain was worth it as we came back to win "The Game", 30-27.

"One of my biggest thrills was preparing for the Harvard game. On our last Thursday practice of the year, the underclassmen would carry out a long-standing Yale tradition by making a long double line, and the seniors would run through the line and get high fives and slaps on the back from the rest of the team. Like the Jim Croce song, *If I could save time in a bottle*.

Kelly Ryan uncorks a bomb at Cornell in '86. Yale's Chris Martin (75) is on the ground and captain Ken Lund (67) is blocking. In photo is Cornell's Tom McHale (94).
(YALE ATHLETICS)

Kelly Ryan (quarterback) '85, '86, '87 (captain)

TRADER FOR THE CHICAGO BOARD OF TRADE
GLEN ELLYN, ILLINOIS

In 1987 Kelly Ryan won the Asa A. Bushnell Cup as the Ivy League's Most Valuable Player and was an All-Ivy first team selection. He passed for sixteen touchdowns that year and completed a then Yale-record 170 passes for a completion percentage of .603, which currently ranks fourth in team history. Against Army in '86 he passed for 426 yards. Only Joe Walland (437) and Alvin Cowan (438) have passed for more yards in a game. During his career he passed for 4,309 yards including twenty-two touchdowns.

Brother Mike

"I was very fortunate that I had the chance to play two years with my brother Mike at Yale. Mike was a linebacker and the proverbial big brother. In the third game of my sophomore year in '85 against Holy Cross, I went in late in the game at quarterback for Mike Curtin, who was injured. Before I got to the coaches, Mike grabbed me and said sternly, 'You better get the job done.'

"There were about two minutes left in the game and we were trailing 15-12 in a third-and-10 situation. I threw a pass to Dean Athanasia for the first down. We drove down the field and scored to give us a 19-15 win.

"Playing football with my brother was a great experience. The oddity of it all was that in my junior year I called the plays on the offensive side of the ball and he called the defenses. The *New York Times* did a piece on us, using the theme of brothers calling the plays on both sides of the ball. There were times we scrimmaged against each other and Mike would hit me. To be honest, I think he took care of little brother.

Running the Steps

"In the summer of '86, Mike Flannery, Bob Shoop, and I stayed in New Haven and trained together. Bob and I used to go to the Bowl and work out after the work day ended from our summer jobs. We'd go up and down the field like we were driving the ball against Harvard. We made up plays and spent an unbelievable amount of time together. When we

finished we ran the steps. I can honestly say that I've seen the whole stadium.

"My biggest disappointment at Yale was the knee injury I suffered before my junior season in the annual Blue-White scrimmage to help us prepare for the '86 season. Knowing that my brother would be a senior, I wanted to play a full season with him in good health.

"I tore my posterior ligament when a teammate accidentally hit me during our scrimmage. Before the scrimmage I had asked coach Cozza if I could play without wearing the yellow vest that quarterbacks usually wore so they wouldn't get hit. I wanted everything to simulate game conditions as much as possible and Coach allowed me to play without the vest. I don't know if wearing the yellow vest would have prevented the injury from happening, but I know I didn't want to be the only player on the field wearing a yellow vest.

A Miracle in the Bowl

"The time I spent with Shoop proved helpful our senior year, especially in the Penn game, the most unusual game I ever played in.

"We entered the game 3-2 (1-1 in the Ivy). Two of our wins were of the last second-variety, against UConn (30-27) and William & Mary (40-34). At the time, Penn was the team to beat in the Ivy and we were looking for a turnaround game for our program. We led 21-7 in the last quarter when Penn came back and took a 22-21 lead. They had the ball at midfield with about thirty seconds left in the game, and we were out of timeouts. All they had to do was take a knee, but their quarterback fumbled the snap and Mike Browne recovered the fumble.

"We took over on our 42 and I passed 12 yards to tailback Mike Stewart. I then hit Shoop on a quick-out pattern ('77 Pass'), and he ran out of bounds in front of the Yale bench. We ran the same play to Shoop, which brought the ball down to the 32 with 18 ticks on the clock. We figured if we got about 10 more yards, Dave Derby, our kicker, had a good shot at winning the game with a field goal. We called the same play to Shoop, but this time he faked his out pattern and went up and deep along the sideline. He was told to go as far as he could before stepping out of bounds to stop the clock in the closing seconds of the game. Well, I hit Bob again and he ran along the sideline. But when he was about to get tackled with about 6 seconds remaining, instead of stepping out of bounds and putting the game in the hands of Derby, he turned toward the middle of the field and headed toward the end zone. If he makes it into the end zone, we win the game. If he gets tackled before crossing the end zone, we lose since time would run out. A Penn player just missed tackling Bob before he crossed the goal line. We kicked off, and they had one play from scrimmage and the game ended. It was the most improbable win in my career and perhaps in Yale football history.

"I didn't know that Shoop had scored. I was lying on the ground and looking at the sky. I didn't see anything, but I knew we won the game when I heard the roar of our fans and saw two Penn defensive linemen standing over me, one of whom was cussing.

"After the game we went up to the room under the stands where we held our pregame, halftime and postgame meetings. Coach Cozza said a few words and then the whole team sang the Yale fight song, *Bulldog, Bulldog, Bow, wow, wow, Eli Yale.* The place was rocking. I then went back out to the field where my parents were waiting for me along with my brother, Mike, and my sisters Molly and Katy. We took some pictures and I still have them. These are memories that money can't buy.

The Freeze Bowl

"It seemed like there were so many bizarre games in '87. We played Princeton in New Jersey in 70-degree weather on November 14. Thanks to some great blocking, we had one of the best offensive games of our season in our 34-19 win. We completed 21 of 30 passes for 329 yards and three touchdowns and no interceptions. The Princeton quarterback that game was Jason Garrett, who went on to coach the Dallas Cowboys.

"It's hard to believe that one week after playing Princeton in unusually mild weather, we played Harvard on what some have said was the coldest day in the history of the state of Connecticut. The temperature was in the low teens, but if you include the wind chill factor it might have been 20 below. It was beyond cold. The newspapers called it the 'Freeze Bowl.'

"Despite the frigid weather, a large crowd turned out for the game. We were losing 14-10 late in the game and were driving. I wondered if there could be one more great come-from-behind win. Then we fumbled and our season came to a disappointing end. We were 'one miracle short,' as coach Cozza recalled in his book, *True Blue.* But the season had been a special experience for our entire team, and while losing our final game was heart-wrenching, it didn't take me long to realize how lucky I had been to be a part of an extraordinary group, the men of Yale football.

"When the game was over, Harvard captain Kevin Dulsky hugged me and said, 'You could be my quarterback any time.'

A Special Gift

"My relationships went beyond the football program. I befriended a man who worked in maintenance. Before I graduated he gave me a gift I will always treasure. He presented me with a walking stick that he carved from the back of a broken bleacher from the Bowl. He engraved my name, class, and statistics. It's a piece of the Yale Bowl, and I love it."

Jon Reese (linebacker) '87, '88, '89 (captain)

FOUNDER OF "MAKE IT COUNT FOUNDATION" (PROVIDES RESOURCES FOR OPTIMAL HOUSING, HEALTH AND EDUCATION)
WEST ISLIP, NEW YORK

Jon Reese, a linebacker from West Babylon, New York, started every game but one in his three-year varsity football career and was captain of Cozza's last Ivy title team in 1989. He won the Ted Blair Award as team MVP that year and was chosen first team All-Ivy. He had 122 career tackles. He played on a total of four Ivy champion teams in lacrosse and football and won the William Neely Mallory Award as the top athlete in his class. An outstanding lacrosse player, he was elected to the National Lacrosse Hall of Fame in 2011.

Thanks to leadership gifts from Jon and his brother Jason Reese '87, Jamie and Cynthia Kempner '79, Kevin Genda '87 and Karen Yarasavage '87 together with an anonymous $1 million challenge match made by a former player to the Yale Soccer Association and many other donors, Yale in recent years has significantly upgraded its soccer-lacrosse stadium. It was renamed Reese Stadium in 2006 and dedicated in 2011.

Halloween Night Accident

"It's inexplicable and perhaps a miracle that I was able to play the final three games of the '89 season, considering the accident I was in on Halloween night. We were really fired up that week following an emotional 23-22 win over Pennsylvania on the last Saturday of October. We were undefeated in the Ivy with three games to play—Cornell, Princeton and Harvard.

"After practice on Tuesday night five of my teammates were loaded in my car as we headed back to the campus for the training table. There were three guys in the back seat and my two roommates, Tony Guido and Bob Bennett, were sitting in the front. Guido

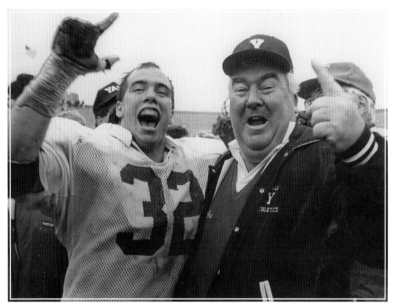

Jon Reese celebrates a victory with Harold McGrath who worked security for many years in the Bowl.
(SABBY FRINZI)

was sitting on Bennett's lap. We were on Edgewood Avenue when a drunk driver ran a red light and hit us almost head-on. My face went through the front windshield, and I broke my jaw in two places. My upper jaw was shattered like an eggshell. I also broke my nose, tore ligaments in my elbow, lost several upper teeth, and had a lot of stitches on my upper lip. I suffered a concussion and lost consciousness. When I awoke in the Hospital of St. Raphael, Carm was in the room. I was barely able to talk. Although I don't remember saying it, Carm said that I said I was sorry. He couldn't understand what in the world I was sorry for.

"The expectation was that I would never play football again. I should have been thankful just to be alive, but I was already thinking how quickly I could get out of the hospital and get back in uniform with the team. During my Yale career I had never missed a game from the start of the '87 season through my senior year. But the chance of playing against Cornell on Saturday was a long shot at best.

"My jaw was wired shut and I just drank fluids. They transferred me to the Yale Health Center, and on Friday I was allowed to visit my teammates at practice. I worked it out with my brother or father to sign me out. I remember how much pain I was in. My face was so swollen I couldn't recognize myself from photographs that were taken.

"My teammates all huddled around me at the practice in the Bowl. I could not speak to them and it was a very emotional experience.

"I dressed with the team on the day of the game, thinking that my chances of playing were remote at best. In the first quarter Kevin Skol, my replacement, got injured. I ran down to Carm and looked at him. I could not speak but he knew that I wanted to go in. He paused and said, 'Just don't get hurt.'

Darth Vader

"Subsequent to my injury, Joe Levatino, who was on the equipment staff, trainer Bill Kaminsky and 'Sweet Lou' Scigliano had designed a special helmet for me with a black visor, not knowing if I would ever use it. I looked like the reincarnation of Darth Vader. In the heat of battle on the field, the enclosed helmet began to fog up with condensation. And with all the work done on my face, and with my elbow in a cast, it was problematic putting on and taking off the helmet. We got the helmet off and I grabbed a hammer and smashed one of the two upper panels of the mask. This would allow air to get through, but I did look pretty ugly, as noted by one of the Cornell players.

"I was somewhere between tentative and painful. Every time I made a hit, I was afraid to take out my mouthpiece because I thought my teeth would be lying in it.

"In retrospect, it was pretty insane for me to be playing that day even though Yale kept an oral surgeon on the sideline to monitor my situation. But I had two healthy legs and one healthy arm. I was confident in my effort and I did a pretty good job,

making nine tackles and causing a fumble. Most important, we won the game 34-19 and remained undefeated in the Ivy.

"Following the game I went back to the hospital because my whole body was cramping up, since I hadn't eaten anything in several days.

Wall Street

"There was a positive side to the injury in that it was responsible for my getting my first job on Wall Street. I interviewed for a position at Lehman Brothers, and the guy who interviewed me was rude and obnoxious. He had his back turned to me for a time and kept challenging me with questions. He finally said to me, 'What makes you more qualified than the 500 or so applicants that are seeking the same job?' I told him my accident story and how a man's effort was so important in life. I looked him in the eye and said with confidence, 'If you teach me, I'll do the job better than any of your applicants.'

"Apparently I blew the guy out of the water. He immediately summoned one of the managing directors. We spent time talking and then he called in another managing director. By 5 p.m. I had the job.

"Unfortunately, I have continued to suffer the effects of my injuries from that accident. Between 2008 and 2010, I had to have my six top front teeth removed, and then the oral surgeon had to remove dying bone and then rebuild and replace the bone. After that healed, an orthodontist wired my jaw to realign it the way it was before the bone started decaying. After about a year the dentist removed the temporary teeth, screwed in titanium posts and implanted my new pearly whites!!! At least I lost 20 pounds during the process—which I have recently found.

"A lot of people sympathized with me but actually I'm proud of the ordeal.

A Maximum Effort Guy

"In '88 we beat Harvard 26-17 at Harvard Stadium. I had an excellent all-around game and my teammates carried me off the field. How often do you see a football team carrying a defensive player off the field? Every time I look at that photo in Carm's book *True Blue,* it gives me a warm feeling. But my biggest thrill at Yale has nothing to do with a game or a championship. It is what I learned about myself through what Yale provided me educationally and athletically as a football and lacrosse player. I learned from my coaches and teammates that it was important to give everything you've got. In the process of doing that, it was OK if you lost.

Make it Count

"On September 11, 2001, my life changed as a result of the terrorist attacks in New York City, when I lost my best friend and twenty other close friends. Rich Lee, one of my teammates at Yale, lost his life on 9/11. A defensive tackle, Rich was a gentle giant. He had an office at Cantor Fitzgerald, a bond-trading company located on the 104th floor of the World Trade Center's North Tower.

"The horrific events of 9/11 inspired me to deliver the message that life is short and it's important to make it count while we are on this earth."

Rich Huff (cornerback) '87, '88, '89
BUSINESS SYSTEMS ANALYSIS, SENIOR SPECIALIST
KELLER, TEXAS

No relation to NFL Hall of Famer Sam Huff, Rich was selected to the 1989 All-Ivy first team. In '89 he had seven interceptions, a single-season pass interception record he shares with Clint Frank (1936) and Mark Wallrapp (1995).

Rich Huff blocks an Alan Hall punt in the 1988 Harvard game. Kevin Brice (26) and Bob Stokes (29) converge on Hall. Brian Hennan recovered the ball at the Harvard 35 and scored. It was the first blocked punt return for a TD in the history of the Yale-Harvard series.
(SABBY FRINZI)

Molly

"Anyone who has been around Yale football has seen and likely been a part of the post-game tradition of inviting fans to the field to mingle with players. I had my first taste of this as a sophomore and it was pretty heady stuff for a young player, being asked for an autograph.

"It was during one of these sessions that someone different showed up. I was on one knee, chatting and signing, when I caught sight of a girl, younger and smaller than most that day and looking not too sure of herself. She made a couple of steps forward, but was nudged by larger kids and backed off toward mom and dad. So, wrapping up with one kid, I turned directly to her and said hello. She was a bit shy, but offered up a program for me to sign. She had been so patient and had been overrun by others for a while, so I made a point of spending a little more time with her, asking her name (Molly) and asking questions. Her folks explained that they were big fans of Yale football and that in order to make games more interesting for all of their kids, they had each child pick a favorite player to watch. Molly had settled on me. Did I mention that these sessions were ego boosters?

"Well, Molly and the Jennings family continued to come to games and I always made a point to look for her and spend some time. She warmed up a bit, flashed more smiles and chatted more. There came a game when Molly couldn't make it because she had some issues with asthma.

"I didn't consider this to be that big a deal, really, until I got a letter at Yale Station. It was from Molly's parents and in it they thanked me for taking time to chat with their daughter. I was pretty floored. It was just what I thought anyone should do in my place. In any event, I think we both made an impression on each other. We exchanged a couple of letters and I got a care package or two. To be honest, I think I got far more out of it than Molly could have. But the story doesn't quite end there.

"Years later I wound up coaching at Brown. I was just a part-time assistant and stuck up in the booth during the games. Coming down the bleachers after one game, someone called my name. I was now face to face with the Jennings family again. Molly's older brother attended Brown and they were in for Family Day. It was an incredible coincidence and brought back all the memories from afternoons in the Bowl. I confessed that all of her notes and drawings had been kept and thanked her again.

The Leaper

"In 1989 we added a new scheme for PAT and field goal blocks called the leaper. Chris Brown and I had some decent jumping ability, so we switched from a traditional approach from the edge to a full frontal assault. 'Brownie' and I would set up as middle linebackers and wait for the snap. The guys up front—Scott Wollam, Bruce Bottorff, Carmine Perelli and others—would go low to force the offensive linemen to stay down. A couple of steps forward, and Chris and I would launch with hands up. We got at least three that season, maybe as many as five.

Sam Huff

"A great many of my memories of Yale football are rooted in things that happened outside of the game itself. The road trip dinners, with Vic Meglio asking, 'You gonna eat your fat?'; the pack of old timers, die-hard football fans asking about my being related to Sam Huff, the NFL linebacker/Hall of Famer and my leaving them guessing by saying, 'I don't want to comment on that; I'm trying to make my own way'; the weekly pilgrimage to Phil's barbershop to see Sabby Frinzi's photos from the previous Saturday.

"The most enduring of those memories is my five-year-old friend, Molly!"

Darin Kehler (quarterback) '88, '89, '90

DIRECTOR OF OPERATIONS/HIGH SCHOOL FOOTBALL OFFICIAL
HERSHEY, PENNSYLVANIA

Quarterback Darin Kehler rushed for 1,643 yards and passed for 1,816 yards during his Yale career. He was selected to the All-Ivy first team in 1989.

A Phone Call from Carm

"I played defensive back on the '87 freshman team and a little quarterback but decided to concentrate on baseball my sophomore year.

"Yale opened the '88 season with a 24-24 tie against Brown before getting spanked by UConn 41-0. The next two games on our schedule were Navy

Darin Kehler (13) was a double-threat quarterback.
(SABBY FRINZI)

and Army. Coach Cozza was concerned because his three quarterbacks, Bob Verduzco, Mark Brubaker, and John Furjanic, were all struggling with injuries. Two days after the UConn game, coach Cozza called my room and asked if I would be interested in helping the team at quarterback. At the time I was playing fall baseball. Freshman football coach Joe Benanto, knowing the dilemma that coach Cozza was in with the injured quarterbacks, suggested to Coach that he call me.

"I was surprised and in disbelief by the phone call. I think it was the only time in Carm's thirty-two years at Yale that he tried to recruit a player off the campus. I was interested but concerned how the rest of the team would feel, since I did not go through the drudgery of the preseason two-a-day sessions and it was already Sept. 26. I didn't want to come in during the middle of the story. Carm told me to come to his office and that he would talk to the team about it. The team endorsed the idea, and instead of going to baseball practice that day, I traded in my sliding pads for shoulder pads.

A Developing Quarterback

"We lost to Navy 41-7 and Army beat us 33-18, but we didn't play badly. The Monday before the

Army game I played in the JV game against Milford Academy and got my feet wet. Carm was watching the game from the tower. Fortunately, my first action in over a year produced very good results, as we scored on every possession that I was behind center while my baseball teammates cheered me on. I got in the Army game for a few plays and was making steady progress. Buddy Zachery scored on an 82-yard run that game. On that same day, Columbia beat Princeton and broke a 44-game losing streak, the longest in the nation. Carm was able to breathe a sigh of relief, because we had Columbia next and he was worried that Columbia would end their streak against us.

"We beat Columbia 24-10 and I got sufficient playing time. I wanted to be able to manage the game and stay within myself, which I think I did. I got my first start of the season in Game 7 against Dartmouth. We were losing 13-12 when we put together an 82-yard drive from our 11-yard line. The drive concluded with a 24-yard field goal by Scott Walton. Buddy then ran 57 yards for an insurance TD and we won 22-13. I think that was the defining game for me because it solidified the respect of the team toward me.

"We then lost to Cornell and Princeton but beat Harvard in Boston, 26-17. To me that game was the springboard for the '89 season. Brubaker came in that game and engineered an important two-minute drive that some people might forget.

A Talented Lot

"I thought of the three years I played, the '88 team was the most talented offensively. We had a big line with guys like Jeff Rudolph (guard), Art Kalman (tackle) and Mike Ciotti (center). Rudolph and Kalman were first-team All-Ivy selections. Zachery and Kevin Brice were outstanding running backs. Unfortunately, the coaching staff did not have enough time to prepare an offense that would utilize my running skills. But they did for the '89 season and it proved to be successful. Fortunately, Nick Crawford transferred in from Davidson, which gave us two effective option quarterbacks.

The Wishbone

"The wishbone was made for a quarterback like me. I was only 5 feet 9, 165 pounds. If I dropped back, my vision would be obstructed. I enjoyed running the option, which I did in our opener against Brown when I ran for 107 yards in our 12-3 win.

"The following week against Lehigh, Hurricane Hugo came through and we won 33-17. I scored three touchdowns, ran for 186 yards and completed 11 of 15 passes. The sky got black and it started pouring in the third quarter. The student section was chanting, 'Hugo, Hugo, Hugo' as the water came running down the steps. It looked like Niagara Falls in the Bowl.

"I was awarded the 'Gold Helmet' award by the *Boston Globe* as the top player in New England that week, an award that I am proud of.

Carm's Last Title

"We were 8-1 going into the '89 Harvard game. Harvard coach Joe Restic employed his Multiflex offense and jumped on us for a 21-0 lead. The Multiflex changes formations on virtually every play. The idea is to confuse the defense. Carm once said, 'When you play Harvard, you have to be able to defend the United States.'

"We climbed back and got to within 21-20 but missed the extra point. I think that deflated us and

we lost our momentum. Harvard went on to win 37-20. Although we lost, we did gain a share of the Ivy title in '89 which was Carm's last Ivy League championship.

MIT Prank

"A strange thing happened in that game when some MIT students attempted to pull off a prank. We were huddled in our own end zone opposite the scoreboard when somebody set off a charge that was intended to propel something out of the goal post behind us. Something was supposed to unfurl but it didn't. However, some light smoke came out of the post. Where else could you experience that type of incident during a college football game?"

An earlier incident concocted by MIT students occurred in the second quarter of the 1982 Yale-Harvard game. After a Harvard score, a huge black weather balloon surfaced at midfield in Harvard Stadium. The balloon had been installed underground with vacuum motors and freon gas that inflated it to a diameter of almost 6 feet. The letters "M-I-T" appeared across its girth before it exploded, spraying talcum powder on the field.

Going Out with a Flourish

"In '90 we finished 6-4, 5-2 in the Ivy, good for third place. But we did win the H-Y-P 'Big Three' title by beating Princeton and Harvard. Although I was an option quarterback, I enjoyed throwing to Ya-sin Shabazz that year. I suffered a freak back injury in the Lafayette game that set me back. Somehow my head landed in the stomach of a Lafayette tackler and when he leaned on me it compressed my spine and created a pinched nerve in my hip. It actually put my hip to sleep for about two weeks and slowed me down.

"The Princeton game in the Bowl was played in front of only 5,500 rain-soaked fans. This was my final game ever in the Bowl and we made the best of it, winning 34-7. After the game we had some fun doing belly-flops in the mud near the Yale bench. I remember sliding through the mud with the Michalik twins, Rob and Chris. My Yale Bowl swan song was certainly an unusual one.

"The following week at Harvard I was the most focused I ever was going into a game. I didn't want to go out with a loss. I was really dialed in, particularly because of losing to Harvard the prior year, which spoiled our undefeated league season, and our 34-19 win was a feeling of accomplishment. In my two varsity seasons we went 14-6. There was so much emotion when Carm took me out of the game. We hugged and I'm sure we both felt a sense of satisfaction, thinking of the day he called my room."

REMEMBERING KEVIN CZINGER

CARM COZZA

"If I picked my All-Yale team, I would have to pick two or three at each position. Pound for pound, Kevin Czinger was unreal. He bench-pressed more than twice his weight. He could press 400 pounds. He was extremely quick, extremely aggressive and extremely bright. He scored close to 1,600 [the maximum then] on his SATs.

"Kevin was quiet, yet he had a way of intimidating people. He was the kind of guy that, when he got on the bus, everybody got quiet. He had a tryout as a linebacker with the Cleveland Browns. They were impressed with him, but ultimately he was too short at 5-feet-10."

KEN HILL

"I lockered next to Kevin Czinger because he was No. 40 and I wore No. 42. I was a quiet Southern kid and Kevin didn't say much to anybody. One day we were having a conversation at the field house when I looked up and saw a bunch of guys looking at us, surprised that we were having a conversation. Czinger stories are legendary. He had some temper. He was a short kid and unbelievably strong. He probably had a Napoleon complex."

LEN FASANO (RUNNING BACK) '78, '79, '80—ATTORNEY, STATE SENATOR; NORTH HAVEN, CONN.

Len Fasano is the son of the late Dr. Len Fasano who lettered in '47, '48 and '49.

"Normally we were quiet at halftime. But in one game against Columbia we didn't play well in the first half. Czinger lost it at our halftime meeting. He started punching the wall, yelling, 'We shouldn't be losing to this team.'

DAVE KELLEY—DEFENSIVE LINE COACH, 1973-96

"I've had the privilege to coach many great players, but in my opinion Kevin Czinger was

Len Fasano signs a young fan's game day program.
(YALE ATHLETICS)

memory and told him the page number. The next day defensive coordinator Buddy Amendola and I were at the Ray Tompkins House when we received a call from the offensive coordinator at Florida State, BC's next opponent. In his deep Southern drawl he said, 'Coach, we've been watching this guy (Czinger) and we think he's the best football player we ever did see. How big is that boy, 220?' I answered, 'No, 190.' He replied, 'He's a son of a bitch. I don't know if our boy at middle guard [Ron Simmons, a consensus All-American] could beat him out.'

the best modern football player at Yale. He was not just a great football player, he was a brilliant student who held everybody to a higher standard. If he looked you in the eye, he would burn holes through you with his glare.

"He did things that nobody his size (5-10, 190 pounds) with his ability should be able to do. Czinger was strong and his intensity was on another level. At St. Ignatius High School in Cleveland, he wrestled heavyweight at 190 pounds and pinned future middle guards at Michigan and Michigan State.

"In 1980 Boston College beat us up there 27-9. He played head up on the guard and head up on the center, depending on which defense we were in. Both the center and the guard he played against went on to have a lengthy career in the NFL. In the first half he had five sacks and four tackles, three in the backfield. The BC kids couldn't block him, and they were embarrassed.

"In the second half they started tackling him. They ran eight straight plays where they illegally tackled Kevin because they couldn't block him. So Kevin went to the official and not only complained, he quoted the holding rule by

Czinger's Summer Workout Program

"When he returned for his senior year ('80) Czinger looked immaculate, like he just came out of an Allegeheny Steel plant. During the first meeting with my linemen I asked them how they made out with the summer physical training program I gave them. Kevin said, 'Coach, I didn't use it.' I asked, 'What did you do?' He said, 'My mom and I worked out every day. My mom got in our car and I pushed the car up and down the street.' I then asked, 'How many times did you do this?' He said, 'Until I dropped.'

An Arm-Wrestling Challenge

"One time a recruit challenged Kevin to an arm-wrestling match. That was a mistake. Dennis Tulsiak, a 6-foot, 240-pound kid from Pittsburgh, had won a 'Strongest Man' contest. During his visit to Yale he was at a party when Czinger walked in to the room. 'Is that Czinger?' he asked. When he was told that it was, he went up to Kevin and said, 'Let's do it. I want to arm-wrestle you.' Czinger replied, 'What's wrong with you, man?'

"Tulsiak looked at Czinger like he was a piece of meat he could chew and spit out. Everybody in the room knew what was going to happen except for Tulsiak. They got ready, and Czinger put Tulsiak down faster than you can say Albie Booth. Tulsiak complained that it was an unfair start. So they did it again, and again Czinger put him down in a flash and bruised his arm. Tulsiak looked up at him and said, 'I gotta come here. This is amazing.' Dennis ended up as a three-year starter as a defensive tackle and was an All-Ivy first-team selection in 1980.

"Czinger and Tulsiak got to be good friends. One night they were walking down Broadway by the Yale Co-Op and were taking parked cars and bouncing them to the middle of the road."

JOE BENANTO

Czinger and Crowley

"When I coached the freshman football team, I had Czinger and Bill Crowley, two former great Yale players, as volunteer assistants. Bill was a Rhodes scholar and two-time first-team All-Ivy selection (1977-78). Crowley helped coach the linebackers and would come to practice in suit and tie directly from his workplace. Czinger, who was in graduate school, was a physical fitness nut. He was also as ferocious of a coach as he was as a player. He used to put the kids through some very intense drills. He wasn't there every day, which brought a sigh of relief from the players. When they saw him coming, they would let out a collective 'Oh, no' groan.

"Czinger, who was undersized, had aspirations of playing in the NFL. Apparently a pro scout told him that he should be a linebacker because nobody scouts nose guards. When he returned for his senior year in 1980, he wanted to play linebacker. This put Carm and Dave Kelley, the defensive line coach, in a delicate situation. But they worked it out, and Kevin agreed to play the nose guard or middle guard position as he had in the past.

"As for Crowley, one day we were playing at Princeton on a Saturday morning. The game had started and I couldn't find the defensive team. I soon noticed that Crowley was having them scrimmage on another field."

THEY REMEMBER THE 1980S

JON STEIN—*NEW HAVEN REGISTER* REPORTER

"Regarding Yale's win over Navy in '81, *Register* writer George Wadley, who was on the Jets beat but who followed Yale football, saw Rogan's winning pass to Curt Grieve at 30,000 feet, on a flight to the West Coast. It was one of ABC'S highlights."

SEB LASPINA—YALE OFFENSIVE COORDINATOR (1974-96)

"One of my most satisfying games was when we beat Navy in '81. I called three touchdown passes that game-two went from John Rogan to Curt Grieve and the other went from Rogan to Tom Kokoska."

Tom Mercein (30) scores one of his two TDs in the '86 Yale-Harvard game.
(YALE ATHLETICS)

Game day program cover for the September 28, 1985, Yale-UConn game that was never played because of Hurricane Gloria.
(YALE ATHLETICS)

CARM COZZA—YALE HEAD COACH

"Beating Air Force in '80, which was my 100th win, and Navy in '81 were the biggest non-Ivy wins of my coaching career.

"A real tough loss was the '81 Princeton game. We went down there undefeated, and we weren't a bad defensive team. We had beaten Princeton 14 straight years. We had a bad pass interference call in the end zone. If the rules were like they are now, we would have won that game. At the time, if there was a pass interference call in the end zone, the ball was placed on the 2-yard line. Now it's a 15-yard penalty"

VITO DEVITO—FRESHMAN BACKFIELD COACH (1974-91)

"Rich Diana had a great career as a running back and a baseball player. I'll never forget the game he had against the Harvard freshmen at Harvard in '78. We always had a tough time up there. But that day he scored on an 87-yard pass

play and went 67 yards on a punt return, and we won 30-0. The following day the varsity beat Harvard 35-28. It was a great weekend.

"Rich went on to become an orthopedic surgeon and did two knee replacements on me. Looking back, you can say that maybe I played a small part in helping Rich develop into a great college running back. But he played a bigger role in my life by giving me the ability to walk again."

SABBY FRINZI—YALE FOOTBALL PHOTOGRAPHER

"When Pat Ruwe was the captain in '82, my hand got hit with an errant pass while I was standing on the sidelines. Ruwe, who would become an orthopedic doctor, came over and took a look at my hand. He asked, 'What finger do you snap the camera with?' I told him and he said jokingly, 'Since it's not the finger you use to snap with,

Linebacker Jeff Rohrer was an All-Ivy first team selection in '81. He was a member of the Dallas Cowboys from 1982-88. (YALE ATHLETICS)

you're fine.' He's been my doctor ever since.

CHUCK MERCEIN

"My son, Tommy, who played at Yale ('84-'86) also wore my No. 30 and played the same position. My biggest thrill was not as a player but rather as a father when I saw him score two touchdowns against Harvard in '86. It was Tommy's last game as a senior at Yale."

TOM PEPE

"Would you believe that my first day on the job as sports turf supervisor was September 28, 1985, the weekend of Hurricane Gloria? The Bowl was ready for play, but one of the reasons the Yale-UConn game was canceled was that the traffic lights weren't working. The Yale officials didn't want any intoxicated fans driving on streets without traffic lights."

"The Yale-UConn game became one big party. It wasn't just UConn students filling up Lot D; it became a social event for the local colleges as well. If there were 30,000 to 40,000 fans in the Bowl, there were another 15,000 or 20,000

1981 captain Fred Leone at 2011 Yale-Harvard tailgate party. The former defensive end was a first team All-Ivy selection in 1980 and 1981. (RICH MARAZZI)

in the parking lots. The athletic department would subcontract a company to install portable toilets in Lot D that would serve as a separation between the regular fans who parked there and the partying students. One year there were eighty or so portable toilets, and a horde of UConn students ran down the line of toilets and knocked them over, door side down, with people in them.

The Freeze Bowl

"One of the most unusual cleanups we had was following the frigid '87 Harvard game, when some reports said the wind chill was 45 degrees below zero. That day fans were leaving at the end of the first quarter because of the horrible weather conditions. By halftime any food they left (soda, apples, bananas) was frozen. My eyeballs hurt for three days after that game. I had to have borderline frostbite on my eyes."

DESPITE WINNING AN Ivy League championship in 1989, it would be another ten years before the Bulldogs would enjoy another Ivy League title. Carmen Cozza retired following the 1996 season after thirty-two years as Yale's head coach. He was replaced by Jack Siedlecki, who led the Elis to an ivy championship in his third season.

YALE BULLDOGS
GAMEDAY

125th Year of Yale Football

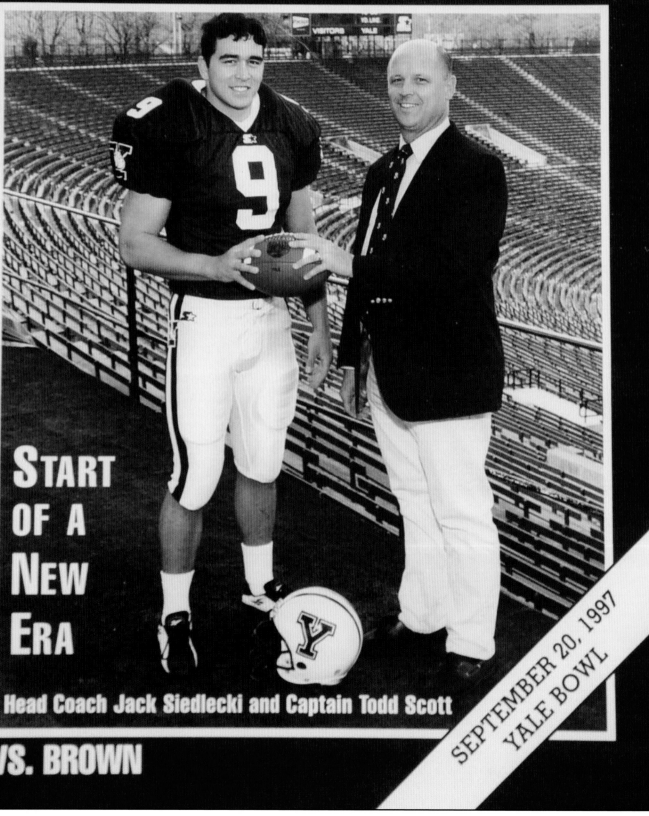

START OF A NEW ERA

Head Coach Jack Siedlecki and Captain Todd Scott

VS. BROWN

SEPTEMBER 20, 1997
YALE BOWL

CHAPTER 21

THE 1990S—A LONG WAY BACK TO GLORY

"I have spent my entire career trying to get this job. I want to be with the best student-athletes because it's fun to coach guys who have that kind of intellect. I have an unbelievable amount of respect for the Yale football tradition."

—Jack Siedlecki at the December 19, 1996, press conference when he was introduced as Yale's new head coach.

AFTER A DECADE of excellence in the seventies, followed by the up and down (and up again) eighties, the nineties were a time of significant changes for Yale football. In 1993 the Ivy League made freshmen eligible for varsity football for the first time since the 1940s. At the end of the 1996 season Carmen Cozza retired after thirty-two seasons as Yale's head coach. He was the winningest coach in Ivy history but the program floundered in his final five years when Yale was an anemic 17-33. The Bulldog had lost its bark. The splendid days of Dowling and Hill, of "Pags" and "Spags," were fading memories. The nineties were the only losing decade the Bulldogs ever suffered in the Bowl.

A front-page editorial in the *Yale Daily News* called for Cozza's resignation or discharge. Many readers thought it was a joke—maybe part of a parody issue of the *Daily News* wrought by Harvard hands. But it was no joke. (The editor of the *Daily News* at the time was Theo Epstein, who went on to become general manager of the Boston Red Sox and is currently the President of Baseball Operations for the Chicago Cubs.)

Cozza was succeeded by Jack Siedlecki, who was to head the football program through 2008. In Siedlecki's maiden season, his youthful team went 1-9. Injuries forced the Bulldogs to open the season with a freshman, Mike McClellan, at quarterback—the first freshman to start at the position since Art Dakos in 1945.

The Yale-UConn rivalry came to an end in '98, when the scholarship Huskies smothered the Bulldogs, 63-21. It was the most points an opponent had ever scored against Yale. In their forty-nine-game series, which began in 1948, Yale held the edge, 32-17.

Failure is sometimes the fire that forges the steel of success. In 1999 the Bulldogs rose from the depths to regain their proud position on the Ivy vine

sharing the League title with Brown while going 9-1 behind the passing of southpaw QB Joe Walland and the receiving of future NFL tight end, Eric Johnson. Yale's only loss came against Brown the first game of the season. It was the second time Brown spoiled a perfect season for the Elis in a season opener; the first time was in 1976.

Walland got up from a sick bed to lead Yale to a 24-21 victory over Harvard. His final TD toss went to Johnson with 29 seconds left. Entering the 2014 season, this was the last time Yale beat Harvard in the Bowl.

Johnson, a fidgety 6-foot-3, 225-pound receiver, had 21 catches and 244 receiving yards, both single-game Yale records. Steve Conn, the Yale Sports publicity director, wrote of Johnson, "God must have put in overtime to create this Yale player."

Corner back Todd Tomich and safety Than Merrill were both two-time All-Ivy first-team selections in 1999-2000. Merrill played defensive back for the Chicago Bears in 2001.

THE PLAYERS

Chris Kouri (fullback/tailback) '89, '90, '91 (captain)

ATTORNEY
CHARLOTTE, NORTH CAROLINA

Chris Kouri was an All-Ivy first team selection in 1991, when he rushed for 1,101 yards. During his Yale career he rushed for 2,006 yards (4.6 per carry) and had 16 touchdowns.

"My dad passed away during my junior year in high school and my years at Yale were difficult dealing with that loss. There's no replacement for your father, but the coaches at Yale, as a group and individually, gave me a sense of security at a tough time. The coach that left the most indelible impression on

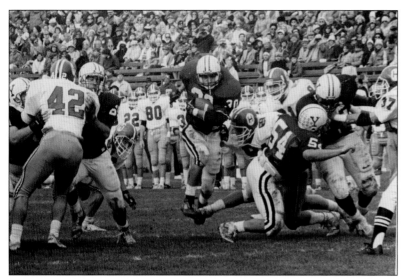

CHRIS KOURI GAINS VALUABLE YARDAGE IN THE 1989 YALE-HARVARD GAME. ROB
MICHALIK (65) AND DAVE RUSSELL (70) DOUBLE TEAM HARVARD'S ERIC DRURY
(42). MIKE CIOTTI (54) AND TERRY JOHNSON (72) ALSO CLEAR THE WAY FOR
KOURI.
(SABBY FRINZI)

me was Rich Pont, who coached the running backs. He had a quiet, steely way that emanated from Cozza. Coach Pont was wise, funny, and underestimated in his humor. He was a great observer and had nicknames for everybody. He called me 'Zebra-able' saying I was quick, agile like a Zebra—powerful animal. He referred to Dave Sheronas as 'The Plug,' and called Dave Kelley 'Tomcat F-14.' The nicknames and military terminology he preferred made us all laugh.

"Coach Seb LaSpina had a funny, quiet way of sounding tough. He would say, 'You've got to give him the shillelagh,' if he wanted a crushing block or a tackler punished. I played at 5-11, 195 pounds and he always wanted me to put on weight. He would quip, 'Chris, how about if you go and eat a sandwich?'

"I was so nervous during the preseason two-a-days my sophomore year in '89. We stayed at the Old Campus, and I don't think I slept a wink the entire week that ended with a scrimmage against the University of New Haven. I had two long runs that game and perhaps that impressed the coaching staff, since I became a starter thereafter. So fatigued and sleep deprived, I got sick and was hospitalized immediately following

that UNH scrimmage. I remember and appreciate Cozza's visit with me as I recovered.

"Unfortunately, we lost to Harvard that championship season. I remember catching a pass over the middle in 'The Game' of '89 and got speared in the lower back—it really laid me out. While on the ground in a fog of pain, I heard the crowd erupt in cheer —the pain and confusion blended together. Coach Cozza came out to check on me, as he always did with his injured players. After the game, I learned the great cheer resulted from MIT's attempt to pull a prank that backfired near our huddle in the south end zone—happening almost simultaneously with me getting injured.

"I had a 90-yard touchdown run against Princeton in '91—that was a thrill. We were in a Power-I formation and I ran almost up the gut. We isolated their left inside linebacker and I shot the hole. There was a lot of contact and a lot of shifting. The play glided to the right side of the field and I was able to hide behind some traffic and take off. I got some great blocking and glided past the wall. But despite our dominance in many parts of the game, it was one we let slip away, 22-16.

"The most frustrating loss, though, was the Dartmouth game my senior year in '91. We masterfully executed an eight-minute drive in the last quarter to pull ahead 24-21 with 1:48 left in the game. Then Jay Fiedler, Dartmouth's great (and future NFL) quarterback, engineered a 79-yard scoring drive to win the game 28-24.

"I played and battled with some great teammates and friends like Kevin Allen, Nick Crawford, David Russell, Ya-Sin Shabazz, Maurice Saah, Scott Wagner, Carm Perrelli, Eric Drury, Adam Lenain, Eric Kaup—I could go on. Dave Russell (whom we affectionately called Otis) tragically died of esophageal cancer. We miss him.

"It bothers me that we never beat UConn, but we did beat Harvard and Princeton two out of my three varsity years. The '90 game in Boston might have been the most complete game of that season—we won 34-19. That year we also beat Princeton to take the Big Three title for the first time since '84.

"Hey, it was a great experience!"

Dave Sheronas (fullback) '90, '91, '92 (captain)

DEPARTMENT OF DEFENSE EMPLOYEE
ASHBURN, VIRGINIA

"Taking the field for the first time with the Yale freshman team at Clint Frank Field was the greatest thrill I ever had at Yale. Something unusual happened to me before the first freshman game I ever played. Dave Kelley, a teammate and the son of assistant coach Dave Kelley, was pumped, and he smacked my head so hard that it took me until the middle of the first quarter to get my bearings. In my four years at Yale I was never hit that hard.

"We had some outstanding players in '92 but couldn't put it together. It's difficult for me to talk about it. But in my career I was fortunate to play with such talented players as defensive back John Furjanic, offensive linemen Kevin Allen and Bart Newman, defensive tackle Erik Lee, quarterbacks Nick Crawford, Steve Mills and Chris Hetherington, running backs Keith Price and Chris Kouri, and linebackers Milt Hubbard, Kevin Hill and Ben Heim.

"My senior year my shoulder got ripped out its socket in the Princeton game and I wasn't supposed to play against Harvard. I assured [our team physician] Dr. [Barry] Goldberg and the coaching staff that if they allowed me to get in just one play, I would make sure that I would stay away from contact. I

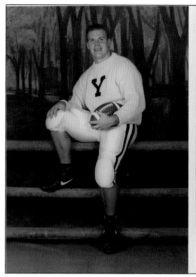

1992 captain Dave Sheronas
(SABBY FRINZI)

went into the game as a wide receiver with my arm taped up. The Harvard D-back on my side held his arms up like 'What's going on here?' We called a running play, and I ran right at the D-back and gave him a forearm shiver. When I ran off the field, Dr. Goldberg yelled, 'You asshole, Sheronas.'

"I felt a need to serve our country, so I enlisted in the Army in '99 and went to Officer Candidate School. I was in the military for six and a half years. My shoulder injury continued to plague me, so I went to the Army Medical Center at Landstuhl, Germany, for an MRI and I got the surprise of my life. I went into a room to get an injection before the MRI, and in walks Chuck Wennogle, who was now Dr. (Major) Chuck Wennogle. Chuck was a kicker at Yale from 1988-90. He stared at me and said, 'Dave Sheronas?' He stuck me with a needle full of dye as we caught up on old friends and our football days. Not quite the training room, it brought back memories of heating pads and ice baths."

John Saunders (outside linebacker) '91, '92, '93 (captain)

CEO AND FOUNDER OF A FOOD COMPANY
CASTLE ROCK, COLORADO

Carm Cozza chats with Harvard coach Joe Restic before Restic's final game in 1993. Also in photo is Yale captain John Saunders (36) and Harvard captain Brian Ramer (58).
(SABBY FRINZI)

A Trip to Disney World

"My greatest thrill as a Yale football player was also, in the end, one of my greatest disappointments. In 1993, Yale had been given a great opportunity to have a very competitive road game with a very tough and up-and-coming team at Central Florida. For us, this game represented something very close to the Super Bowl. To top it off, we were going to play the CFU team at a terrific field, the Citrus Bowl in Orlando.

"After arriving in Orlando on Thursday evening, the entire Yale football team was the star of the Disney World parade during the day on Friday. As usual, Coach Cozza was very sensitive to his team losing focus and getting caught up in the pomp and circumstance. We anticipated a great game but knew it would be a tough battle, especially since we had lost our All-America candidate at running back, Keith Price, who was out for the season with a very bad ACL injury in our first scrimmage.

"It began to sink in that we actually had a good chance of winning this game! With less than a minute left, we began our last defensive stand with the lead still in hand. Without a doubt, this was the hardest-fought game in my Yale career, and although we ended up losing 42-28, the entire Central Florida

team, fans and stadium were stunned by the game they had just witnessed.

"Beating Harvard three out of four times was special. We truly had respect but always forged against a deep desire to always stick in Harvard's face on the football field. My final Harvard game in '93 was an important one because it was the year that Joe Restic was retiring and would be the twenty-third[rd] time he and Carm Cozza had met each other across the field. It was also the 110th time Yale had played Harvard, so there was plenty of focus on the game and how the Ivy League continued many of its education-first initiatives, such as no athletic scholarships for athletes. For me it was extra special because I had undergone a serious brain surgery in early January, which had jeopardized my ability to play my final season at Yale, let alone the final Game.

"I have a condition called Arnold Chiari malformation, which means the base of my brain is extremely large and extends a little bit out the hole where my spinal cord comes out. I had always had minor headaches, but after my junior season they became severe. After going through my options with several neurosurgeons, I decided to do a 'relatively' simple surgery, which essentially just made more room for my brain by cutting out a crescent-shaped piece of my skull and first three vertebrae. Outside of having to cut through the muscles in the back of my neck and the rehab associated with that, it really wasn't too bad, so I was ready to play by the time two-a-days rolled around.

" In the end, we won The Game 33-31, with Harvard's last-second 'Hail Mary' pass being deflected by Martin Feeney and Carl Ricci. The moment is imprinted in my mind and I will never forget those fall days that occupied so much of my young life. Boola Boola!"

Carl Ricci (linebacker) '92, '93, '94 (captain)

Attorney
North Kingstown, Rhode Island

Linebacker Carl Ricci was an All-Ivy first team selection in 1994.

Taking a Punch from Goofy

"When we played Central Florida they were very good and were ranked in the top 10 in Division I-AA. We arrived on a Thursday night and the following morning, we went to Disney World, which I'm not sure was a good idea on a very hot day after a flight. I had been there before, so I just found a hotel on the grounds and relaxed with a teammate.

"We had a parade with the Disney band that went up Main Street and took photos with the characters. I was teasing Goofy, and he wasn't happy about it. He hit me with an uppercut in the solar plexus area and really stung me. I tried not to react like it hurt, but it did.

"There were many Yale alumni down there for the weekend. They really made a big thing out of it with the usual tailgate parties etc. And the Citrus Bowl had the nicest locker room I was ever in.

"We entered the game 0-2, starting the season with losses against Brown and UConn and were heavy underdogs in front of a hostile crowd. The game had upset written all over it as we were ahead 28-27 entering the final minute. Central Florida was driving, and they were on our 9-yard line when they fumbled. The ball went up in the air and a wide receiver picked it off and scored. We got the ball back with about thirty seconds left and threw an interception. It's hard to believe that we were ahead by one point with a minute to play and lost by 14. If there was a positive from that game, it taught us that we could play in big games against good teams.

1994 Yale captain Carl Ricci gives interview on the road (Yale Athletics)

Yale's Last Win Over UConn

"In '94 we opened with wins over Brown and Holy Cross. Our next game was against UConn, a team that was bigger and more physical than we were. This was Skip Holtz's first season as UConn's head coach. As the Yale captain, I went to my first press conference, which was in Hartford. I was just hanging back, since most of the attention was focused on UConn. A woman reporter from Channel 8 came up to me and said, 'Are you a player?' I said, 'Yes.' She asked, 'How can Yale beat UConn, since they are bigger, faster and stronger?' I found that to be very depressing.

"I answered, 'We're not going to play the game in the weight room. And you didn't necessarily say they were better than us. That's why we're going to play the game.'

"We got an early lead and held onto to it. After our first touchdown we recovered an onside kick, which was a key play in a game that we won handily, 28-17. After the game I was walking back to the field house when the same Channel 8 reporter, who didn't give us a chance, stopped me and said, 'Carl, I can't believe you did it.'

"My biggest thrill at Yale was beating Brown my senior year, 27-16. It was my first game as captain, and being from Rhode Island, I felt it was special. It was Mark Whipple's first game as the head coach at Brown. I had five interceptions that season and three of them came against Brown. I returned one for a touchdown. I returned another one for a TD but it was called back because my roommate, Mark Wallrapp, was called for clipping. If he didn't clip, I don't think I would have scored because I was running out of gas as I headed downfield.

"My biggest disappointment was the losing. We were 18-22 during my career. We lost to Princeton all four years, but we did beat Harvard three times, including my junior and senior years. It was nice to walk off the field for the last time with a 32-13 win at Harvard Stadium in '94."

Rob Masella (defensive back) '93, '94, '95, '96 (captain)

ORTHOPEDIC SURGEON
CALDWELL, NEW JERSEY

Defensive back Rob Masella, a versatile performer, was an All-Ivy first team selection in 1996. When he returned the opening kickoff against Brown in 1993, he was the first freshman since 1946 to carry a football for Yale. He ranks third among Yale players in career kickoff return yardage with 1,143 yards, behind only Chris Smith (1,484) and Robert Carr (1,401). His 95-yard kickoff return TD vs. Brown in 1994 led to Yale's 27-16 win.

"My greatest thrill was returning an interception for a touchdown at West Point my senior year. It gave us a lead in the second quarter. I still have a vivid memory of picking off the pass thrown in the flat and taking it to the end zone untouched, with our fans in that corner and turning around to see the entire stadium of cadets quiet and speechless. "My greatest disappointment was our home record (7-15) at the Bowl during my four years of varsity.

Carm's Last Captain

"The 1996 season was for me the greatest spectacle that I was ever a part of. I was Carm Cozza's last Yale football captain, which was my greatest honor. The media frenzy started in preseason camp when Coach Cozza came to us and told us that he was retiring. The press conference in the Smilow Field Center was televised over many networks and was the first of eleven I would be a part of. We beat Brown (30-0) to start the year off right. I had a big day personally in the win vs. Bucknell, playing against a former high school teammate and All-Patriot League player, Hunter Adams. At the press conference after the Columbia game I sat next to future NFL All-Pro Marcellus Wiley.

Rob Masella picks off Army pass and runs for TD in '96 game at West Point.
(YALE ATHLETICS)

"I'll never forget the '96 Princeton game, coach Cozza's last in the Yale Bowl. Having all but I think two of Carm's captains lined up on the 50-yard line before the game, and my being the only one to still have the ability to play, was a special feeling. It is only a select few young men who get to be the Yale football captain, and I was one of Carm's 32 captains. For that, I am thankful I chose Yale football.

An Unusual Game Day Ritual

"The strangest and most unusual thing happened my freshman year at our preseason scrimmage against Union at the Bowl. I happened to find myself close to captain John Saunders at the front of the tunnel because I came off the field last from pregame practice. While the seniors were getting everyone pumped up for the game, I hear retching, and then vomit hits me in the calf. Saunders then looks back, as I do, and Dave Dixon looks at him and says, 'Ready.' I came to find out that Dave had been doing that for his entire career. It was a game-day event that I became accustomed to and even looked forward to. Crazy, but that's Yale football.

"That scrimmage against Union was marked by season-ending injuries to three of our best players—Keith Price, running back; Dave Feuerstein, wide receiver; and Chris Hetherington, quarterback. Dave was our primary threat on kickoff returns. When the next kickoff return came about, the coaches were scrambling for a replacement and I happened to be standing next to Cozza when he said, 'Masella, get in there.' Wouldn't you know it; they kicked the ball to me and I brought it back 90-plus yards and got tackled on the 1-yard line. I wasn't stretched out, having watched the previous hour of play. To this day, coach Dave Kelley still rides me for getting caught on that play. By the way,

I was so nervous, my roommate and QB Blake Kendall told me, that I didn't even put in my mouthpiece, which he saw flopping out as I ran past our sideline."

Peter Sarantos (defensive end) '96, '97, '98, '99

SALES FOR A MEDICAL EQUIPMENT COMPANY
HERMOSA BEACH, CALIFORNIA

Defensive end Peter Sarantos was an All-Ivy first team selection in 1999. He was a part of the "three-headed" defensive end rotation with Eli Kelley and Jeff Hockenbrock. Both Sarantos and Hockenbrock earned All-New England honors. Sarantos had 18 career sacks and Hockenbrock had 22, second only to Kevin Czinger.

"The record books show that the 1999 football squad went 9-1 and captured a piece of the Ivy League title. The team established some impressive stats, but it's not the numbers that we remember when we gather together and reminisce; it's the stories. To quote author Tim O'Brien: 'Stories are for joining the past to the future. Stories are for those late hours in the night when you can't remember how you got from where you were to where you are. Stories are for eternity, when memory is erased, when there is nothing to remember except the story.'

"For example, any picture of the defensive unit from the 1999 squad will show lineman Andy Tuzzolino with a cast on his right hand. The cast is unremarkable, and most probably wouldn't even notice it, but it's hard to forget why he had to wear it. He broke his hand in preseason by punching an offensive lineman in the face. Repeatedly. It was a fellow Bulldog player, and the lineman was wearing a face mask. I don't know if you've ever been punched in the facemask while wearing a helmet, but it doesn't hurt at all. Nice going, 'Tuzz.'

Peter Sarantos tackles Harvard's Chuck Nwokocha in Yale's 24-21 win in '99. Yale's Than Merrill (8) and Josh Phillips (27) are in photo. (YALE ATHLETICS)

"The Big Nerd"

"Before he was a star tight end in the NFL, Eric Johnson was terrorizing opposing Ivy League defenses with his crisp routes and ridiculous hands. Eric was an Academic All-American and one of the nicest guys around. His nickname was 'The Big Nerd.' Therefore, it was inherently more hilarious and completely unforgettable on the one occasion he managed to get into trouble. A freak snowstorm had blown through around the time of spring practice, and as we were waiting for the coaching staff to make their way to the field, Eric uncharacteristically tried to draw some laughs and lob a snowball in their direction. I'm sure he intended the projectile to come up short, but he pelted Steve Plisk, the strength coach, square in the face from about 60 yards away. I'll bet his athleticism didn't help him much on the 10,000 miles he probably had to run as punishment. But he definitely got some laughs!

Bizarre Ending vs. Brown

"And who could forget the seesaw of emotions in the '99 Brown game? It was our season opener, and the game went back and forth all afternoon. The ending was something even Hollywood couldn't script. In the last minute of the contest, we were winning 24-17. Brown scored but Ben Blake blocked the game-tying extra point-only to have the holder pick up the ball and advance it toward the end zone. We managed to bring him down short of the goal line, but not before he blindly pitched the ball back to this fullback [Bob Scholl], who looked to be 400 pounds and waddled in for a 2-pointer, giving Brown a 25-24 win.

"We even managed to get in field goal range to win the game because Brown drew two unsportsmanlike-conduct penalties that were enforced on the kickoff. But our 47-yard field goal attempt by Mike Murawczyk came up short. We ran the table and won the rest of our games including a share of the Ivy League title and fell just short of being the first team to go undefeated and untied since the great 1960 team 39 years earlier.

"Another iconic figure from the 1999 team is the revered quarterback Joe Walland. He had a magical touch, an uncanny ability to make spot decisions, and a pair of legs that helped him get out of dozens of sticky situations. Joe would be the first guy to tell you so. However, if he tried to tell you so back then, you probably wouldn't have been able to understand it. Joe had what could best be described as a "unique dental arrangement." To be more specific, Joe had about eighty-five teeth in his mouth. Captain Jake Fuller swears that he had to act as interpreter in the huddle after Joe would make the play calls. I'm not sure if he grew all of those extra teeth to intimidate opponents, but I know he scared the hell out of me! He has since pared back to the normal 32 adult teeth and now has a model's smile. But his mouthpiece still exists as testament to what was once freakishly awesome."

Jake Borden (wide receiver) '96, '97, '98, '99

COMMERCIAL REAL ESTATE BROKER
BOSTON, MASSACHUSETTS

"In '97 against Valparaiso at Soldier Field in Chicago, coach Jack Siedlecki sent in Joe Walland to replace our starting quarterback, Chris Whitaker, who suffered a concussion in the second quarter. Walland's first play was a short pass completion. It was now third and 12 at midfield and Siedlecki sent in a sweep play. Walland asked me if I was open on the previous play, and I said, 'Yes.' So Walland, a sophomore quarterback, in his second varsity play, shrugged off Siedlecki's play and threw me a pass for a first down. We scored 27 unanswered points in the second half and won 34-14, our only win of the season.

"We entered the '98 season having lost thirteen straight Ivy League games. Our last Ivy win had been the opening game of the '96 season when we beat Brown 30-0. In '98 we opened with Brown at Providence. We were losing 28-24 when Walland threw a

Jake Borden makes TD catch in the '98 Penn game at Franklin Field.
(YALE ATHLETICS)

'Hail Mary' pass into the end zone on the final play of the game and I caught it to give us a 30-28 win. We called the play 'Big Ben.' It was a thrill because not only did we win the game, but my parents, brother and a couple of friends were there at Brown Stadium. We beat a Brown team that was a favorite to win the Ivy, and when we got back to New Haven we partied at Toad's."

Joe Walland (quarterback) '96, '97, '98, '99

MANAGER FOR A MEDICAL DEVICE COMPANY
MANHATTAN BEACH, CALIFORNIA

Some achievements fade into the mists of time, but what Joe Walland did in the '99 Harvard game endures. He came out of the infirmary and completed 42 of 67 passes for 437 yards leading Yale to a 24-21 victory. In the second half he uncorked the genie. Walland's 20-for-33 third quarter and his 33-for-51 second half, set Division I-AA records for attempts and completions. His final TD toss went to Eric Johnson for a touchdown with 29 seconds left. His performance earned him a Gold Helmet award from the New England Sports Writers.

The runner-up to Brown QB James Perry for the Ivy League Player of the Year Award in '99, Walland still holds Yale records for attempts and completions in a game, and only Alvin Cowan has passed for more yards in a day (438 in 2003). Walland's career interception rate, only 1.65 percent in 787 attempts, is another Yale and Division I-AA record. Over his career, Walland passed for 4,832 yards and 35 touchdowns. He remains tied with Brian Dowling for throwing touchdown passes in 14 consecutive games.

"The final 24 hours of my Yale football career might be a subject for Ripley's *Believe it or Not*. It virtually was a trip to hell and back. My family arrived in New Haven from Ohio in the middle of the week for the '99 Harvard game, and we planned a weekend of revelry and fun together. The weather was cold that week and I wasn't feeling well. I practiced on Friday

Yale QB Joe Walland (7) escapes Harvard's Mike Sands (99) in Yale's 24-21 win over Harvard in 1999.
(Sabby Frinzi)

but felt awful. After the Friday practice, Dr. Barry Goldberg, our team doctor, sent me to the infirmary, where it was discovered I had a 103-degree temp and was admitted. I think I had the flu but never did know.

"They kept me on IV's all night to keep me from dehydrating. In the middle of the night I had to use the bathroom and I was so weak I needed assistance from a nurse to get there. Kickoff was less than 12 hours away and I couldn't make it to the lav on my own power. Throughout the night I had to gargle and take antibiotics. Obviously, I was not confident that I would be playing against Harvard.

"Dr. Goldberg picked me up early on Saturday morning. I was weak, and I think I lost 10 pounds. I normally played at 205, but that day I would say I was down to 195. Kickoff was five hours away and I was swallowing horse pills every three hours. After I got taped I sat outside because I was burning up from my fever. Fortunately it was a seasonably warm day for late November.

"Miraculously, I started the game on about two cylinders. But I gained steam late in the second quarter when my fever broke. Once I got caught

up in the game, I wasn't thinking how I felt. It didn't matter that I hadn't eaten any food in the last 24 hours. Maybe my adrenalin took over—whatever; it was all about beating Harvard at that point.

"In the second half we decided to go with the no-huddle shotgun offense, using four wide receivers—Eric Johnson, Jake Fuller, Jake Borden and Tom McNamara. It was a no-huddle, check-with-the-QB offense. With the exception of the first play of the second half, when I handed off to Rashad Bartholomew, every play was designed to be a pass play. I think I had to run the ball three times and was sacked once or twice, but we beat them with our passing game. Ironically, I had a ligament tear in my throwing thumb that was shot up with cortisone. Not many knew about that injury.

"As the game wore on, we noticed that one of Harvard's cornerbacks was vomiting from exhaustion, having to chase our receivers all over the field with limited rest in between plays. So we worked on him. Harvard's defense was sucking wind and, knowing they were tired, we went at them relentlessly.

"The Catch"

"With twenty-nine seconds to go we were trailing 21-17 when I hit Eric Johnson in the end zone. The pass was deflected by Harvard's left tackle and it fell short, but Eric caught it just above the ground and we won the game 24-21. We ran the same play earlier in the year against Penn. Johnson had the ability to get inside the defender and block him off, which is what he did on that play. After the game Harvard coach Tim Murphy admitted to me that his defense was gassed.

"It's been well publicized that I came out of a sick bed that morning, but I don't think any one knew that I broke a big toe in the third quarter when a lineman fell on the back of my heel as my foot was in a vertical position, snapping my big toe back. I also got cleated pretty bad on my other big toe. When the game was over, they had to take a heated scalpel and put it under my toenail to relieve the hematoma. That was the most painful experience of the day.

"Following the game I went back to the infirmary to get checked. I was released and returned to my apartment, where my family and friends joined me and ordered pizza, a far cry from a nice dinner at a good restaurant. The next morning I went to the Yale New Haven Hospital for X-rays on my broken toe. Then I went back to Cleveland with my parents, since there were no classes the following week. That was a fun ride, eight hours on the Pennsylvania Turnpike. Physically, I was a mess. If we had a game the next week, I wouldn't have been able to play. But beating Harvard made it all worthwhile."

In his story for the New York Times, *headlined "Walland Quits Sick Bed to Give Share of Title to Yale," Jack Cavanaugh summed up the quarterback's achievement this way: "Quarterback Joe Walland earned a place in the Yale Bowl pantheon today with one of the greatest performances in the annals of Eli football."*

Josh Phillips (cornerback) '97, '98, '99, '00

ASSISTANT STRENGTH AND CONDITIONING COACH, UNIVERSITY OF CALIFORNIA AT BERKELEY
DANVILLE, CALIFORNIA

"I thought I would win a championship and die the same day. Here is what happened.

"On the final play of the 1999 Harvard game, Ryan LoProto intercepted a pass to seal the win.

When I saw the ball go into his hands, that was a big moment. I ran over to Ryan to congratulate him when suddenly my teammates piled on and fans rushed the field. I was completely pinned under a whole bunch of people. I couldn't breathe and couldn't move my limbs. It was so frightening for a minute or so. I was yelling for people to get off.

"The 24-21 win over Harvard was my biggest thrill. Conversely, my greatest disappointment came in the final game I ever played in the Bowl—on November 11, 2000, when Princeton beat us 19-14. I was assigned to cover Chism Opara, an exceedingly athletic 6-3, 210-pound receiver.

"In the last two minutes of the game, we were winning 14-12. Princeton had the ball in their own territory. On third and long, quarterback Jon Blevins threw the ball to a little back out of the backfield. He ran for 10 yards as Ray Littleton and I were converging on him. I got there two steps before Ray and could have made a solo tackle and knocked him out of bounds. But if I did that it would stop the clock, so I tried to stand him up. Ray knocked him toward the side, and he ran for another 25 yards.

"Princeton was now on our end of the field and threw a deep post to Opara. The ball hung up in the air and he had box-out position on me. I could have tried to undercut him and attempt an interception, but I decided to play it safe and strip him. He went up in the air, caught it, and came down in the end zone with sixteen seconds left on the clock. Blevins then attempted to rush for two points but failed. My final game ever in the Yale Bowl resulted in a 19-14 Princeton win with me falling into the end zone with Opara. In retrospect, if I had to do it over again, I would have made the solo tackle on the back who caught the ball out of the backfield, even if meant stopping the clock.

Josh Phillips
(SABBY FRINZI)

Locker-room Fun

"The locker room was a place we had fun. Mike Murawczyk, our kicker, was one of the cockiest kickers I ever met. He loved to play practical jokes. He used to frequently tape the lock to my locker and would do this with others. Nobody could determine who was doing this, and we were all blaming each other. Then I figured it had to be Mike, because he had the free time to pull this prank while the rest of the players were at their individual team meetings. Also, he was done with practice before anyone else and would come into an empty locker room. But I had the last laugh. One day I put four rolls of tape on his lock.

"My junior year we had a 'pose down' muscle-man contest in the locker room. Five or six guys entered. The winner would be judged by the entire team. They flexed their muscles in fun. In mockery of it all, Todd Tomich, who was a skinny white kid, came out in a jock strap carrying two 5-pound dumbbells. The team chose Derek Goeriz the winner. He was from Texas and came out oiled-up wearing Hanes underwear and cowboy boots performing to the tune of heavy metal music.

"One unusual thing I remember about practice was that women's soccer coach Rudy Meredith would practice with us one day each year during spring ball. He did the individual and tackling drills.

LoProto's Strange Death

"I graduated in 2001, and the tragic realities of life have struck like a Mack truck. Ryan's [LoProto] death on July 10, 2005, has always bothered me. We

were very close. We were in the same Bible study group and the same defensive backfield. He apparently fell off a bridge in Spain. People just don't fall off bridges. It's unclear how it occurred. I know his dad tried to get the investigators to look deeper into the case. Another teammate, Jim Keppel, died in his sleep in New York City on May 9, 2003. They found that he had a heart defect. Jim owns the Yale running back record for catches in a game (9), season (32) and career (65).

Post-Season Games

"If I had a complaint, it's that Ivy League schools cannot participate in post-season football games. They are allowed to in other sports, but not football. I once questioned past President Richard Levin about that. He answered, 'There are three reasons: (1) It would cheapen the significance of the Harvard game, (2) it would interfere with final exams, and (3) we might get embarrassed.'

"I say, let the athletes decide that."

Tom Gioia (Nose tackle) '97, '98, '99

PRIVATE EQUITY INVESTOR
ATLANTA, GEORGIA

"I was a spot player. I played defensive line, goal-line defense, you name it. My biggest thrill was the '99 Penn game, when I got to play about three quarters of the game. [Assistant] Coach Duane Brooks said, 'I can't find anybody to stop the run.' But I went in and did the job. That game was key in our winning the Ivy League title.

"My biggest disappointment was being injured my entire freshman and senior years. During my freshman year I hurt my wrist just before the first game of the season, which would have been Jack

Tom Gioia
(SABBY FRINZI)

Siedlecki's first game as Yale's head football coach. I had to have my wrist reconstructed in '97, and my senior year I blew out a disc in my spine.

"What added to my disappointment as a freshman was that I didn't get a lot of attention from the coaching staff. When I came out of surgery at Yale-New Haven Hospital, there was one guy there waiting for me as I was being rolled out, and that was Ben Johnstone, a wide receiver. That one visit from Ben, a guy I didn't really know, kept me connected to the team. I didn't get a visit or a phone call from any other player or coach. I never felt I was doing those early-morning workouts for the coaches.

"My first semester at Yale I was only able to use my left hand for three months. That made it difficult for writing assignments and taking tests.

"But I don't want to sound like sour grapes. I have a lot of respect for Siedlecki and I loved Brooks, my position coach. We still keep in touch.

"As for Ben Johnstone, I never did tell him how much that visit meant to me. But I will."

THEY REMEMBER

JACK SIEDLECKI—HEAD COACH, 1997-2008

From the Outhouse to the Penthouse

"After going 1-9 in '97 we had nothing to hang our hat on, so I hung a sign on every player's locker that read, 'Believe without Evidence.' I think our opening-game 30-28 win against Brown in '98 turned things around when Jake Borden caught that great 'Hail Mary' pass from Joe Walland. We finished 6-4, including wins over Princeton (31-28) and Harvard (9-7). Winning the 'Big Three' championship with a second-place finish in the Ivy seemed inconceivable after winning one game the previous year. Then in '99 we shared the Ivy League championship, going 9-1 and again won the H-Y-P title. We climbed from the unlikelihood of the outhouse to the penthouse in two years.

"Our wins against Princeton and Harvard were pulsating. We truly began to 'believe without evidence,' and those signs hung for several years.

"There is no doubt that my biggest thrill at Yale was beating Harvard in '99 and winning the Ivy title. Quarterback Joe Walland was in a sick bed the night before with a 103 fever. I saw him in the training room with Dr. Goldberg in the morning and he didn't look good. But it was one of those situations where you weren't going to tell him he wasn't going to play because it was his team. Dr. Goldberg said that Joe should see the effects of the antibiotics around halftime. Joe started slow that game but picked up steam, making a great drive just before the half. Dr. Goldberg was right.

A Performance for the Ages

"We started the second half trailing 7-3. The first play Joe called was a running play for Rashad Bartholomew, and that was the last running play he called the rest of the game. It was also the last time we huddled because we went into our 'Shotgun Lightning Check-With-

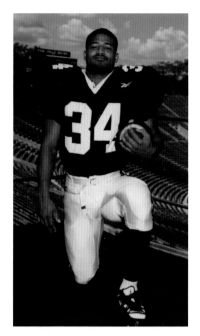

Rashad Bartholomew rushed for 3,015 yards during his Yale career (1998-2000) ranking him third on the all-time rushing list. (SABBY FRINZI)

Me' offense. The 'Me' was Joe himself. We lined up on the ball every other play and never huddled. I signaled change in the formation a few times, but Joe called the plays. We practiced this all the time. Our quick, lightning style exhausted the Harvard players. In the last quarter their linemen where on their hands and knees. Of all the players I coached, Walland probably had the best understanding of the offense. He had very little ego on the field and was very confident of himself. I wasn't afraid to let him go and call his own game.

"My philosophy was if I called a play from the sideline, I probably would have a four-out-of-five success rate of calling a play that had a chance. If you have a quarterback who really knows the offense and can make a good read on the line of scrimmage, now the chance of having a successful outcome of a play increases to five-out-of-five.

"I'm sure Rashad was upset about not carrying the ball in the second half. Here's a guy that in his Yale career averaged 4.7 yards per carry, scored 25 touchdowns, and racked up over 3,000 yards in three years. He was a transfer from the Air Force Academy and when he first got here, we were very reliant on him. I had to use a fullback, Konrad Sopielnikow, as our blocking back for Walland in the Harvard game and Rashad had to sit in the second half. In retrospect, that game taught our tailbacks a lesson. Simply stated, if you want to play, learn how to pass block. For

Future NFL tight end and first-team All-Ivy wide receiver Eric Johnson makes "The Catch" in Yale's 24-21 victory over Harvard in '99. (BILL O'BRIEN)

the remainder of my tenure, that is what they did.

The Greatest Pair of Hands

"Eric Johnson, who had an excellent NFL career with the San Francisco 49ers, had the greatest pair of hands of any kid I ever saw. He never wore gloves. One day Paul Pawlak, a Patriots scout, came to practice and Eric caught a pass where he had to reach behind his body. He snared the ball and pinned it against his leg. Pawlak said, 'That's was one of the greatest catches I ever saw.' I said, 'Paul, that happens every day.'

BILL O'BRIEN
A Historic Photo

"My most famous photo as a Yale free lance photographer is when Eric Johnson caught the touchdown pass from Joe Walland with 29 seconds to go in the 1999 Harvard game. I was standing in the north end zone with the scoreboard behind me and was literally leaning on the goal post. As Walland was driving the team down the field, I knew it was going to be an exciting finish one way or another. I debated what lens to use—wide or telescopic? I decided to use a wide-angle lens, which opens the field, and as luck would have it Johnson caught the pass from Walland down into the goal post area, just a few feet from where I was standing. Johnson caught the ball, fell and rolled over. And would you believe it was the last picture on my strip of negatives? If I didn't get it with that shot, I wouldn't have gotten it at all.

Unlike the contemporary digital camera that can take thousands of shots, it wasn't like that in '99. Today that photo hangs in the offices of the Yale president, Athletic Director Tom Beckett, Sports Information Director Steve Conn, and Don Scharf, who heads the athletics outreach program.

THE TIJUANA CAPER

Following the 1999 game in San Diego, several Yale players crossed the border to Mexico. The story gains legs with the passage of time.

PETER SARANTOS

"For our third game of the season, the Bulldogs eked out a 17-6 defensively-led win against the University of San Diego. (It felt like our defense was on the field for 59 of the 60 minutes). I don't recall the scoring, but I do remember that after the game about half the team squirreled away to Tijuana. No one knows for sure what happened in Mexico, but legend has it that an unnamed teammate punched a

man over the railing on the bridge at the border. e vehemently denies the story every time I see him, but we still call that man 'The Murderer.' uly trust in his innocence, but man! What a catchy nickname!) The truth is Dan Searle and this drunk Mexican guy got into a verbal altercation, and friends of the Mexican guy pulled him away and in doing so, the guy fell off a small bridge—which turned into a 10-foot fall. The bridge was in 'no man's land,' somewhere between the U.S. and Mexican borders.

PETER LEE

"There was a rumor that some of the players were going to go to Tijuana, Mexico, after the game. Coach Siedlecki gave us strict orders not to go, but some guys didn't listen. Nobody really slept that night. I went to a beach party, and the guys who crossed the border came back wearing ponchos and sombreros. The coaches were steaming. At our next practice we ran, ran, ran. "

JACK SIEDLECKI

"I wasn't there to deal with it, since I was in flight returning to Connecticut. Frankly, I didn't learn much about it until weeks later. Let me explain.

Dave Iwan (4) sweeps around end in Yale's 21-0 loss at Cornell in 1993. (Sabby Frinzi)

Dan Iwan (3) turns the corner in Yale's 31-27 win at Holy Cross in 1993.
(SABBY FRINZI)

Former Yale QB Chris Hetherington (right) enjoys a moment with his dad, Ray Hetherington, at the Bowl. Hetherington, who lettered at Yale from 1992-95, played 11 years in the NFL, mostly as a fullback.
(BILL O'BRIEN)

"We could not get a flight back for the entire team after the game because it would have been too late, so we arranged for a post-game reception at the Marriott for the players, family and friends. Most of the coaching staff, including myself, flew home immediately after the game. If the coaches had stayed, it would have affected our preparation for the Holy Cross game the following week, since we wouldn't get back to New Haven until early Sunday night.

So we decided to leave coach Larry Ciotti and Athletic Director Tom Beckett with the team. I understand the revelers, wearing sombreros, returned from Tijuana about 5 a.m. on Sunday morning and were greeted by Beckett in the hotel lobby. Nobody told me about the incident for quite some time. I always kidded Ciotti about the team crossing the border to Mexico under his supervision while he slept into the night."

DURING MOST OF the 1990s, the Yale football program had more than its share of dark storm clouds. However, the decade ended with sunshine and an Ivy League championship. But it would be eight years before another championship banner would hang on the inner walls of the Yale Bowl.

YALE BOWL

Than Merrill

Defending
the trophy
and
tradition

Yale
vs.
Dayton

CHAPTER 22

FROM 2000 TO 2009—AN ERA OF RECORD BREAKERS

*"In 2006 our only loss (34-31) came
at the hands of Princeton in the Bowl.
I was surprised at the reaction of the
alumni. They were crying and complaining. No one gave us a chance
against Harvard the next week, but we
beat them, 34-13."*

—Former Yale coach Jack Siedlecki

W HEN YALE OPENED the 2000 season, it was in a nose-to-nose race with the University of Michigan to become the first college football team to win 800 games. On the morning of September 16, 2000, the Bulldogs had 799 career victories to the Wolverines' 798. Later that day, Yale crossed the finish line first, defeating the University of Dayton in the Bowl, 42-6. When the game was no longer in doubt, coach Jack Siedlecki told his team, "'Hey fellas, you're a part of history. You got the 800th win.'" (Michigan was upset later that day by UCLA, 23-20.)

One of the darkest events in history occurred just over a year later. It, too, had an effect on the Yale football program. Rich Lee, a former defensive tackle for Yale, was in his office at Cantor-Fitzgerald on the 104th floor of the World Trade Center's north tower on the morning of September 11, 2001. He was among those killed when two hijacked airliners struck the Twin Towers, causing them to collapse. The 9/11 attacks, which brought transportation almost to a standstill, forced the cancellation of Yale's 2001 opening game at Towson State in Maryland. On October 7, U.S. and British air strikes against Afghanistan began on the day of Yale's first Sunday football game—against Dartmouth in the Bowl, an event planned as the windup of a gala celebration of Yale's 300th anniversary. Admission was free, but the turnout on a sunny afternoon was just 19,996 as many Americans stayed by their TVs to monitor news of the war. And Dartmouth won.

After beating Fordham at the Bowl the following week, the Bulldogs' season went steadily downhill. Yale had beaten Harvard for the third successive time in 2000, but the dismal 2001 season saw Harvard begin a string of five consecutive victories against Yale. A couple of four-time All-Ivy

players, linebacker Dante Balestracci and running back Clifton Dawson, were thorns in Yale's side.

The 2002 and 2003 teams had ho-hum 6-4 seasons but the Bulldogs ran off a string of four straight wins against Princeton from 2002 through 2005. Yale's 27-24 overtime victory against Princeton in 2003 was set up by Chandler

Rich Lee lost his life during the terrorist attacks in New York City on September 11, 2001. (YALE ATHLETICS)

Henley's acrobatic catch with no time remaining in regulation. The following week Dawson's touchdown in the third overtime gave Harvard a 30-24 victory in the Bowl. The loss haunts Yale coach Jack Siedlecki more than any other in his career.

WAR OF PRANKS

Yale and Harvard have had an endless "Battle of Pranks," and even MIT has gotten into the act, often at the expense of its neighbor on the Charles River. As the *Harvard Crimson* reported, "MIT students launched a rocket carrying an MIT banner over the goalposts in 1990, and in 2006 replaced the 'VE-RI-TAS' logo on the Harvard Stadium scoreboard with 'HU-GE-EGO.'"

The "Mother of All Pranks," a plan conceived and coordinated by Yale students Michael Kai and David Aulicino, was executed with the help of twenty classmates at the 2004 Yale-Harvard game in Boston.

A satirical article in *Maxim* said Yale perpetrated "the greatest prank this side of the Mason-Dixon line since the Boston Tea Party ... and caused dozens of stoic, blue-blooded Harvard men to spit port wine all over their smoking jackets." Here's what happened:

Yale won the Battle of Pranks but Harvard won "The Game" in 2004. (YALE ATHLETICS)

The students, costumed as a Harvard "pep squad," handed out placards, either white or crimson, to about 1,800 fans in a section near the middle on the Harvard side occupied mostly by Crimson alumni. The fans were told that when they lifted the placards on cue they would spell "GO HARVARD." Instead, when raised on high, the placards spelled "WE SUCK."

But again, the Bulldogs fell on the sword at Harvard Stadium, 35-3.

From 2001 to 2004, Yale quarterback Alvin Cowan set multiple passing records in Jack Siedlecki's high octane air-it-out offense. But in 2005 the paradigm changed with the arrival of Mike McLeod, a powerful 5-foot-11, 200-pound running back from New Britain, Connecticut. McLeod, the Ivy League Rookie of the Year as a freshman, was a preminent Ivy player during this era. He earned first-team All-Ivy three times and was the Ivy MVP in 2007. Yale's attack mode shifted from pass happy to three yards and a "McLeod of dust" (a phrase coined by Norman Bender '68). From 2005 to 2008 he gained a school record 4,514 yards and scored fifty-four rushing TDs, more than any Yale player since 1900. He also had one touchdown pass reception. He topped 100 rushing yards in twenty-two games leading the Bulldogs to a 23-7 mark over his last three years. McLeod was named a first team Football Championship

Subdivision (Division I AA) All-American in 2007, joining tight end Nate Lawrie (2003), and tackles Rory Hennessey (2004) and Ed McCarthy (2006) for similar honors during the decade.

Yale beat Penn 17-14 in overtime in '06 in the Bowl. The following year the Bulldogs broke the hearts of the Quakers at Franklin Field with a 26-20 win in three OTs.

The Elis won their last Ivy championship in 2006. Following an opening season loss to the University of San Diego, a team coached by Jim Harbaugh, the current coach of the San Francisco 49ers, the Elis ran off seven consecutive wins before losing to Princeton, their only Ivy loss.

Siedlecki's '07 team was perhaps his best. The Bulldogs came into the 124th edition of The Game at 9-0, poised for their first perfect season in forty-seven years. But again they ran into a Harvard mine field when the Crimson coming in at 7-2, exploded for a 37-6 win. It was the fifth time since 1920 that Harvard spoiled a perfect season for the Elis (1921, 1968, 1974, 1979, and 2007).

Siedlecki retired after the 2008 season and was replaced by Tom Williams, who stepped into controversy the first time he faced Harvard in '09. The Elis led 10-7 with 2:40 remaining and Harvard was out of timeouts when he made a mind-numbing decision to go for a first down on fourth and 22 on the Yale 28. The move backfired and the Bulldogs ended on the short side of the 14-10 game.

Peter Lee (quarterback) '99, '00, '01

VICE PRESIDENT AT BARCLAYS WEALTH
CHICAGO, ILLINOIS

A transfer from Wisconsin, Peter Lee set Yale records in 2001 for completion percentage (.619) and avoiding interceptions (1 in 236 attempts).

Peter Lee
(SABBY FRINZI)

"I grew up in Chicago and didn't know that they played football in the Ivy League. I wanted to play in the Big Ten, so I went to the University of Wisconsin, where I redshirted my freshman year in '97. We beat UCLA 38-31 in the '99 Rose Bowl, and I was hoping to compete for the quarterback job my sophomore year. But Brad Childress, who recruited me, went to the Philadelphia Eagles with Andy Reid. Childress was the offensive coordinator at Wisconsin, but after he left they put in a different system. Head coach Barry Alvarez and I agreed it wouldn't work out.

"I decided to take a step up academically and still play in some big-time games like Yale-Harvard and Yale-Penn, so I transferred to Yale in '99. If I transferred to Duke or Stanford, I would have had to sit out one year, but since Yale was a non-scholarship Division I-AA school, I was eligible to play immediately.

From Rose Bowl to the Yale Bowl

"I remember visiting the huge Yale Bowl and saw where it held around 70,000. I thought it would be the same kind of atmosphere on game day as at Wisconsin, or perhaps as in the Rose Bowl, the last football field I walked on. Was I in for a surprise!

"We opened the '99 season against Brown on September 18. When we ran out of the tunnel there were only about 5,000 fans. I couldn't believe it. I was expecting the Bowl to be full. I thought there was an error in the schedule.

Lee to Johnson

"One of my best games was against Columbia in 2000, when we beat them in the Bowl, 41-0. It was one of the windiest days I ever played in. I threw four

touchdown passes, three to Eric Johnson. He was a remarkable talent.

"In that Columbia game, Ryan LoProto, our safety, intercepted two passes that he returned for touchdowns on runs of 67 and 17 yards. He was the first Yale player to score twice on interceptions in one game. He was a great guy who embodied everything you would want in a teammate.

The Right Decision

"I was fortunate to have David Swensen, who runs Yale's endowment and heads up the Yale investment office, as an academic mentor. In my opinion, next to Warren Buffett, he is the greatest institutional investor in the country. During my senior year I had the privilege of studying his playbook. That experience inspired my professional career.

"No doubt, I made the right decision to transfer to Yale, even if the Yale Bowl wasn't filled every week."

THE PLAYERS

Alvin Cowan (quarterback) '00, '01, '03 (captain), '04

HIGH SCHOOL FOOTBALL COACH/ACTOR
LOS ANGELES, CALIFORNIA

Alvin Cowan holds Yale records for touchdown passes in a career (41) and for completions (227) and passing yards (2,994) in a season; he is tied with Jeff Mroz for most touchdown passes in a season (22). Against Harvard in 2003 he threw for 438 yards, another record. A medical redshirt most of 2002, Cowan set Yale records for total offense in a career (6,024), a season (3,429) and a game (464). As a fledgling actor, he has appeared in two independent movies and had a role in an ABC-TV Private Practice episode.

Cowan to Plumb

"Oddly enough, my greatest thrill at Yale was a loss against Penn at Franklin Field in 2003. Entering the

Ralph Plumb stiff arms a defender.
(RON WAITE/YALE ATHLETICS)

game, we were 4-1 and undefeated in the Ivy. Our only loss was to a very strong Colgate team. Penn was the big bad guy on the block at the time, and we were getting blown out 31-10 when we came to life late in the third quarter. We were virtually unstoppable in the fourth quarter as we staged a rally that tied the score.

"Penn lost one of their outstanding defensive backs, and the player who took his place wasn't in his

Alvin Cowan runs the ball in the 2003 Yale-Harvard game. No. 8 for Harvard is Gary Sonkur.
(SABBY FRINZI)

class. Ralph Plumb simply ate him up. Ralph kept coming back to the huddle pleading for me to throw him the ball. He used some colorful "F-bombs" in his classic Portsmouth, R.I., tongue. Ralph was a super wide receiver. He still holds the Yale record for most catches in a career (195) by a wide receiver and most yards gained by a receiver in a career (2,396).

"The game went into overtime, and we kicked a field goal that was blocked. The ball rolled into the end zone and my roommate, Chad Almy, fell on the ball, but the play was nullified because the offensive team could not legally touch a kick that had crossed the neutral zone. Penn then kicked a field goal to win the game, 34-31.

We were all exhausted, but I never saw our fans and the Yale band so excited after a game, even though we had lost. We received a hero's welcome in defeat, and it was touching beyond belief.

A Talented Lot

"I know I hold several Yale passing records, but with all due respect to the quarterbacks who played before and after me, I think I might have had the best group of skilled players to throw to. Aside from Plumb, who was like having a tight end and a wide receiver, we had Nate Lawrie, an All-Ivy and I-AA All-America tight end who played in the NFL; P.J. Collins, another talented wide guy; and Ronnie Benigno, a great slot player. Then there was Robert Carr in the backfield, who had two 200-yard games in '02. I think he was sick and tired of all the passing we did in '03, but he never complained. And there was the elusive, sure-handed Chandler Henley, a backup receiver as a sophomore in '03. That year we also had two first-team All-Ivy tackles in Rory Hennessey and Jake Kohl. Hennessey was a I-AA All-American in 2004.

Robert Carr (2001-04) ran for 3,393 yards, second on the all-time Yale rushing list. (YALE ATHLETICS)

"Benigno and Henley were pretty sharp guys with a good sense of humor. If we had a comfortable lead, they would often bring the play in from the sidelines and try to screw me up. If the play was called 'Queen's Right, Kansas-Brown,' they might say 'Brown-Right, Kansas-Queen's.' They would say it and run quickly to their wide receiver spots so I couldn't ask for a clarification. One time I had to call a timeout because I was confused, but I refused to throw them under the bus with the coaching staff.

"The coaching staff was wonderful as well. I spent a lot of time with quarterback coach Joel Lamb, who taught me how to attack different defensive looks. We spent a lot of time discussing philosophy from an offensive perspective.

A Big Day

"We opened the 2002 season, my junior year, against San Diego, a game we won 49-14 in the Bowl. That day I scored three running touchdowns and passed for three touchdowns. In the second game that year I broke my leg in the Cornell game in Ithaca that we won 50-23 and was a medical redshirt the remainder of that season.

"If I have any regrets, they're never winning the Ivy League title and beating Harvard only once in my four years; we defeated them in 2000. I never bought a Yale ring because I always wanted an Ivy League championship ring. But looking back, the experiences I had at Yale were invaluable. Because I went to Yale, it opened a door for me to spend some private time with President George W. Bush.

Visit with President Bush

"During my junior year I was invited to a birthday party at the Bush ranch in Crawford, Texas. The Bushes (George W.) had twin daughters, Barbara and Jenna, who were celebrating their twenty-first birthday. I'm from Austin, Texas, and dated a girl who was friends with Barbara. When the President heard I was a Yale student, he gave me a tour of the ranch at five in the morning. We talked about his days at Yale and DKE, the fraternity he was in.

"Barbara and I entered Yale in 2000 and as freshmen we went to a Willie Nelson concert together in New York City.

The Barn

"For a time I lived with twelve guys in an eleven-room house we called 'The Barn' at 174 Park St. in New Haven. When we first got there, P.J. Collins opened a closet and a bat flew out. My senior year Ken Estrera, Barton Simmons, Bryant Diefenbacher, and I moved to an apartment at 73 Edgewood Ave. We called ourselves the 'Four Redshirts' since we had all been redshirted during our football careers.

"A bunch of new guys moved into The Barn, a combination of football and hockey players. One of the football players was Will Blodgett. To my angst and surprise, a competitive rivalry ensued between the new occupants of The Barn and the Four Redshirts.

"When we lived at The Barn, my parents had a neon beer sign made that read, 'The Barn: Est. 2002.' When we moved to Edgewood, we took the sign with us. One day when I wasn't home, some of the new residents of The Barn came to our apartment on Edgewood and pilfered the sign. They thought the sign should stay at The Barn. I didn't think this was right, since my parents had given it to me. Thus, the seeds for battle were planted for a prank war that escalated beyond my wildest imagination.

"We didn't want to forcibly take it back. Instead, we wanted them to eat some humble pie and return the sign. So Estrera designed a clever scheme called, 'The 12 Days of Christmas,' to pressure them to return the sign.

"On Day No. 1 we threw eggs at The Barn and left a note that read: 'On the first day of Christmas my true love said to me, one dozen eggs. Return the sign to 73 Edgewood or the second day of Christmas will begin tomorrow.' They retaliated by egging our house the next day.

"Day No. 2: We still had the keys to The Barn so we went back armed with dog crap. Kenny got the idea from an Adam Sandler movie titled *Billy Madison*. We scooped up some dog excrement and put it in two paper bags. We quietly entered The Barn and placed the smelly brown bags in the living room. Knowing that some of the residents were in the house, we lit the bag on fire to trigger the fire alarm. The idea was to have someone come down and step on the bags of dog shit to extinguish the fire. We left a note that read, "On the second day of Christmas my true love said to me, one dozen eggs, two bags of dog shit ... and we'll be back for Day No. 3 if we don't get the sign back." They were pissed but stubbornly refused to return the sign.

"The next day I returned home from classes and found Kenny holding two rats, both the size of New York subway rats. He had gone to a pet store to find the two largest rats he could find. He wrote the number "1" on the body of one rat and the number "3" on the other one. The idea was to make them think that there were three rats. We snuck into The Barn late in the afternoon and released the rats while

spreading cat food on the floor. We left a note saying, 'On the third day of Christmas my true love said to me, one dozen eggs, two bags of shit, three huge rats ... and we'll be back for the fourth day if you don't return the sign by noon the next day.'

"They were livid but did not react to our ultimatum. So on Day No. 4 we went back to The Barn and stole every sign on the walls except "The Barn" sign. We were adamant about them returning the sign. We wrote another note that read, "On the fourth day of Christmas my true love said to me, one dozen eggs, two bags of shit, three huge rats, all of your signs... and we'll be back for Day No. 5 if the sign is not returned."

"Our persistence had paid off. That night they put their arms down and returned the sign."

Jeff Mroz (quarterback) '01, '02, '03, '05

EMPLOYED BY A PRIVATE EQUITY FIRM
NEW YORK, NEW YORK

Jeff Mroz is tied with Alvin Cowan for most passing touchdowns in a season (22 in 2005) and ranks second in Yale history for single-season pass completions (216) when he threw for 2,484 yards in 2005. He threw five touchdown passes against Cornell in '05 tying a Yale Bowl collegian record shared by Yale's Pete Doherty (vs. Columbia in 1966) and Dartmouth's Greg Smith (2001). He is tied with Patrick Witt for second in career passing TDs (37). Mroz signed free-agent contracts with the Dallas Cowboys (2006) and Philadelphia Eagles (2007). He played in the Arena Football League for the Columbus Destroyers (2008) and Alabama Vipers (2010).

Locker Room Hijinks

"Will Blodgett, a freshman wide receiver on the team, was the unfortunate victim of many pranks and jokes. One day the team was already stretching, but without Will. With his loud voice, strong opinions and engaging personality, it was easy to notice when

QB Jeff Mroz makes toss in Yale's 28-19 win over Holy Cross in 2002.
(RON WAITE/YALE ATHLETICS)

Stephen Schmalhofer (defensive line) '05,'06,'07

BUSINESS DEVELOPMENT FOR A NEW YORK-BASED TECHNOLOGY COMPANY
NEW YORK, NEW YORK

The Tale of Scottie Moore

"Millions of football fans have sat in the Yale Bowl on a gorgeous fall Saturday. Precious few have seen what happens on the day before the game. Yale players take the field in shorts and jerseys to jog through drills, walk through a few plays and enjoy tossing the football around.

"On a Friday in late September 2004, we laced up our cleats and walked to the Yale Bowl. Click-clack, click-clack past the tennis players volleying in the sun. Thump, thump, thump ... we lumbered down the tunnel of the Bowl, which also doubled as our defensive halftime room. The Ivy League champion banners were rolled up on one side. The smell was musty like my grandfather's farmhouse basement.

"The Bowl was empty. The rows of blue seats calmly circled the stadium. Strength coach Mike Ranfone began the warm-up drills as we tried to shake the fatigue and soreness from our legs.

"The tedium of warm-ups drew to a close. Captain Rory Hennessey ('05) gathered the team around him. Rory was from Ohio, where people have self-respect, and what he wanted was to inspire his team. He was confident because he was dominant. Rory could pick up his opponent and put him in the stands if he so desired. He was a composed, stoic leader who used glances and stares to convey his message to his teammates and coaches.

"Knowing that Rory would be watching, the team enthusiastically broke huddle and split into position groups. I jogged to the north end zone and noticed

Will was not there. The entire team, coaches, and trainers all watched as Will came running out late. Will informed the team what everybody had already known: his helmet had been stuck to his locker with rolls of tape, which took him a long time to get off.

"Later in the practice, we were doing a two-minute drill. We would start near our own goal line and drive the length of the field until we scored or were stopped by our defense. We got to the opposing 20-yard line when I took the snap and dropped back. Will was running a post pattern. With everybody covered, I threw the ball away through the back of the end zone to avoid taking the sack. Everybody knew I was throwing it away-except Will. He sped up, seeing the ball was thrown in his direction, eyes wide open as he was tracking the ball and hoping to score a TD to end the practice. Running as fast as he could, eyes fixed on the ball, Will was almost there, until WHACK-Will ran square into the goal post at the back of the end zone and dropped straight back to the ground. The goal post may still be shaking to this day."

Stephen Schmalhofer attacks Columbia QB Craig Hormann (14) in Yale's 21-3 win in 2006.
(SABBY FRINZI)

everyone in their usual groups. The defensive linemen relaxed by catching passes in the corner to the right of the Bowl's scoreboard. The tight ends practiced dropping long passes. The O-linemen avoided catching glimpses of coach Keith Clark's crotch as he demonstrated a variety of ninja kick techniques uncomfortably close to their faces. And the wide receivers were running footwork drills. Why is their story worth telling?

"Scottie Moore, a 6-5 freshman with an extra few inches of lankiness, had such great skills that he was the only wide receiver Yale recruited in 2004. Having played against several BCS-level players at Central Dauphin, an AAAA- level school in Pennsylvania, Scottie often overmatched his JV competitors. He challenged himself by refusing to increase his speed beyond a light jog during games. The sideline was his sanctuary, as he would routinely snag six to eight receptions while toeing the line and stepping out. He refused to give enemy defenders the pleasure of tackling him.

"But Scottie's languid demeanor drew the ire of his coach. Pacing his charges through a set of drills, coach Matt Dence threw a routine ball to Scottie. In

a most casual manner, Scottie declined to catch the pass and instead punched it to the ground before jogging back into line. Coach felt a mix of anger and embarrassment creep up his neck.

"The next time Scottie appeared at the front of the line, coach Dence unleashed a quick volley of two passes. Scottie's eyes lit up in anticipation. A challenge! A dare! He hauled in both passes with ease.

"Coach Dence, encouraged by the flash of brilliance from his otherwise slothful star, stood passively waiting for the return of the footballs. Scottie lazily cocked back and lobbed a slow, high-floating pass toward his coach. As Dence traced the arc of the ball, his eyes drifted upwards, losing sight for just a moment of young Mr. Moore. What his eyes could not tell him, the stinging pain from his groin would soon relay.

"Scottie had followed his first rainbow pass with a laser-guided missile directed at Coach Dence's most tender region. This is known as a 'high-low.'

"Coach Dence called Scottie back to the front of the line. With a powerful swing of his milk-white leg, he thundered a drop kick into the stands of the Yale Bowl. 'Go fetch!'

"Legend has it that Scottie Moore went to retrieve that football and never came back. He just kept walking up and out Portal 12."

Scott Moore played on the JV team his freshman year and never played again.

Chandler Henley (wide receiver) '02, '03, '04, '06 (captain)

OFFENSIVE GRADUATE ASSISTANT FOOTBALL COACH AT VANDERBILT UNIVERSITY
NASHVILLE, TENNESSEE

"The 2006 season was pretty special, we got blown out in the first game of the season against San Diego and then ripped off 7 straight victories-including 2

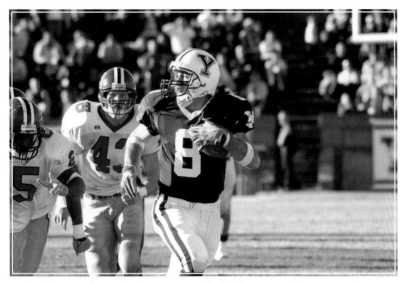

Chandler Henley makes reception off a hitch route in the 2003 Yale-Harvard game. Harvard's Mante Dzakuma (25) and Bobby Everett (43) chase Henley.
(YALE ATHLETICS)

overtime wins and a come from behind win at Brown. All this set up the seniors' final game in the Bowl against Princeton with a chance to clinch an outright Ivy title which would have been Yale's first since 1980. After jumping out to a 28-14 lead at halftime, we went flat in the second half and ended up losing. As disappointed as I was, I ran into Rich Diana the Tuesday of Harvard week at Mory's. He told me the story of his team that had the same exact scenario his senior year-and his message to me was don't feel sorry for yourself that you lost a chance to win an outright title...but feel sorry for Harvard that they were the next team standing in our way of what we had worked so hard for. It changed my mindset as a captain and I relayed the story to the team. We went out and took it out of Harvard from the first drive, beating them on their own field (34-13) to win an Ivy League Championship in the last game of football most of us ever played. I can still taste the satisfaction in the cigar I smoked on the 50 yard line at Harvard stadium."

Brandt Hollander (nose tackle) '04, '05, '06, '07 (captain)

UCLA LAW SCHOOL
INDIANAPOLIS, INDIANPOLIS

Hollander was an All-Ivy first team selection in 2006 and 2007.

Disgusting Tactics

"I always liked getting into the faces of my opponents. On occasion I would literally do it by vomiting on the opposing center. I have kind of a weak stomach and could work myself up to it. The greasy food we ate in the dining room helped to set up the big splash. I would do it against opposing centers when they were long snapping for a punt or maybe a field goal. The centers would cuss me out and they would go crazy, but I didn't care. I wasn't the first to do it. I got the idea from reading an article where a pro football player did that from the perspective of upchucking on the long snapper.

"My tactics weren't always so disgusting, but they were weird. A week before a game, I would go on Facebook and get the name of the girlfriend of the guy I was going to play against. On the day of the game I would talk to him about his girlfriend. It wasn't appropriate, but I wanted them to know who I was. I wanted them to think of me the entire game.

Bashing Princeton

"Princeton was my first choice of schools, but they said I wasn't tough enough. Obviously, I did not like their head coach, Dr. Roger Hughes, because he ruined my dream by not giving me the respect I deserved. Well, during my football career we beat them three out of four years. Our only loss came in '06 when they nipped us 34-31. But we bounced back the following week and beat Harvard. Yes, there is a genuine dislike between us and Princeton.

"For some reason we used to scrimmage Princeton every year. I never understood why. The scrimmages were controlled but the players weren't. We would

2007 Yale captain Brandt Hollander
(SABBY FRINZI)

purposely start a fight and there would be a huge dog pile. This would give us a rest from the drills we had to do.

"Playing in the Yale Bowl was a unique experience. One time we were playing Princeton and I busted through the line and sacked the quarterback. As I got up I was disoriented, but I could hear the crowd roaring. It's strange—during the play everything goes quiet and after the play all your senses come back.

"But I creamed the Princeton quarterback.

"Looking back, I'm sure there were some Princeton players and coaches who wanted to vomit on me!"

Casey Gerald (cornerback) '05, '06, '07, '08

DIRECTOR OF STRATEGIC DEVELOPMENT FOR REBOOT; ATTENDED HARVARD BUSINESS SCHOOL
NEW YORK, NEW YORK

Casey Gerald, a Rhodes Scholar finalist, was selected as a National Football Foundation scholar-athlete in 2008.

The Clash of the Titans

"In 2007 Harvard came into the Bowl with two losses but was undefeated in the Ivy. The game was being billed as 'The Clash of the Titans.' I gave a speech and said something like, 'Bullshit, we are the real titans.'

"We thought that we were going to win our second straight championship, but we had nothing that day. The week of practice was awful. The practice field was terrible, so we practiced on the lacrosse field. We were so confident, however, that I think we were lulled to sleep as Harvard whipped us 37-6. We blew

coverages and missed tackles. They were hungry for it. We just thought it was time to eat.

An Incredible Twenty-four Hours

"During my senior year ('08), I found out the week of the Brown game that I was a finalist for a Rhodes Scholarship. It was a great honor, but my interview was scheduled in Houston on Nov. 21, the day before the Harvard game in Boston. I had to make the agonizing decision of playing the last game of my college career or interviewing for a Rhodes scholarship. I leaned toward playing with my teammates against Harvard, but I decided to go to Houston after talking to Jack Ford and Yale Athletic Director Tom Beckett.

"Ford said, 'Casey, I love Yale football as much as anybody. But one of my regrets was not to put myself in a position to compete for a Rhodes Scholarship.' I then met Tom in his office and I told him that this was the toughest decision of my life. He paused and said, 'Casey, you have to go. The Rhodes Scholarship will mean more to you as years go by.'

"At that moment we both started to cry. Mr. Beckett was not a hugger, but we gave each other a hug.

"I now knew that I would miss the Harvard game and my playing career was over. It is a tradition the day before the Harvard game that every senior says something to the team. My teammates were aware that week that I was going to Houston. So I gave my speech on Wednesday afternoon at practice. I said, 'Fellas, the greatest honor of my life has been playing with you.'

"On Thursday the athletic department arranged my transportation. They had a Town Car take me to

Casey Gerald
(SABBY FRINZI)

Newark Airport. I got to Houston about midnight and checked into a hotel.

"I was the first one to interview on Friday, and after the first day of interviews we met at the house of one of the judges for a reception. I wanted to get out of there, as my heart and mind were with my teammates in Boston.

"Then this one judge arranged for me to leave and get back for the game. I would later find out that Mr. Beckett worked it out so I would be able to get to Boston in time for the game.

"I got to Newark Airport at 1 in the morning. Yale arranged for a car to drive me to Boston, and I arrived at the team hotel at 5 a.m. At 7:30 a.m. Tony Reno, my position coach, woke me up to attend a team meeting.

"Tony walked me downstairs to the ballroom. When my teammates saw me, they all started hugging me. After the meeting we went to Harvard Stadium, and on the bus coach Reno gave me some cold waffles, not a very good breakfast after a long night and for a guy who was about to play a football game.

"As for the game, it was a bloody, cold Boston day along the Charles and we lost 10-0. Gino Gordon ran 168 yards and scored Harvard's lone touchdown. It was one of the toughest games we had. We couldn't move the ball.

"It was tough knowing that I wasn't going to put the pads on again after playing ten years of organized football. And as I left the field, I was curious how I had done in my interview the day before. Procedurally, as soon as the interviews are done the judges make their decision, so I knew it wouldn't be long before I got the result. I got into the locker room and found a text message from the guy who had interviewed me for the Rhodes. He informed me that they gave the Rhodes to two other individuals.

"In a matter of moments I walked off the football field for the last time as a player and learned that I did not receive the Rhodes Scholarship. It was the first time in my life that I had dedicated myself to something that didn't go my way. But I learned that it's not whether you fail, it's whether you recover. It proved to be the biggest lesson I learned at Yale.

"I spent the night in Boston with Andrew Berry, a Harvard player who was a friend. His twin brother was a receiver at Princeton. We didn't talk too much, as he obviously knew I was tired and down for several reasons. To add to my already trying day, the heat went down in the Harvard dorm I stayed in. I ended up sleeping in my Yale sweats in a cold dorm, one day after interviewing for a Rhodes Scholarship. Welcome to the real world!"

Bobby Abare (linebacker) '05, '06, '07, '08 (captain)

SALES (IBM)
BOSTON, MASSACHUSETTS

Bobby Abare was a first team All-Ivy and All-New England selection for three years (2006-08), during which time he was Yale's leading tackler. Abare joins Dick Jauron and Mike McLeod as Yale's only three-time All-Ivy first team selections. He had ten career interceptions, the most of any linebacker in Yale history, and more touchdowns (4) than any previous defensive player at Yale. On November 4, 2006, he picked off three passes and returned one for a TD in a 27-24 victory at Brown.

A Twin Ruse

"My brother Larry and I are fraternal twins. On the day of my final practice at Yale, Larry and I decided to have a little fun. We switched jerseys, shoulder pads and helmets and went to each other's position drills. I gave him my No. 44 and I wore his No. 32. We did it for the first 20 minutes, and the coaches and several players didn't have a clue what we were up to.

Abare twins, Bobby and Larry, before the 2008 Harvard game, the last game they played together.
(THE ABARE FAMILY)

Fisticuffs at Practice

"I wasn't very happy with the way our practices were going when we began as freshmen. There was very little intensity as compared to what I was used to in high school. Then something happened during one of the preseason two-a-day drills that changed things. We were practicing special teams punting when my brother Larry and Casey Gerald got into a scuffle.

"Larry was the gunner, the guy who is supposed to make the tackle on the punt return. But as Larry went downfield he was held a couple of times by Casey. Larry had enough and the two went at it. I sprinted forty yards and found myself in the middle, pulling Casey away from my brother. I think the fight changed things for the better. It helped us bond as a team, and we played more spirited football.

"My first varsity start came my freshman year against Harvard in '05. What a thrill it was going onto the field that day! When the Yale Bowl fills up there's nothing like it. The crowd noise was deafening. That's the game they beat us in triple overtime, the longest game in Yale football history.

"I'll never forget the day my sophomore year (November 4, 2006) when I intercepted three passes and we beat Brown (27-24). My dad, who played for

UConn and who has meant so much to Larry and me, couldn't make the game, but he watched it on TV while he was in Texas.

Throwing Out the First Pitch at Fenway

"Growing up twenty miles outside Boston, I've been a Red Sox fan all of my life. On September 2, 2008, the Red Sox invited Harvard captain Matt Curtis and me to throw out the first pitch at Fenway Park before the Red Sox-Orioles game. The idea was to promote the playing of the 125th Yale-Harvard game that year. My eighty-four-year old grandparents and other relatives and friends were there. It was a thrill!"

Larry Abare (strong safety) '05, '06, '08, '09, (medical redshirt '07)

COACH DESJARLAIS' MOTIVATING SPEECH
ACTON, MASSACHUSETTS

"Coming into the 2006 Harvard game, our season could be summarized as an early-season loss against San Diego, which was led by their star QB, Josh Johnson. Johnson tore apart a young Yale defense that was simply not ready for their offensive arsenal that day. However, after our initial loss against San Diego, we rallied off seven straight wins before suffering a horrible loss to Princeton at home. We had a two-touchdown lead at halftime and let it slip away as Princeton came back to win 34-31, dropping us into a tie for first. Therefore, we would have to beat Harvard to clinch the Ivy League championship.

"Needless to say, the Princeton game was a huge letdown for our squad and coming into the Harvard game, if we had lost any confidence, it was cemented and restored back to its original level after the speech that special teams coach Jason DesJarlais gave us. "Before the game, we had our usual pregame rituals taking place in our hotel. We watched film, had our meetings with our position coaches and talked about our game plan against Harvard. However, the night before the game coach DesJarlais gave a powerful motivational speech. He retold the story of how Muhammad Ali had changed his name from Cassius Clay. Before his title fight in 1967 against Ernie Terrell, Terrell had taunted Ali, calling him Cassius. Essentially, coach DesJarlais likened Terrell's disrespect for Muhammad Ali's name change to how Harvard had no respect for the name "Yale" and rightfully so, considering that the seniors on that team had never beaten Harvard in their four years.

"Coach DesJarlais highlighted the pounding that Ali gave Terrell that night in the ring in 1967, referencing countless times Ali's chant to Terrell in the ring, yelling, 'What's my name, Uncle Tom? What's my name?' DesJarlais challenged us to rise up and give the same pounding to Harvard that Terrell suffered at the hands of Ali. You could hear how badly coach DesJarlais wanted us to win that game and how badly he felt like we (Yale) needed this win after years of losing to Harvard. "Like Ali, we rose up that day in 2006, shutting down Clifton Dawson and Harvard's running game and pounding their QB, Matt Pizzotti, all day. Offensively, Mike McLeod ran wild and Chandler Henley had a remarkable day, continuing to lead as he had done all year. "To this day, Muhammad Ali's title fight, coach DesJarlais' speech, and our 34-13 pummeling of Harvard are synonymous with each other. "On a deeper level, I think coach DesJarlais' speech was incredibly fitting, considering it was one of his first years as the special teams coach. I

believe coach DesJarlais, as well as Chandler's leadership, was vital in providing the leadership and vision we needed to become Ivy League champions that year.

A Controversial Call

"In the 2008 Harvard game we were trailing 3-0 when Harvard punted deep to around our 10-yard line. An official, who I understand was a long distance from the play, ruled that the ball struck me. A Harvard player fell on the ball and Harvard took over and scored. Harvard won the game, 10-0.

"The play has been a subject of controversy and probably always will be. The truth is I have no recollection of whether or not the ball glanced off me, but I do not believe it did. However, given the fact that I sustained a concussion during the game, I do not recall many plays and I have never watched the tape.

Fourth and 22

"It is easy to say in retrospect that we shouldn't have gone for it on 4th down against Harvard in 2009. However, as a young head coach, I'm not sure if Coach Williams had acquired the experience to make a decision like that in his Yale coaching career and as they say, you only learn through experience. Perhaps he would have made a different decision if he were head coach today.

"Looking back at that season, I can actually see why Coach Williams went for it that day. The fake punt was something we had practiced a number of times and we had done pretty well in executing other surprise special teams plays. Namely, we had a couple great onside kicks that we had recovered and earlier that year, we successfully ran a fake punt against Lehigh, which amounted to the game-winning touchdown by our captain Paul Rice. All this being said, I was really hoping that Coach Williams would elect to punt. The play itself was run to the short side of the field that gave John Powers little running room. I believe he actually gained about 15 yards on the play and thus, if it was 4th and 15 he would have gained a first down. I also believe that John would have made the first down had the play been run to the wide side of the field. Given that we had arguably the best punter in Yale history in Tom Mante (who would later have several NFL tryouts and play in the UFL for a season), I think Tom would have been able to bury Harvard deep in their end and it would have been up to our defense to stop Harvard. Of course I'm biased and believe we would have been able to stop Harvard's offense, but I can see why Coach Williams may have had his doubts, especially considering that in Harvard's previous possession, our defense had given up a long drive after we had several chances to turn the ball over on fourth down.

"I can understand why most people would question Coach WIlliams' decision in that fourth and 22 situation, but the decision was not that clear cut when you consider how the game was going and what had transpired earlier that season with our success running special teams trick plays.

"The mood after the game was obviously one of disappointment. Our team felt that we had outplayed Harvard for most of the game and had let the game slip away from us in the fourth quarter. I cannot speak for everyone, but for me, it didn't really matter how we lost to Harvard. The mere fact that we had lost to our traditional rival is what really stung. I don't think the 2009 loss was any more painful than 2005, 2007, or the 2008 games. Coupled with the loss, there was a sense of melancholy as most of our football playing careers were over."

In addition to the Abares, other noted twin siblings who lettered at Yale include Dick and Bob Jacunski (1960) and Chris and Rob Michalik (1988-1990).

Tom Mante (punter, place-kicker) '06, '07, '08, '09

MBA CANDIDATE AT VANDERBILT'S OWEN GRADUATE SCHOOL OF MANAGEMENT; UFL PUNTER
WESTFORD, MASSACHUSETTS

Tom Mante was an All-Ivy first team selection in 2009. His 54-yard field goal against Cornell in 2009 tied the Yale record held by Otis Guernsey in 1915. He averaged a Yale record 40.1 yards per punt in his career.

"Although I might be best remembered for tying the Yale and Ivy League record for the longest field goal (54 yards) and some booming punts, the play that I am most known for is the fake punt against Harvard in 2009. In the fourth quarter, we were leading 10-0 when Harvard drove 76 yards on six plays in just 1:50 to pull to within 3 points. We were leading 10-7 and had the ball, fourth and 22 on our own 28 with 2:40 on the clock, when Paul Rice, the personal protector in the punt formation, brought the play in from the sideline that called for a fake punt reverse. The word 'Bulldog' was the code word for fake and was part of the name of the play. Needless to say, the players in the huddle were very surprised. One said, 'Really? This play, right now?' Another asked, 'Are you sure we want to do that?'

"The idea for the play came from the sidelines, with head coach Tom Williams giving the green light. I was absolutely surprised with the decision, especially at that point in the game. I would have been much more comfortable had we called it earlier in the game.

"My assignment was to pick up the most dangerous man downfield, but a lineman from Harvard sprang free from his block on the line, so I cut my assignment short to help seal him off. The man I was supposed to block ended up making the

Tom Mante (8) kicks his record tying 54-yard FG against Cornell in 2009. The holder is Richard Scudellari (18). The long snapper is Matt Kelleher (not in photo).
(YALE ATHLETICS)

tackle on John Powers a few yards short of the first down. Harvard took over on our 40 with 2:25 on the clock and scored three plays later when quarterback Collier Winters hit Chris Lorditch across the middle to give Harvard a 14-10 victory. Harvard linebacker Jon Takamura finished the game with an interception.

"When the game ended we were stunned and dazed in the locker room. We sat in disbelief because we had the game wrapped up and lost. We were flabbergasted, and there were a lot of tears, myself included. But there were no hard feelings toward the coaches, players, or anyone else. To coach Williams's credit, that call caught Harvard completely off guard. I thought it was a good surprise call, but we didn't execute. We were playing to win, not to lose. I know that Tom will be second-guessed forever because the play came against Harvard.

"It appeared that the coaching staff didn't have much confidence in our defense at that point in the game because Harvard had scored so easily on their previous series. However, I thought overall our defense played well that game. You can argue that Harvard was out of timeouts, but to counter that, the wind was blowing in my face.

Good Boots

"My biggest thrill at Yale came in the 2006 Harvard game, a game we won 34-13 at Harvard Stadium. I was a freshman, and two of my four punts were downed within the 5-yard line. One of the punts resulted in a shank by the Harvard punter when they went three-and-out, and the ball ended up on the 8-yard line; Travis Henry may have tipped it. Mike McLeod then went in untouched, which set the tone for the rest of the game. Contributing to an Ivy championship and seeing our fans storm Harvard's field–I'll never forget that.

"Of course the 54-yard field goal I made against Cornell in the Bowl in 2009 was special. Cornell had a 7-3 lead with seconds remaining before the half. In warm-ups I was hitting from 58 and 59 yards. Coach Williams asked me if I could make it and of course I said yes. The line, my holder, Richie Scudellari, and snapper, Matt Kelleher, did a great job, and the kick cleared the bar by about 9 yards. After I made the field goal, I was so excited that I ran to the sideline and jumped up to celebrate with my best friend, Tim 'The Bear' Handlon, who was 6-feet-2 and 226 pounds, and got knocked on my ass. Unfortunately, we lost the game 14-12.

"In our 2008 game against Holy Cross, I kicked a 34-yard game-winning field goal in our 31-28 overtime win, and that's something I'll never forget.

Pizza and Practice

"For many years the kickers had a tradition, on the last Thursday practice before the Harvard game, of ordering pizza from the Yorkside restaurant on Temple Street. The streak was stopped when Alan Kimball, our veteran kicker, chickened out his junior year. I vowed to continue the streak my senior year, which I did. Alan Barnes, Philippe Panico, and I rode around in a golf cart eating pizza all practice. Coach Williams even ate a slice with us.

Jack Siedlecki, Head coach, 1997-2008

MADISON, CONNECTICUT

The Greatest Kid I Coached at Yale

"The 19-14 Princeton loss in 2000 was very disappointing. At the post-game media conference, Dave Solomon, the late *New Haven Register* writer, asked a question about the loss. Peter Mazza, the captain of the team, stepped right up and took the blame, saying that Princeton's winning touchdown was his responsibility. He thought that a Princeton player running up the sideline on the Princeton side, heading toward the north goal line, was going out of bounds, so he let up. I don't think Peter was the only one, but he took the blame. Peter was maybe the greatest kid I ever coached at Yale. He was calling our defenses from his linebacker position as a freshman and was first-team All-Ivy his senior year. If I had one player I'd want in a foxhole with me, it would have been Peter Mazza.

The Events of 9/11

"Over the years Yale coaches have had to deal with wars and other non-football-related issues. I'll never forget the events of 9/11. The night before, we had our annual kickoff dinner at the Yale Club in New York City with Governor George Pataki in attendance. The next morning my secretary said, 'Something awful has happened.' We hooked up a TV and followed the tragic events of the day. I remember seeing New York Mayor Rudy Giuliani and Pataki, who were on national television. To think that I was with the governor the night before was kind of weird.

"We were scheduled to open with Towson State but canceled the game. Yale was one of the first schools to cancel their game that weekend. We did practice during the week, but a couple of practices were shorter and lighter than normal.

Mike McLeod (2005-08) is Yale's all-time rushing (4,514 yards) and rushing touchdown (54) leader. (SABBY FRINZI)

A Galling Loss to Harvard

"My most disappointing day at Yale was the triple-overtime 30-24 loss to Harvard in 2005. We led 21-3 in the third quarter and had played so well in many ways. Jeff Mroz, our quarterback, played great. However, on a third and 3 we ran a pass play that Jeff loved to throw, but he made one of the worst throws of his career. A Harvard player picked it off and ran it back for a touchdown. Clifton Dawson rushed for 128 yards for Harvard and scored the winning TD from 2 yards out in the third overtime. Following the game Harvard coach Tim Murphy, a longtime friend, shook my hand and said, "We didn't deserve to win. We made too many mistakes." But Harvard won for the fifth straight year, and it hurt.

"That day was a disappointing day for the Siedlecki household as well. At halftime we led 14-3 and my wife, Nancy, confident that we would win, left the game to see my daughter, Amy, play for Hand High School in the state championship field hockey game. Well, Hand lost the game, 1-0, to make the day a double whammy. After that Harvard triple-overtime loss, we won our next five overtime games from 2006-08, with two of them coming against Penn. But I might trade one or two of those for that triple-overtime loss to Harvard.

"We bounced back in 2006 and tied for the Ivy League title with Princeton. This was especially satisfying since we were picked to finish fifth in the Ivy. Our only loss (34-31) came at the hands of Princeton in the Bowl. I was surprised at the reaction of the alumni. They were crying and complaining. No one gave us a chance against Harvard the next week, but we beat them, 34-13.

Yale Lays an Egg

"Of course losing to Harvard 37-6 on the final day of the 2007 season was almost as disappointing as the triple-overtime loss. What happened? To this day, I have no idea. To lay an egg like that was inexplicable. We flat-out got our ass kicked. Early in the game Steve Santoro batted a ball that deflected into the hands of a Harvard player who was on the ground. We had no energy and never recovered.

McLeod

"Mike McLeod had his share of long runs, but he was the greatest short-yardage running back I ever had. In the 2007 game against Princeton we went on a crucial fourth down and needed a yard or two. We missed a block and it looked like Mike was going to get nailed in the backfield for a 2- or 3-yard loss, but he literally carried the Princeton defensive lineman 4 or 5 yards to get the first down.

"Mike was also the best pass blocker I ever had. He understood blitzes and what was coming. Larry Ciotti always did a great job coaching the backs in that department. I know I was criticized for using McLeod as often as I did. He had 1,063 carries, or 325 more rushing attempts than Robert Carr, who had held the record. Some said that we became too predictable. My answer to that is we were 23-7 in Mike's last three years (2006-08). That's the best three-year Yale record since the 1979-81 teams under Carm [Cozza] that went 25-4. Using McLeod often is what we were.

An Unheralded Quarterback

"During those years our quarterback, Matt Polhemus, was not in the class of Walland, Lee, or Mroz as a passer. He had a strong arm but was not accurate. But Matt had good running ability, and he offset McLeod. Polhemus had more big plays running with the football himself than he had big pass plays. We found a way to win with Matt. His two years at quarterback we were 17-3 and I had lost the tag of 'Air Siedlecki.'

"Matt had the craziest pair of legs you ever saw, and he was fearless. He never really got to air it out because of the freezer of well-hung McLeod meat we kept in the backfield at that time. He also had to wait his time. His sophomore year ('04) he finally got a few late snaps against Columbia. Coach Keith Clark pulled him aside and, just to mess with him, called a front-side run play. Just as Matt turned to take the field, Clark grabbed him, stared him in the eyes, licked his lips and grunted, "I bet you don't have the *balls* to change the play!"

"Well, Matt goes in and switches the play to a naked boot off the run and picks up a nice little gain on the keeper. We pretty much used the same strategy when he became our regular quarterback."

BOB BARTH—PA ANNOUNCER FOR VARIOUS YALE ATHLETIC EVENTS; SHELTON, CONNECTICUT

I normally work basketball, baseball, and soccer, but in 2003 I worked as a spotter for PA announcer Mark Ryba for the Harvard game. There was a banner attached to the scoreboard. As I remember, Yale students from the Marching Band are the one's that put it there as it was going to be part of their halftime show. Yale personnel walking around the perimeter of the Bowl hours before the game was scheduled to begin noticed a black box behind the scoreboard that looked out of

place. The police were notified and kept everyone out of the Bowl. They stopped traffic around the area while the Bomb Squad investigated. I think nobody fessed up to the incident for fear of reprisal by the Yale Administration."

The 2003 Yale-Harvard game drew the largest crowd (53,136) in the Bowl in 14 years. Harvard won 37-19 behind the arm of quarterback Ryan Fitzpatrick, who threw for 230 yards and four touchdowns. Fitzpatrick, who would be the Ivy League MVP in 2004, went on to a successful NFL career with the St. Louis Rams, Cincinnati Bengals, Buffalo Bills, and Tennessee Titans.

Top: Todd Tomich and his family; Below: Tomich runs back punt return vs. Harvard in 1998. Harvard's No. 97 is Artie Jones. Tomich was an All-Ivy first-team selection at defensive back in 1999 and 2000.
(YALE ATHLETICS)

The Yale team erupts in jubilation after Alan Kimball kicks a walk-off 35-yard FG to beat Penn 17-14 in overtime in 2006.
(BILL O'BRIEN)

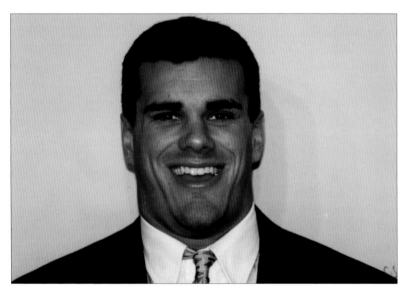

Than Merrill, who played with the Chicago Bears in 2001, was a two-time first team All-Ivy selection at safety and defensive back.
(SABBY FRINZI)

2010 Yale captain Tom McCarthy (48) attempts to knock down a pass by Harvard's Collier Winters (16) in the 2009 Harvard game. Ben Sessions (57) blocks McCarthy.
(YALE ATHLETICS)

Jack Siedlecki inherited a floundering Yale program in 1997 that had only won seventeen games the previous five years. During his tenure (1997-2008) his teams produced a 70-49 record, including two Ivy League titles. But the unofficial mandate for a Yale coach is to beat Harvard. Siedlecki's 4-8 mark vs. the Crimson, losing seven times in his last eight tries, clouded his accomplishments and created unrest among old Blues. He was replaced by Tom Williams, Yale's first African American head football coach. Williams's stay lasted only three years.

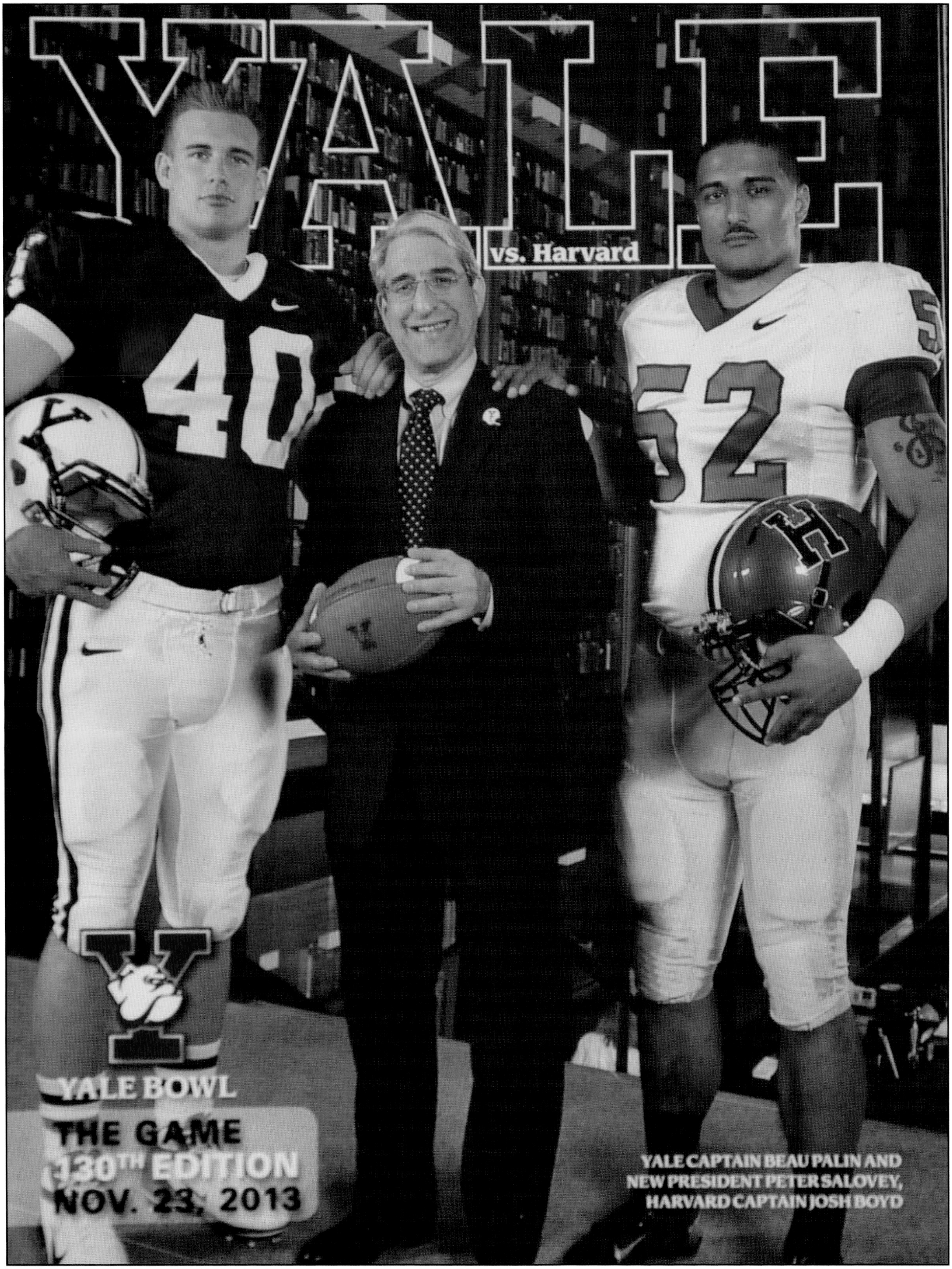

YALE

vs. Harvard

40

52

YALE BOWL

THE GAME
130TH EDITION
NOV. 23, 2013

YALE CAPTAIN BEAU PALIN AND
NEW PRESIDENT PETER SALOVEY,
HARVARD CAPTAIN JOSH BOYD

Chapter 23

2010-2013—A CHANGE IN CULTURE

"I think the most important thing that happened in the last 12 months was we changed the culture here. The guys have become one football team and guys that play for each other and with that mentality, and it's been really great to watch."

—Yale football coach Tony Reno (October 2013, Telegram.com)

THE SECOND DECADE of the new millennium began on a promising note for the Yale Bulldogs. The 2010 team, under second-year head coach Tom Williams, finished a tidy 7-3. But the next season, the program took a step backward, both on the field and as a result of allegations against a player and the coach. As if that weren't enough, Yale suffered its worst loss to Harvard in twenty-nine years, losing 45-7 in front of a home crowd. And The Game was played under the cloud of a pre-game tailgating accident, which resulted in serious injuries and one fatality. By necessity, the 2012 and 2013 seasons were devoted to rebuilding and changing the football culture at Yale.

All of that lay in the future in 2010, and Williams had reasons for optimism. Besides, Williams had fun coaching. He was known for his practice gimmicks, which were part of his persona. For example, he was concerned that Yale's 2010 game with Fordham, which came between Dartmouth and Penn on the schedule, could be what he called a "trap game"—a game that his players might take too lightly. To get their attention, he attached a mousetrap to the baseball cap he wore in practice the week of the game. Yale edged Fordham 7-6.

Chris Smith
(YALE ATHLETICS)

In the Bulldogs' 27-24 win at Brown, Chris Smith, Yale's all-time kickoff return yards leader (1,726), ran back two straight kickoffs (79 and 83 yards) for TDs in a span of 2:23 to set an Ivy League record.

Expectations were high for 2011 with the return of veteran quarterback Patrick Witt, a transfer from the University of Nebraska. Witt, the son of airline pilots, was to set Yale career records for pass completions (549) and passing yardage (6,033) and completion percentage (.601). Witt was joined by senior running back Alex Thomas and a cadre of other skilled backs and receivers. But the team finished a disappointing 5-5, enduring a fifth successive loss to Harvard.

Patrick Witt (2009-11) passed for thirty-seven TDs, second most in Yale history.
(YALE ATHLETICS)

On October 29, 2011, Yale beat Columbia 16-13 in New York amid a blizzard that crippled much of the Northeast. The Great White Way that day wasn't Broadway but the northern tip of Manhattan.

CONTROVERSY AND TRAGEDY AHEAD OF THE GAME

Distractions and disaster marred the week of the 2011 Harvard game. Three weeks earlier, reports had circulated that Witt faced a tough choice: playing against Harvard or going to Atlanta for a Rhodes Scholarship interview. The story drew national media attention. It later developed that Witt was not on the final interview list, rendering the question moot.

It was revealed that early in the 2011 season a female student filed an informal complaint against Witt to the University-Wide Committee on Sexual Misconduct. The case never went any further. The Rhodes Trust informed Yale and Witt that his candidacy was suspended unless the university decided to re-endorse it. It is unknown whether or not Yale University re-endorsed Witt's candidacy, since it treats such matters privately.

Ironically, a Rhodes scholarship controversy led to coach Tom Williams' resignation. Williams had allegedly stated that he had faced a situation whether to interview for a Rhodes Scholarship while playing at Stanford in the 1980s or play in a game. The story drew scrutiny from the *New York Times.* The paper quoted an official of the Rhodes Trust as saying there was no record that Williams ever applied. Two days before the Harvard game, Williams told Jim Fuller of the *New Haven Register* that a faculty advisor at Stanford had encouraged him to apply for the Rhodes, but he never went as far in the process as Witt had. Asked if he had been a Rhodes finalist, Williams replied, "No, nor did I intend to [be]. If I misrepresented that, it wasn't my intention."

Further, published biographies of Williams had stated he had been on the practice squad of the NFL's San Francisco 49ers. The scenario that emerged was that he had taken part in a three-day tryout camp but never signed a contract with the 49ers or took part in their summer training camp.

On December 21, 2011, after an internal investigation by Yale, Williams resigned. He left with a 16-14 overall mark. "I'm the same man I've always been," said Williams upon his departure.

Horror in Lot D

The Witt decision and the Williams controversy paled in comparison to the incident outside the Bowl in Parking Lot D hours before the 2011 Harvard game. Three women were struck by a keg-laden U-Haul truck that Brendan Ross, a 21-year-old Yale student, was driving to a Sigma Phi Epsilon tailgate party. Nancy Barry, 30, was killed and her friends, Sarah Short and Elizabeth Dernbach, were injured. Ross initially was charged with negligent homicide, a charge later reduced with the Barry family's agreement. Ross pleaded guilty to driving unreasonably fast and unsafe starting and was granted accelerated rehabilitation that called for 400 hours of community service. This gave him the chance to avoid a criminal record and possible prison time, but did not rule out civil suits.

THE RENO ERA

Following Williams's resignation, Yale hired Tony Reno, who had been a Yale assistant under Jack Siedlecki but had joined Tim Murphy's staff at Harvard after Siedlecki left. Reno was introduced to the media as Yale's 34th head football coach on Jan. 12, 2012. Dismissing the undercurrent of discord that preceded him, he said confidently, "I'm the man for the job."

The Reno era began in high gear on September 15, 2012, with a 24-21 Yale victory at Georgetown. The feature play was a 98-yard touchdown pass from freshman quarterback Eric Williams to Cameron Sandquist, who caught a ball batted by Hoya safety Malcolm Caldwell-Meeks. Williams was the first Yale freshman quarterback to start and win a season opener since seventeen-year-old Art Dakos engineered a win over Tufts in 1945. Another newcomer, Tyler Varga, scored two touchdowns and rushed for 103 yards. Varga, a ferocious 5-11, 220-pound running back in the mold of Rich Diana, transferred from the University of Western Ontario in Canada.

After Varga had played three games, the NCAA received an anonymous challenge of his eligibility. He was held out of the Dartmouth game, before being cleared to play the remainder of the season. The situation remains a nettling question. If he was properly cleared to start the season, how could the NCAA act in such a manner?

The Bulldogs finished 2-8 in a season that was hampered by injuries and inexperience. Reno's top three quarterbacks all went down with injuries in the Penn game. Ironically, Yale's 27-13 victory over the Ivy champion Quakers was the Bulldogs' only league win.

Tom Williams
(YALE ATHLETICS)

In the 2012 Princeton game played in the Bowl, Yale running back Mordecai Cargill threw a pass to quarterback Henry Furman that was picked off by Princeton defensive back Trocon Davis who returned it for a 100-yard touchdown in the Tigers' 29-7 win. It was the longest interception return in Yale Bowl history.

In 2012 there was no Yale captain on the program cover for the Harvard game. Will McHale, the elected Yale captain, had surrendered his captaincy because of an off-campus altercation in May of that year.

The Bulldogs came out of the gate with fierce determination in 2013 winning their first three games before losing their next three and finishing 5-5. The season became a war of attrition suffering long term losses to key personnel like receiver Chris Smith, QB Henry Furman, and Varga. Their 24-10 win over 18th ranked FCS power Cal Poly at San Luis Obispo, California, was one of the great road wins in Yale football history. The last time Yale beat a nationally ranked team on the road was in 1947 when the Elis downed AP No. 11 ranked Columbia at Baker Field, 17-7 when both schools were classified as University Division Major College programs.

The year's best individual performance was turned in by Deon Randall in the Bulldog's 38-23 win over Cornell at the Bowl. The 2014 captain-elect scored four consecutive touchdowns in the second half that earned him the Ivy League Offensive Player of the Week and the Gold Helmet (top D1 player) by the New England Sports Writers. His 32-yard rushing TD with nineteen seconds left against Brown was Yale's most memorable run of the season and the game-winner. He was called on to play defense on the Bears' last attempt to even the score as time ran out, knocking down a pass in the end zone.

A human interest story emerged when Yale beat Columbia 53-12. Tate Harshbarger, a 5-foot-9, 153-pound walk-on, entered the game in the fourth quarter and carried the ball 10 times, including a 14-yard touchdown. In a most unusual sight, the entire Yale team raced to the south end zone in the Bowl in jubilation. The Elis received an ensuing excessive celebration penalty but nobody cared. Yale QB Hank Furman labeled it, "the best moment of the season."

THE PLAYERS

Jesse Reising (linebacker) '08, '09, '10

JURIS DOCTOR CANDIDATE AT HARVARD LAW SCHOOL;
PRESIDENT AND CO-FOUNDER, OPERATION OPPORTUNITY
FOUNDATION
CAMBRIDGE, MASSACHUSETTS

Yale's 2010 season ended with a 28-21 loss at Harvard. Late in the game, Yale linebacker Jesse Reising, who aspired to a career as a Marine officer, suffered a serious neck injury. The Game became just "a game" while Reising lay motionless. The injury was to change the course of his life.

"On November 20, 2010, I left Harvard's campus on a stretcher, wondering whether my service to my country was over. I have been fortunate enough to return to Harvard as a law student, hoping that my service has only begun.

"I had curl/flat responsibility on what would turn out to be the last play of my football career. The receiver I was covering ran a flag route. By the time

Jesse Reising is a profile in courage.
(YALE ATHLETICS)

I saw the Harvard quarterback's eyes shift to his running back, Gino Gordon, on the underneath route, I had already dropped deep into the secondary. I did not want to leave Gordon — the Ivy League Player of the Year — enough time to make a move after he caught the pass, so I sprinted 10-15 yards full speed to try to make contact with him as soon as he caught the ball. I ended up making contact just as he dropped his shoulder pads to protect himself from the hit I was about to deliver, and his helmet hit my right shoulder pad, which pushed my shoulder down and snapped my head to the opposite side, tearing two nerves in my neck. I think I broke a few bones in my shoulder as well, but the main concern was the nerves in my neck.

After the hit, I was face down on the field, unable to move. I heard the footsteps of the trainers and doctors running out onto the field, and I heard someone say, 'He's paralyzed.' Upon hearing that, I immediately tried to get up, and I did move a bit, but the doctors made me stay put. I thought my arm was dislocated and I just wanted someone to place it. "As reality set in about the potential severity of my injury, I feared losing my ability to serve in the Marines. The low point for me after my injury was the conversation with my recruiter, dis-enrolling me from Officer Candidate School. Losing the Marine Corps left a hole in my heart.

"But the human spirit has remarkable capacity to triumph over the body. I had to ask myself *why* I wanted to become a Marine, and *how* I could accomplish those ends through different means. For me, this meant that I would find whatever way I could to serve my country to the best of my ability—whether that meant going to Afghanistan to support the counter-insurgency effort as a civilian; serving those serving in the military in my place by launching the Warrior-Scholar Project (an 'academic boot camp' designed to help veterans transition from the military to college); or working toward my law degree to serve and represent the United States as a federal prosecutor.

"Six months after my injury, I still had virtually no movement in my arm, so a team of three surgeons at the Mayo Clinic took a nerve from my leg and grafted it into my neck. They also diverted part of a nerve that normally helps curl my fingers and used it to help curl my entire arm. I was given a very high dose of anesthesia because I had to be put to sleep for almost half of the day for the surgery. I was over 200 pounds, and I drank beer and whiskey, which built up my tolerance.

"I was supposed to stay in the recovery room for a couple of hours after I woke up, but I started hitting on my nurse within minutes and distracted her from attending to the other patients, so they ended up rolling me out of the recovery room almost immediately.

"Today, people barely notice anything is wrong with my arm. I still have to boost my right arm with my left in order to shake someone's hand, and I can't raise my hand above my head. But I'm very lucky in that I am still able to carry on a perfectly normal lifestyle. My recovery has been near-miraculous. Unfortunately, many people with brachial plexus injuries like mine are not so lucky, and I pray for them daily.

"A bum arm is not the only permanent reminder of my four years of Yale football. Football has shaped me into the man I am today and taught me some of life's most important lessons, and I would not trade my four years of Yale football for anything. The friendships forged will last a lifetime."

Don Scharf on Jesse Reising

"Our student athletes are wonderful. When Jesse found out that he was dis-enrolled for Officer Candidate School because of the injury he suffered in the 2010 Harvard game, he was crushed. When he learned that he was never going to be able to raise his arm above his shoulder, he knew that his dream of becoming a Marine pilot and officer was over. Jesse became very depressed. I sent Jesse a couple of e-mails and asked if he would come in to see me. We talked for about an hour. I told him that there were still opportunities for him if that's what he wanted. I knew I was able to put him in touch with about a half dozen alumni in Washington who would introduce him to the right people in the CIA and Secret Service. He spent a couple of days in Washington with these alums, He actually got a little taste of the military, spending a year in Afghanistan auditing U.S. Government contracts

I hooked up Jesse with Dick Torykian, who is unbelievably connected. His son Rich lettered in football ('89-'91) and lacrosse at Yale.

Pat Moran (defensive tackle) '08, '09, '11

ALEXANDRIA, VIRGINIA

"I will never forget playing in that snowstorm at Columbia in 2011. Can you imagine having a pre-Halloween snowstorm with 4 to 6 inches of snow on the ground? I was expecting a mix of rain and snow, so I wore my turf shoes because Wien Stadium has artificial turf. But when we were going through warm-ups, I couldn't get traction. We got through the game and fortunately won 16-13. Near the end of the game, Beau Palin came into the huddle all fired up. He had heard that Brown broke Penn's Ivy League winning

Pat Moran
(YALE ATHLETICS)

streak with their 6-0 win. Beau got into a squat position and kept yelling 'Yeah ... Yeah,' and he was shadow boxing. This gave us a chance for the Ivy title. At the time Harvard was the only undefeated team in the Ivy, and Brown and Yale had one loss in the league.

"After the game all we were thinking about was taking a warm shower. But when we got back to the locker room the showers were ice cold. One bay had lukewarm water, and about 60 guys converged on that bay. Two out of the three showers were frigid. That was a final 'F - - - you' from Columbia!"

Mordecai Cargill (tail back) '09, '10, '11, '12

CLEVELAND HEIGHTS, OHIO

"Playing in that blizzard at Columbia had to be the most unusual day of my Yale career for many reasons. Being from Ohio, I had played in a lot of cold games but never played in a game when it snowed

Mordecai Cargill
(YALE ATHLETICS)

continuously. I carried the ball 42 times for 230 yards that game and scored two TDs. Defensive end Matt Battaglia said, 'You didn't carry the ball 42 times in practice the last two weeks.' I had to carry the load because Alex [Thomas] was injured and didn't play that day. For me it was tunnel vision. I wasn't thinking of being tired.

"Playing on Field Turf helped. I wore my molded cleats, which is what most guys wear on turf fields. Playing on grass, most players wear the screw-in cleats. I wasn't worried about balance. I just got the ball and ran. Our offensive line did a super job opening holes for me. In playing conditions like that, I think the offense has the advantage over the defense because the offensive player knows the direction he is going and the defense must react to that.

"Another thing that stands out in my mind was the day coach Williams lost his hat in an early-morning practice in 2010. Coach was yelling at Josh Grizzard about something when he dramatically threw

his hat in the air and the wind took it over the wall and into the graveyard adjacent to the practice field. Everyone laughed."

Cameron Sandquist (wide receiver) '10, '11, '12

POLITICAL SCIENCE MAJOR
REDMOND, WASHINGTON

Beat Dartmouth

"Even as a freshman in 2010, I was able to pick up on the newly acquired disdain for Dartmouth leading up to this game. One way or another, our two teams had really begun to hate each other, and this game really saw it magnified. It was a heated game that came down to the wire. As the game reached its end, I remember Chris Stanley, a senior, had a strip fumble that was nothing short of miraculous. He somehow pulled the ball out while on the run without breaking stride. The turnover set up the game-winning field goal attempt by Philippe Panico.

"To this point in the season, (Game 4) we had

Cameron Sandquist stretches out for catch in Yale's 37-17 win over Cornell in 2011.
(YALE ATHLETICS)

been absolutely heinous on field goal conversions. I want to say it was the first one we had made all year, and Philippe really made it dramatic. As time expired he banked in the kick [off the right goal post] and immediately took off to celebrate. Naturally, the whole team chased him down to join him. None of us really noticed, but Philippe had beelined straight for the center of the field, where we all began mobbing him in celebration. Next thing we knew, both teams were completely face to face on the 50-yard line, with Dartmouth fully ready to defend their turf in brawling fashion. The coaches successfully de-escalated the situation and it quickly became one of the most awkward handshake exchanges I have ever been a part of.

"The locker room celebration was unbelievable. Players were climbing lockers, Coach Williams was dancing, and chants were breaking out everywhere. I can still remember the 'Fat Daddy' chants for Joe Young as Coach Dub gave a memorable speech about the intensity of the game. The feeling after that has stuck with me to this day. There really was nothing like playing in such a heated game as a freshman, coming back to win it on a last-second field goal, and then celebrating with all my new best friends.

Move Over, Gary Fencik

"In the opening game of the 2012 season against Georgetown, Eric Williams, our freshman quarterback, connected with me on a 98-yard touchdown pass, breaking the school record of 97 yards—Don Gesicki to Gary Fencik in 1975 at Princeton. All preseason, coach [Kevin] Morris had talked about trying to go after that record and that we were going to take chances. With under a minute left in the first half, it was the perfect chance to give it a shot. All I was running was a simple go route and hoping to be open. To be honest, it wasn't my best route, and Eric

will tell you it wasn't his best throw, but it all worked out. When the ball got tipped by a Georgetown defender, my only focus was to bring it in, but about the time I reached the 10-yard line I was almost laughing that it had happened and even more that Eric's first TD was for the record. I cracked a little joke to Eric in the end zone, just saying welcome to college ball, because I thought it was too funny this is how he was starting his career.

"At that moment we just wanted to switch the momentum going into halftime, but it's becoming a cooler thing to be a part of the further I get from it. Being associated any way with Yale football is a blessing. Seeing all the names that have played in the Bowl before me, it is really just the highest honor to be part of a play that is in the history books with them."

Tyler Varga (TB) '12, '13

PRE-MED STUDENT
KITCHENER, ONTARIO

Tyler Varga was selected to the All-Ivy First Team in 2012.

"My journey to Yale is an interesting one. I was recruited by a number of schools in Canada and the United States. I had a lower leg injury (compartment syndrome) the final game of my senior year in high school. I suffered trauma to my leg that induced swelling and bleeding. The nerve function got shut down in my leg. I didn't get the necessary surgery that was recommended to recover from the injury, so a lot of doctors were saying I never would be able to walk again, never mind play football. A lot of schools that were interested in me fell off the map, and my college football career was in doubt.

"I ended up staying in Canada. In 2011 I played at the University of Western Ontario. But we parted ways. Coach Reno called me shortly after he was

Tyler Varga makes yardage against Cornell in 2012.
(YALE ATHLETICS)

Alex Thomas rushed for 1,701 yards from 2009-11.
(YALE ATHLETICS)

Gio Christodoulou returned punts for a record 834 yards in his career (2007-2011).
(YALE ATHLETICS)

hired. Both Harvard and Yale recruited me when coach Reno was at Harvard. When he found out I was looking to transfer, he called me. I committed officially to attend Yale in June of 2012.

Eligibility Issue

"I played the first three games of the season against Georgetown, Cornell, and Colgate. Then my eligibility became a question because I had transferred. I don't know who challenged it. I thought everything was cleared up [before the season started]. Our coaching staff was under the impression that I was eligible to play [in 2012] and the NCAA had ruled on it earlier.

"I did not play in the Dartmouth game, and it was really frustrating. I also didn't know how many years of eligibility I would have. I wanted to be able to plan my life. Having four years at Yale vs. three is a big difference. I was subsequently declared eligible and a sophomore.

"I'm a pre-med student. Before my leg injury I was sure I wanted to be an eye surgeon. If you can save somebody's vision, that's one of the most important things you can do. An eye surgeon can get quick satisfaction. But I got interested in orthopedics from my leg injury. I spent a lot of time with orthopedic doctors. I decided why fight it. By staying in orthopedics I could remain close to football and do something I love."

Kahlil Keys (tailback) '12, '13

POLITICAL SCIENCE MAJOR
PETALUMA, CALIFORNIA

On November 2, 2013, Yale upended Columbia 53-12. Junior Kahlil Keys scored his first varsity TD on a 94-yard run establishing a new school record. The old record (93 yards) was held by Denny McGill in 1956.

"The play was called '37 Boss.' My job was to read the defensive line and either run off tackle or behind the center. I hit the seam and made the play. It was a testament to how well we blocked up front and how the receivers blocked on the perimeter

"I ran ninety-four yards untouched. I was pretty gassed by the time I got to the Columbia 20-yard line. It was at that point I knew I was going to score.

"My parents listened to the radio broadcast in California. They were thrilled. That night I hung with some of my teammates and celebrated Halloween. We went to Toad's and other places.

"It's a day I'll never forget

Kahlil Keys makes his historic run vs. Columbia in 2013.
(YALE ATHLETICS)

THE GLORY AND grandeur of Yale football as a national program vanished long ago. The exploits of Kelley and Frank, McGill and Ward and Dowling and Hill have faded in time along with raccoon coats and trolley car rides to the Bowl.

The student athletes who now walk through the tunnel about to engage in battle in the historic Bowl are well aware of their inherited proud legacy cultivated by generations of champions. Because of that, they continue to play for pride with the understanding that Yale, though no longer a national football power, remains a Goliath in the classroom.

Will coach Tony Reno and his staff restore the Yale program to its perch at the top of the Ivy echelon?

Old Blues and Yale fans wish him well!

PART IV

The Yale Bowl

The Braintrust

YALE BULLDOGS

NOVEMBER 16, 1996 / YALE BOWL G A M E D A Y   VS. PRINCETON

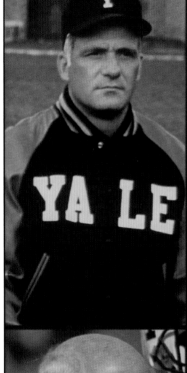

A LEGENDARY ERA COMES TO AN END

The November 16, 1996, Yale-Princeton Game Day program cover. This was the last game Carmen Cozza coached in the Yale Bowl.
(YALE ATHLETICS)

Chapter 24

CARMEN COZZA—THE SHEPHERD OF YALE FOOTBALL

"One reason why Carmen was such a successful coach was that his philosophy and idealisms were glove-in-glove with Yale's traditional thoughts of education and football."

—Dave Kelley, former defensive line coach

CARMEN COZZA, YALE'S 31st head football coach, enjoyed a thirty-two-year tenure. Yale's most decorated coach recorded 179 wins against 119 losses and 5 ties. His Ivy League mark stands at 135-85-5 and includes ten championships, four outright. His teams were 22-10 against Princeton and 16-15-1 vs. Harvard. His teams were 116-66-1 in the Yale Bowl and 63-53-4 on the road. Cozza, the patriarch of Yale football in the modern era, joins Walter Camp, Howard Jones, and Tad Jones as former Yale head coaches who are enshrined in the College Football Hall of Fame.

During the 1976-77 school year Cozza served as both football coach and athletic director. His agreement with Yale President Kingman Brewster stipulated that he would resign the football position at the end of the '76 season and be a full-time athletic director. Brewster did not think it was possible to hold both positions and do the necessary job. Several days after the season ended, Cozza decided to remain as head coach and resigned as athletic director.

Carmen Cozza is one of four Yale coaches enshrined in the College Football Hall of Fame.
(YALE ATHLETICS)

Carmen Cozza (Head football coach, 1965-1996)

ORANGE, CONNECTICUT

"I'm often asked who was the greatest influence on my coaching career? I played for Woody Hayes and Ara Parseghian at Miami of Ohio. Woody was a holler guy and was very demanding. He was an English major and a big history buff. He would scream at you a lot, but he had a real caring for his athletes. Woody was a bug on academics and proctored the study table. I struggled a little my freshman and sophomore years, and I'll never forget him being there. If you got a little tired, he would wake you in his own way.

"Ara was very young, about twenty-five years old, when he got the coaching job at Miami. He had been an outstanding athlete. Ara had a way of needling you a little bit, and yet he could relate extremely well with us because he was only a few years older than we were.

"I also got a lot from John Pont, my roommate at Miami. I talked to Bo Schembechler a lot. Bo was a teammate of mine at Miami, along with Bill Arnsparger and John McVay. But to be honest, I learned more from my players, probably, than anybody else. I always told my staff if I didn't know what quarterback to start, somehow the players would let you know.

Practice Stories

"In '68 there was a gentleman named Benjie, who was slightly impaired. He had a tricycle with an ice cream box in the back. Near the end of practice I spotted him and bought Popsicles for all the players. They thought that was the greatest thing since sliced bread. I didn't pre-plan it. I just happened to see the truck, and it was hot as hell and the kids were working real hard. I got more feedback on that than you could imagine.

"Perhaps the most unusual thing that happened in practice involved a free-spirited defensive back named Dave Holahan ['69, '70] and his dog, named Fred. Dave would take Fred, a mutt, to practice every day and tie him to a bench near the field. Fred was very obedient and would quietly watch practice. The players loved him, and he became our mascot. He was fed as well as anybody on campus. One day, a player was hit and landed on Fred, breaking his paw. I told the manager to take him to the vet and I would pay the bill. Fortunately, Fred recovered without any complications.

"Believe it or not, Holahan took Fred to the team banquet, which was held in the elegant President's Room in Woolsey Hall. Fred was seated in a regular chair with a bib. I noticed Fred and waited for the players to react, which they never did. I was sitting next to Yale President Kingman Brewster, and I spent the evening trying to block his view of this rather unusual circumstance. Kingman didn't say a word. He had two black Labs and liked dogs.

Biggest Wins

"In '65 we beat Brown, 3-0, on Danny Begel's field goal. It was my first-ever Ivy League win, and I rate that game as one of my top Ivy League wins. Beating Dartmouth 56-15 in '67 was big. They came into the Bowl undefeated and had beaten Harvard the week before. Keith Jackson and Bud Wilkinson broadcast the game. The win at Princeton that year and the '67 win over Harvard also rank high. The '87 win against Penn, when we trailed and Penn had the ball with thirty-five seconds to play, is up there, as is the 30-0 win at Brown in '96, my final season.

Carm Cozza chalks up another victory.
(Yale Athletics)

"Beating Air Force in '80, which was my 100th win, and Navy in '81, were the biggest non-Ivy wins of my coaching career. Air Force was a good team that had tied Illinois the week before. Navy was a good team that almost beat Michigan the week before. They took a 12-0 lead and were running through us at will before we began to stop them and started to move the ball. John Rogan completed 16 of 30 passes for three touchdowns, and Curt Grieve caught two of them. Ara [Parseghian] was doing color for ABC-TV and was making all kinds of excuses for us when Navy was having their way. He said we didn't have spring practice or give scholarships.

"Following the game, I ran up to the press box to see Ara after I got done talking to the kids, but he had left early because he and Al Michaels had to catch a flight. But he called me the next day. It was a thrill to beat Navy with Ara in the Bowl.

Blackman and Restic

"In retrospect the two coaches that were the most difficult to prepare for were Bob Blackman (Dartmouth and Cornell) and Joe Restic (Harvard).

Dartmouth is the only team in the league I had a losing record against. What Blackman did better than any one else is that he wrote to every high school in the country to get names of prospects. When we first got here, you could not initiate contact with an athlete. We had to rely on alumni. Now the alumni are taken out of recruiting. The biggest challenge I had as the head coach was recruiting.

The Quirky Kickers

"I personally coached the kickers, who were always a little different. Tony Greblick, who kicked for us in '82, was a barefoot kicker and a real character. During his freshman year he was playing at Harvard on a very cold day, and to keep warm he zipped himself into one of the ball bags. The problem was that the zipper handles were on the outside of the bag, so when coach Harry Jacunski called for him to kick, he couldn't get out. Finally someone saw the bag moving and let him out, but by then it was too late to send him in.

"The best conventional field goal kicker I ever had was Brian Clarke ('71-73). He drove me crazy for four years, but he was a very good straight-ahead kicker. As far as strength, I would probably pick Tony Jones ('79-81), who kicked field goals and punted for us. When we beat Air Force, we were inside our own 20, and he punted the ball 60 yards and got us out of the hole and we won the game.

Final Game in the Bowl

"Coaching my final game in the Yale Bowl on November 16, 1996, against Princeton was very emotional for me. When I saw all my past captains, I ran over and hugged them all. In all honesty I'm not sure I coached a lick that day. My mind wasn't there. It was hard.

"I liked my players at Yale. I had a chance to go to the University of Virginia when they hired George Welch (in 1982). I made my demands strong because I think, subconsciously, I didn't want to leave. When I was thinking about going, my middle daughter heard about it and she had tears in her eyes. I said, 'No, it's not worth it.' Coaching is coaching, no matter where you go. I didn't pursue the job.

My Best Teams

"The '67-'68 teams that won 16 in a row have to be near the top. The '79-'81 teams were my best defensive teams. Perhaps one of the most gratifying coaching years we ever had was in '69. Nobody gave that team much of a chance, and we ended up gaining a share of the Ivy League title. Because we had so many big leads in '68, the kids on that team got a lot of playing time. One thing the players knew how to do on that ['69] team was win, and you know how important that is.

The Impact of Going I-AA

"The Ivy League went from Division I-A to I-AA in '82. I didn't think at the time that it would have the impact it did. But all of a sudden we were no longer on the regional network of ABC-TV. We weren't considered big time any more. When we were I-A we played Boston College, Rutgers, Miami of Ohio, and the military academies. I think going to Division I-AA affected recruiting and attendance. A lot of kids liked the fact that we were in I-A. The image of being I-AA hurt the league. But we still played Central Florida, the University of Hawaii, and UConn.

An Amazing Statistic

"One thing I am very proud of was our graduation rate. Of the more than 2,000 players I coached, I think we only had seven who did not get degrees. I don't think that with any one of them, not getting a degree had anything to do with academics. Some of them didn't graduate in four years, but they came back to get their degrees.

A Tribute to Carm

"I've received many honors over the years. Being inducted into the College Football Hall of Fame was wonderful, and being the winningest coach in Ivy League history is great, but the relationships with the players will be everlasting to me. In 2010 I had a birthday golf outing, and to see so many players who showed up was overwhelming.

MANY OF **C**ARMEN Cozza's players attended his 80th birthday party in 2010 at the Yale Golf Course. Former player Paul Sortal ('73) wrote an ode to honor his beloved former coach. An abbreviated version follows:

AN ODE TO COACH CARMEN COZZA ON HIS 80TH BIRTHDAY

You'd have had success at scholarship schools, or like Jauron, in the pros;
Yet you chose the Ivy ideal, instead of "anything goes",
You set Ivy records in games, championships, and wins,
Frankly, that's only where the Cozza legend begins!

Rather, you were dignified, commensurate with our school;
You innately and clearly were—thus didn't have to act—cool;
You regaled us with tales of Eli gridiron glory,

Returning Yale to national ranking as part of that story!

So, College Football Hall of Fame Coach (that has such a genuine ring),
Imagine your charges, a thousand strong, huddled to sing,
First "Boola", then "Bulldog" followed by a rousing "Down the Field";
Last, "Happy Birthday, Dear Carm", as the Harkness bells pealed.

THE PLAYERS REMEMBER CARM

BRIAN DOWLING '66, '67, '68

"Have I been haunted by the memories of that tie game with Harvard in '68? No. Like Frank

Champi said in the movie, *Harvard Beats Yale 29-29*, 'We were all winners.' I spoke at the luncheon on the weekend they premiered the movie in 2008, and I said, 'We're all winners.

Harvard said they were winners because they made the comeback, and we were winners because we got to play for Carmen Cozza.'"

TED LIVINGSTON '65, '67, '68

"On Monday nights during the '68 season, Carmen Cozza made presentations to the students and faculty at a lecture hall in one of the classroom buildings. It was like a "Football 101" course, and those sessions were largely attended. He would show film of the past Saturday's game and review some of the finer points."

JACK FORD '69, '70, '71

"The '71 game at Princeton was interesting. They were heavily favored, coming off their win against Harvard. The night before the game we had dinner at one of the dining halls at Princeton after our workout at Palmer Stadium. While walking back to our rooms, I decided to infuse a little Yale spirit into the Princeton campus. I got the biggest linemen I could find, and in the middle of Nassau Street I led the group, singing Yale fight songs and stopping traffic. I was like Leonard Bernstein conducting the New York Philharmonic Orchestra and really having fun when my teammates suddenly stopped singing. I looked around and here comes Carm. He leaned toward me and said, 'You better win tomorrow.'

"The epilogue to the story is we beat Princeton 10-6 and were overjoyed. Carm then said to me, 'Do you think you can do that next week against Harvard?'

"I had the honor of emceeing Carm's retirement dinner on Nov. 16, 1996. It was difficult on a number of levels. Everybody wanted this to be a storybook ending of a storybook career. But

"Four Decades of History" Front Row L-R: Rich Diana, Jon Reese, Carm Cozza, and Jack Ford. Back Row L-R: John Spagnola, Chris Hetherington, Dick Jauron, and Calvin Hill.

Princeton won that day, 17-13, and I knew Carm was crushed about the loss.

"At the dinner, however, it didn't take long to dispel that curtain of gloom. We were there to celebrate such a marvelous life. It went from a wake to a celebration."

DICK JAURON '70, '71, '72

"Carm was a great athlete who beat me in handball. We still have a terrific relationship. I have so much respect for the man and the university. They fit so well. My father, who was a great coach, taught me about all the legendary coaches, and that includes Carm."

JOHN PAGLIARO '75, '76, '77
An Emotional Meeting with Carm

"When we beat Harvard in Boston in '76, the players carried Carm off the field, thinking it might be his last game, since it appeared that he was going to be the full-time athletic director and would resign his coaching position. His emotional post-game speech and the atmosphere in the locker room are something I will take with me forever.

"It was a very difficult time. Although we won the game and walked off the field as Ivy co-champs, we felt as though we were losing a huge part of who we were. Carm was never one to get very emotional, but that was the first time I saw him show true emotion and strong feelings about what was happening. To me, it didn't seem like he wanted to go and leave his players and coaches. I never felt comfortable with his decision about leaving, and I never felt comfortable about him to not be allowed to be both the coach and athletic director.

"I decided to meet with Carm personally. It was not a long conversation. I was nervous when I went in. We talked a bit and I think he knew I was uneasy about something. Then I came right out and asked him if he would coach me one more time. I think that got to him, and it opened his mind to what he would be missing—the players whom he loved so dearly. He loved being on the practice field and the Yale Bowl. That was Carm's life for so long, and I truly feel he did not think about how much he would miss it. It got a bit emotional, and honestly, I did not know what he was going to do until he finally decided to come back to coaching soon after our meeting. It certainly was not just me who influenced him; it was Carm himself. He finally came to grips with what he truly wanted to do, and we were thrilled about it. He led us to another Ivy League title."

Coach Cozza and Gary Fencik
(YALE ATHLETICS)

KEN HILL '77, '78, '79
The Recruiting Wars

"I was heavily recruited by LSU and several other major-college teams. Many of the star players showed me a good time and tried to influence me to go there. Some of the stuff that was offered me was ridiculous, like a car, building my parents a home and other things. At age 16 or 17, this put a lot of pressure on me. I remember LSU head coach Charlie McClendon and his staff took me into a room and showed me LSU football highlight films. I was advised ahead of time not to sign anything.

"Because of my large family, I had a sense of familial responsibility. I tried to make a decision that would help relieve some of the financial burdens they had to deal with. I signed a letter of intent with LSU, because at that time the national commitment date for scholar-athletes was significantly earlier in the year than the date the Ivy League schools sent out their acceptances or rejection letters. I had to protect myself.

"My parents placed the decision in my lap, which bothered me. My brother Charlie was at Yale and was on the football team, although he didn't play varsity. He influenced me to go to Yale. Charlie told the Yale people I was interested, but they didn't believe him. They knew I was a high school star and one of the centerpieces of the SEC recruiting circle. They thought that Charlie was trying to pull a fast one just to get me a free visit.

"Rich Pont, the offensive backfield coach, hurriedly put together a visit. I had made the circuit with some of the most esteemed college coaches in the country. But Carmen Cozza was different. I found him to be a genuine man. Unlike my earlier recruiting experiences, Yale did not offer anything outlandish. Pont kidded me and said, 'I'll buy you a pair of sneakers for graduation in 1980.' I never got the sneakers.

"I made it clear that I wanted to play offense at Yale, and to some degree Carm gave me a voice in the decision. At Yale I never played one down on defense, even though I was a defensive back in the NFL."

MIKE SULLIVAN '77,'78, '79

"So much of my identity is associated with being one of Carm's boys. More than his polish and commanding presence, I admired Carm for his genuine interest in our well-being, the respect he showed his coaches, and his constant humility. All of his captains had these traits, including our great '79 captain, Tim Tumpane. I grew up in Orange, Conn., and shared many junior high school classes with Carm's youngest daughter, Karen. There's no better evidence of a man's character than the vigorous respect of a discerning fourteen-year-old daughter."

LEN FASANO '78, '79, '80
Jack-in-the-Box

"Carm got very nervous before games, but he also knew how to have fun.

Every Sunday night we met with Carm. If we won the day before, we could get a little lighthearted. At one Sunday meeting we were a bit giddy, especially Bob Krystyniak, who decided to have a little fun. He found a container with a lid on it in the area behind where Carm was talking to us. Every now and then he would pop up out of the can, acting like a Jack-in-the-box.

"The players began laughing and Carm couldn't understand it. I think he caught Krystyniak, because he sat on the can so Krystyniak couldn't pop up."

TOM GIELLA

"I always admired the classy way Carm handled both victory and defeat. He never took praise when we won, and he never blamed it on the kids when we lost. We either won or lost together as a team."

JON REESE '87, '88, '89

"I was recruited by many schools. My decision to attend Yale was made when Carm Cozza sat with me and my dad at our living room table during a recruiting visit and said, 'You will some day be our Yale captain.' My father was a high school football coach, and that statement by Carm carried a lot of weight. When I was elected captain he called my father and said, 'Walt, Jon has been elected captain of the 1989 Yale football team. I told you that would happen.'"

ROB MASELLA '93, '94, '95, '96

"In the early part of the 1996 season, a former player and fellow New Jersey recruit, Nick Adamo '96, died in a small-plane crash. Coach

Cozza wanted to take the entire team down to New Jersey for the wake. Like most things at Yale over his 30-plus years, when coach Cozza asked for something, the football people around him got it done, and two buses of Yale football players and staff left New Haven for New Jersey."

CARMEN ILACQUA '82, '84, '85
A Rowdy Table

"I like to think I did my job to the best of my physical ability as the team captain. However, things managed to get a bit out of hand one evening at the 1986 annual Walter Camp All-America dinner held in the Freshman Commons. I was with some of my senior teammates, whose names will be withheld to protect the innocent (Shannon, Curtin, Skwara, Tjarksen, McKenna, and Koze). At the cocktail hour we asked the waitress if we could each have a few beers to take to our table. So we all walked into the dining room with beer stashed away inside our tuxedoes. Then we started pulling them out once seated at our table, only to discover we had collectively smuggled what was probably a case of beer. I'm sure this was embarrassing for some at the event, as it was a quite a sight.

"We left the dinner when it was about three-quarters over, while the luminaries were giving speeches. A couple of years before, Illinois coach Mike White had been honored, and his photo was hanging on a wall. One of my teammates, who was from Chicago, was an Illinois fan and he yanked the photo off the wall as we exited the Commons. The photo was taken to a party, where it was destroyed under unusual circumstances.

"The following morning there was an article in the *Register* that reported how the Yale captain's table was rowdy and how his group left early and grabbed the photo of coach White. I was humiliated and knew I was going to face the wrath of coach Cozza in short order. Sure enough, my phone rang inside a half an hour and things went from bad to worse. It was Coach Cozza. He wasn't a happy camper and wanted to know about the picture. He demanded that I be in his office in half an hour. I called him back before I went to his office and said, 'I think I know where the picture is.'

"When I arrived in his office I was never so scared in my life. I was shaking in my socks. I had all the pieces of the picture in a plastic garbage bag. Carm stared at me and asked, 'Who took the picture off the wall?' I dug the hole deeper when I fibbed with a straight face and said, 'It fell off the wall.' Carm's face was getting redder and redder. He wanted to know how it happened, but I refused to throw my friends under the bus. Finally he said in disgust, 'Get out of my office.'

"My teammates called me 'Carmen' or 'Carmine' after Carmine Ragusa, the actor from the TV series *Happy Days* and *Laverne and Shirley*. They would never call me 'Carm.' There was only one Carm!"

SEB LASPINA—ASSISTANT COACH (1965-1996); VENICE, FLORIDA

"I was Carm's offensive coordinator for almost his entire tenure as Yale's head football coach. When we first started, the coaching staff would have extremely heated arguments, which was healthy. Carm would let us go but he kept things under control. He wouldn't stifle us.

"We also had our share of fun. The coaches would stay late into the night in their offices at the Ray Tompkins House, and Carm would go from meeting-to-meeting. We used to have contests to see which coaches would stay the latest. On a couple of occasions we scared the life out of Carm when he left before us. Buddy Amendola, Bill Narduzzi, Neil Putnam and I were in on this. This is what we did:

"In the photography area on the bottom floor of Ray Tompkins House, there were these old light bulbs that the coaches got hold of. A couple of times we threw the light bulbs from the second floor at Carm in the parking lot when he left the building. When they hit the ground, it was like bombs going off."

DAVE KELLEY—DEFENSIVE LINE COACH, 1973-96; GUILFORD, CONNECTICUT

"When I was hired in '73 from Allegheny College, Yale assistant coach Seb LaSpina met me at the airport and brought me to meet Carmen Cozza for the first time. Carmen said, 'You will do whatever you have to do and you will learn what you have to teach. I will not interfere with you. The main thing is that you must take care of your boys.'

"One reason why Carmen was such a successful coach was that his philosophy and idealisms were glove-in-glove with Yale's traditional thoughts of education and football. Football at Yale is part of a Yale education, not apart from education. He nurtured quality thinking with quality people."

JACK SIEDLECKI—YALE'S 33RD HEAD FOOTBALL COACH (1997-2008); MADISON, CONNECTICUT

"Following Carmen Cozza, a Yale and Ivy League coaching legend, was not a big deal because of the way he handled it. He was involved in the interview process, but after I was hired he basically stayed away from the program for a year. He has no ego- he's such an easy-going, first-class guy. He didn't come to practices and he left me alone. When Carm went on the air as a radio color commentator with Dick Galiette on WELI, he came to practice one day each week to help in his own preparation. My last couple of years he traveled on the team bus with us because he always felt more comfortable with the coaches and players than he did with the media guys. And as a color commentator, he never said anything negative about the players or coaches."

JOE BENANTO—YALE VARSITY BASEBALL COACH/HEAD FRESHMAN FOOTBALL COACH (1981-90); SHELTON, CONNECTICUT

"Carm was the right guy at the right time for the job. He never wanted to rock the boat, but he also had a way of finessing the administration at times, which might have helped him. His greatest asset was that he had the ability to not let things bother him. If he was upset over losing a recruit, he would never let on. And I don't think he ever used his prestige in dealing with the admissions people.

"Unfortunately, many Yale alumni live in the past and don't understand the athletic climate at Yale in the 21st century."

THEY REMEMBER CARM

JOEL SMILOW ('54)

"My 1988 gift to endow the position of Yale's head coach of football was my first seven-figure gift and has proved to be the forerunner of what has become a 25-year dedication to philanthropy-primarily on behalf of Yale, Boys & Girls Clubs of America and numerous medical institutions. My football coaching endowment was a first for Yale. I'm very proud of the fact that Yale now has 17 varsity sports that are led by head coaches in endowed positions as a result of the domino effect of "the first."

"At the time I endowed the position, I knew Carm, but not very well. When I made the gift it was suggested that I come out to practice, watch the team, and take some pictures with the coach. I was walking across the practice field when Carm came over and handed me a Yale cap with the big Y. It had mesh on the sides. I still have it to this day and keep it as a souvenir.

"I call it my million-dollar hat!"

DON SCHARF '55

"Before Carm was being honored at a banquet, I received a phone call from Dick Torykian. He asked if Carm would like a letter from every living United States president. Today the letters stand on the wall in the Cozza suite at the Smilow Athletic Center."

BILL KAMINSKY—YALE TRAINER

"During my forty-two years at Yale, I spent twenty-seven of them with Carmen Cozza as the head coach. He was a Hall of Fame person before he was a Hall of Fame coach. One day Tony Barzilauskas, Fritz's son, got into a fistfight in practice. Carmen threw him off the field."

JON STEIN

"I saw Carm cry twice, an emotion he restrained after the 1968 Harvard debacle. He cried after announcing his retirement to become AD at the 1976 captain's banquet, only to change his mind two days later and remain Yale's coach for two decades more.

"I saw Cozza cry again after his 23-19 win over Liberty Bowl-bound Navy in 1981. He had his smallest line ever that season and was overcome with emotion about how they protected John Rogan, his great passer. Then he composed himself and did his press conference."

SABBY FRINZI

"I've been taking Yale football photos since 1965, Carmen Cozza's first year as Yale's head coach. Several years ago Carm suffered a heart attack while vacationing in Florida. I spend the winters in Florida, so I decided to visit him. When I walked in the hospital room he said to the nurse while staring at me, 'I can't get rid of him.'

"I took the team picture for twenty-five years. When Jack Siedlecki took over for Cozza in 1997, he brought his own photographer. That cost me about $7,000 to $8,000 a year. I sold a lot of team pictures over the years because parents would buy photos for family and friends."

RICH SCHYNER

"I succeeded Bill Humes as the superintendent of Yale's athletic fields. During my twenty-six years I got to know many wonderful people at Yale. One of my favorites was Carmen Cozza, a true gentleman in every sense of the word.

"In the late seventies a pregnant tiger cat was living above the halftime room under the stands. I used to feed her a can of tuna fish under the visitors' tunnel. She wouldn't let me pet her, but she let me feed her. When she gave birth, I found her baby by Portal 17. It was a boy and I named the cat "Carm" because of my admiration for Carm Cozza."

ERIK AABOE—ASSISTANT COUNTY MANAGER FOR SANTA FE COUNTY; SANTA FE, NEW MEXICO

Erik Aaboe was the Yale Bulldog mascot in the Fall of 1976.

"During my junior year at Yale, a friend who was a senior said, 'You're tall. You want to be the mascot?' At the end of the year, he handed me the black plastic bag with the head and costume in it. He said, 'Just give the stuff to Peter (something-or-other) after your stint.' That was my training. It was pretty fun. You run

around and act like a fool in front of thousands of people and nobody knows who you are. Like an anonymous court jester.

"I remember jumping around along the sidelines, making stupid, overly dramatic gestures, as all mascots do. You know, putting your hand to your ear and leaning in to the crowd. The usual. I recall one game in the Bowl, against Colgate. Their halftime band was walking along in formation, pretty conservative (quite unlike the Yale Precision Marching Band). I walked around while their band was doing their formation marching. I would walk along next to someone and say, '3, 7, 14, 2, 6' while they were trying to march along in their formation. I don't remember messing anyone up. However, Carm Cozza came up to me at the start of the next game and very brusquely said, 'Don't mess around with the other band.' He was clearly bothered by it and by me."

RON VACCARO

"It's a pleasure working with Carm in the broadcast booth. As long as Carm is doing color for the games, I'm going to make sure I'm in the booth with him. We've become quite close and drive together on road trips. His football knowledge speaks for itself. But what many do not know is how well-read he is in all areas. Carm has a thirst for knowledge. He's a Renaissance man."

JOE DECROSTA

"On November 16, 1996, legendary Yale football coach Carm Cozza led his Bulldog players onto the Yale Bowl gridiron for the last time. The Princeton Tigers would have the honor of facing

Cozza in this Ivy League tilt. It was a sunlit day with a brisk autumn chill. The Yale faithful would feel a different kind of chill later that afternoon. The less-than-half-full Bowl was to be a harbinger of disappointment.

"Cozza led his Elis onto the field to the familiar strains of *Bulldog, Bulldog, Bow, Wow, Wow, Eli Yale.* The fans that were in attendance wanted nothing more than a victory for Cozza. Most of this contest would be a grind-it-out affair. With a gallant effort the Yale Bulldogs would claw their way to a 13-10 lead. During the fourth quarter, I felt a pang of hope for a storybook finish. I even imagined coach Carm being carried off the field by his players after I 'dreamt of victory.' But the Bulldogs would fail to hold onto that lead for Cozza losing to Princeton, 17-13. There would be no fairy-tale ending to Carm Cozza's last game at historic Yale Bowl.

"Players, coaches and fans swarmed around the grand gentleman Cozza to console him. I watched misty-eyed as he rather melted into the crowd to the strains of *Auld Lang Syne*. His kind would not be forgotten. The winningest football coach in Yale history would see the 1996 season end with a disappointing 2-8 record. The hand-picked successor of former Bulldog coach John Pont deserved a better fate."

Erik Aaboe, the Yale mascot, at Harvard Stadium in 1976 for the Yale-Harvard game.
(New Haven Register)

If **Walter Camp** is considered the High Priest of Yale football, Carmen Cozza was its Godfather. When Carm spoke, people listened.

Yale and college football in general have benefited from his impeccable character, dignity, and coaching skills. His kind seldom passes our way.

Former Yale player Howard Jones coached two seasons at Yale, compiling a 15-2-3 record. He subsequently coached at several universities including the University of Southern California where he won two national championships.
(Yale Athletics)

CHAPTER 25

THE COACHES

Fans like to compare Yale with Stanford. The typical cry is: Why can't Yale be like Stanford, a school that also strongly emphasizes academics and student athletes, yet plays big-time football? The answer is that Stanford gives out 85 full football scholarships. They made a commitment to be in the Pac-12 Conference and compete."

—former head coach Jack Siedlecki

OVER THE PAST fifty years, Carmen Cozza has been the coach most associated with the Yale football program. But others have influenced Yale football in significant ways.

HEAD COACHES
Jack Siedlecki, Yale's 32nd Head Football Coach (1997-2008)

MADISON, CONNECTICUT

Jack Siedlecki's record as Yale's head football coach from 1997-2008 was 70-49. He was 47-37 in the Ivy League, winning two championships. He was named the New England Sports Writers' Coach of the Year in 1999, when he led the Elis to a 9-1 mark and their first Ivy championship in 10 years. He won the award again in 2007 when Yale finished 9-1. Only Carmen Cozza served as Yale's head football coach longer than Siedlecki.

Before coming to Yale, Siedlecki was head coach at Worcester Polytechnic and Amherst, two Division III colleges in Massachusetts. His Worcester Poly teams went 36-11-1. At Amherst, inheriting a program that was 1-14-1 over the preceding two seasons, he had a 20-11-1 mark over four years. At both schools he was voted District 1 Coach of the Year by the American Football Coaches' Association.

"My dad was a high school coach in Johnstown, New York, and he taught me the history of the game. He would take me to Archbold Stadium in Syracuse to watch the Orangemen play. Ben Schwartzwalder was the Syracuse coach, and I saw great players like Jim Brown, Ernie Davis, and Floyd Little. I also learned about Yale's great football history, and having the opportunity to coach in the Yale Bowl was special. My father had back-to-back undefeated seasons before he left coaching to become a high-school principal. I

think every coach would like to leave under those conditions. Unfortunately, my dad died at the age of 62 and never got to see me coach in the Bowl.

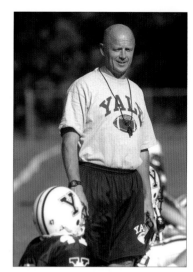

Jack Siedlecki
(YALE ATHLETICS)

Following a Legend

"Coach Cozza and I both had dreadful debuts as the Yale head coach. His '65 team lost to UConn, something no other Yale team had done, and on September 20, 1997, Brown whipped us 52-14 in my first game. All of our quarterbacks and receivers were injured. We had to start a freshman, Mike McClellan, at quarterback. That first year we finished 1-9, and if it weren't for Valparaiso, we would have been 0-10.

"When I took over the head coach's job, the football program was under-recruited and underfunded. We started six freshmen, and that's usually a red flag. Several of my assistant coaches, like Rick Flanders, Duane Brooks, and Rob Neviaser, all had Ivy League experience, and they could not believe the morbid state of Yale football in 1997.

"The program had been neglected, and the blame lay in multiple areas. When Yale went from Division I to Division I-AA in the early '80s, I think support in several areas really changed and rules were put in place affecting the number of players you could recruit. I found that Yale lagged behind the rest of the Ivy League in fund-raising by far. We had a budget that wasn't very large, and the academic index, which all the Ivy League schools have, was restrictive.

"I think maybe Carm resented the fund-raising part of the job, but the changes at Yale no doubt affected his program. You can divide Carm's tenure into two 16-year periods. The first 16 years his teams won or shared the Ivy title eight times. The last 16 years his teams shared the Ivy title twice.

The Challenges of a Yale Football Coach

"In the '60s and '70s and before, you might have 100 players come out for the freshman team. After Yale went Division I-AA in the early '80s, Yale was allowed to recruit fifty freshman football players. When I got there in 1997 the number was reduced to thirty-five and in 2003 it was lowered to thirty. Richard Levin, when he was president, stated publicly he would like the number to be twenty-five.

"You can have 120 players in your program over the four classes. When the number went to thirty-five freshman recruits, that's when the banding started. The players are put into "bands" based on SAT scores and high school grade point averages. Of the 120 players in the program, you can have eight in the lower band, twenty-eight in the second, fifty-two in the third and thirty-two in the fourth. To leave space for possible transfers, we seldom recruited thirty freshmen. Yale usually recruits 180 freshman student-athletes for its 36 varsity teams.

"Fans like to compare Yale with Stanford. The typical cry is: 'Why can't Yale be like Stanford, a school that also strongly emphasizes academics and student athletes, yet plays big-time football?' The answer is that Stanford gives out eighty-five full football scholarships. They made a commitment to be in the Pac-12 Conference and compete. In essence, the admissions people, the administration and the coaching staff are all on the same page at Stanford. This is not true at Yale, which is a non-scholarship program. The stringent academic requirements that Yale must adhere to in the Ivy league and the unbalanced financial aid do not put Yale on an equal playing field with its opponents. Because of that, there are so many high school players out there who are unrecruitable. My teams for several years were not competitive in the area of financial aid, which affected how we competed. Sometimes we really didn't have a chance to compete against Harvard or Penn because there were so many hurdles to overcome.

"Harvard and Penn have been falsely accused of bending the rules. What they do is legal, and Yale needs to make the commitment and be more like them. You need players to win. If we'd never had Mike McLeod between 2005 and 2008, I don't know where we would have been.

"What's the answer? It's an institutional decision. All entities—from the president, to the board of trustees, to the admissions people, to the athletic director and the coach—must all be in sync. I understand and admire Yale's academic philosophy, but when the football team loses to Harvard, the Old Blues get nervous.

On-the-Field Meetings

"One thing that caught the fans' attention my first year was our on-the-field team meetings following games. The reason we did it was that we didn't have enough locker room space to talk to the whole team at the same time. We worked out of three different locker rooms at the Smilow Field Center, the old Lapham Field House. Having coached at two Division III schools with limited locker room space, that's how I met with the team after games. If I had to do one thing over again, I would have fought harder to get our own locker room at Yale. Fans might be surprised to learn that at halftime, the offensive team met in a small room under the stands while the defensive team met in the tunnel. The current Kenney Center is beautiful. I wish we'd had it.

Battling Deafness

"I learned that our on-the-field meetings drew quite a few curious fans who crept within earshot. I am sensitive to strained hearing. When I was in high school I got hit carrying the football and suffered nerve damage in my right ear. My hearing has gotten progressively worse over the years. I am now totally deaf in my right ear and thirty-five percent deaf in my left ear. The reason I wear only one hearing aid is that the right ear is uncorrectable. I think people sometimes misinterpreted my reserved or aloof behavior as being non-friendly. But the truth is I didn't wear a hearing aid when I coached and sometimes had trouble hearing people when they talked. The sight of me fumbling with my headset on the sideline was common—the reason being I was struggling to hear my assistants.

A Bevy of Talent

"I've been blessed with many great players, too many to mention. During my 12 years, a Yale player was selected to the All-Ivy first team 38 times. One that wasn't was defensive nose guard Andy Tuzzolino, who was unblockable and very disruptive. Some said he was in the Kevin Czinger class. Looking back, we were fortunate to have some quality transfers in the early years, such as Rashad Bartholomew (Air Force), Than Merrill (Stanford) and Peter Lee (Wisconsin). There are coaches out there who think they can coach my wife and win. You don't win without players.

"I'm tired of Yale and Yale is tired of me"

"I kind of sensed my eventual demise when I met with Tom Beckett after the 2006 season to discuss my evaluation. He asked me about my expectations. I said, 'I think I should be getting a contract extension, but I probably won't because this is Yale and we have unrealistic expectations.' I did not get the extension. Beckett was fair to deal with, but he had a tough time losing and shaking losses. Coaches can't let a loss linger, but that's one of the hard things about being an athletic director.

"The following year we finished 9-1, and the atmosphere around the program was not good. Obviously our nightmare game against Harvard in 2007 did not help. But for a non-scholarship program, it was just wrong to have that attitude.

"I had one year remaining on my contract when I resigned the head football coaching position at the end of the 2008 season. At the time, I said, 'I'm tired of Yale and Yale is tired of me.' The job was no longer fun. We were 23-7 my last three years, and during that period we shared an Ivy League title, beat Harvard once and defeated Princeton and Penn twice.

"We lost the 2008 game to Harvard. A critical call occurred when an official, who was forty yards away, called Larry Abare for touching a punt on our 10-yard line that Harvard recovered. We were trailing 3-0 and the call gave Harvard the ball. They scored shortly after, making the score 10-0, which proved to be the final score. When I met with Tom after the season, I had made the decision to resign. The first thing he asked was, 'Did Abare touch the ball?' I said, 'You could watch the film 100 times and you'll see that he didn't touch it.' I then asked him, 'If I decide to get out of coaching, would I have a job as an assistant athletic director?' He answered, 'As long as you want.' I discussed it with my wife and resigned.

"I now coach the quarterbacks at Wesleyan and love it. I'm having fun again!"

JOSH PHILLIPS—CORNERBACK; '97,'98,'99,'00

"Coach Jack Siedlecki had a custom of holding our postgame meeting on the field. It could have been a more private deal to meet in the locker room, but by getting the meeting out of the way, it gave us more time to socialize with our family and friends on the field. I got to like Siedlecki more the longer I was there. In a social setting he was quiet.

"He got the job late and played a ton of freshmen in '97, when we went 1-9. We used to call each other the "01 rejects" because a lot of schools had passed us up before we got recruited by Yale. But Siedlecki turned it around, going 9-1 in '99 to win the Ivy League title and a second straight H-Y-P (Big Three) title."

STAN CELMER

"Perhaps my greatest honor as a Yale fan came before the first game of the '97 season. This was Jack's first year as Yale's head coach. I had gotten to know him from attending practice every day, and the upperclassmen told him about me. I was standing outside the Bowl and shaking hands with the players before they entered the Bowl to wish them luck. Jack looked at me and said, 'You're coming with us. You're going to lead us into the Bowl.' I was stunned. I attended the pregame meeting and then led the team into the Bowl to the 50-yard line. What a thrill!"

"In 2001 I suffered a serious head injury when I fell in my house. I broke a bone in my neck and shattered my forehead. I was in an induced coma for five weeks in St. Raphael's Hospital in New Haven. The injury left me with no sense of smell, but I'm alive. I woke up in the Montowese Health and Rehabilitation Center in North Haven. I have no recollection of being in St. Raphael's.

"While I was recuperating at Montowese, Siedlecki presented me with a signed football from all the players. Of all the Yale coaches I knew, he was the friendliest. When I returned to practice at the end of the season, all the players lined up and gave me a hug while the coaches all shook my hand. The 2001 Harvard game was the only game I saw that year.

"At the end of the season I was invited to the team banquet at the Yale Commons. I didn't want to go, because I was still wearing a hockey helmet because of my injury. But I decided to go and my wife drove me there. When Siedlecki gave his speech he said in reference to me, 'The reason for the poor season (3-6) was because Stan wasn't at the games.'"

Tony Reno, Yale's 34th Head Football Coach (2012-)

MADISON, CONNECTICUT

A graduate of Worcester State College where he was a three-year starter at free safety, Reno began his Yale tenure as head coach in 2012 when his fledgling Elis went 2-8. Their only Ivy League win came against league champion Penn. Reno's first coaching job was defensive assistant coach at King's (Pennsylvania) College in 1997 before serving as defensive coordinator at Worcester State from 1998 to 2002 when the Lancers went 27-5 and were the 2001 ECAC Northeast champions. He then spent six years as a Yale assistant under Jack Siedlecki helping the Bulldogs win the 2006 Ivy League title coaching the defensive secondary. The 2007 and 2008 Bulldogs were No. 1 in FCS scoring defense.

Reno, who is the first Yale football head coach from Massachusetts since Ted Coy in 1910, was the Harvard special teams coordinator and defensive secondary coach under head coach Tim Murphy from 2009-11 helping to engineer Harvard's undefeated Ivy League championship team in 2011. He is the first to leave the Harvard staff to take the head coaching position at Yale.

"When I served under Jack Siedlecki we recruited a very talented freshman class in 2005 with players like Mike McLeod, Bobby Abare, Casey Gerald, Kyle Hawari, and Steve Santoro. We played Penn at Franklin Field on Oct. 22 and got our clocks cleaned (38-21) playing in a downpour. We had turnovers everywhere. At 8:00 a.m. the next morning, all 30 Yale freshmen held a closed door meeting and decided that our play was unacceptable. From that point on that changed the Yale football program.

"We trounced Columbia the following week and two weeks later beat Princeton 21-14. We tied the game with 1:14 left when Brendan Sponheimer forced a fumble after he hit Brian Shield who just caught a pass from Jeff Terrell with 47 seconds remaining in the game. Bobby Abare caught it in the air and ran back 27 yards to the 1, which set up Jeff Mroz's game-winning touchdown. We scored two touchdowns in twenty-seven seconds. The following week we lost to Harvard in three overtimes but tied for the Ivy League championship in 2006.

Harvard Domination

"Before the 2014 season Harvard has won twelve of the last thirteen games played against Yale. They've had great teams there for many years and their success is more than just beating Yale it's been against the entire league. They've gone after top level players and have been able to yield them.

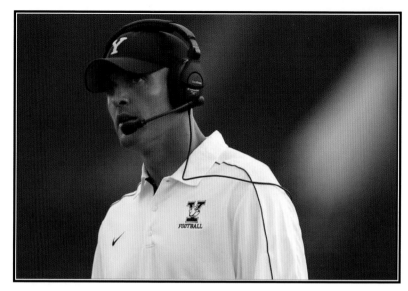

Tony Reno
(John Coleman)

First Year Woes

"Winning our first game against Georgetown in 2012 was a thrill. My wife and kids were there along with my parents. But we faced a great deal of adversity my first year as head Yale football coach. We lost four quarterbacks to injuries and quarterback John Whitelaw left the team before the start of the season. And our captain, Will McHale, was involved in an off campus altercation several months before the season began and his captaincy was suspended.

"We wanted to be a 3-4 defense and realized that wasn't working. We took our whole defensive playbook and scrapped it after the third game of the season. We needed to be in a five-man front. That gave us a better chance to defend the run and the best chance to win games.

"Offensively we started to hit stride when we beat Penn and then we got the wind knocked out of our sails when all of our quarterbacks went down that game. For the next two weeks we had to operate out of the single wing.

Tyler Varga Controversy

"Tyler is a very talented transfer from the University of Western Ontario in Canada. Someone in the league contested his eligibility the day before the 2012 Dartmouth game. We had to sit him out until the NCAA resolved the issue. The Ivy League had never seen a Canadian transfer for football. In Canada there is only Division I football. Under the 'one time transfer rule,' Ivy League rules allow transfers from a scholarship program to become eligible immediately if they are transferring to a school that doesn't give scholarships.

"I did not agree with the protocol that the NCAA took. Tyler sat out the Dartmouth game while they made a ruling that said he was eligible. I'm extremely satisfied the way the Yale administration handled it.

Tradition

"The history of Yale football is important to me. I see my job as not only respecting the great Yale football tradition, but building on it. We are changing the culture. We're not going to draw 60,000 fans every week but nationally we ranked fourth in FCS football attendance. I'm excited about the future."

REMEMBERING HARRY JACUNSKI

HARRY JACUNSKI—ASSISTANT COACH, 1948-1980

An all-state center at New Britain High School in Connecticut, Harry Jacunski was a left end on Fordham's famed "Seven Blocks of Granite" lines, which included Vince Lombardi, and Alex Wojciechowicz. He captained the 1938 Fordham Rams and played six years for the Green Bay Packers as a teammate of Hall of Famer Don Hutson. He was on two NFL championship teams (1939 and 1944).

After brief spells as an assistant coach at Notre Dame and Harvard, Jacunski joined the Yale coaching staff in '48 and remained for thirty-three years, serving head coaches Herman Hickman, Jordan Olivar, John Pont, and Carmen Cozza. Under Hickman and Olivar he coached the ends; on Pont's staff, the guards and centers; under Cozza, he was head coach of the freshman team. His freshman squads were 59-37-3 over 16 seasons and included nine future NFL players.

Jacunski's twin sons, Robert and Richard, were reserve ends on Yale's undefeated '60 team.

Harry died February 20, 2003, at the age of eighty-seven.

SEB LASPINA

"Harry loved Yale songs. On road trips he used to pass out the lyrics to his players and they would sing on the bus. Harry used to keep his pep talks on little cards and use the same ones every year."

MIKE CAVALLON ('55, '56, '57)

"When I was playing, I wasn't playing for my girlfriend in the stands or my father in the stands or for dear old Yale. I was playing for Harry Jacunski. He was the one who made it fun."

DAVID LEIWANT ('73 FRESHMEN TEAM)

"At the end of practice on the day before the Brown game, Harry called us all together and asked us to think about one thing for the next day's game. He said, 'What's the color of horseshit? Brown, Brown, Brown.'"

STEVE WOODSUM ('73)

"One time he gave us a rousing halftime speech. We were all pounding each other on the shoulder pads and helmets. And just before we were to take the field to do battle, he told us all to get on the floor and pick up all the orange peels that had been left around."

BOB PERSCHEL ('70, '71, '72)

"I remember running the linebacker agility drill some people called the "carioca," I suppose in honor of the footwork required in the South American ballroom dance of the same name. Harry would holler across the field, 'OK, gentlemen, time to carry your oka.'"

GREG HALL ('74, '75, '76)

"Harry wanted to use a vocabulary that would impress Yale students. He would say, 'Yale will face a formidable opponent today.' Harry would sit us down to offer profound coaching points. One time he was giving us a pregame lecture and he said, 'Fellas, three things can happen today: You can beat the other team, they can beat you or the refs can beat you.'

"Harry's locker was on third floor of the Lapham Field House. He would play a scratchy old record of Yale fight songs before and after every practice. He had incredible respect for the players. Harry was beloved by all."

DREW PACE ('78)

"I can still see Harry wearing that blue flannel jacket with gray leather sleeves and YALE across the front, with the Y baseball cap, always a little bit crooked. As all of us knew he turned us from Bullpups into Bulldogs in more ways than one."

PAT O'BRIEN ('77, '78)

"One time a fight broke out in practice freshman year between Bill Crowley and somebody. Harry called us together, not to talk about sportsmanship but to say—somewhat in disbelief that he would even have to tell us— that if you were going to hit somebody in the head with your bare hand, you should rip his helmet off first. That's when I realized Coach was something more than special."

JED DUNCAN ('80, '81, '82)

"My favorite thing about Harry was his goofy sense of humor. He would say, 'Let's go down to the ghoul line.' He always used to remember my name by saying, 'If anybody can, Dun can.'"

JUDY HALL HOWARD ('77)

"I worked in the office of Yale football for my four years of college, sharing a large open office space with Harry Jacunski and Grace, Carm Cozza's secretary. He truly loved his players and wanted them all to succeed, not only on the playing field, but in the classroom and life. He was their champion and he was mine too.

"I doubt that Carm ever knew that one time Harry 'borrowed' three football uniforms for me and my roommates to wear on Halloween at the King's [President Kingman Brewster Jr.] annual block party, and that he sneaked into Carm's office to get me one of the Yale football T-shirts that were given only to the players."

ASSISTANT COACHES

The assistant coaches are listed chronologically by their hiring date at Yale.

Seb LaSpina, Assistant Coach (1965-1996)

VENICE, FLORIDA

A 1958 graduate of Miami University of Ohio, Seb LaSpina lettered in football and track. He was an all-conference football player and conference shot put champion.

"My job as offensive coordinator was to design plays. Up until 1973 the quarterbacks called the plays. Then we came to the conclusion that we needed greater control of what was going on. We would work 70-80 hours during the week on a game plan, and the quarterback would not necessarily follow it. We finally realized that the quarterbacks had classes and labs to deal with. Our philosophy was contrary to that of the president of Boston University, who was promoting the idea of having the coaches sit in the stands because they had too much control.

"During games I would call the plays. I would have two or three of the backup quarterbacks near me on the sideline and they would relay my call to the quarterback on the field by using hand signals. One of the quarterbacks at my side was the dummy QB, meaning he would give dummy signals that didn't mean anything.

Coaches and Sons

My son, Mike, lettered at Yale between 1983 and '85. It's always difficult coaching when your son is on the team. I'm not the only one to experience that at Yale. Several assistant coaches have had sons play for Yale while they were active coaches. Harry Jacunski's sons, Dick and Bob (1960), Rich Pont's son, Joey (1981-83) and Dave Kelley's son, David (1990-92) all played at Yale when their fathers were coaching. But we never had to coach our own kids with the

L-R: Head coach Carm Cozza, and assistants Seb LaSpina and Buddy Amendola celebrate the Bulldogs 24-7 win over Harvard in '77. Amendola was a longtime defensive coordinator under Cozza. (YALE ATHLETICS)

exception of Jacunski because they all played positions assigned to other coaches.

"We always had to deal with the players one on one because as coaches we were part-time counselors. We had to help them deal with deaths in their families and their lives on campus. I once had a former player return after he graduated, and he tried to change my religion. He didn't succeed."

Dave Kelley, Defensive line coach, 1973-96

GUILFORD, CONNECTICUT

Dave Kelley became the defensive line coach in 1973 and the defensive coordinator in 1982. He earned All-Yankee Conference honors three times at the University of Massachusetts as a fullback and a monster back. The top scholar athlete at UMass, Kelley was also a standout in wrestling and lacrosse.

The Hawaiian Warrior

"In '92 I made a recruiting trip to Hawaii to meet with a fullback named Kena Heffernan, who played for us from '93 to '95. Kena was one of the top three men in the warrior class in Hawaii. He came from a poor family of fishermen who would go out on a weekly basis, make their catch and return. He lived in a one-room house that had shutters on the sides, one bedroom that sixteen people would sleep in, and a large kitchen.

"Kena was a 6-foot, 215-pound fullback, a bronze god who was tough as nails. He lived in a coastal town called Laie but went to Punahou School in Honolulu, thirty-seven miles away. It was the best high school academically in Hawaii, like Choate in Connecticut. He had a full scholarship based on need. A hard-working kid, he worked two jobs in addition to playing football. He wanted to study the Japanese language because he was concerned that the Japanese were taking over the golf courses and recreation areas in Hawaii.

"Kena stayed with my family in Guilford, Connecticut, during the Thanksgiving and Christmas holidays. He only went home at the end of the school year. He loved my wife and adopted her in his heart. When he saw something that needed repair, he did it on his own.

"When he graduated he worked an extra job to help pay for his parents' air fare. His parents stayed with us but refused to sleep in any of our beds. Instead, they carried their beds, which looked like fish nets you could roll up. This is how they slept at home.

"After Kena graduated, he invited my wife and me to his home in Hawaii and took us to the cultural center, where he performed native and warrior dances. Part of the dance was to walk over hot coals. I asked him if it was hocus-pocus and he assured me that it wasn't. Following his performance he took me to the top of a cliff that was located 60 feet above a body of water. When we got there he walked me to the edge of the cliff. He placed his hands on my shoulders and said, 'You are one of us.' He then unexpectedly jumped off the cliff into the water. I was startled and didn't know why he did this. I soon learned that was his way of symbolizing how he would give his life for me.

"At Yale he was 6-1 and 210-215 pounds. He grew to 275 pounds and became the third-ranking sumo wrestler in the world. Kena Heffernan didn't have money but he had character, integrity, and parents who loved him.

Count Bassi

"In '74 I recruited Keith Bassi, who was an outstanding fullback and linebacker out of Ringgold High School in Monongahela, Pennsylvania. He was the valedictorian of his class and the MVP of his team. We called him 'Count Bassi.' His coach, Joe Gladys, said he could play for anybody.

"We looked at film and noticed the quarterback seldom passed, playing out of the wishbone. I think he passed twelve times the whole year. The quarterback was a guy named Joe Montana.

"Look at the (Bleepin') Scoreboard"

"I have had many headset conversations with coach Buddy Amendola over the years. He would be down on the field and I would be up in the press area. There was one exchange that will always stay with me.

"A United Airlines commercial flight flew over Harvard Stadium during the middle of the game. The pilot picked up his mike and thought he was talking to the press box when he asked, 'What's the score?' For some reason this was transmitted into Buddy's headset, and he thought it was me asking him the question. He snapped, 'Look at the fuckin' scoreboard.'"

L-R: Ron Darling, Gerry Harrington, and Rich Diana at a 2013 Yale-Harvard tailgate party.
(RICH MARAZZI)

Vito DeVito, Freshman backfield coach (1974-91)

ORANGE, CONNECTICUT

"Before I was a freshman backfield coach, I served as the freshman basketball coach under Joe Vancisin for 17 years. I then coached football, mostly with Harry Jacunski, but I also worked with Joe Benanto and Larry Ciotti. So overall I coached thirty-five years at Yale. When freshman football was dropped, I lost my job. Carmen Cozza petitioned the NCAA three times to give him an extra varsity coach, but the NCAA wouldn't allow it.

"I had coached football at Jonathan Law High School in Milford, Connecticut, for many years. I am very proud that two of my players, Bob Perschel and John Kerecz, played and started at Yale. Perschel, who captained the '72 team, was a first-team All-Ivy selection that year.

"I was fortunate to work with so many great athletes in both basketball and football during my tenure at Yale. Brian Dowling's legacy is that of a great quarterback, but he was also the star of my freshman basketball team. Calvin Hill was also an outstanding basketball player. But we practiced from seven to

nine at night, and he said that his studies came first and decided not to play.

"Coaching freshman football was a wonderful experience. Every Tuesday we would help the varsity prepare for Saturday's opponent by running their plays we got from the scouting reports. Sometimes the practices would be intense and a scuffle would break out.

"Ron Darling, who made his mark at Yale and in the major leagues as a pitcher with the New York Mets, was an outstanding defensive back on the Yale freshman football team in '78. He was originally a quarterback, but we were so deep in the position that we switched him to defensive halfback. Darling came to me after the season and told me that he was going to concentrate on baseball. I guess he made a good decision."

Joe Benanto Shelton, Connecticut

Joe Benanto was the head freshman football coach from 1981 through 1990, compiling a record of 46-13-1. He was also varsity baseball coach from 1979 through 1990; his teams went 248-237, winning the Eastern Intercollegiate Baseball League title in 1981.

"I'll never forget the first freshman game I ever coached. It was at West Point and we got lost going up. We were taping players as we were getting out of the bus. The people at West Point wanted to start the game at 4 p.m. sharp and weren't about to give us any extra time.

"To make matters worse, on the kickoff we lost three players to injury. My cousin Jimmy [Benanto], who used to help me, arrived a little late and asked how things were going. I said, 'Whatever could go wrong has gone wrong.' But we beat Army that day, (30-22) so what started out as a nightmarish day had a happy ending.

1985 coaching staff: L-R: Joe Benanto, Bill Samko, Dave Kelley, Seb LaSpina, Bob Estock, Don Martin, and Rich Pont
(YALE ATHLETICS)

The Challenge of Coaching at Yale

"Coaching at Yale is an honor, but it's also a real challenge. I think many problems started with the arrival of Frank Ryan as the athletic director. His job was to cut budgets within the athletic department, including football. You can go back to Yale President's Bart Giamatti's famous speech when he talked about de-emphasizing sports. And there's the academic index, which is based on a student's SAT or ACT scores and class rank and can get tricky. Since Yale, Harvard, and Princeton are required to have higher mean scores, it puts those schools at a disadvantage."

Larry Ciotti, Freshman coach 1991-92; currently assistant head coach and running backs coach

MADISON, CONNECTICUT

Larry Ciotti, who captained the 1965 Southern Connecticut State University football team as a center/linebacker, was the head football coach at Hand High School in Madison, Connecticut, for nineteen years where he won five state titles. He coached the Yale freshman team for two

years guiding the Bullpups to an 8-4 record. He then coached the inside linebackers for two years and running backs for two years on the varsity level under Carmen Cozza. Subsequently he coached the running backs for 12 years under Jack Siedlecki. He received the Walter Camp Foundation Lifetime Achievement Award in 2011.

"When Carmen Cozza called and asked if I was interested in the freshman coaching job, I said, 'Give me five seconds to think it over.' At the time, I was the athletic director at Hand High. He added that the 1991 season might be the last year for freshman football at Yale. But the program lasted two more years. My '92 team, the last Yale freshmen team, won the mythical Ivy League championship going 5-1.

"At Hand we had seven Division I players one year. When I came to Yale, I knew we could not live with the quarterbacks we had. One day in practice I was

Joe Linta
(YALE ATHLETICS)

2013 Yale coaching staff: Front Row (L-R): Nick Kray, Larry Ciotti, Tony Reno, Rick Flanders, Steven Vashel, Kevin Morris. Back Row: Chris Gennaro, Emil Johnson, Joe Conlin, Dwayne Wilmot, Kevin Cahill, Paul Rice, Patrick Hatch. (YALE ATHLETICS)

watching Chris Hetherington, a 6-foot-3, 245-pound wide receiver chucking the ball back on a rope after he made a catch. I asked him if he ever played quarterback. He said, 'No, but I wouldn't mind trying.' I gave him some drills and he wound up having a great varsity career before going on to play in the NFL as a fullback and a special teams player. At Yale he still ranks in the top ten in career total offense and career passing yards.

"When Jack Siedlecki was hired he let all of Carm's coaches go except me. He said, 'Do you know why I kept you?' I said, 'No.' He said, 'Because I would have someone my age to talk to.'"

Joe Linta (defensive tackle '82) NFL agent/president J.L. Sports

HAMDEN HALL FOOTBALL COACH
BRANFORD, CONNECTICUT

"It was a great experience working with Larry Ciotti, a legendary high school coach. I was surprised to

find that he was a bit superstitious. Before our first game with Brown he told me to sit down. He pulled out a rabbit's foot and said, 'Rub it for good luck.'

"Our final game of the season was against Harvard, the final Freshman game Yale ever played. We played on a field adjacent to the Harvard Stadium. About an hour before the game, Larry and I walked over to the varsity stadium and buried the rabbit's foot on the 50-yard line.

"We won the game, 26-6!"

ALL OF THE men profiled in this chapter have all played an integral role in the success of Yale's football program. Their talents should be appreciated and never forgotten.

PART V

Extra Points

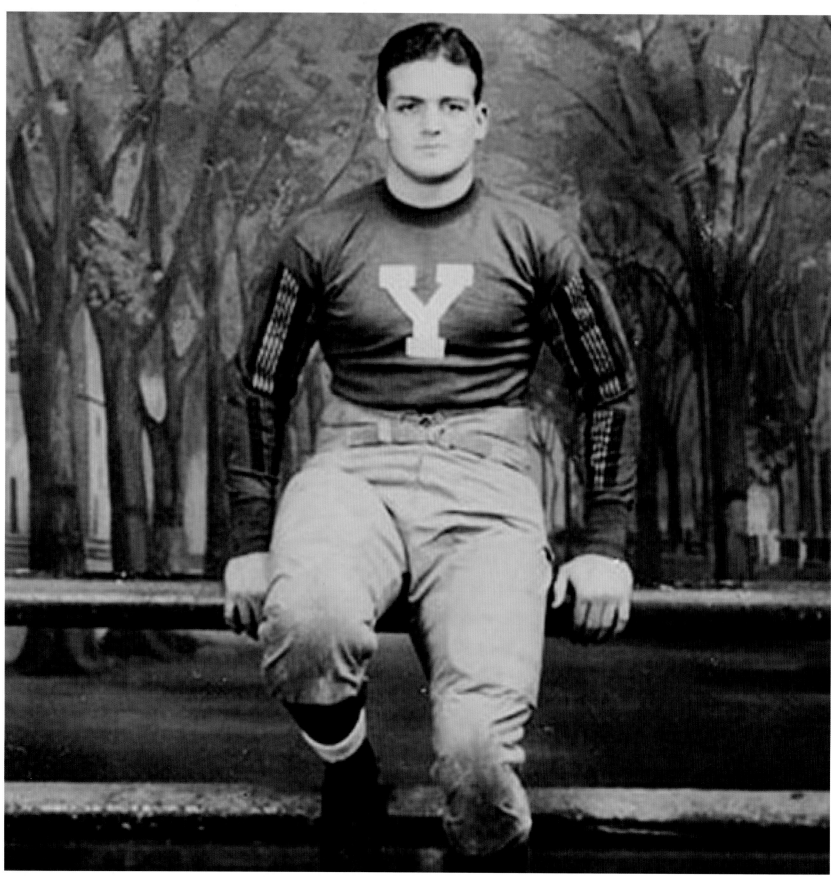

Clint Frank
(YALE ATHLETICS)

Chapter 26

THE YALE FENCE

*"Men of all tastes were there together.
They sat on a common rail..."*

—Walter Camp

Walter Camp captained the 1878-79 teams.
(YALE ATHLETICS)

I**N 1875, YALE** football captain William Arnold was photographed in front of the Yale Fence. Considered a totem of athletic captainhood, the fence has served as the backdrop for generations of Yale captains in all sports, including Walter Camp and future president George Herbert Walker Bush. It is a Yale tradition that has endured to the present day.

The original Yale Fence, which existed from 1833 to 1888, was a three-rail structure that stood at the intersection of College and Chapel Streets in New Haven. It ran along the Old College in front of Old Brick Row. The fence was the preferred spot where many Yale seniors posed for their oficial classpicture.

There are different accounts of the original fence's demise. Judith Ann Schiff, the Chief Research Archivist at the Yale University Library, wrote in the summer 1998 editon of the *Yale Alumni Magazine,* "…[T]he fence was gradually removed as buildings went up. On May 19 (1885) the (Yale) Corporation voted to remove the fence. Two days later three whole sections vanished without explanation, leaving nothing but the post holes… On June 29 (1888), amid the grand jubilation of Yale's crew victory over Harvard, every remaining rail was torn out."

Other sources explain that the fence was pretty well demolished during freshman rush week in 1879 and was subsequently dismantled over the next ten years and removed.

The Yale Fence is normally reserved for Yale captains but tradition was snubbed when three-time (1889-91) All-American guard William "Pudge" Heffelfinger was photographed in front of the Fence.
(YALE ATHLETICS)

George H.W. Bush, the 41st U.S. President, captained the 1948 Yale baseball team.
(YALE ATHLETICS)

Pach Brothers

The Pach Brothers studio was founded in New York City in the post-Civil War era, at a time when photography had become increasingly popular with the general public. The prominent photography company recognized the business opportunities of taking photos of the college scene and set up outposts in various college towns, including New Haven. Aware of the local importance of the Yale Fence, a Pach Brothers employee reportedly salvaged an eight-foot section of it for use as a prop in their New Haven studio before the entire fence vanished.

On November 16, 1929, the Yale Fence was reported missing from the Pach Brothers studio. It had been raided by students from the *Harvard Lampoon,* the longest-running undergraduate humor publication. The fence was returned more than a week later after Yale's 10-6 loss at Harvard.

Eight years later, *Life* magazine described the theft this way: "Pach Bros. called in the police, said it valued the fence at $10,000. The *Lampoon...* returned the fence after having posed its janitor up against it in sacrilegious mockery of Yale's captains."

Good Fences Make Testy Rivals

In 1931, illustrator A.B. Savrann drew a game-day program cover which depicted John Harvard unceremoniously sitting on Yale's sacred fence. Some Yale alums were so outraged that they recommended suspending the Yale-Harvard football series altogether. Tongue firmly in cheek, Paul Barnett, the director of athletic publicity at Yale, had a more welcoming reaction: "There would always be a seat for John Harvard on the Yale fence."

The following year Savrann struck again, this time depicting the Princeton Tiger dancing atop the Yale Fence in mocking fashion for the November

Harvard Cantab sitting on Yale Fence on cover of 1931 Yale-Harvard game day program. (A.B. Savrann / Harvard Athletics)

1932 Yale-Princeton game day program
(A.B. Savrann /Princeton University)

Yale-Harvard game day program
(Jim Fogelman /Yale Athletics)

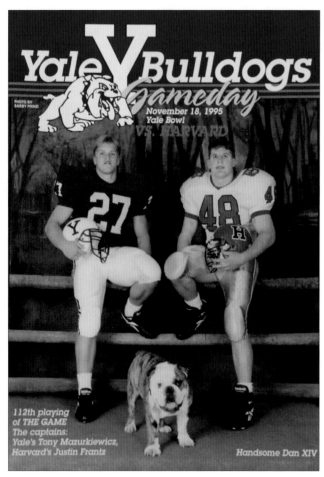

1995 Yale-Harvard game day program
(Yale Athletics)

George Weber: Documenting Yale Football

George Weber was the official Yale football photographer from 1933 to 1963. He played a significant role in photographing and filming Yale University's football history, and is integral to the story of the Yale Fence. Weber took over the Pach Brothers business and studio around 1945. The studio, located on

Longtime Yale Football Photographer George Weber
(New Haven Register)

24, 1932, game day program at Princeton. The Tiger is also on the Fence for the 1945 Yale-Princeton program.

Artist Jim Fogelman took a less incendiary approach. Fogelman depicted captains Cotty Davison of Yale and Vince Moravec of Harvard sitting together on the fence about to break a wishbone on the front cover of the 1947 Yale-Harvard game day program. This was the first time the captains of the two schools were depicted together. The opposing captains would not be shown together on the venerated Fence again until 1995. Tradition was ignored in favor of sportsmanship when Harvard captain Justin Frantz was pictured with Yale captain Tony Mazurkiewicz on the cover of the November 18, 1995, game day program.

1066 Chapel Street, is where he shot the Yale sports captains for many years leaning against the fence.

In addition, Weber filmed 259 consecutive varsity football games and 150 freshman contests. In 1963 he co-directed with John S. Ellsworth, chairman of Yale's Audio Visual center, a ninety -minute film, *Football at Yale-Story of a Tradition*. The film chronicled the first eighty-eight years of Yale football history.

Weber cut his teeth working at MGM's film exchange in New York City before working under internationally-known photographer Joseph Reed, who had been filming Yale games since the 1920s. The fun- loving photographer then served under Leroy Phelps whom he succeeded before the end of the 1933 season.

"My father was not a Yale alum but when he was around Yale sports teams, students and staff, he was the center of attention due to his sense of humor and his stories," said Ernestine Weber McKinnon, daughter of George Weber. "Those who knew him, loved him! He was my hero ! He worked closely with all of the football coaches from Tad Jones to Jordan Olivar. After each football game, my parents and I rushed to get the film developed and back to the coaches within two and a half hours."

Weber's granddaughter, Karen McKinnon Brown, has fond memories of the old fence. "I used to play on the original fence in my grandfather's studio where he photographed many Yale legends including Albie Booth and Levi Jackson," said Brown.

"At the Yale Bowl press box I remember his camera was on a tripod, the place was smoky and I could hardly see the football players but I loved being with him. I hung on to his leg and used to keep my hand in his back pocket. Funny, the things you remember."

Another granddaughter, Catherine McKinnon, added some historic insight. "The first game he

1952 captain Joe Mitinger was the last Yale football captain photographed on the original fence.
(YALE ATHLETICS)

photographed as the official Yale Football Photographer was the 1933 Yale-Harvard game," she said.

"To avoid missing plays due to the camera jamming, he carried five 16mm movie cameras to every game. If a camera jammed he put it aside and used another camera. He was tough. The 1942 Princeton game was so cold that all the other photographers gave up after the first quarter, but not our Papa. He hung in there for the entire game despite the fact his hands suffered a severe case of frostbite that took many weeks to heal."

Yale Fence II

Since 1953, the Yale sports captains have been photographed against a fence located on the bottom floor of the Ray Tompkins House at Yale. But it is not the same fence that was used in portraits taken in the period from 1875 to 1952. Judging from comparative photographs, it appears that Joe Mitinger,

Yale captains have been photographed in front of Yale Fence II since 1953.
(Bill O'Brien)

1953 captain Joe Fortunato was the first captain photographed in front of Yale Fence II.
(Yale Athletics)

the 1952 Yale football captain, was the last captain to be photographed in front of the original fence. All photos taken after 1952 show a fence in which the middle post is not cracked. Joe Fortunato, the 1953 Yale captain, was the first captain photographed in front of the current fence—Yale Fence II.

It is believed that Weber took photographs using Yale Fence II until his death in 1964. But little is known about the origin of this second fence.

The Original Fence

Much more, however, is known about the original eight-foot fence that currently sits in an undisclosed location for security purposes. Its authenticity is supported by the irregularities in the rails of the fence, including the elongated fracture on the middle post and the knot in the upper right hand corner of the top post.

The fence has gone through several hands, including the late Frank Conti, who co-owned Kavanaugh's restaurant (formerly Jocko Sullivan's) with Michael Kavanaugh on Chapel Street in New Haven.

"It is my understanding that L. Raymond Pratt, a photographer who headed the New Haven office of the Pach Bros studio, ended up with the fence when the studio went out of business in the 1940s," said John Conti, the brother of Frank Conti. "It's possible that George Weber either gave the fence or sold it to Pratt some time in 1952. Pratt then loaned the fence to Adam Fusco, the proprietor of the Adam House, a restaurant in East Haven. Pratt subsequently got the fence back and in 1966 sold it to Clarence Whitney who had it for many years. It was then sold to my brother, Frank, in 1977 or 1978. He displayed the fence in his restaurant where it occupied a position of honor. On occasion a Yale grad or student would come in and sit on it. Isn't it strange that the fence found its way back to Chapel Street?"

The original Yale Fence.
(JOHN CONTI)

The fence is currently owned by Frank Conti's son, Michael, who captained the Ithaca College football team in 2011.

The story of the Yale Fence leaves several unanswered questions. How or why did the original fence escape the hands of George Weber? And what is the derivation of the current fence, the one used since 1953 at the Ray Tompkins House?

According to Michael Lotstein, a Records Services Archivist at the Yale University Library, the fence that is currently in the Ray Tompkins House (Yale Fence II) is "a piece of the actual Yale Fence" that ran along the Old College. Its provenance, however, is unknown.

Nearly every college sports program has its own unique traditions. Ohio State has its Buckeye helmet decals, Penn State its generic football uniforms, Notre Dame its golden dome. But there is nothing quite like the Yale Fence. As Walter Camp put it, "Men of all tastes were there together. They sat on a common rail..."

1948 Football Y Association Barbecue L-R: Dan Parker, John Cluney, Chick Kelley, Herman Hickman, Hugh Fullerton, captain Bill Conway and George Trevor.

CHAPTER 27

THE PRESS BOX—WRITERS AND BROADCASTERS AT THE YALE BOWL

"The Yale Bowl is a mite squalid for a shrine."

—Red Smith, in reference to the Yale Bowl
Press Box

Bob Barton is the resident historian of Yale football.
(BILL O'BRIEN)

THE YALE BOWL press box has been graced by some of the most talented journalists in sports history. Bob Barton ('57) kicks off this chapter by detailing the history of the print media in the Bowl press box.

"In the history of the Yale Bowl press box, November 2, 1986, was a watershed.

"That was the day the place burned.

"What burned on that calm Sunday morning was the wooden press box, held up by posts and metal struts, that dated to the 1920s. In its place was erected a concrete edifice fashioned for a new era. In many respects, change was overdue.

"The old place had been crowded, open to rain and wind, reachable only by ascending 113 wooden steps on the outer slope of the Bowl, devoid of creature comforts beyond the halftime ham-and-cheese sandwich. Retrofitting had been needed to equip the box for Western Union teletypes and then for fax machines. Radio and television announcers worked from shacks on its roof that offered minimal protection. When the 1963 Yale-Harvard game was postponed after President John F. Kennedy was shot, Red Smith opined in the *New York Herald Tribune*, 'There'll be other days to shiver in that crepe-gray heap called Yale Bowl....' Gray heap? Such indeed was the old press box.

"The new place has things that the old box didn't: bathrooms, a food counter, booths for the broadcasters and for coaches, and areas that Yale can use as skyboxes to entertain dignitaries and donors. In recent years, with the construction of the Kenney Family Field Center, an elevator has replaced the wooden steps. Computers and the internet permit instant reporting and instant statistics. The flip side is that the new box – already 25 years old- is far less spacious or weatherproof than the enclosed press suites at, say, Boston College or UConn's Rentschler Field. On a frigid November day, the Bowl is still unkind to mortal flesh.

"In other respects too, the new box inevitably is lacking. The old box looked down on the exploits of Albie Booth, of Larry Kelley and Clint Frank, of Levi Jackson, of Brian Dowling and Calvin Hill-athletes whose like may never again be seen in New Haven. The old box smacked of history, with plaques in memory of the writer George Trevor, of statistician Ernie Anderson, of radio color man Tiny Markle and of Bolt Elwell, the 1940s lineman whose classmates and teammates chipped in to spruce up the old box in 1959. And the old box had been the domain of some media giants – nationally known columnists such as Grantland Rice, Westbrook Pegler and Paul Gallico; eminent New York writers such as Smith, Trevor, Dan Parker and Stanley Woodward. Today the press rows are populated, for the most part, by New Haven and campus media types. Few Connecticut newspapers now send staffers to cover Yale. That's sad.

"It's also a testament to the rise of the University of Connecticut—a team Yale once was guaranteed to beat—to big-time status since Yale and its Ivy League confreres dropped in the 1980s to the lesser echelon known then as Division I-AA. The Ivies' insistence on doing things right, keeping academics at the fore and scholarships under control, has cost them recruits and fans and media exposure. As newspaper circulation and staffs shrink, editors cover the events that draw the most.

"In the days when Yale football used to pack 'em in, so did its press box. The Bowl was part of the regular beat for the New York papers. A Saturday in the 1950s might find Parker on hand for the *Mirror,* Til Ferdenzi for the *Journal-American,* Bob Cooke or the authoritative Jesse Abramson for the *Herald Tribune,* Joe Sheehan or the peerless historian Allison Danzig for the *Times.* Red Smith, the Pulitzer-winning columnist who served the *Tribune* and later the *Times,* lugged a typewriter to the Bowl press box, as did Bill Wallace, a Yale grad who started at the *World Telegram* and wound up as the *Times* NFL expert. One who didn't haul a typewriter up the steps was Trevor, an Old Blue (class of 1915) who was the *Sun's* football guru. He wrote his copy by hand. So did the *Herald Tribune's* courtly Al Laney, who would print neatly in pencil on sheets of yellow Western Union paper and hand them to one of the kids who stood ready to run his prose to a telegrapher.

"A Harvard game would cram the Bowl press box with Boston writers—Bill Cunningham, Jerry Nason, Tim Horgan, Bob Hoobing, Joe Concannon, among others –and never was The Game described more colorfully than when John Powers and Leigh Montville were there for the *Globe.* Ned Martin, better known for broadcasting the Red Sox, worked games from the roof of the Bowl press box, as did Mel Allen, longtime radio voice of the New York Yankees.

"Several Connecticut writers were familiar sights at the Bowl for decades. Hank O'Donnell of the *Waterbury Republican* covered Yale from the 1920s to the '70s, and Lou Black handled Yale sports for

thirty-three years for The Associated Press. The *New Haven Register* and *Journal-Courier* had their own legends: Dan Mulvey, whose coverage of a Depression-era Yale game might run to 5,000 words; Bill Ahern, the jolly elf always identifiable by his ten-gallon hat; Charley Kellogg, the tweed-jacketed *Register* columnist whose metaphors came often from horse racing; and, starting in the late '60s, the ever-inquisitive Jon Stein. Others who seemed to have been around just short of forever were Don McDonald and Gus Langner of the statistics crew and Jack Casey, whose typewriter produced play-by-play accounts that could be published verbatim.

"In the old box, you never knew if someone sitting unnoticed next to you might one day be among the rich and famous. An undergraduate who did odd jobs such as spotting for radio stations in the 1960s, Dick Ebersol, became president of NBC Sports. The student announcer who handled the press box PA in the early '50s, Joel Smilow, became chairman and CEO of Playtex and one of Yale's leading benefactors.

"From 1943 to 1968, denizens of the press box were shepherded by Charley Loftus, Yale's longest-serving director of sports information. Loftus was acclaimed for his magazine-length game programs and for the volume of stuff he provided to writers-lineups and depth charts, the typed play-by-play, statistics and the occasional suggestion of a *mot juste,* such as a Shakespearean 'thwacked' instead of 'beat.' Once, though, he landed Yale in a controversy that couldn't happen today.

"The year was 1954. Under Loftus, the Yale press box was a male-only preserve. The one woman allowed to start up the 113 steps—and she had to get off at the 97th—was the telephone operator, who occupied a booth out of sight beneath the box. For the fourth game of the 1954 season, Loftus made an exception. The *Cornell Daily Sun* staff had chosen a female sports editor, Anne Morrissey, and she was allowed to sit in the press box because of her rank.

"Three weeks later, *United Press* assigned a woman, Faye Loyd, to cover the Yale-Army game. She had covered Notre Dame-Navy in Baltimore the week before, but Loftus was adamant in barring her, saying that UP wanted to exploit her sex for publicity. He offered her a seat in the top row of the stands, where she balanced a typewriter on her knees and filed her report, with someone handing statistics to her through the scaffolding that supported the press box.

"Five years later, when Yale played Dartmouth in the rain, a woman asked for a press box seat and Loftus didn't say a word. She was Mary B. Griswold, wife of Yale's president."

The three plaques currently in the press box are dedicated to statistician Ernie Anderson, writer George

John Altavilla (*Hartford Courant*) and Chris Hunn (*New Haven Register*) are popular writers who currently cover Yale football.
(SAM RUBIN)

S. Trevor, and broadcaster Tiny Markle. Noticeably lacking is a plaque for the longtime radio voice of Yale football-Dick Galiette.

THEY REMEMBER

WILLIAM N. WALLACE ('45 W, '49)

"Regarding the Faye Loyd matter, Charley Loftus, for all his genius as a creator of magnificent programs and as a schmoozing publicist to all sports writers on all matters:

Yale was wrong on this one. There was an uproar from other journalists and publications, all critical of Yale (and Loftus). He soon changed his tune and the policy was altered—all are welcome.

"The old wooden press box in the Bowl had become increasingly decrepit. Yale's finances were in

deficit mode. The Yale Class of 1945, abetted by the 1947 football captain, Endicott 'Cotty' Davison, then working for Yale in development, raised money to do a renovation in memory of classmate Bolt Elwell, a three sport Yale athlete ('42,'45,'46) and a World War II veteran who died too early (about 1955) and who had been a three-sport star at Yale and a football teammate of Davison. The renovation helped some.

"The press box burned down the morning after the '86 Dartmouth game. Yale went without a press box for not quite two full seasons. The scribes sat in the top-row seats, which had temporary table tops out over the row in front and a tent-like structure above. The electronics were piped in and it was adequate- barely.

"The athletic director, Frank Ryan, and the provost (name lost) got into a battle, it was said, about who was to build/design /pay for a replacement. Stall.

"Finally the new box was built. No one of any experience with press boxes or of some authority was consulted or asked to check up on the design. The result was an open, impractical, uncomfortable disaster.

"The new press box was unveiled at the November 21, 1987, Harvard game. It happened to be the coldest day—or one of the coldest—in Yale Bowl annals. In the two inadequate one-toilet bathrooms, the pipes were frozen and nothing flushed.

"I covered that game for the *New York Times.* I found my Southport, Connecticut, neighbor, Gibney Patterson, (Yale '44), snooping about. Patterson headed a Bridgeport construction company. 'Look,' he said. ''Don't complain to me. We built it. But we didn't design it.'"

JACK DOLAN

"The Bowl press box was the first sports press box to provide reporters with a two-deep player roster; a play-by-play recap and other innovations created by Loftus, who also coined the now-popular term "tailgate" for the pregame parking lot parties at the Bowl.

"After the passing of Charley Loftus, it was co-named for him and Elwell. The [pre-fire] wooden press box had a plaque on the rear wall noting that the great sportswriter Grantland Rice had covered Yale games there."

GEORGE GRANDE

"From a media perspective the Bowl was not perfect. Anyone who covered Yale football in the old days will tell you about the spartan conditions of the old press box. There was a leak in the roof, and every time it rained I would leave with a big stain on my shoulder."

PETER EASTON

"I hated that inadequate [wooden] press box with no bathroom and no protection from weather. I almost drowned during a Yale-Colgate game in the Mark Van Eeghen days. [Van Eeghen set Colgate's single-season rushing record in 1973 and had a stellar NFL career..]"

DAN MULVEY JR.

"From about 1944 to 1950, I attended every Yale game in the Bowl with my mother while dad worked in the press box. We sat on the 50-yard line. Every now and then my father would stick his head out and say hello. My mother always wanted me to go to Cornell because she loved the Cornell fight song, *Give My Regards to Davy,* which is set to the tune of George M. Cohan's *Give My Regards to Broadway.* But I went to Providence."

TOM PEPE

On November 2, 1986, I was driving to the Bowl at 5:30 on the morning following the Dartmouth game to supervise the cleanup. I was on Central Avenue when I noticed this glow underneath the press box. I went immediately to a telephone to report this. Within 20 minutes the press box was totally engulfed in flames. It looked like paper burning; it was all dry wood. The cause of the fire was faulty wiring in an electrical box. "

JOEL ALDERMAN ('51) REMEMBERS CHARLEY LOFTUS

"When Charley was appointed the Yale SID at the age of 25 in 1944, he became the youngest person to hold such a position at a major college.

"Charley ruled and virtually dominated the Bowl's press box, thumping the long and creaky wood floor with his slight limp while pacing from end to end, checking on the needs of the journalists. He would serve them only meager halftime refreshments, usually a cup of bullion broth, a dry roast beef or ham-and-cheese sandwich, a bag of peanuts and an apple. Not even coffee. He probably figured the men (before women were allowed in) were there to work, not to dine on elegant food.

"Among his innovations were to provide the media with a written play-by-play shortly after each quarter, and to host and popularize weekly amplified telephone interviews with opposing coaches on the Tuesday before each game. He was to gain national recognition and numerous awards for his artful and informative game programs and team brochures, many of which are now valuable collectors' items.

"To some he could be intimidating. But to many others he was a confidant and friend. He regularly held court with the biggest names in the business. He would meet once or twice a year with writers Red Smith, Grantland Rice, Frank Graham, and Tim Cohane, cartoonist Willard Mullin, caterer Joe Stevens and Yale coach Herman Hickman as the 'Village Green Reading Society'—a name he created. Its main purpose was certainly not to read.

"Most of us easily accepted Charley's shortcomings and overlooked his idiosyncrasies and phobias, such as: (1) He obtained a vanity personal phone number that was just a succession of 7's, a number now used by a local cab company; (2) He would often go to and from the Bowl under a police escort, not to gain attention but to protect against some personal and probably imagined fears; (3) He had a psychological inability to venture outside New Haven, preventing him from attending Yale games away from the Bowl. Instead he would send his capable assistant, first Stan Venoit and later Peter Easton. Stan went on to become an outspoken city reporter for the *New Haven Register,* and Peter eventually followed Charley as the sports information director.

"Right after his death at the age of 55 in 1974, noted sports columnist Red Smith wrote, 'When it came to making friends for Yale, informing and assisting the press, beating the publicity drums and selling tickets, no college ever had a better press agent than Charles Randall Loftus.'

"His name is perpetuated each fall at the annual Yale football banquet with the presentation of the Charles Loftus Award to the team's outstanding freshman."

The 1986 press box fire
(Tom Pepe)

Broadcasting Yale Football on the Radio

LEE DEFOREST, 'THE father of modern radio,' built a wireless transmitter at City Point in New Haven. He reportedly did an amateur broadcast of the 1916 Yale-Harvard game. The first live commercial radio broadcast of a college football game took place on October 8, 1921, when KDKA in Pittsburgh carried the West Virginia- Pittsburgh game with Harold W. Arlin behind the mike. Franklin M. Doolittle, ('15) broadcast the November 12, 1921, Yale-Princeton game over his amateur radio station, IGAI.26. Radio stations WDRC of Hartford and WPAJ picked up the broadcast of the game, won by Yale.

That broadcast was executed in an unusual way. *New Haven Register* sports editor Dan Mulvey attended the game and described the action over a telephone to Doolittle, who was at home with his transmitter. Doolittle repeated the information into his homemade microphone.

According to Yale football broadcasting historian Joel Alderman, the first professional broadcast of Yale football is generally considered to have been at the October 14, 1922, Iowa game in the Bowl, carried on WOR (Newark, N.J.). That season AT&T radiophone station WEAF (New York), the predecessor of WNBC and today's WFAN, carried Yale games against Brown, Princeton and Harvard. There were on-the- field microphones to pick up the bands, cheering on both sides, and crowd noise.

Bill McGeehan, sporting editor of the *New York Herald,* called Yale's 1922 game at Princeton on WGY. The following week McGeehan broadcast the Yale-Harvard game on WGY, working from an enclosed glass booth, described as a telephone booth, at the Bowl and using a wireless. The broadcast was reportedly heard as far west as the Pacific Coast and as far south as Cuba.

The Yale-Harvard broadcast included a thirty-minute pregame show featuring McGeehan, Walter Turnbull and another "well known football critic," identified as Daniel (quite possibly Dan Daniel of the *New York World Telegram).*

The 1925 Yale-Harvard game at Boston reportedly had the largest radio audience of any college game ever broadcast up to that time stretching as far west as St. Louis on a thirteen-station hookup. Graham McNamee of WEAF in New York called the game with Phillip Carlin joining him in the booth.

The 1927 Yale-Harvard game from Soldier's Field (Harvard Stadium) was sent to the Harvard Club of London. By arrangement with the Postal Telegraph Co., a wire was set up in the press stands running to New York, then connecting through a transatlantic cable with the Commercial Cable Co. in London and thence to the Harvard Club. "It is not explained in news reports if the announcer's voice was actually transmitted or just telegraphic play-by-play written scripts were sent," Alderman said. "But the 1931 Yale-Harvard game was actually heard over the BBC. Unfortunately, reception was lost after 30 minutes and reported 'thousands of British auditors sitting around their evening firesides' (*New York Times,* December 6, 1931) missed Albie Booth's field goal in the final minutes of Yale's 3-0 win.'"

Radio ushered in the use of sports as an advertising vehicle. From 1936 through 1951 the Atlantic Refining Company sponsored Yale football broadcasts and other leading college football games in the East, South and Midwest. In '36, six games in the Bowl were broadcast. In '37, Bill Slater, a West Point graduate and headmaster of Adelphi Academy in Brooklyn, broadcast Yale home games on the Yankee Network while Bob Hall, a Yale quarterback in the late '20s, and Yale athletic director (1950-53) provided the color.

BROADCASTING PIONEERS AND LEGENDS

Several of the pioneers and the celebrities of sports broadcasting have "called" Yale football action on the air from the Bowl.

Two legendary announcers were in the radio booths on October 24, 1931, when Yale and Army played to a 6-6 tie. WABC and a coast-to-coast Columbia network carried a broadcast by Ted Husing, while McNamee, assisted by Floyd Gibbons, announced the game over WEAF and an extensive NBC network.

Husing's broadcast was synchronized over W2XAB in New York, an experimental visual broadcasting station that used in-studio graphics to describe the action. In 1931 CBS opened W2XAB and used a mechanical television system.

Yale closed the '31 season with a 51-14 win against Princeton in the Bowl, broadcast over WOR radio by Ford Frick, who later became National League president and baseball commissioner.

In addition to Husing and McNamee, such broadcasting luminaries as Bill Stern, Mel Allen,

1943 Yale-Army broadcast: L-R: Lieut. John Dillon (spotter for Army), Red Barber at the mike, injured Yale player Walt Brown (spotter for Yale). (YALE ATHLETICS)

Red Barber, Ernie Harwell, Jim Britt, Red Grange, Tom Hussey, Leo Egan, Marty Glickman, called Yale games at the Bowl. Van Patrick worked the Giants-Lions exhibition game in 1960. Marv Albert anchored the Giants' radio broadcast over WNEW when they played in the Bowl in '73 and '74. Sam Huff and Chip Cipolla did the color.

The Yankee Network—not associated with the New York Yankees baseball team— was a regional network that ironically carried Yankee baseball games with WNAC (AM 1230) in Boston as its flagship station. WICC in Bridgeport and occasionally WOR in New York carried Yale games via the Yankee Network.

THE LOCALS BEHIND THE MIKE

Yale graduate Howard Eaton covered Yale games on WELI (AM, 960) in New Haven from 1950 to 1962. For several years Joel Alderman did color with Eaton. Former Red Sox announcer Ned Martin called Yale football for a time in the early '60s with

Mel Allen
(RICH MARAZZI)

Ernie Harwell, the longtime voice of the Detroit Tigers, worked games in the Bowl.
(RICH MARAZZI)

L-R: Herbert Korte (WELI engineer), Joel Alderman and Howard Eaton in the radio booth at the Yale Bowl.
(JOEL ALDERMAN)

L-R: Carm Cozza, Kevin Guarino (spotter) and Ron Vaccaro, the current voice of Yale football.
(YALE ATHLETICS)

Dick Galiette as his color man. But for most of five decades, excluding a window from 1988 to 1996, Galiette was the voice of Yale football over WELI, WICC, and several affiliates. He worked with a cadre of color commentators including Tiny Markle, Jon Stashower, Bob Norman, Joe Benanto, and Carm Cozza. For a time George and Carlo Grande and Bill Gonillo were in the booth before Galiette returned. Ron Vaccaro succeeded Galiette upon his death in 2005 and has worked alongside Cozza since then. G

Beginning in 2013 Yale games were carried ESPN Radio 1300 as part of a network of Buckley Radio stations in Connecticut.

WYBC has broadcast Yale football since the late '40s. The station is run primarily by Yale undergraduates, but there is some community involvement. The station first started in 1941 as WOCD and was run by the *Yale Daily News*. They subsequently purchased WNHC through the bankruptcy court, and operated at 1340 AM.

JOEL ALDERMAN ('51)

"Howard Eaton, who worked in the advertising industry, was not a full-time broadcaster but had unique ideas. He used an egg timer as a reminder to give the score when the timer emptied. He had a pocket adding machine to keep the cumulative rushing and passing yardage of the teams. He also had a homemade slide rule as an aid in determining the exact yardage made on any play. Charlie Wright did color before me and Bud Finch pinch-hit on occasion. Joe Celello from Naugatuck, Conn., was one of his spotters.

"In the mid-'60s Eaton and I formed the Ivy Alumni Network, which lasted until 1983. The idea was to extend Ivy League football to different radio stations across the country. Our dream was to have a coast-to-coast radio network of Ivy League football contests. In later years we broadcast to Yale and Harvard alumni clubs throughout the country, which would have meetings on the day of the game. The blossoming of television proved to be the demise of the network.

"On our level, we never had the equipment or resources to go "high tech." But we did the next best thing. Our engineer had strung an extremely long broadcast line from his remote equipment in the press box, extending down to the ground outside the Bowl, then running through the players' entrance and on to the tunnel opening onto the field. All we needed then was a connecting line with a microphone.

"William "Pudge" Claffey, a Wilbur Cross High School student who was our helper, would hold the microphone and point it in various directions so we could bring in those colorful sounds without battling the bad acoustics of the public address system. Syd Jaffe was a longtime public address announcer and Jack Casey had the same assignment for the writers on the press box PA, and later I also did that for a couple of seasons. That assignment is currently handled by Steve Conn."

BUD FINCH

"I was at WELI from 1939 to 1996. There was a time when I put together a network of 10 stations. For a time in the '50s and early '60s, nobody wanted to cover Yale games until Dick Galiette took ownership of the network. "

JOEL SMILOW ('54)

"As sports director of WYBC, the Yale Broadcasting Co., during my senior year, I did play-by-play of Yale football's away games that '53 season. When Yale played at home, I ran the public address system in the press box. That wasn't as much fun, but I got paid $20 a game and I needed the money."

GEORGE GRANDE

"Professionally, both my brother Carlo and I broadcast many games from the Bowl, and I know this made our dad proud. I grew up listening to Yale football on 960 WELI. For a time, WELI did not carry the games, so a group of us worked behind the scenes to return Yale football broadcasts to the station. Broadcasting with Carlo, Tiny Markle, Dick Galiette and Bill

Gonillo was a wonderful experience. One of the most joyous parts of my career has been the link to the Yale Bowl. Every broadcaster who ever worked there understood the history, the lore and the essence of what Yale football stood for- the melding of athletics and academics."

JOE CASTIGLIONE

"A native of Hamden, Connecticut, I entered Colgate University in '64. The reason I applied to Colgate is that I wanted to go to a school that played Yale. The following year I broadcast the Yale-Colgate game from the Yale Bowl over our college station. Here I was, sitting atop the Bowl on the visitors' side in the tiny white broadcast booth, waxing nostalgic. Memories of sitting with my dad and all the games I had attended ran through my mind. It was a chilling experience. This was Carmen Cozza's first year as the head Yale coach and Colgate prevailed that day, 7-0.

"Looking back at my Yale football experience, I guess I can say, like so many: 'Thanks, Dad!'"

A TRIBUTE TO DICK GALIETTE

RON VACCARO ('04)—PRESENT YALE PLAY-BY-PLAY BROADCASTER

"On October 15, 2005, Yale was defeated by Lehigh in overtime, 28-21 in Bethlehem, Pennsylvania. At the time, I was working the

Dick Galiette was the voice of Yale football for thirty-three seasons over WELI and WICC. He died on October 21, 2005 at age 72.
(YALE ATHLETICS)

sideline for Yale football broadcasts with Dick Galiette and Carmen Cozza in the booth. I had broadcast games over WYBC when I was a student at Yale. On the Monday after the Lehigh game, Steve Conn called to tell me that Dick was ill in the hospital and to stand by and be ready to do the Penn game the following week in Philadelphia.

"The morning of the Penn game, I did a taped interview with Yale coach Jack Siedlecki at the Renaissance Airport Hotel in Philadelphia. At the end of the interview Jack gave Dick heartfelt best wishes for a good recovery. Carm was not far away and heard what Jack had to say. He immediately informed me that Dick passed away and I would have to omit the Siedlecki get-well message.

"Going on the air that day was very difficult. Nothing I do in my life will be as pressure-packed or as hard as that. This was the first Yale broadcast without Dick in many years. It was morbid, and the rainy weather added to the gloom at Franklin Field. As soon as I went on the air I announced that Dick had died. It was not publicly known that he was sick.

"I had become very good friends with Dick. When I was a student I worked as a spotter for him. I would take the team bus to road games and on occasion would ride back with Dick. It's amazing how close he was to the players, even though 50 years separated him from them. He attended practice almost daily and loved the kids.

"Dick was my mentor. The No. 1 thing I learned is that you can never be overprepared. You need to talk to people and be informed."

BOB NORMAN—BROADCASTER, MAYOR OF EAST HAVEN, CONNECTICUT (1985-91) NEWSCASTER AND ANCHORMAN FOR OVER 20 YEARS AT CHANNEL 8 NEWS

"I worked with Dick Galiette, doing color on WELI broadcasts from 1968 to 1973. Dick was the ultimate pro. He really did his homework, accumulating as much information as possible. He knew who was good and who wasn't. He knew whom to watch.

"We used to have weekly meetings with Carm Cozza, who was fantastic to work with. On Friday afternoon we would meet with Buddy Amendola, one of Carm's assistants, and he would give us the scouting report on the next day's opponent.

"I'll never forget one embarrassing moment I had working a game in the Bowl with Dick. It was a quiet day and I was giving the Ivy League scores. Every score we had was 0-0 (nothing to nothing). After I gave the scores it was time for a station break. Instead of saying, 'We'll take a break on the Yale Football Network,' I said, 'We'll take a break on the Yale Football Nothing.'

"The game I'll never forget was the 29-29 tie game at Harvard in '68. When the game ended, Dick and I were stunned. We looked at each other like 'What the hell happened here?' Following the game we drove back to Connecticut, found a watering hole and drowned our sorrows."

Bob Norman died on January 19, 2013.

THE SPOTTERS

FRANK STOLZENBERG ('53)

"I worked with some of the most legendary announcers in sports history, including names like Mel Allen, Russ Hodges, Ernie Harwell, and Bill Stern. Mel would bring his brother, Larry, to be a spotter for the opposing team. Usually the opposing team would have an injured player do the job.

"My fee was $5 a game. The first time I worked with Mel, I thought I was getting stiffed by the great Mel Allen, the longtime voice of the New York Yankees. When it was time to pay me, he said he didn't have his wallet but promised he would have his secretary send me a check. True to his word, I received a check for $20, four times what I usually made.

"The first time I worked with Stern, I noticed that he didn't stand for the national anthem. I was perplexed but was afraid to say something. But he soon took away all anxiety by explaining

Frank Stolzenberg during his college days at Yale.
(THE STOLZENBERG FAMILY)

that when he got to a game, he'd take off his prosthetic leg to relieve the soreness. Standing up for him was difficult. I learned that his left leg was amputated above the knee because of an injury he suffered in an auto accident in 1935.

The Work of a Spotter

"I used a 2x2-foot piece of cardboard with Yale's players arranged according to position.

I had blue pins for Yale and red pins for the opposing players. A pin would be next to the players who were in the game. On a given play the announcer would glance at my board and I would use a pencil and point to the appropriate pin or pins. Then the announcer would look to the other spotter for similar identification. The announcers would be constantly moving their heads from side to side.

"The key was the moving of the pencil. It wasn't that complicated because most players went both ways. During that era, maybe 30 players or so combined from both teams would play in a game.

Phantom Player

"I once put a player in the game who really didn't play. Before a game I promised him that he would be announced on the radio as actually playing. I did this because the player's mother had never heard his name on the radio. I simply moved my magical pencil and pointed to the pin that identified him as the player that was involved in the play.

Interesting Guests

"We worked from an old radio booth on top of the press box that was very small. There was room for an announcer, two spotters and a guy with a microphone and headset. At halftime there was usually a guest. I remember meeting Broderick Crawford, Maureen O'Sullivan and Harold Russell.

"I only worked one television game during my career as a spotter, and it was during the 1950 season when WPIX carried Yale games. A temporary booth was built above the press box on the Yale side. Dan Peterson did the play-by-play."

GEORGE MARTELON

"I have worked as a spotter for Yale Bowl public address announcer Mark Ryba since 2007. It's the world's best job. I first attended a Yale game in 1958 with my dad. Today, as I work with Mark in the press box and we stand for the national anthem and face the flag above Portal 8, I think back on those days with a great deal of positive thoughts."

Some of the PA announcers from the 1950s to the present include Syd Jaffe, Ron Rohmer, Bob Chatfield and Mark Ryba, who has been there since 2003.

Spotter George Martelon (standing) and Mark Ryba, the Bowl's PA announcer
(SAM RUBIN)

TELEVISION

THE FIRST TELEVISED college football game took place during the "experimental" era of television history when Fordham University met tiny Waynesburg College at Randalls Island in New York City on September 30, 1939. Bill Stern called the action over station W2XBS (now WNBC) as a demonstration of this new medium at New York's World's Fair

The first Yale football game ever televised was on Oct. 12, 1940, at Franklin Field in Philadelphia, where the Elis faced a strong Penn team that was coming off a 51-0 victory over Maryland. The Quakers pummeled the camera-shy Bulldogs, 50-7.

The first TV game from the Yale Bowl was the Oct. 9, 1948, Columbia contest, in which the Lions edged the Elis, 34-28. WNBT, an NBC outlet in

New York, carried the game with Bob Stanton calling the action. It was televised along the Eastern Seaboard.

The first Yale-Harvard telecast was on November 19, 1949, when the Elis won 29-6 in the Bowl. The game was shown on NBC national/regional TV. This was Levi Jackson's final game in a Yale uniform and he went out in a blaze of glory, scoring two touchdowns.

In 1950 Yale had seven home games. Six were carried by either WPIX on Channel 11 or WABD, Channel 5, the Dumont station in New York.

For many years Yale wore its blue jerseys for the Harvard game and Harvard wore crimson. This stopped in the mid-'50s when the NCAA, because of the growing popularity of television, mandated that the home team wear the dark-colored jersey and the visiting team wear white. If both teams wore dark jerseys it would be too confusing for the viewers watching black-and-white TV. Subsequently the NCAA has given the home team the option of wearing the jersey color of their choice. The color of the Yale jersey has gone from a true blue to a very dark blue.

Some noted broadcasters who worked TV in the Bowl included Lindsey Nelson, Jim McKay, Jim Simpson, Keith Jackson, Al Michaels, Sean McDonough, John Sterling, and Charlie Steiner, plus distinguished color analysts like former coaches Bud Wilkinson, Ara Parseghian, Terry Brennan and Frank Broyles. Former Giants' kicker Pat Summerall worked the Giants' telecasts in '73 and '74.

Dick Galiette was host of a Sunday afternoon TV show with Yale coach Carmen Cozza in the late 1960s on WNHC-TV.

TV Stations and Yale Football

In the addition to WPIX, Dumont and NBC, Yale football has been televised by ABC, CBS, ESPN, PBS, Sports Channel America, Pay Per view, MSG, ESPN 2, ESPN 3, NESN, YES, DirecTV, NBC Sports, formerly Versus, NBCSN and FOX College Central. Brian Dowling produced a closed-circuit broadcast of the Yale-Harvard game every year from 1980 to 2004.

Historically, the Yale Bowl has been filled to the brim with talent on the field as well as the press box. Just as the Bowl has been a playground to many of college football's all-time greats, the Yale press box has been by the most noted sportswriters and broadcasters in the world of sports.

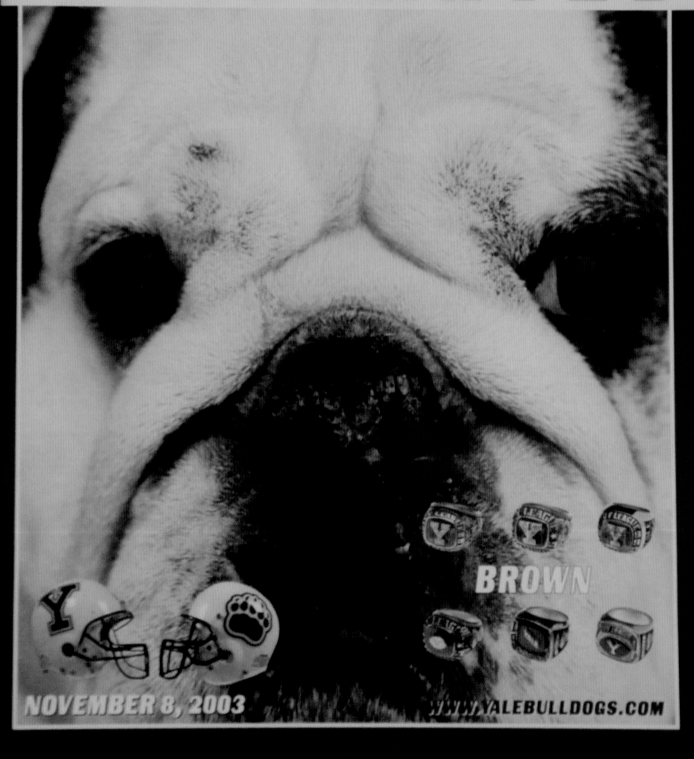

Handsome Dan is considered by many as the first live college mascot. The lineage of the seventeen Handsome Dans goes back to 1889. (YALE ATHLETICS)

CHAPTER 28

HANDSOME DAN

"Dan is the mascot against which all other mascots are judged, and what does this humble creature ask in return? A college to call his home and a scratch behind the ears."

—The Yale Herald

Handsome Dan I
(Yale Athletics)

whenever Yale scored. The bulldog was befriended by the players and students and is believed to have been the first live college mascot.

Graves returned to his native England after graduating, but Dan stayed on campus with Graves' brother. Prior to football and baseball games he would be led across the field, drawing applause from the crowd. A fine specimen, Handsome Dan I went on to win awards at some thirty dog shows, including a first prize at a Westminster Kennel Club show. In 1897 he crossed the Atlantic to be reunited with his master. He died a year later.

Graves had him stuffed by a taxidermist and returned him to Yale, where he was displayed in the old gymnasium and served as an inspiration for Cole Porter's Yale fight song *Bulldog*. He spent time in the Peabody Museum before being transferred to one of the trophy rooms at Yale's Payne Whitney Gym.

In January 1979 he disappeared. Shortly afterward, a ransom note appeared in the *Yale Daily News*, demanding $1 million and a six-pack of beer for his return. Many feared that Dan had been spirited off to Harvard. Mysteriously, he was returned on Labor Day weekend of 1980. He now is in a sealed glass case where, according to former Yale faculty member Stanton Ford, "he is the perpetual guardian of the treasures which attest to generations of Yale athletic glory. Handsome Dan's fervent anti-Harvard proclivities became a requirement for all his successors."

After an interval of thirty-seven years since Dan I roamed the Yale sidelines, Yale acquired a Handsome Dan II. In 1933, the freshman class purchased this bulldog from the Trapp family in Branford, Connecticut, as a gift to coach Raymond "Ducky" Pond. On the eve of the 1934 Yale-Harvard game, Dan II was dognapped, apparently by Harvard students. (Coincidentally—or not—members of the Harvard swim

L EGEND HAS IT that in 1889 a Yale undergraduate, Andrew B. Graves, purchased a white bulldog from a New Haven blacksmith for $65. However, an article by Bob Baumann in the October 18, 1980, Yale-Columbia game day program challenges the history of the purchase. He claims Graves bought the dog from a breeder named Ned Porter, an 1880 Yale grad. His argument is based on a letter Graves sent to the Yale Alumni Records Office in 1930 in which he makes reference to Porter as a breeder and not a blacksmith.

Graves said the dog looked like "a cross between an alligator and a horned toad," as reported by the *Hartford Courant*. The dog followed his master to classes and to games, and tradition says it barked team had stayed at the Ray Tompkins House as guests of the Yale Athletic Association shortly before Dan's disappearance.) This embarrassment was exacerbated when hamburger grease was put on the boots of John Harvard's statue in Cambridge and a picture was circulated of Dan licking Harvard's boots. Eventually Dan II was returned. United Press reported the incident this way on March 25, 1934: "Shortly before 11 p.m. a large sedan occupied by two Harvard campus policemen, stopped before the headquarters of the Yale campus police. Dan was later escorted to the Ray Tompkins House, from where he disappeared ten days ago. Three 'rescuers,' apparently content to return Dan to his hometown, sped away." Dan died in 1937 three weeks after he suffered a broken leg.

Dan IX, owned by John E. Sanders, an assistant professor of geology at Yale, became a national figure when he appeared on the cover of *Sports Illustrated*'s November 6, 1956, issue. About a month after his picture appeared, Dan IX died of a kidney ailment.

Although the Yale mascot is traditionally a male, the custom was broken with Dan XII, a.k.a. Bingo. Owned by Yale history professor Rollin Osterweis, Bingo was the only female Handsome Dan ever among the seventeen Dans. Dan XVII is currently the property of Yale alum Chris Getman. (Dan XVII has the distinction of having had his picture

Former Yale president Richard Levin, former president George H.W. Bush, Chris Getman, and Handsome Dan (YALE ATHLETICS)

taken with both a former president—George H. W. Bush—and a Beatle—Sir Paul McCartney.)

THE BRONZED BULLDOG

The popular Yale mascot took on a new incarnation on November 11, 2011, when a quarter-ton bronze statue of the original Handsome Dan was unveiled outside the Jensen Plaza at the western entrance to the Bowl. Yale grad Mark Simon, a founding partner at Centerbrook Architects & Planners in Essex, Connecticut, commissioned the statue for Yale. The bronzed bulldog is bolted down with threaded rods connecting it to a granite base, which weighs a few tons and is connected to a concrete base. It appears to be well protected from the Harvards and Sons of Old Nassau.

MEMORIES OF HANDSOME DAN

JIM TRAPP—TEACHER; MILFORD, CONNECTICUT

"In 1933 my late grandfather had a farm in the Momauguin section of East Haven, Conn.

He had a bulldog that my cousin Bobby Gilman was in charge of, and I can remember as a three-year-old pulling the dog's line. Shortly after that, the bulldog was purchased with pennies donated by the freshman class and given to coach 'Ducky' Pond. The dog became Handsome Dan II."

CHRIS GETMAN '64—THE MAN WHO WALKS THE DOG

"I have been the owner and caretaker for Handsome Dan XIII, XIV, XV, and XVII. All of them have lived in my home and each one had his own individual traits and characteristics. Maurice, who was Handsome Dan XIII, was the longest-serving mascot (1984-95; 97), a total of twelve years. He was from Bronxville, New York, and was very athletic. He would climb the giant steps at East Rock.

"Maurice would head-butt anybody in a costume, including the Yale Bulldog, the UConn Husky, the Brown Bear, and the Princeton Tiger.

"I had arranged for Margaret and Caitlin Fitzgerald and Jonathan Massey, all family friends, to walk Maurice at the 1985 game at Army. But all sideline passes were rescinded and the Yale band was told they couldn't play because the officials at West Point did not approve of the band's halftime script. It basically read, 'Army had been infiltrated by communists'—the reasons being General Patton subscribed to *Redbook* Magazine, General Eisenhower was a Cincinnati *Reds* fan, and General MacArthur donated to the American *Red* Cross.' The Army guys didn't get the tongue-in-cheek, satirical spirit of the Yale Precision Marching Band. We got around [the ban] by having the kids dress in Yale

Chris Getman walks Handsome Dan XVII in the Yale Bowl at the 2013 Cornell game.
(BILL O'BRIEN)

cheerleading outfits. They marched right in and were told to say if questioned, 'I'm a child prodigy in Calhoun College.'

"Army won the game in a blowout, 59-16, and every time they scored they shot off a cannon, which scared Maurice. Before we left the field at the end of the game, I tried to have Maurice relieve himself to prepare for the long trip home, but he wouldn't cooperate. On the way back to the bus we passed the home of the commandant of the United States Military Academy, where Maurice took a healthy dump on his lawn. It was great revenge for what he had been through.

"Over the years Harvard students have come to my home, posing as Yale students. Their goal is to kidnap Handsome Dan. They get nowhere. Handsome Dan and I can sniff a Cantab a mile away."

Yale coach Tony Reno flanked by 2013 captain Beau Palin (40) and senior Willy Moore (66) lead the Bulldogs on the traditional pregame walk from the Smilow Field Center to the Bowl.
(JACK WARHOLA)

CHAPTER 29

THE TUNNEL AND THE BOWL— PLAYERS' MEMORIES

"The Yale Bowl is a cathedral to intercollegiate football, in much the same manner that Cameron Indoor Arena or Fenway Park are to college basketball and major league baseball, respectively. It was as if the friendly ghosts of Yale legends past welcomed you as you walked through the tunnel onto the field."

—Calvin Hill

Ted Livingston (75) joins Carm Cozza in leading the team onto the field in 1968.
(YALE ATHLETICS)

"Because there are no dressing rooms in the Yale Bowl, I always thought it was an exciting part of the day to watch the players walk from the field house to the Bowl before the start of games," said former assistant coach Sam Burrell.

Once the players reach the Bowl, the walk from the tunnel to the field is a special experience reserved for only players and coaches. The tunnel walk bonds teammates forever. It is a timeless memory.

What follows are quotes from former players, in which they describe the playing in the Yale Bowl and the unique experience of walking through the tunnel.

THERE ARE NO dressing rooms in the Yale Bowl, and so players must don their uniforms in the Joel Smilow Field Center and walk to the Bowl. This is a part of the Yale Bowl experience that is a unique feature for players and fans. Before the game, it's common for fans to wish the walking warriors well as they prepare to do battle. Following the game, it's common for players to give away their chin straps and sign game day programs for appreciative fans. This connection between players and spectators is unheard of in most major college football venues, where clubhouses are built within the stadium and players enter and exit cut off from the people who watch them play.

The walk through the tunnel has been a visceral experience for generations of Yale players.
(BILL O'BRIEN)

NELSON TALBOTT JR. '43

"My fondest memory of the Bowl was simply going through the tunnel and running on to the field while looking up at the stands."

BILL LOVEJOY '56

"My father, Winslow, who was a Yale All-American center in 1924, said to me, 'You're never going to realize how little you feel when you go into the Yale Bowl when it's full.' He was right. You don't see the stadium; you see the ocean of people and all those little heads around the top."

PAUL LOPATA '57

"I loved playing in the Yale Bowl. It was one of the nicest stadiums in the country. And since we drew so well, we played most of our games at home. In the twenty-seven scheduled games from 1954-56, twenty-two were played in the Bowl. We only alternated home and away games with Columbia, Princeton, and Harvard."

DICK WINTERBAUER '58

"I loved playing in the Yale Bowl. Running onto the field as a nineteen-year-old sophomore in '55 for the Army game before over 60,000 fans and two weeks later entering the Bowl for the Harvard game in front of close to 56,000 on a snowy day sent chills down my back."

KEN WOLFE '61

"For me the Yale Bowl represents playing Ivy League football and getting a great education. I used to feel inadequate when I talked to some of my friends at Penn State. But as I got older, I realized that the Ivy League does it right."

JIM LITTLE '62

"When I visited Yale, Gib Holgate, the freshman football coach took me out to the Bowl. It was a beautiful day in late fall after the football season. He unlocked the gates and the two of us walked toward the empty Bowl. He took me down the tunnel that led to the field. When I walked out of the tunnel onto the field, I looked around at that huge 65,000 seat stadium with so much football history and took in the beautiful grass football field. It was overwhelming and, based on a totally visceral reaction, at that moment I decided that I was going to go to Yale."

HANK HIGDON '63

"The first time I was ever in the Yale Bowl was in 1946 when Yale defeated the Coast Guard 47-14. I was so impressed that from that moment on all I wanted to do was play football for Yale. The Bowl of course is an icon for college football, not just Yale football, and has been the venue of some incredibly exciting games.

"Walking out of the Bowl after games was special. There were always kids asking for autographs and chin straps. It was no problem signing autographs, but because chin straps were not that plentiful, we used to hide them in our pants."

CHUCK MERCEIN '65

"The Yale Bowl is full of tradition and was a great place to play football. It was a vibrant, exciting place. The setting was beautiful, with colorful, sparkling fall foliage on West Rock overlooking the Bowl beyond the scoreboard. I used to say, 'Thank God for letting me be here.'"

WATTS HUMPHREY '66

"Playing in the Yale Bowl, where my father (Bud) played with Larry Kelley and Clint Frank and my brother (George) played center and captained the '63 team, was the biggest thrill of my college career."

BRIAN DOWLING '69

"Playing in the Yale Bowl was special because we were playing well and drew large crowds. But because of the dwindling attendance today, I suggested during the renovation of the Bowl the possibility of eliminating the end zone seats and having grassy hills at both ends where monuments or plaques could pay homage to former players. I would also shape the stands diagonally. This would make a crowd of 20,000 look large. With the current small crowds, if there are 10,000 in the Bowl, it looks like 500 people."

ANDY COE '70

"It was kind of a dream come true to play football for Yale in the Bowl, and playing there with the success we had in the late '60s was unforgettable. The Yale Bowl was an important part of the first twenty-five years of my life."

DICK JAURON '73

"The Yale Bowl connected us to all the players before us. The meeting room in the Bowl was dismal, old, and dusty. But it was better that way because it gave it a feel of nostalgia. To be on the field in a game in

that stadium was a thrill. The connection, the sense of history, and the Bowl itself made it an atmosphere like no other."

DON GESICKI '76

"I am a New Jersey native and a lifelong New York Football Giants fan. My first trip to the Yale Bowl was in late August 1971, just before I began my senior year in high school. A group of friends and I made the trip from New Jersey to New Haven to attend a preseason game between the New York Jets and the Giants.

"It was a very hot, sunny late summer day and there was a capacity crowd in excess of 70,000. The Bowl was filled with raucous Giants and Jets fans. I was impressed by the enormity of the Yale Bowl and the deafening sound generated by the huge crowd. Little did I know that a few months later I would return to the Bowl as a prospective student-athlete.

"When I visited Yale, coach Seb LaSpina took me to the Bowl. There was a coating of snow on the ground when we drove out to see the spectacular football stadium. Coach parked close to the Bowl and we slowly walked to one of the portals. The only sound was the snow crunching under our feet. Coach LaSpina opened the gate, and the creaking noise echoed throughout the vast empty Bowl. We silently moved down the portal and looked out on the eerily quiet stadium. Needless to say, I was awestruck by the serene setting—quite a difference from my first visit in '71."

JOHN PAGLIARO SR. '78

"I was ten-years-old when I made my first trip to the Yale Bowl with my dad and his friend Pete

Garofalo. At the Bowl I sat in the end zone, first row, and was in awe of the place. I remember walking in the Bowl and being moved by the size and beauty of the field. It was the most beautiful football field I had seen. That day I watched Brian Dowling and Calvin Hill perform their magic and I just dreamed of what it would be like to play on that gorgeous field.

"Just a few years later I found myself playing on that same field. As a player, the most powerful moment for me was always entering the Bowl. When it's just before a game, the adrenalin is flowing and you enter through this dark, narrow tunnel leading you into the beautiful sea of blue and green of Yale Bowl. Without a doubt, a very special and powerful walk."

JOE ZURAW '79

"The Yale Bowl was familiar to me long before I entered the university, since I worked there as an usher when the New York Giants played there in '73 and '74. Walking through the Walter Camp Memorial Gate columns and running onto to the Yale Bowl field was an incredible experience that all Yale players enjoy."

JOHN SPAGNOLA '79

"The Yale Bowl was a very special place. It's like sacred ground going back to 1914. We walked on hallowed ground, following the likes of Clint Frank and Larry Kelley. But it seemed like it rained every Saturday. I liked that because it made everybody as slow as I was."

BOB KRYSTINIAK '79

"It was great playing at such a venue as the Yale Bowl where many great players had played over

the years. Not only did I play football in the Bowl, I played Frisbee. During the spring a couple of my friends and I used to climb the fence and sneak into the Bowl when it was supposed to be closed and have Frisbee contests. We used to try to throw the Frisbee through the uprights of the goal posts."

MIKE SULLIVAN '80

"My Yale Bowl roots go back to my dad, who played for Hillhouse against West Haven in that famous Thanksgiving Day game in 48 that drew over 40,000 fans. As a kid I followed the Dowling-Hill and Dick Jauron teams. Just to be a part of a rich football tradition at Yale was special."

KEN HILL '80

"The Yale football program is steeped in tradition, and the Yale Bowl embodies that. Being in that building and going through that tunnel and that little halftime room was special. The magnitude of the structure's presence made it an amazing experience, bigger than walking onto the field at the Rose Bowl when I played in Super Bowl XXI with New York Giants in '87. Not to anthropomorphize a building, but playing in the Bowl it was an unbelievable experience because of the presence of history and greatness that you could feel. Opponents knew when they walked into the Bowl that they were in for one heck of a fight and were probably going to lose."

CURT GRIEVE '82

"I recall the Bowl in the early 1980s as crumbling in some parts but still retaining its classic dignity.

Like other elements of the Yale athletic fields complex, the Bowl made me feel I'd been transported back in time."

RICH DIANA '82

"Growing up in the shadows of the Yale Bowl in Hamden, it was an honor for me to play there."

MIKE CURTIN '86

"During my recruiting visit, Carm Cozza took my father and me to the Yale Bowl in his blue station wagon. He drove through the tunnel on the east side of the Bowl where the visiting team enters. We got out of the car and looked around the massive Bowl. The monumental history of the university and the tradition of the football program hit me immediately. I looked into the corner of the south end zone where Curt Grieve caught the touchdown pass that beat Navy in '81. I looked around the Bowl and saw the atypical scoreboard. I felt the extent of the opportunity and made my decision that day in the Bowl that I would attend Yale. This was a big step for a kid from Salt Lake City who was the son of Irish immigrant parents. I was enthralled by the opportunity and experience. That said, I think my father enjoyed it more than I did."Walking from the team meeting room in the Bowl down to the field was a unique multisensory experience that every Yale player has enjoyed since 1914. In the 1980s there were wooden stairs coming out of the team room. It wasn't a well-lit area, and there was always dampness in the air. Soon the characteristic sounds of cleats on the wooden boards gave way to the concrete in the historic tunnel that led to the field. At the top of the tunnel the lighting was poor. As we

drew closer to the field you could smell the turf from about a 30-foot distance. The turf always seemed moist, particularly after the grass had been cut. And then we stepped onto the same surface that so many great players had graced before us. We were welcomed by the Yale band's traditional playing of Cole Porter's *Bulldog*. Taking the field was overwhelming and a chilling experience. It was a magical place and distinctly different from any place else we played.

"I have sometimes thought about returning to the Yale Bowl and taking that walk one more time from our meeting room to the field. But if I did that I wouldn't be wearing the cleats I wore to walk on that concrete in the tunnel nor would I be walking with the same group of guys into the Bowl that I loved dearly. In truth, that reality wouldn't do justice to the memories, and those memories are great ones."

KELLY RYAN '88

"I grew up in Springfield, Illinois, and never was on an airplane before my senior year in high school. When I arrived at Yale in the fall of '84, Troy Jenkins and I decided to take a shuttle bus to the Bowl. I had seen the exterior of it during my recruiting trip but was never inside. When we walked into the Bowl I was overcome by the majesty of the whole thing. It was bigger than life. Troy and I played catch and soaked in every minute. Who would think that almost four years later we would be playing Harvard there before a packed Bowl with a chance to win the Ivy title?

"The '87 Harvard game triggered many emotions. I couldn't help but think about the day Troy and I played catch in an empty Yale Bowl when we were freshmen and saw the Bowl for the first time. And now on this day before 66,000 fans, we walked out of the Bowl for the last time together."

DAVE SHERONAS '93

"The sheer power of the Yale Bowl is intriguing. Walking into the Bowl is a humbling but very empowering experience. There are moments you catch yourself looking around and wondering what game was played here fifty years ago. And then you realize that you are connected to something very historic. You can't prepare, nor can you expect what hits you when you come through the portal for the first time. The Bowl does not look as massive as it is until you enter the field from the portal. Some days you don't hear the crowd at all regardless of the size because you're intensely focused on the game itself.

"The great Yale tradition and the Bowl lend themselves to mysticism. Some players would actually bury their sweat bands and locks of hair under the Bowl turf. The gathering on the field after the games is a magical time. With dusk approaching, the bands playing and kids running around the field, it is a very special happening for Yale players.

"I was in Iraq in 2003, where I was an intelligence officer working with special and Iraqi police forces. One night about 11:30 p.m. Baghdad time, I got a surprise when my father called my cell phone from the Yale Bowl in the second half of the 2003 Yale-Harvard game. He was sitting with six or seven of my former teammates and passed the phone around. Here I was, standing on the other side of the world, talking to my dad and my closest friends who were in the Yale Bowl.

"The Yale Bowl has followed me all over the world."

ROB MASELLA '97

"The Yale Bowl is an icon to the entire football world. It is football history. The way it was constructed in 1913-14 was unique, with a steam shovel reportedly buried under the playing surface. Its age is astonishing, and you could feel the ghosts of the famous players who have played on its hallowed ground. Just being in the Bowl in present day means I am having a great day."

JOSH PHILLIPS '01

"The Yale Bowl is the Goliath of college football venues. Before I got recruited by Yale, I didn't know much about Yale football and its history being from Florida. But once you step into the Bowl and realize how many great players played there, the experience of being a Yale football player becomes special. You learn about the founding fathers of college football like Walter Camp and others."

BRANDT HOLLANDER '07

"I'll never forget my first trip to New Haven. I drove with my parents from Indianapolis and we got lost. We got directions to the Yale Bowl, but the only field I could see on Route 34 was the baseball field. My heart sank. That is not how I imagined the Yale Bowl.

"We were pointed in the right direction and I finally got to the Bowl, where several coaches took us up to the press deck. It was a gorgeous sight—the blue seats and the pristine green grass. I was always awed by the empty Bowl, even on Friday practices the day before the game. The Bowl has so much presence. You're constantly aware of it. It's like being in a church during off hours."

BEAU PALIN '14

"There's so much tradition. It's pretty cool to play there and represent the 'Y' when it's so old and there were so many players before you. But when I walked out of the Yale Bowl for the last time, I looked to my right and to my left and saw guys that I've worked with and trust."

IT IS NO easy task to summarize 140 years of Yale football history and a century at the Yale Bowl. I believe most Yale players and fans, however, will relate to the following sentiment that was published in the November 21, 1981, Yale-Harvard game day program. It is titled *Ode to the Fantastic Football Fan,* written by Charlie Murray.

When my number's up
And I go on to greater things
I hope I wind up
In that great big Stadium in the Sky
Watching footballs slowly floating by
And if I've done my part
On this good earth
If I've played the game
And proved my worth
This one request, please
Grant me
If it's all the same:
Please ... Put me on the "Fifty"
At a Yale-Harvard game.

Yale Football, Yale Bowl Records (Entering the 2014 season)

Games played in Yale Bowl: 600

Record in Yale Bowl: 377-201-22

Yale Football Records by Decade in Yale Bowl

***1914-1919: 18-7

1920-1929: 54-13-5

1930-1939: 36-22-8

1940-1949: 40-26-1

1950-1959: 43-19-5

1960-1969: 41-19-2

1970-1979: 46-10-1

1980-1989: 35-24-0

1990-1999: 23-31-0

2000-2009: 30-20-0

2010- 2013: 11-10-0

BIBLIOGRAPHY

Beech, Mark. *When Saturday Mattered Most: The Last Golden Season of Army Football.* New York: St. Martin's Press, 2012.

Bergin, Thomas G. *Gridiron Glory: Yale Football 1952-72.* New Haven: Football Y Association, 1978.

Bergin, Thomas G. *The Game: The Harvard-Yale Football Rivalry, 1875-1983.* New Haven: Yale University Press, 1984.

Bernstein, Mark F. *Football The Ivy League Origins of an American Obsession. Philadelphia, PA: University of Pennsylvania Press, 2001.*

Bertagna, Joe. *Crimson in Triumph: A Pictorial History of Harvard Athletics, 1852-1985.* Lexington, Mass.: The Stephen Greene Press, 1986.

Boda, Steve Jr., ed., *College Football All-Time Record Book.* New York: The National Collegiate Athletic Association, 1969.

Buck, Polly Stone. *We Minded the Store: Yale Life and Letters During WWII.* Hamden, Conn.: Self-published, 1972.

Cahn, Neil R., Ronald Feiman and Christopher Vizas II, eds. *The Blue Football Book.* New Haven: Yale Banner, 1970.

Cohane, Tim. *The Yale Football Story.* New York: G.P. Putnam's Sons, 1951.

Corbett, Bernard M., and Paul Simpson. *The Only Game That Matters.* New York: Crown Publishers, 2004.

Cozza, Carm with Rick Odermatt. *True Blue: The Carm Cozza Story.* New Haven, Conn., Yale University Press, 1999.

Danzig, Allison. *The History of American Football: Its Great Teams, Players and Coaches.* Englewood Cliffs, N.J.: Prentice-Hall, Inc., 1956.

Elliott, Len. *One Hundred Years of Princeton Football,* Princeton, N.J., Princeton Athletic News, 1969.

Goldstein, Richard. *Ivy League Autumns: An Illustrated History of College Football's Grand Old Rivalries.* New York, St. Martin's Press, 1996.

Jones, Wilbur D. *Football! Navy! War.* Jefferson, N.C.: McFarland & Co., Inc., 2009.

MacCambridge, Michael, ed. *ESPN College Football Encyclopedia: The Complete History of the Game.* New York: ESPN Books, 2005.

McCallum, John. *Ivy League Football Since 1872.* Briarcliff Manor, N.Y., Stein and Day Publishers, 1977.

Newhouse, Dave. *After the Glory: Heisman.* St. Louis, MO, Sporting News Publishing Co., 1985

Olderman, Murray. *The Pro Quarterback.* Englewood Cliffs, N.J.: Prentice-Hall Inc., 1966.

Pierson, George W. *Yale: A Short History.* New Haven: Yale University, 1976.

Rafferty, Kevin, ed. *Harvard Beats Yale 29-29.* New York: The Overlook Press, 2009.

Roberts, Randy. *A Team for America.* New York: First Mariner Books, 2012.

Rubin, Sam. *Yale Football: Images of Sports*. Charleston, S.C., Chicago, Portsmouth, N.H., San Francisco: Arcadia Publishing, 2006.

Shribman, David. *One Hundred Years of Dartmouth Football*. Hanover, N.H.: Dartmouth College Board of Trustees, 1980.

Smith, Walter W. *To Absent Friends From Red Smith*. New York: Atheneum Publishers, Inc., 1982.

Summers, John D. *Yale Bowl and the Open Trolleys*. Pittsburgh: Dorrance Publishing Co., 1996.

Trudeau, Garry, *Bull Tales*. New Haven: Yale Daily News, 1969.

Wallace, William N. *Yale's Iron-men*. Lincoln, Nebraska: Universe, Inc., 2005.

ACKNOWLEDGMENTS

I could not have completed this triple overtime project with lesser hands. I may have carried the ball for the tough yardage but the following eight man line cleared the way for me to cross the goal line. A special thank you and high five to:

Bob Barton ('57) considered the resident historian of Yale University football; **Steve Conn**, Associate Athletics Director, Director of Sports Publicity at Yale, who allowed access to historic Yale photos and archives; **Don Scharf** ('55), who heads the Department of Athletics Outreach Office at Yale, for critical alumni contact information; **Joel Alderman** ('51), for his contribution to Yale broadcasting history; **Don Kosakowski**, a New York football Giants historian for his input and 1940s player reasearch; **Sabby Frinzi**, the Yale football photographer from 1965 to 1996; **Bill O'Brien,** a free-lance photographer who provided numerous photographs and allowed me to research his extensive library of Yale game day programs; and **Wes Moyer,** a former Yale player (2009-11) who was most helpful in the photo search of this book.

Thanks also to

Niels Aaboe, my editor at Skyhorse/Sports Publishing; **Sam Rubin,** Assistant Director of Sports Publicity at Yale; **Tom Peters,** who suggested the appropriate title for this book; **Judith Schiff**, the chief research archivist of manuscripts and archives at Yale's Sterling Library; **Michael Frost** and **Claryn Spies,** public service assistants at the Sterling Library; **Michael Lotstein**, Records Services Archivist, Yale University Library; **Ed Mockus,** the Senior Associate Athletic Director Facilities Operation;

Tim Williamson Director of Harvard Athletic Communications; **Marlene Crockford,** Accounts Representative at Cornell University; **Craig Sachson,** Assistant Director of Athletics Communication at Princeton University; **Mike Kowalsky,** Associate Director of Sports Information at Columbia University; **Boo Coorigan,** Athletic Director at the United States Military Academy at West Point; **Alice Zhao** of *The Harvard Crimson;* **Christopher Humm***,* Director of Athletic Communications at Brown University; **Emily Watlington** and **Maryrose Grossman** of The John F. Kennedy Presidential Library; **Don and Roy Couture** of Aerial Photography of Don Couture; **Peter Brown and John Woodruff** of Woodruff/Brown Photography; and **Ted Livingston** for photo assistance.

I also wish to thank the *New Haven Register* **staff** including **Sean Barker**, sports editor; **Angel Diggs**, Librarian; and **Vern Williams.**

L-R: Bill O'Brien, Wes Moyer, Joel Alderman, Don Kosakowski, Rich Marazzi, Bob Barton, Don Scharf and Steve Conn (Sabby Frinzi)

And a note of gratitude must go to **Ed Casey** of the West Haven Veterans Museum and Learning Center; **Andrew Rizzo,** the Executive Director of Office of Building Inspection and Enforcement in New Haven; **Carmine Capasso** of G.L. Capasso, Inc.; **Michael H. Schreiber,** the curator of the Shore Line Trolley Museum Collections in East Haven, Connecticut; and **Mark Guarino** of the Guymark Studio in Hamden, Connecticut.

Finally, my thanks to **Loisann Marazzi,** my wife, for her unconditional support and all the tailgate lunches she prepared; **my sons**, **Rich** and **Brian,** for their interest and support; and **Trisha and Rachel,** my daughter-in-laws for their support.